Jaguar Books on Latin America

Series Editors

WILLIAM H. BEEZLEY, Neville G. Penrose Chair of Latin
   American Studies, Texas Christian University
COLIN M. MACLACHLAN, Professor and Chair, Department
   of History, Tulane University

Volumes Published

John E. Kicza, ed., *The Indian in Latin American History: Resistance, Resilience,
   and Acculturation* (1993). Cloth ISBN 0-8420-2421-2
   Paper ISBN 0-8420-2425-5

Susan E. Place, ed., *Tropical Rainforests: Latin American Nature and Society in
   Transition* (1993). Cloth ISBN 0-8420-2423-9   Paper ISBN 0-8420-2427-1

Paul W. Drake, ed., *Money Doctors, Foreign Debts, and Economic Reforms in
   Latin America from the 1890s to the Present* (1994).
   Cloth ISBN 0-8420-2434-4   Paper ISBN 0-8420-2435-2

John A. Britton, ed., *Molding the Hearts and Minds: Education, Communications,
   and Social Change in Latin America* (1994).
   Cloth ISBN 0-8420-2489-1   Paper ISBN 0-8420-2490-5

Darién J. Davis, ed., *Slavery and Beyond: The African Impact on Latin America
   and the Caribbean* (1994). Cloth ISBN 0-8420-2484-0
   Paper ISBN 0-8420-2485-9

David J. Weber and Jane M. Rausch, eds., *Where Cultures Meet: Frontiers in
   Latin American History* (1994). Cloth ISBN 0-8420-2477-8
   Paper ISBN 0-8420-2478-6

Gertrude M. Yeager, ed., *Confronting Change, Challenging Tradition: Women in
   Latin American History* (1994). Cloth ISBN 0-8420-2479-4
   Paper ISBN 0-8420-2480-8

Linda Alexander Rodríguez, ed., *Rank and Privilege: The Military and Society
   in Latin America* (1994). Cloth ISBN 0-8420-2432-8
   Paper ISBN 0-8420-2433-6

Rank
and
Privilege

Rank and Privilege

The Military and Society in Latin America

Linda Alexander Rodríguez
Editor

Jaguar Books on Latin America
Number 8

A Scholarly Resources Inc. Imprint
Wilmington, Delaware

Scholarly Resources Inc.
104 Greenhill Avenue
Wilmington, DE 19805–1897

Library of Congress Cataloging-in-Publication Data

Rank and privilege : the military and society in Latin America / Linda
    Alexander Rodríguez, editor.
        p.   cm. — (Jaguar books on Latin America ; no. 8)
    Includes bibliographical references.
    ISBN 0-8420-2432-8. — ISBN 0-8420-2433-6 (pbk.)
    1. Civil-military relations—Latin America. 2. Latin America—
Armed Forces—Political activity. I. Rodríguez, Linda Alexander.
II. Series.
UA602.3.R36   1994
306.2'7'098—dc20   94-14393
                                                                    CIP

⊗The paper used in this publication meets the minimum requirements of
the American National Standard for permanence of paper for printed
library materials, Z39.48, 1984.

Contents

Linda Alexander Rodríguez, Introduction, **ix**

1 Jorge I. Domínguez, International War and Government Modernization: The Military—A Case Study, **1**

2 Christon I. Archer, *"La Causa Buena"*: The Counterinsurgency Army of New Spain and the Ten Years' War, **11**

3 Linda Alexander Rodríguez, Authoritarianism and Militarism in Ecuador, **37**

4 William F. Sater, The War of the Pacific, **55**

5 Frederick M. Nunn, The South American Military Tradition: Preprofessional Armies in Argentina, Chile, Peru, and Brazil, **71**

6 Stanley E. Hilton, The Armed Forces and Industrialists in Modern Brazil: The Drive for Military Autonomy, 1889–1945, **95**

7 Daniel M. Masterson, Caudillismo and Institutional Change: Manuel Odría and the Peruvian Armed Forces, 1948–1956, **143**

8 Peter Calvert and Susan Calvert, The Military and Development, **155**

9 Gabriel Marcella, The Latin American Military, Low-Intensity Conflict, and Democracy, **189**

10 William S. Ackroyd, Military Professionalism and Nonintervention in Mexico, **219**

Suggested Readings, **235**

Introduction

Linda Alexander Rodríguez

Scholars have been preoccupied with the role of the Latin American military since the 1960s. Most studies have focused on the twentieth century and on topics such as the nature of civil-military relations, the professionalization of armies, or the political role of the armed forces. Researchers not only have given less attention to these issues in the nineteenth century, but they have also tended to ignore questions like the role of the martial institution in the areas of national defense, internal security, and social and economic development. Since most studies examine a limited number of topics during a short period of time, they often provide a distorted image of the Latin American military. Many scholars, for example, assume that Latin American armed forces have had no legitimate defense functions, that military professionalization and developmentalism are exclusively contemporary events, and that a multifaceted definition of national security is a post-World War II phenomenon.

Although it is difficult, and in some cases impossible, to distinguish the national army from other armed groups in the early nineteenth century, historical context is necessary to understand the evolution of the martial institution. The formation of armies, like that of other organizations, is best understood as a complex nonlinear process that occurred at different rates in the various states of the region. Although the professionalization of the Spanish American armed forces began in the late colonial era, periods of professionalization were followed by events that diminished those gains. After independence, for example, the irregular forces of the new countries replaced the relatively professional Spanish colonial armies. During the nineteenth century, the absorption of the victorious irregular forces into the national army after a rebellion, or in extreme cases the destruction of the institution, disrupted the process of professionalization. Mexico is an excellent example of this process. As a result of the country's first turbulent decades, the army was restructured on numerous occasions. The institution became stable and professional in the final decades of the nineteenth century under Porfirio Díaz, only to be dismantled by the revolutionaries who gained power after 1913. It would take decades to return to the level of professional competence achieved by the Mexican military at the end of the nineteenth century.

While historical context is essential to an understanding of the military's role in Latin America, it is also necessary to discard the widely held belief that the armed forces of the first world are apolitical. As long as we maintain the fiction that the militaries of countries such as the United States, France, Germany, Great Britain, and the former Soviet Union are professional, that rank is obtained solely on merit, and that respect for civil authority is unchallenged, we will view their Latin American counterparts as predatory, unprofessional, and comic opera institutions. We cannot comprehend the nature of the Latin American armed forces unless we realize that they, like those of the first world, function within a political system. The differences between Latin American militaries and those of the so-called developed countries are the result largely of the strength and cohesiveness of the civil institutions and power structures within these two groups of nations. In all countries, domestic civil-political considerations are as important in determining the actions of the armed forces as strictly martial factors. England's decision to go to war with Argentina over the Malvinas (Falkland) Islands or the United States' invasions of Panama and Grenada, for example, cannot be divorced from the context of internal politics and the delicate balance between civil and military power within the two North Atlantic states. It is therefore not surprising that domestic politics are crucial in determining whether the armed forces in a particular Latin American country wage war, against either their neighbors or their own people.

National defense has been of paramount importance in Latin America since the 1770s. The formation of a colonial army in Spanish America during the last decades of the eighteenth century grew out of Spain's disastrous experience in the Seven Years' War and the realization that the Crown was incapable of defending the region. The Bourbon monarchy created a modern military, first in Spain and subsequently in America, as part of an effort to meet external challenges through political, institutional, and economic modernization. The Bourbon military reform entailed strengthening the regular army, creating a militia, and expanding the institution's political and economic role.

The Spanish monarchy reformed the military to counter growing external challenges, yet internal threats to political stability quickly became important factors in shaping the militarization of Spanish America. Although the nature of regional responses to internal threats differed considerably, some general trends are discernable. Throughout Spanish America economic considerations mandated a growing reliance on local militias and reserves, and a lower dependence on Spanish regular army units, to suppress rebellion. Internal challenges to authority often involved scattered low-intensity conflicts rather than conventional warfare. The fragmented insurgency engulfing important regions of three viceroyalties in the last decades of the empire profoundly affected the armed forces. The Comunero rebellion in Nueva Granada (1781), the Tupac Amaru revolt in Peru (1780–1783), and the guerrilla struggle in New Spain (1810–1821) forced military commanders and administrators responsible for colonial defense to redirect their efforts from external defense toward counterinsurgency and pacification programs.

In New Spain, regional army commanders imposed martial law and levied war taxes in the eleven-year struggle against Miguel Hidalgo, José María Morelos, and their heirs. This expansion of military authority challenged and, in many regions, supplanted civilian control. Not surprisingly, Mexican independence resulted, in part, from the army's fear that the restored constitutional government in Spain threatened its new privileges and expanded authority. Mexico, unlike Spanish South America, achieved independence through a political compromise in which most of the royal army switched sides.

Spanish South America pursued a very different path to emancipation. There patriot forces, which included professional soldiers as well as irregular forces, fought against armies that remained loyal to the Crown. Only in the newly established viceroyalty of the Río de la Plata and the Captaincy General of Chile did the Americans gain relatively easy victories; in other areas of Spanish South America the struggle was protracted and brutal. Northern South America achieved liberation at a very high cost, the creation of a praetorian tradition that would haunt the countries of the region for decades.

In the nineteenth century, attacks by Spain, the United States, Britain, and France reinforced the new countries' belief that national defense was a legitimate priority. Mexico, for example, was invaded five times between 1829 and 1861, losing half its national territory to the United States in 1848 and its independence to a French-imposed monarchy from 1862 to 1867. Although only the states of Central America approached that level of pillage by extraregional powers, South American countries also suffered. Venezuela and Argentina lost territory to the British; England and France blockaded Argentina; the Spanish attacked Peru and destroyed Chile's major port, Valparaiso; and almost all the newly independent states endured humiliating incidents in which European countries and the United States used military might to press their claims. Such episodes led to increased domestic pressures for improved armaments and training, and prompted Latin American countries to spend substantial sums on their armed forces. In some cases, weapons had to be employed to defend the nation from the very power that supplied them. For example, at midcentury Mexico purchased French armaments that subsequently had to be used against an invading French army in the 1860s.

Danger did not come solely from extraregional powers. During that century, Ibero America endured six major intraregional wars: one between Peru and Gran Colombia over unresolved boundary disputes; two involving Argentina and Brazil over competing territorial claims that were eventually resolved with the founding of Uruguay; two in which Chile defeated Peru and Bolivia to prevent the creation of a more powerful coalition and to settle territorial differences; and one in which Argentina, Uruguay, and Brazil eviscerated Paraguay, taking one third of that country's territory and killing a majority of its adult males. These were only the most prominent armed confrontations between sister nations; countless other conflicts undermined regional stability and established patterns of enmity and suspicion in the area. From independence to the present, border disputes and the competition for regional dominance fostered high defense expenditures, enhanced intermittent efforts to modernize the armed forces, and resulted in the expansion of the military's role in national life.

Classic rivalries—such as those among Peru, Bolivia, and Chile, and between Brazil and Argentina, Peru and Ecuador, and Chile and Argentina—developed in the first decades of the national period. Since their initial clash in 1825 over the area that eventually became Uruguay, the two largest South American countries, Brazil and Argentina, have competed for military superiority. Mutual distrust, which expressed itself in two nineteenth-century wars and countless border incidents, shaped the two nations' strategic policy and engendered an escalating arms race in the area. Similarly, the competing claims of Chile and Argentina to Patagonia, the Beagle Islands, and Antarctica were not resolved and sparked an arms race at the end of the nineteenth century. Regional conflicts were also prominent in northern South America. As early as 1830, Gran Colombia and Peru went to war over competing territorial claims. That conflict was only the first of a series of contests that have continued into the twentieth century between Peru and Ecuador, one of the three states to emerge from Gran Colombia in 1830.

The fortress mentality engendered by confrontations with non-Latin American states and the more frequent struggles among the sister nations of the region strained government budgets and frequently provided ambitious military officers with an excuse to supplant civilian administrations. Even countries like Chile, which had demonstrated its military prowess by defeating the combined forces of Peru and Bolivia on two occasions, believed themselves vulnerable. The anxiety of vanquished countries bordered on hysteria. Great conflicts, like the Paraguayan War (1864–1870) and the War of the Pacific (1879–1884), inevitably exposed institutional and organizational weakness within both victorious and vanquished armed forces, prompting reassessments of civil-military relations and reorganizations of military training.

Intraregional confrontations that did not end in war could be equally important in stimulating military reform and rearmament. The competition between Chile and Argentina over the Beagle Islands at the turn of the century touched off an escalating arms race. Such weapons purchases and institutional reorganizations, while important, should be interpreted not as breaks with earlier practices but as extensions of previous institutional reforms. After independence, the new states began buying European weapons, founding military academies, employing foreign military advisers, and utilizing martial texts—first from Spain and later translations of French and German works—to train the armed forces. By the 1850s countries like Mexico were sending officers to Europe for advanced training and were modeling their forces on European institutions.

In the last decades of the nineteenth century most Latin American countries renewed their efforts to professionalize officer training by establishing or expanding military schools, employing foreign advisers, and sending officers to Europe for advanced education. The victors in the Paraguayan War, Argentina and Brazil, turned to Germany and France for weapons and advisers. After the War of the Pacific, Chile adopted German training, organization, and armaments, while Peru modernized its military under the direction of French advisers. Subsequently, the Bolivians sought help from both the Germans and the French. Mexico, whose experience with foreign intervention was particularly painful, refused to employ foreign missions. Instead, the country reformed and expanded military training and sent officers abroad for advanced training. El Salvador and Guatemala founded military schools and employed European advisers. Expanded education increased social mobility and redefined the military's societal role. As the officer corps gained technical expertise, armed forces personnel frequently were employed in economic and social development projects ranging from road construction to the provision of medical care. Such activities reinforced the belief that the martial institution was uniquely qualified to promote modernization and define and defend national interests from the inept and misguided policies of civilians.

Professionalization had the long-term effect of politicizing the armed forces to defend their corporate interests, which they identified as synonymous with those of the nation. In Central and South America professionalized armies became the arbiters of politics, while in Mexico the military emerged as an important interest group. Even Brazil, which had escaped the postindependence instability that afflicted Spanish America, faced growing politicization in the army as a result of the Paraguayan War. A generation of officers emerged from that conflict determined to protect institutional interests and to improve professional training. The officers developed a corporate spirit and shifted away from an unconditional support of the monarchy. In so doing, they prepared the way for the next generation of better-educated officers to project their new vision of corporate interests into the political arena, resulting in the overthrow of the Brazilian monarchy in 1889.

During the nineteenth century internal threats to political stability, and at times to national survival, plagued much of Ibero America and fostered the militarization of politics. As in the colonial period, many of these internal struggles involved guerrilla warfare. In northern South America, where independence was achieved through military victory and, in Mexico, militarized by a decade of preindependence counterinsurgency, "generals" dominated national politics in the first decades. Although there were significant differences among Latin American states—ranging from Chile, where civil authority consolidated relatively rapidly, to Peru, where military leaders retained control throughout the century—in most of the continent lack of political consensus and the willingness of civilians to seek military support to enhance their political position blurred the boundaries between civil and military authority.

As in the better-studied twentieth century, nineteenth-century soldiers were frequently drawn into politics as various political groups sought to achieve with force what they could not accomplish through parliamentary debate. Many Latin American countries, such as Mexico, Argentina, Guatemala, Colombia, Venezuela, and Ecuador, endured civil wars pitting federalists against centralists and liberals against conservatives who threatened to dismember the new republics. Mexico, Chile, and Argentina also subdued unincorporated indigenous populations on their frontiers. These internal conflicts had varying impacts on the armed forces of the region. Protracted guerrilla warfare weakened civil authority, sapped national budgets, and enhanced the role of military politicians. Such struggles frequently disrupted efforts to professionalize the military in countries like Bolivia, Ecuador, and Peru. In other countries, such as Argentina and Chile, campaigns against indigenous groups stimulated the modernization of the army and enhanced the stature of the institution. At the end of the century, messianic rebellions in countries such as Mexico and Brazil could be quelled only by the modern weapons of the armed forces.

External threats continued to preoccupy Latin American states in the twentieth century. Binational conflicts resulting from unsettled boundary disputes have led to war on five occasions; direct interventions by extraregional powers, particularly the United States, have continued to plague the area; and the arming and provisioning of dissident political groups, both of the Right and of the Left, by regional and extraregional powers has increased domestic political instability. The United States has been particularly active in using force to pursue its goals in the region. In the first two decades of the twentieth century, the United States averaged one armed intervention per year in the area, with U.S. forces occupying some countries for periods as long as thirteen years. The rate of U.S. intervention declined in the 1930s and 1940s, but overt and covert use of force has escalated in the last three decades.

Although direct U.S. interventions were confined largely to Central America and the Caribbean, no Latin American country considered itself immune from external threat. Germany posed a danger in both world wars; German submarines and raiders threatened Latin American shipping. Indeed, Mexico declared war on the Axis powers, not because of pressure from the United States, as is generally believed, but because German U-boats sank several unarmed Mexican ships in the summer of 1942. After the development of the Cold War and the Cuban Revolution, several Latin American states came to view the Soviet Union as a potential danger. Although a direct Soviet threat materialized only briefly during the 1962 Cuban missile crisis, another European power, Great Britain, did intervene in the region. The 1982 Malvinas/Falklands War between Great Britain and Argentina demonstrated that the United States would not protect Latin America from all extracontinental threats despite the provisions of the Río treaty, which stipulated that aggression against one American state by an outside power would be viewed as aggression against all of them. Therefore, even large, relatively developed countries required strong and professional military forces to protect their national interests. In the face of such real and imagined extraregional threats, the armed forces of Latin America have responded, as in the past, by reforming and modernizing training, expanding the military's mission, embracing institutional reform, seeking to increase armed preparedness, and, where possible, establishing military superiority through either the purchase or the production of advanced weaponry.

In recent years, the armed forces of some Latin American countries have entered the world arms market as suppliers. Although the international arms trade continues to be dominated by countries such as the United States, Russia, France, Great Britain, Germany, and China, Latin

American states also sell weapons on the international market. Brazilian, Argentine, Cuban, and Chilean sales of tanks, aircraft, personnel carriers, missiles, and other weapons amount to more than $1 billion annually. Thus while the region's armed forces, with the exception of Cuba's participation in Angola and Ethiopia, have had only limited experience in extraregional combat, Latin American countries play an indirect role in international conflicts by supplying arms to regular and irregular forces throughout the developing world. Brazil, which has emerged as the leading military power of Latin America and the region's major weapons producer and exporter, has benefited from the desire of Third World countries, including other Latin American countries, to diversify arms sources. Despite increasing weapons exports, the region as a whole continues to be a net importer of armaments. At the end of the 1980s countries in the region were spending $3 billion annually for imported weapons.

Many twentieth-century intraregional conflicts, such as territorial disputes in northern South America and the struggle for military superiority in the Southern Cone, are essentially continuations of nineteenth-century contentions and unresolved animosities. During the twentieth century the unresolved dispute between Peru and Ecuador spawned low-level conflict on numerous occasions between 1910 and 1991, and sparked a major confrontation in 1941. The 1941 war provided the Peruvian armed forces with an opportunity to re-establish their reputation in the wake of their 1933 defeat by Colombia. Then, Peru's military had been humiliated by the superior Colombian forces that ousted them from the Leticia region claimed by both states since independence. In 1941, Ecuador was defeated by a larger, better-equipped, and better-prepared Peruvian force. The bloodiest territorial struggle of the period pitted a larger Bolivian force against a better armed and trained Paraguayan army for control of the Chaco. Almost four hundred thousand men (240,000 Bolivians and 150,000 Paraguayans) participated in the war that lasted from 1932 until 1935, leaving fifty-six thousand Bolivians and thirty-six thousand Paraguayans dead. The 1938 treaty ending the war awarded two thirds of the disputed lands to Paraguay. Similarly, competing Chilean and Argentine territorial claims have continued to shape twentieth-century military policy in the two countries. Argentina, for example, failed to commit its best-prepared troops during the 1982 war with Great Britain, in part, because it feared that Chile not only actively supported the British but also might use the war as an opportunity to resolve pending boundary disputes by opening a second front.

Recently, indirect interventions through foreign sponsorship of domestic subversion have become important in defining national security issues and in reshaping the nature of military preparedness. Although indirect aggression—the arming and provisioning of dissident political groups within sister nations—began in the nineteenth century, especially in Central America, Colombia, Ecuador, Peru, and in the Río de la Plata, the practice has become the principal mechanism for bilateral conflict since 1959. This phenomenon has blurred the boundary between intraregional and non-Latin American intervention as the United States and the Soviet Union used their clients to subvert the governments of recalcitrant states. Honduras, for example, became a base for United States-sponsored attempts to overthrow "radical" regimes in Central America during the 1980s, while Cuba, armed and supplied by the Soviet Union, aided leftist movements in Latin American countries during the 1960s and 1970s. These events, which culminated in the Sandinista Revolution in Nicaragua and the civil war in El Salvador, prompted the region's armed forces to revise national security doctrines. Such intervention became the justification for the militarization of Latin American politics and a significant factor in stimulating a regional arms race.

Internal threats to political stability have continued to spur military professionalization, modification of military doctrine, and the redefinition of the institution's civic role and mission. The wave of military coups that washed over the region in the 1920s, 1930s, and 1940s were directly related to efforts to modernize the region's armed forces. Although the success of military modernization varied, the process entailed expanded military, scientific, and technical training for officers, structural reorganization based on European and U.S. models, the development and implementation of a system of promotion based on merit, the purchase of sophisticated arms and equipment, and the establishment of universal conscription. Since military modernization frequently outpaced social and political modernization, many professional officers came to view their country's underdeveloped economies and unintegrated societies as threats to institutional development and military preparedness.

Latin American armies became increasingly politicized as governments used them to control rebellions, strikes, political dissidents, and other mass movements in rural and urban areas during the first decades of the century. At the same time, conscription expanded the size of the armed forces creating both the potential and the need for a more diversified institutional role. Since conscripts were primarily from the lower classes, the military expanded its role in many areas, from education to health care. By the 1920s military officers in most Latin American countries were convinced that institutional strength was inextricably linked to economic and social development. Reform movements such as those in Chile (1924), Ecuador (1925), and Argentina (1943) were led by young professional officers who believed that they were uniquely qualified to purge the political system of corrupt and inept civilian officials and to foster national regeneration. The officers were disdainful, both of civilian governments that had failed to promote economic and social change and of senior military officers who held their positions because of political rather than professional criteria.

The military coups of the 1960s and 1970s, like those of the first decades of the century, were frequently institutional responses to heightened internal tensions and polarization as well as to the widely held belief that civilian governments were incapable of meeting such challenges to internal order. These movements, however, occurred in a new international and domestic environment. After the Cuban Revolution of 1959 and Fidel Castro's subsequent attempts to foment armed insurrection in the region, the military forces of most Latin American countries identified both leftist political groups and poverty as the most dangerous threats to internal security. As a result, Central and South American nations restructured officer training, emphasizing the maintenance of internal order as well as an expanded civic action role for the armed forces.

In the 1960s many officers in Latin America found that their concerns with internal security were becoming fashionable among military and civilian policymakers in the United States, as that country began to reorient its Cold War strategy to emphasize counterinsurgency. Armed forces on the continent sought to exploit their northern neighbor's heightened interest in regional security to obtain modern weapons and advanced training. As in the past, this new wave of modernization contributed significantly to the militarization of politics. By the mid-1970s, fourteen of the twenty-one Latin American states had military governments. Most were more adept at restricting political participation than at solving complex domestic problems, such as poverty and social atomization.

Analyses of the military coups of the 1960s and 1970s focused principally on issues such as professionalization, class identification, and the level of national development in their efforts to determine key factors in civil-military relations. Scholars of the military provided two competing visions of the institution in the 1960s. One group argued that the armed forces' political role would diminish as economic, social, and political modernization occurred. A second maintained that the military could play not only a central but also a constructive role in the modernization process because officers essentially defended middle-sector interests and were unlikely to employ excessive force that would erode their power base. Although the military governments that came to power in Peru (1968) and Ecuador (1972) seemed to conform to the second progressive model, the military regimes in Brazil (1964), Chile (1973), and Argentina (1976) quickly shattered those expectations. The most developed countries of the region spawned repressive military governments, destroying the assumption that development and democracy had a simple, linear relationship. In the early 1970s researchers adopted the concept of authoritarian regimes in an effort to explain the unexpected resurgence of militarism by the most professional armed forces of the region.

Reflecting scholars' general dissatisfaction with models that failed to explain either contemporary events or diversity within the region, empirical studies of the armed forces of individual countries gradually replaced broader theoretical works. Indeed, many researchers concluded that it was futile to construct theoretical models with inadequate comparative data. Recent empirical studies have interpreted the coups of the 1960s and 1970s as a new form of institutional militarism, resulting from both professionalization and a heightened awareness of corporate interest. However, a closer examination of the historical record indicates that many of these movements continued patterns established in the nineteenth century and the first decades of the twentieth century. As in earlier periods, the militarization of politics in the 1960s and 1970s frequently occurred at the behest of civilian groups. In Uruguay and Chile, for example, civilian politicians from all ideological groups actively courted the military.

The "new" military belief that the armed forces constituted the most impartial interpreter of national interests and that it was the institution best equipped to promote national unity and development merely reiterated a view enunciated in several countries at the end of the nineteenth century and the first decades of the twentieth century. In both instances, such attitudes reflected the improvements in military education. Similarly, the idea that the failure of civilian politicians to control societal tensions directly threatened internal and institutional security has been a crucial factor in justifying coups since the nineteenth century. The 1925 revolt in Ecuador, for example, demonstrates that all these factors played a prominent role in fostering military coups even in the less developed countries of the region.

Although since the 1960s military coups have exhibited continuities with earlier phenomena, there are also differences. The distinctive features of most recent interventions consisted of their duration and their expanded use of force. The armed forces of Brazil (1964–1985), Peru (1968–1980), Ecuador (1972–1978), Chile (1973–1990), Uruguay (1973–1984), and Argentina (1976–1983) were inclined to retain political control for many years, and the military in the most developed countries—Brazil, Argentina, Uruguay, and Chile—brutally repressed broad segments of the urban population. Previous twentieth-century military governments—with a few exceptions, such as the regimes of Carlos Ibañez in

Chile (1927–1931) and Marcos Pérez Jiménez in Venezuela (1948–1957)—tended to be of short duration and generally restricted the use of violence to rural populations and to marginal urban groups. The repressive nature of recent military regimes must be viewed in the context of the region's increasing polarization, the result of political crises and economic decline, and its attendant spiraling political, economic, and social violence. During the 1970s terrorists of both the Left and the Right wreaked havoc on their societies. In turn, military governments, as well as individual members of the armed forces, responded with unparalleled ferocity to the growing specter of urban violence, kidnapping, torturing, and killing thousands of real and suspected leftists. While the escalating repression of opposition groups was originally aimed at leftist terrorist organizations such as the Tupamaro guerrillas in Uruguay and the Montoneros in Argentina, labor unions, student organizations, human and civil rights activists, political parties, and the press all became targets in these "dirty wars" against subversion.

In the last decade the officer corps of many nations, particularly Brazil, Chile, Argentina, and Uruguay, where the armed forces had seized power and had successfully reduced domestic political violence, began to question the efficacy of directly controlling the government and emphasizing internal security. Argentina's defeat by Great Britain in the 1982 Malvinas/Falklands War appeared to demonstrate that military preoccupation with domestic issues and the assumption of governing responsibilities had eroded the ability of the armed forces to meet their primary responsibility: defending the nation from external aggression. Ironically, the failure of the Argentine military also reduced tensions in the Southern Cone by convincing Brazilian officers that their forces were dominant in the region.

The withdrawal of the military from direct control of the government in the largest countries in South America was a complex process involving delicate negotiations between the armed forces and civilian groups. Despite ideological differences—ranging from the leftist military government of Peru, which carried out a significant land reform, to the rightist military governments of Chile and Brazil, which embraced neoliberal economic solutions and draconian measures to demobilize the population and suppress political activity—all the military governments of the region sought to create mechanisms that would allow the armed forces to continue to form and implement policy in those areas deemed vital to the martial institution prior to relinquishing power to civilians. In many countries, including Brazil and Chile, the transition to democratic rule in the 1980s was achieved by ceding significant areas of authority to the military. Social, political, and economic developments in the region have reinforced this expanded institutional role for the armed forces. For example, the growth of the drug trade, economic stagnation, and internal terrorism by groups like the Sendero Luminoso (Shining Path) in Peru, have created a new awareness of internal threats as well as a reassessment by the military of its mission and its relationship to civil society.

Contemporary scholarly approaches to the study of the Latin American military generally have focused on the armed forces as an agent of social mobility as well as on the impact of generational, class, and ethnic origins of soldiers and officers on the military and its mission. The few works devoted to an examination of these issues during the late eighteenth and nineteenth centuries help to provide a context for the current debate concerning the role of corporate versus class or ethnic identity in defining the military's institutional mandate and role in society. Studies of these issues in the colonial period suggest that, while the army and militia offered opportunities for social advancement in Venezuela and Peru, regional economic and political variations were more important in predicting institutional responses to specific situations than the class or ethnic origins of army personnel. Several twentieth-century students of the military, however, have stressed the importance of the middle-class origins of most officers in determining military attitudes and actions. Other scholars have used a related concept, military generation, which refers to a cohort of armed forces personnel with shared training and career experiences, to explain divisions within the military of a specific country. Such analysts argue that members of a generation may possess attitudes and goals, based on their shared institutional experience, that are more important than a general identification with either the martial institution or their class. For example, in Argentina the 1982 military defeat prompted a reassessment of the organization of the armed forces and its command structure. The restructuring revealed a generational split within the officer corps between those who fought in the Malvinas Islands and the noncombatant officials who made the ill-fated and uncoordinated command decisions. Subsequent military revolts in Argentina during 1987 and 1988 demonstrate that generational factors are critical in forming military attitudes about the role of the armed forces.

At the end of the 1980s the region's armed forces were undergoing changes that may be expected to influence both institutional development and civil-military relations in the 1990s. After a decade of growth, which increased troop strength from 1.5 million to 1.9 million, the size of the region's armed forces was reduced to levels existing at the beginning of the decade. The decline was particularly dramatic in Brazil, which cut its armed forces by 41 percent, and in Chile and Peru, where troops declined by 24 percent and 13 percent, respectively. Although these reductions were accompanied by declining military expenditures, which in some countries, like Argentina, meant real cuts in military salaries, nations in the region continue to vary widely in the percentage of national government expenditures devoted to the armed forces. In some countries, such as El Salvador, Peru, and Bolivia, military expenditures continued to consume between 25 percent and 35 percent of the budget, while other states, such as Mexico and Brazil, reduced their military's share of the budget to just over 2 percent.

Despite the trend toward smaller armed forces, the military in most Latin American countries continues to have significant autonomy. The return to civilian rule has only initiated the process of forming a new power relationship between the military and civilian sectors of society. Because military education throughout the region continues to emphasize a broad definition of national security and institutional responsibility, expanded professionalization can be expected to foster political action by the armed forces. Domestic political and economic problems, including the production and distribution of drugs, increasing poverty, economic stagnation, and the struggle for political control, can also be expected to keep the military politically active. Solutions to these issues will be complicated by the ongoing international political and economic restructuring, which is shattering long-standing ideological, economic, and geopolitical accommodations. Finally, the unresolved boundary disputes and competing claims to resources and territory in the region, which continue to promote instability and discord, will inevitably draw the military into politics for the remainder of the decade and into the next century.

1

International War and Government Modernization: The Military—A Case Study

Jorge I. Domínguez

After the Seven Years' War the Spanish Crown restructured the empire in an effort to exercise greater control over its vast territories. It established a colonial army, reorganized administrative and territorial boundaries, introduced the intendancy system, restructured commerce, and increased taxes. These innovations benefited some regions and groups and harmed others. The discontent they caused subsequently contributed to the drive for independence.

During the second half of the eighteenth century the Crown's growing preoccupation with the empire's vulnerability to external threats made colonial defense a central feature of Spanish policy. In contrast to the previous defensive strategy, which had emphasized coastal fortifications, the new policy required the formation of a colonial army in Spanish America. Since Spain lacked the resources and manpower to defend the empire, colonial defense was entrusted to a small regular army reinforced by a much larger local militia. The Crown introduced the fuero *militar, judicial and military privileges, as an incentive to recruitment. By 1808 the imperial forces numbered some one hundred twenty-five thousand. Although the senior officer corps was made up of a relatively large number of Spaniards, the armed forces were overwhelmingly American and included many blacks. The expansion of the regular army, as well as the militias, provided new avenues for social mobility, particularly for persons of color.*

From *Insurrection or Loyalty: The Breakdown of the Spanish Empire* (Cambridge: Harvard University Press, 1980), 74–81, 275–76. ©1980 by the President and Fellows of Harvard College. Reprinted by permission of Harvard University Press.

The international system was an important reason for Spain's desire to modernize its American empire. Fear of political, military, and economic defeat spurred the Crown toward change. Resources and personnel committed to the military increased. The empire's policies were reflected by the military, including ethnic mobility and the search for private gain through political access typical of a neopatrimonial culture. The military would play a complex role in a society where military-aristocratic values had always been important.

Military strength increased during the second half of the eighteenth century, coinciding with imperial political modernization, with international wars, and with economic growth. The size of the regular army in Chile doubled from 1,279 in 1752 to 2,358 by 1800; in Mexico it rose from 3,032 in 1758 to 10,620 in 1810. In Cuba the increase from 3,591 in 1770 to 15,000 by 1830 resulted from Spain's retreat from the continent of South America. Spain maintained that level of regular troops in Cuba for the next three decades. The size of the militia rose in Mexico from 10,698 in 1766 to 30,685 in 1810 (the peak militia strength was 34,717 in 1784). The militia's size also doubled in Cuba from 8,076 in 1770 to 15,000 in 1830. Militia strength in Chile reached at least 29,639 in the late eighteenth century.

Military participation ratios (see Table 1) are far greater for Chile than for Mexico. Chile's rate of regular army participation is 1.5 times Mexico's; for the militia, it is over six times greater. Cuba's rate of militia participation is just under Chile's for the early nineteenth century, but its regular army participation ratio was almost four times greater. This reflects Cuba's strategic importance for Spain, and Chile's horizontal or parallel ethnic system.

Although no time series is available for Venezuela, it had 918 regular troops and 13,136 members of the militia by 1800. Its regular army participation ratio was lower than Mexico's, much lower than Chile's and Cuba's. Its militia participation ratio was not quite three times that of Mexico, thus a bit lower than that of Chile and Cuba. By the standards of 1960, the rate of militarization of Chile and Cuba falls somewhere between that of Israel and North Korea, higher than France's during the Algerian war.[1] Venezuela is at the level of Czechoslovakia or Spain; Mexico's level was similar to that of Canada. In short, Chile's and Cuba's rates of militarization were extraordinary.

These military participation ratios are explained by international politics, or by the characteristics of ethnic systems; they differ from social mobilization measures. . . . However, military participation ratios are not accurate indicators of repression. Spain had a total military force of about one hundred twenty-five thousand men in America in 1808, but the overwhelming majority of these were not regular troops, but militiamen—citizen soldiers who were mostly Americans.[2]

Table 1. Military Participation in 1800

Country	Regular army	Militia	Total military	Military men per 1,000 persons	Rank order[a] Regular army	Militia	Total
Chile	2,358	29,639	31,997	36	1.5	6.6	5.3
Cuba[b]	3,591	8,076	11,667	32	5.7	4.5	4.8
Venezuela	918	13,136	14,054	16	0.6	2.9	2.3
Mexico[c]	10,620	30,685	41,305	7	1.0	1.0	1.0

Sources: Francisco Depons, *Viaje a la parte oriental de tierra firme* (Caracas: Tipografía Americana, 1930), pp. 179–182; Francisco A. Encina, *Historia de Chile* (Santiago: Nascimiento, 1946), V, 60–61, 73, 162–169, 529–534; Herbert S. Klein, *Slavery in the Americas: A Comparative Study of Virginia and Cuba* (Chicago: Quadrangle, 1971), pp. 218–219; Lyle N. McAlister, *The "Fuero Militar" in New Spain, 1764–1800* (Gainesville: University of Florida Press, 1957), pp. 53, 73, 93–99; Christon I. Archer, *The Army in Bourbon Mexico, 1760–1810* (Albuquerque: University of New Mexico Press, 1977), pp. 22, 110–111, 240; Marcello Carmagnani, "Colonial Latin American Demography: Growth of Chilean Population, 1700–1830," *Journal of Social History* 1, no. 2 (Winter 1967): 183–185; and Timothy E. Anna, *The Fall of the Royal Government in Mexico City* (Lincoln: University of Nebraska Press, 1978), pp. 83–84.

a. Ratios of military personnel per population computed with reference to Mexico, whose score was set at 1.0.

b. Estimates are very conservative because the 1800 population was extrapolated at 362,129 from 1792 and 1817 censuses, but military statistics dated from 1770.

c. Mexican data for 1810.

Military participation in a neopatrimonial elite political culture served to maximize elite political access for private gain in wealth, status, and power. The chief mechanism was the *fuero militar*, military privilege.[3] This removed the military from the jurisdiction of the ordinary court system and established a separate system of military courts with their own privileged jurisdiction. The principle was, in part, the same as that justifying mercantile or mining courts with their own jurisdictions: mercantile courts handled mercantile cases and mining courts handled mining cases, but military courts handled all sorts of cases, military or not (with exceptions to be noted). This was the key to maximizing political access. The *fuero* permitted members of the regular army to enjoy military jurisdiction in civil and criminal cases as well as in strictly military matters. The rights were extended to wives and dependent children, widows and surviving children, and to their domestic servants. They were often passive rights, exercised only when the army officer or soldier was a defendant.

The *fuero* for militiamen varied according to whether a unit was urban or provincial, on active duty or not. When urban or provincial militia units were mobilized, they enjoyed the complete *fuero* of the regular army. When provincial units were not on active duty, the officers and their wives and dependents still enjoyed the complete *fuero*. But enlisted men in inactive provincial units enjoyed only the criminal *fuero*; they were subject to the regular court system for civil cases. The variation in the inactive urban militia was greatest. There was a difference between officers and enlisted men, but the degree of privilege while inactive is difficult to specify. Some enjoyed full privileges, some criminal privileges only, and some none at all. Militia *fueros* were also passive rights, except that the militias of Cuba and Yucatán had the active *fuero*. The latter gave those who enjoyed it the right to bring actions in their own military tribunals against persons of another *fuero*. This concession illustrates the Crown's preferential policies toward Cuba.

Preeminencias, immunities, assured that officers and men of the regular army and their dependents could not be called to discharge municipal duties against their will. They were exempt from providing transportation, lodging, or subsistence for army, church, or civil officials in transit. They were exempt from special money aids to the Crown. They could not be imprisoned for debts, and their arms, horses, or clothing could not be attached for the settlement of private debts. The militia enjoyed the same immunities, except those concerning debts. Upon retirement, regular army and militia officers and men could petition that these immunities and *fueros* be granted for life, to an extent varying by rank, length of service, and circumstances of retirement.

There were general exceptions to military privileges. Cases dating before entry into the service were not privileged. Actions in mercantile law and those related to entailed estates and inheritances were excluded. Malfeasance in public office, sedition, fraud against the treasury, and similar actions were also excluded. These privileges were extended to the military in America in the last third of the eighteenth century because the Crown needed a larger army for imperial defense. The privileges and immunities of the regular army did not pose serious problems because the regular army was small, and lodged in barracks or deployed to remote posts on the frontier. The militiamen, however, because they were more numerous and dispersed throughout the empire, created jurisdictional disputes and enjoyed the fruits of privilege.

The *preeminencias* provided immediate and direct benefits; the benefits of the *fueros* were procedural and substantive. Jurisdictional disputes between military and other courts often occurred. A military man of the regular army or militia who was guilty, or who had lost a civil action, benefited from the delay created by the jurisdictional dispute. Military courts often treated military men more leniently than other courts would have; it was a decided advantage to have one's case tried in courts biased in one's favor. The growth of the military establishment and the efforts by military men to extend the military jurisdiction were serious sources of conflict during the closing decades of the empire. Militia officers in the countryside were often landowners who benefited from courts predisposed in their favor. In the cities many militia officers were medium- and small-scale merchants who benefited greatly from militia privilege.[4]

The military reflected imperial policies and structures in providing a stimulus to the mobility of blacks by providing a means for advancement and for the development of a black elite. The military reflected the larger society by institutionalizing the structural inequality of ethnic groups at the same time that it provided for the advancement of the ethnic strata at the bottom of the social structure. For example, a white sublieutenant's monthly salary in Venezuela was 32 pesos per month; that was higher than a mulatto or black captain's monthly salary (30 and 28 pesos, respectively). For each military rank, whites earned approximately twice as much as blacks. For instance, a white captain earned 60 pesos per month, a black, 28; a white lieutenant earned 40 pesos, a black, 22.[5] On the other hand, mulattoes and blacks in the officer ranks gained status, power, and absolute wealth, although they lagged relative to whites.

The chief reward of black military participation, too, was the enjoyment of privileges.[6] Black militiamen typically did not enjoy *fueros* of any sort when they were inactive, but they enjoyed the full civil and criminal *fuero* when on active duty. Because of the nearly continuous state of war in the empire after 1790, many black militiamen enjoyed the full *fuero* most of the time. There was also a regional variation in the likelihood of mobilization into active duty, and hence in the likelihood of the full enjoyment of the *fuero*. Cuba, coastal New Spain, and coastal Venezuela were most likely to be on alert, so black militiamen in these areas frequently enjoyed privileged jurisdiction.

In order to stimulate black enrollment for imperial defense, the Crown stipulated that black militiamen would be exempt from the payment of the tribute while they were in service. This was especially relevant in New Spain, where such a tax was extensive. Because of treasury protests of loss of revenue, the tribute exemption was limited in the early 1780s: the full exemption was allowed every black in every unit on active service; when they were inactive, only the older, more established provincial militia units continued to enjoy the tribute exemption, not the urban units. However, all militia units on the coast of Veracruz continued to enjoy this exemption at all times because they were frequently on alert. Because these units included most of the black militiamen, relatively few blacks were actually affected by the formal change in the law.

White militiamen had more privileges than black militiamen; Indians were excluded from the military altogether. Therefore, the military reproduced and institutionalized the inequalities of the social structure. Yet it was a crucial instrument for social mobility within the established political system by providing privileges for blacks. Such privileges made military service attractive to blacks and mulattoes and allowed many of them power and status that many whites did not have.

About two fifths of all militiamen in Cuba and Venezuela were blacks; in Mexico, the proportion rose during the 1770s to at least one third, before stabilizing at that level (see Table 2). Thus, a large share of Spain's military force in these colonies was contributed by the black population. The blacks were important to the defense of the empire; and the empire, by welcoming them into military ranks, was important to blacks because it opened up avenues for mobility. Black percentages in the Cuban and Venezuelan militia were about the same. But there were many more free blacks in Venezuela than in Cuba, so it had a lower rate of militarization than the island. Consequently, every third free black adult male in Cuba, but only every twenty-fourth in Venezuela, was enrolled in the militia. The rates of militarization for Venezuelan and Cuban whites were comparable: one out of eight. But this meant that Cuban whites were only about one third as militarized as Cuban blacks, while Venezuelan whites were three times more militarized than Venezuelan blacks.[7] Cuba's free blacks were far more likely to have been co-opted in the imperial system as a result of their direct access to government resources.

Many Cuban blacks were either slaves or members of the military, which sustained and defended a slave system. . . . From the government's point of view this reduced the probability of a coalition of free blacks and slaves in Cuba. Black free men in the military improved their access to job, power, and status, often at the expense of black slaves. In this respect, they were no better—and no worse—than Cuba's white population.

From a comparative point of view, Cuba's high black military participation ratio removed many free black male adults from the active job market and from competition with whites for upper- and middle-income jobs. In Venezuela the army did not serve this function: it absorbed too few free black adult males to affect the upper- and middle-income job market. Given Venezuela's large free black population, competition for these jobs was far more severe than in Cuba, and the white elite of Caracas expressed alarm that blacks might take over jobs in the government reserved for whites. Black pressure for political access in Venezuela was continuous; in Cuba it was diverted to the military. Venezuela, therefore, had a manpower surplus for upper- and middle-income jobs, and a manpower shortage for plantation jobs. The Cuban colonial government coopted freedmen by means of military jobs, giving them income, status, and power, far more than did the Venezuelan colonial government. Cuban black militiamen defended the empire that made their mobility possible. This function was performed less well in Venezuela.

Table 2. Black Participation in the Militia

Country[a]	Total militia	Percentage of blacks	Year
Cuba	8,076	42.2	1770
Venezuela	13,136	41.8	1800
Mexico	10,698	17.6	1766
Mexico	34,717	34.2	1784
Mexico	23,812	33.6	1800

Source: See Table 1.

a. Low estimates for Mexico. Assumed (same proportions across time) that only about 90 percent of the militia units on the Pacific and Gulf coasts and of the Lancers of Veracruz were composed of blacks, and that two thirds of the militiamen in New Galicia-Guadalajara were black. All personnel enrolled in units identified as composed of blacks were added.

Although the imperial military establishment was an army of Americans, it was not so equally everywhere. In Venezuela only about one fifth of the military was Spanish. In Chile the bulk of the soldiers and half the officers were American Chileans.[8] In Mexico, Americans accounted for 76 percent of all enlisted men in the regular troops in 1790, rising to 95 percent in 1800. However, Spaniards held a far higher proportion of the officer ranks than was warranted by their share of the population, thus increasing conflict between Creoles and Spaniards. In 1788, Spaniards filled eleven of the seventeen slots at the rank of captain and above in the Regiment of the Crown, and thirty-eight of its sixty-two slots at or above the rank of first sergeant. In 1800, Spaniards filled ten of thirteen officer jobs in the Guanajuato infantry battalion, and seven of the nine colonel and lieutenant colonel slots in the Bajío militia regiments. Only three of the forty-five senior regular army officers of the Army of New Spain were from New Spain itself at the end of the eighteenth century.[9]

The military establishment in America grew out of international threats to the security of the empire. Its growth reflected the social system within which it developed. The military exhibited the neopatrimonial characteristics typical of other elite institutions. Maximizing political access for private gain was pursued relentlessly. The rate of general militarization varied from colony to colony; its maximum growth is explained by international factors, whether in response to major European powers in Cuba or Indians beyond Spanish control in Chile. The military reflected the structural inequality and flexibility of the empire's ethnic systems. It did so differentially, for the co-opting of black freedmen in Cuba went furthest and had the most widespread effects. In the final analysis, the military establishment reinforced existing trends. It accounted for more government responsiveness to freedmen in Cuba, and it responded to Cubans far more than to other colonials. Its effect on Mexico may have worsened existing elite ethnic differences among officers.

Notes

1. Bruce M. Russett et al., *World Handbook of Political and Social Indicators* (New Haven: Yale University Press, 1964), pp. 74–76.

2. Margaret L. Woodward, "The Spanish Army and the Loss of America, 1810–1824," *Hispanic American Historical Review* 43, no. 4 (1963): 587.

3. This discussion draws heavily from Lyle N. McAlister, *The "Fuero Militar" in New Spain, 1764–1800* (Gainesville: University of Florida Press, 1957), pp. 6–11.

4. Ibid., pp. 14, 33; Lucas Alamán, *Historia de Méjico* (México: Editorial Jus, 1968), I, 58; and María del Carmen Velázquez, *El estado de guerra en Nueva España* (México: Colegio de México, 1950), pp. 154–161, 164, 172–176.

5. McAlister, *"Fuero Militar,"* pp. 11, 45–51; Christon I. Archer, "Pardos, Indians, and the Army of New Spain: Inter-Relationships and Conflicts, 1780–1810," *Journal of Latin American Studies* 6, no. 2 (November 1974): 231–255; and Christon I. Archer, *The Army in Bourbon Mexico, 1760–1810* (Albuquerque: University of New Mexico Press, 1977), pp. 224, 237.

6. Francisco Depons, *Viaje a la parte oriental de tierra firme* (Caracas: Tipografía Americana, 1930), pp. 175–178.

7. Herbert S. Klein, *Slavery in the Americas: A Comparative Study of Virginia and Cuba* (Chicago: Quadrangle, 1971), pp. 218–219; Depons, *Viaje*, pp. 175–178; Ramón de la Sagra, *Historia económico-política y estadística de la isla de Cuba* (Havana: Viudas de Arazoza y Soler, 1831), p. 3; José M. Pérez Cabrera, "Movimiento de población," in Guerra y Sánchez et al., eds., *Historia de la nación cubana*, 10 vols. (Havana: 1852), III, 348. The following facts and assumptions were used in computations. The free black male population over age fifteen for Cuba in 1827 (60.8 percent) was computed directly from the census of that year.

The same rate was applied to the same population stratum in the early 1770s, for which there is a military count for 1770 and a population count in 1774. The 1774 count gave the free black male population from which the adult share was calculated and the military ratio. This is consistent with Lombardi's finding that the Venezuelan population under age six accounted for 28 percent of the population. For Venezuela, the Cuban age structure and an even sex ratio were assumed to apply. Its free black population was taken from chap. 3; then the military ratio was computed. For a justification of the application of Cuban age structure data to Venezuela, see Jorge I. Domínguez, "Political Participation and the Social Mobilization Hypothesis: Chile, Mexico, Venezuela and Cuba, 1800–1825," *The Journal of Interdisciplinary History* 5, no. 2 (Fall 1974): 246–247. See also John V. Lombardi, *People and Places in Colonial Venezuela* (Bloomington: Indiana University Press, 1976), p. 137. For a discussion of Cuban slave demography, see also Jack Ericson Eblen, "On the Natural Increase of Slave Populations: The Example of the Cuban Black Population, 1775–1900," in Stanley L. Engerman and Eugene D. Genovese, eds., *Race and Slavery in the Western Hemisphere: Quantitative Studies* (Princeton: Princeton University Press, 1975); and Stanley L. Engerman, "Comments on the Study of Race and Slavery," in ibid., pp. 509–510.

8. Woodward, "The Spanish Army," p. 587; Francisco A. Encina, *Historia de Chile* (Santiago: Nascimiento, 1946), V, 531.

9. David A. Brading, *Miners and Merchants in Bourbon Mexico, 1763–1810* (Cambridge: Cambridge University Press, 1971), pp. 325–326; Archer, *The Army in Bourbon Mexico*, pp. 195–199, 212–213, 234.

2

"La Causa Buena": The Counterinsurgency Army of New Spain and the Ten Years' War

Christon I. Archer

The Spanish monarchy collapsed in 1808 after Napoleon invaded Spain, precipitating a crisis of legitimacy throughout the empire. In New Spain the Spaniards overthrew the viceroy in order to prevent the American-born criollos from establishing a local government in the name of the king. One of the creole conspiracies to regain control of the government of New Spain inadvertently unleashed a class and race conflict when Father Miguel Hidalgo led a rebellion in September 1810. The colonial army of New Spain was confronted first with the rebellions led by Hidalgo (1810–11) and José María Morelos (1811–1814) and subsequently with a fragmented insurgency.

From 1810 to 1821 the royal authorities developed a strategy to meet this unconventional challenge to the regime. Their counterinsurgency had a far-reaching and unexpected impact on the society and politics of New Spain. Newly arrived officers militarized the country, usurped civil authority in threatened areas, and imposed war taxes in their efforts to extinguish the insurgency. These tactics were successful in some areas, but in regions such as Veracruz the royalists were unable to secure the countryside and defeat the insurgents. The extraordinary financial, social, and political costs borne by the population throughout New Spain to support the counterinsurgency not only eroded loyalty to the royal government

From *The Independence of Mexico and the Creation of the New Nation*, ed. Jaime E. Rodríguez O. (Los Angeles and Irvine: UCLA Latin American Center and Mexico/Chicano Program, 1989), 85–108. Reprinted by permission of The Regents of the University of California.

*but also fostered the careers of provincial leaders who would challenge
the authority of the national elite in the immediate post-Independence
period.*

*The protracted struggle also weakened and exhausted the Spanish
army. Discontent within the military increased when municipalities refused to pay war taxes after the restoration of the Spanish constitution in
1820. Although the fragmented insurgency did not achieve a military victory, eventually many demoralized royalist troops changed sides and joined
the Mexican autonomists in their successful bid for independence.*

> COMANDANTE: "¿Juráis a Díos, y prometéis a la
> Patria, y a la Religión de defenderla hasta perder la
> última gota de vuestra sangre, de mantener estas ricas
> posesiones a Vuestro Augusto Soberano y de
> obedecer a los Cabos, Sargentos, y demas Jefes que
> compongan el Exército?"
> SOLDADOS REALISTAS: "Sí Juramos."[1]

Writing in June 1815, after almost five years of revolution, Bishop
Manuel Abad y Queipo had good reason to believe that he possessed considerable expertise on the *mortífero contagio* of insurgency that
devoured New Spain. During his journey from Valladolid (Morelia) to
Mexico City, where he reported to the king on the origins and state of the
revolution, Abad y Queipo's convoy suffered two violent attacks in which
the four hundred escort troops managed to repulse the insurgents. In the
bishop's view, the royalist struggle against a powerful coalition of rebel
forces was all that stood in the way of a descent into "a frightful anarchy."[2] The revolution of Santo Domingo provided graphic evidence of
the absolute ruin that could destroy Mexico. Abad y Queipo identified a
criollo faction that employed "the most refined Machiavellianism" to convert submissive and pacific Mexicans into *monstruos feroces*. In fifteen
horrendous days during September 1810, more than a million Indians,
Negroes, and mulattoes had been seduced into joining the rebellion.[3]

By identifying a conspiratorial leadership, Abad y Queipo drifted away
from any true understanding of the Mexican insurgency. Like so many
contemporary participants, nineteenth-century observers, and recent historians who have written on the Mexican independence period, the bishop
could not acknowledge the fact that what gripped New Spain was nothing
less than one of the greatest guerrilla insurgencies in modern history. In
response, the royalist army introduced a counterinsurgency program that
was a classic of its type comparable with similar twentieth-century campaigns waged by the French in Algeria, the French and Americans in Vietnam, and the Russians in Afghanistan. The fact that the Mexican
counterinsurgents failed to subdue guerrilla insurgents involved in a to-

tally fragmented people's war of ten years evokes further comparisons with modern wars of national liberation. For Abad y Queipo and Mexico's first generation of historians, proximity to the events and the need to create a Mexican national identity blurred the major themes, creating a generation of national heroes and evil scapegoats. In Mexico, long-term insurgency and counterinsurgency led to decentralization and regionalism and to the enthronement of reactionism over progressive or modern tendencies. After independence, Mexican nation builders, struggling with the heritage of such debilitating factors, had no reason to glorify a deep guerrilla tradition or the continuation of regional centrifugal forces that threatened the existence of the nation.

For Abad y Queipo, the royalist failure to end insurgency quickly appeared to be the direct result of the poor leadership by the army commander, Brigadier Félix Calleja, rather than of a confrontation of monumental proportions between parties that would fight to their death or total exhaustion. No royalist supporter wanted to admit that the army of New Spain had engaged what Calleja described as a "hydra reborn as fast as one cuts off its heads."[4] Abad y Queipo focused criticism on Calleja, whom he described as "a man sold on himself, and very sensitive to flattery."[5] The bishop agreed that initially Calleja had done well enough, leading his Army of the Center to brilliant victories over Padre Miguel Hidalgo's rebel masses at Aculco, Guanajuato, and Calderón. Yet he failed to pursue the rebels with sufficient dedication and energy to liquidate them totally. Calleja's difficulties at Zitácuaro, and in the protracted siege of José María Morelos's army at Cuautla Amilpas, caused many nonmilitary observers to criticize the royalist general and his army. To Abad y Queipo, the fault lay with army commanders who lacked the talent and knowledge needed to prosecute an effective campaign. What was worse, Calleja had convinced Viceroy [Francisco Javier de] Venegas that the insurrection was all but over in 1811, when in fact it was about to enter a powerful new stage. Then, as viceroy, beginning in 1813, Calleja failed to end the revolution. In the mind of the unmilitary bishop, the army appeared to increase its oppression without results. Military discipline declined, many commanders seemed indolent, and the royalist forces controlled only the garrisoned towns and cities. A bloated army of some eighty thousand troops could not handle twenty-five thousand to thirty thousand poorly armed and undisciplined insurgents who were "the true sovereigns of the country."[6] The rebels controlled agriculture, industry, and commerce; they robbed, destroyed, or taxed everything outside the royalist fortifications.

Although there was an element of truth in each of Abad y Queipo's charges against the royalist army, the bishop was guilty of gross oversimplifications and misunderstandings that made him a poor observer of a guerrilla war. It would take time for a conventional army to learn the art of irregular war and to apply a program designed to control, if not to obliterate, insurgency.

Many of the complaints lodged against the royalist army demonstrated little more than the advanced level of petty backbiting, fears, and jealousies prevalent in Mexican society. Calleja, although a brilliant soldier in many respects, lacked training or experience in the area of counter-insurgency. Like most senior officers stationed in Mexico prior to 1810, his major mission had been to prevent a European enemy from landing on the Veracruz coast and, to a lesser degree, to control the northern frontier, where Indian tribes posed regional threats, but never the prospect of total annihilation. The mass appeal of Hidalgo's uprising surprised army officers, like everyone else. In anticipation of a French invasion, many of the provincial militia units, and the few regular infantry battalions, had been mobilized and cantoned in Puebla and near the mountain towns overlooking Veracruz. Administrators and army commanders looked on, dumbfounded, as the insurgency expanded.

Calleja, commander of the Tenth Militia Brigade at San Luis Potosí, possessed no mobilized units even at the company level that could be committed to battle against the insurgents. When he received word of the uprising, at 10:30 A.M. on September 19, Calleja had to create an army from scratch, one not based on an existing force.[7] He met with the commanders of his brigade, assembled green ranch hands from the rural haciendas, and ordered the construction of weapons. The only firearms available in his brigade were ancient worn-out muskets used by the Provincial Dragoon Regiments of San Luis and San Carlos.[8] Ordered by Viceroy Venegas to concentrate his brigade at Querétaro with other royalist units marching there from Puebla, Calleja saw no alternative but to defer. Even the recruitment of Indian bowmen and the mobilization of artisans to construct lances, the most basic weapon used by mounted forces, would take weeks. If there had been a theoretical opportunity for the army to crush Hidalgo's insurgency in its formative stages, neither the provincial units of the cantonments nor Calleja's hastily recruited countrymen were able to act decisively. By October 9, 1810, the Marqués del Xaral del Berrio, commander of Calleja's advance guard, sighted an insurgent force of forty thousand to fifty thousand against San Luis Potosí. They came by roads and through the *barrancas* loaded down with booty from robberies like "a swarm of ants" determined to incite the countryside to rebellion.[9]

Calleja might have viewed many aspects of his situation as humorous if he and his province had not been in mortal peril. He lacked infantry and artillery needed to force the insurgent-occupied passes at Carrasa and Nieto on the road to Querétaro. A junta of artisans knowledgeable about casting iron and bronze promised to make artillery pieces, but produced poor-quality cannon. The first casting failed completely, and the second effort produced one flawed barrel and two others that were so small that they would not do much damage in battle. It was quite obvious, during the experiments, that no one possessed sufficient technical knowledge about casting cannon and that improvements would come only after a period of trial and error. Even after mid-October, only one barrel was ready to be mounted on a carriage.[10]

For all of his efforts to recruit troops, by mid-October Calleja had only fifteen hundred foot soldiers "of the very worst sort," and twenty-six hundred horsemen composed primarily of rural *vaqueros* armed only with lances. Not only did the precipitous nature of the recruitment and training of his soldiers bother Calleja, but also he could not forget the expanding contagion of insurgency and the frequent desertions from his cantonment.[11] Such were the origins of the Army of the Center.

Uncertain about the loyalty of his own troops and civilian populace, Calleja was helpless to prevent disasters befalling the city and province of Guanajuato. On September 23, 1810, Intendente Juan Antonio Riaño of Guanajuato reported that he was in dire straits, surrounded and cut off from provisions. Irapuato had fallen the day before and Riaño knew that his own large urban populations had begun to waver. The *intendente* begged for assistance and information on Calleja's operations and the size of his forces.[12] In reply, Calleja prevaricated with a promise he knew was untrue; he told Riaño to sustain his position with vigor and to expect relief from San Luis Potosí in a week.[13]

Poor Riaño, his lifeline had almost run its course. Far from being able to defend himself, on September 26 he informed Calleja that with five hundred men he had fortified himself in the city *alhóndiga*. He informed Calleja that Dolores, San Miguel, Celaya, Salamanca, and Irapuato had fallen and that Silao was on the point of declaring for insurgency. Guanajuato seethed with discontent, his few cavalrymen were poorly mounted and armed with "glass swords," and his untrustworthy infantry possessed only patched and mended muskets. Riaño told Calleja that ever since September 17, he had not taken off his clothing or been able to obtain minimum rest. For the past three days, he had not managed to sleep for even an hour.[14] By September 27, rebel forces surrounded and besieged the granary. Cut off from news and short of gunpowder, Riaño did manage to send a dispatch to Calleja and another to the *presidente* of Guadalajara requesting relief forces. Despite the hopelessness of the situation, Riaño was certain that the royalist columns, in combination with his garrison, would inflict exemplary punishment upon the rebels.[15] The idea was a good one, but others would have to take up the cause of counterinsurgency. At 11:00 A.M. on September 28, Riaño managed to smuggle out one last runner with a terse note for Calleja: "I am going to fight because I am going to be attacked this instant: I will resist as long as I can because I am honorable: Your Excellency, come to my aid."[16] Riaño was dead within hours, insurgents had sacked the granary killing its European and criollo defenders, and Guanajuato was in rebel hands.[17]

Far from acting decisively to introduce a counterinsurgency program, the royalist commanders staggered before a frightening new power that threatened to sweep aside all military resistance. European Spaniards and other members of the governing elite fled from the provincial cities in *terror pánico* to seek refuge in Querétaro, Mexico City, and in regions distant from the insurgency.[18] At Querétaro, the Conde de la Cadena and the urban government feared dispatching any forces from the city that would allow the sixty thousand inhabitants to launch their own uprising. Cadena placed little confidence in his troops and found that his senior officers exhibited no desire to lead relief expeditions against the insurgent-occupied cities.[19] Large segments of militia units from the Bajío towns joined the rebellion, and Querétaro soldiers who had their wives with them appeared especially untrustworthy. In only two days, seventy-four soldiers of the Provincial Regiment of Celaya garrisoned at Querétaro deserted into rebel territory two leagues outside the city.[20] Cadena asked Viceroy Venegas to transfer loyal troops from Puebla, Veracruz, Tlaxcala, and Toluca. In cities and provinces not yet affected by insurgency, however, recruitment of patriotic militias lagged as men debated terms of service and resisted any suggestion that they might be required to march beyond their city walls. At Veracruz, soon a major center of revolution, residents foiled all efforts to raise a *cuerpo urbano* of one thousand men.[21]

Depression and defeatist attitudes turned to euphoria as the royalists concentrated scattered units and Calleja marched southward from San Luis Potosí. The invulnerability of the Indian and mestizo masses had much more to do with appearance and psychology than with real military might. The massed musketry, grapeshot, and fairly well disciplined soldiers of the Army of the Center crushed the insurgents at Aculco, Guanajuato, and Calderón. Even describing these affairs as battles is misleading since they were so one-sided. The insurgent commanders committed the tragic error of believing that they could engage in conventional battle with the royalist army. They lacked the arms, leaders, and discipline. Once the royalists banished their own fears of rebel omnipotence, they found that they had been combating an illusion of military power rather than a real army. Cadena informed Venegas that after the pacification of the Bajío cities and towns that had supported the insurgency, "I will return to Mexico City without having fired a shot."[22] Upon further reflection and with time to evaluate the true nature of the insurgency, Cadena was less optimistic about a rapid conclusion. In his view, two months more of inaction and paralysis by the military might have been enough to lose New Spain. On the eve of the battle of Calderón, which was to take his own life, Cadena realized that the Hidalgo movement was a general insurrection including all inhabitants and not merely a peasant uprising. Fear and even terror of military retribution might restore order, but in their hearts the Mexicans had come to abhor Spaniards and Spanish rule.[23]

The problem for any counterinsurgent is to balance naked force with a desire to introduce pacific reform policies designed to extirpate the root of insurgency. Calleja could not forget for an instant that his Army of the Center was a force composed principally of Mexicans. He knew that a revolt based simply upon separation from Spain, unencumbered by the racial overtones of the Hidalgo uprising, would appeal to the great majority of Mexicans.[24] From the military point of view, Calleja knew that his victories were flawed to the extent that his green troops wavered when rebel units stood to fight. There was, for example, considerable vacillation in the royalist lines at Calderón before the insurgents broke and turned the battle into a massacre.[25] Worse, the rebels learned very quickly from their disasters and adopted guerrilla warfare and constructed fortifications that would require lengthy conventional sieges. A general proliferation of insurgent bands presented the royalist army with insuperable challenges that would require the introduction of a full-blown counterinsurgency system. Even in 1811 the insurgents had the royalist army running from point to point to meet a multiplicity of minor irritations. In Guanajuato province, the rebel chief Albino García operated with a guerrilla force of about one thousand men out of the steep mountains and canyons of Valle de Santiago. An army division under Major Agustín Viña chased García, but could not engage the guerrillas because of the rough country. When the royalists moved out, the insurgents followed, destroying water tanks, digging pits in roads to prevent the passage of artillery and cavalry, and diverting streams to flood roads. Viña became so frustrated by his inability to engage Albino García's guerrillas that he returned to the town of Salamanca to apprehend and jail some rebel women and children. In Viña's view, they had to be made "to feel the evils of war in every way."[26]

News in 1811 of Morelos's threats to Puebla forced Calleja to move the Army of the Center out of the unpacified Bajío region. Insurgent forces concentrated first at Zitácuaro, fortifying the town and challenging the army to exhaust itself in a debilitating siege. Calleja's critics had no idea about the difficulties entailed in moving approximately five thousand troops. Cold weather caused sickness, and many soldiers suffered from venereal disease "that is endemic in this country and which devours the army."[27] As the provincial soldiers left their home districts, desertion eroded the army's vitality. Supplies of biscuit became precarious, and many units ran short of tobacco, "so essential for soldiers on campaign."[28] As the royalists approached Zitácuaro, the rebels dug great pits in the road, which delayed progress and required considerable energy to fill before artillery and baggage carts could be moved. There was no possibility of living off the land since the enemy implemented an effective scorched-earth policy.[29]

Calleja was not a sanguinary general compared to some other counterinsurgent commanders who served in New Spain. Nevertheless, debilitating dysentery combined with Venegas's impatient demands for rapid movement made Calleja anxious to avoid a lengthy siege at Zitácuaro. He followed his victory with a draconian punishment designed to provoke terror in other insurgent districts. Zitácuaro and eleven Indian villages were razed to ashes.[30] Following the lengthy and debilitating siege of Cuautla Amilpas, on May 6, 1812, Calleja ordered the demolition of the defenses and the burning of the town. At this point, Viceroy Venegas intervened to suspend the order that in his view applied counterinsurgency terror indiscriminately against both guilty and innocent.[31] Unfortunately, either by design or error, Calleja's order halting the sacrifice of Cuautla did not reach Brigadier Ciriaco de Llano, who had been left in charge. Llano informed Calleja that the order containing the "pious resolution" to suspend the destruction had reached him a day late—only the churches and a few other buildings had been spared a fiery end.[32]

It is interesting that, when he became viceroy, Calleja renounced this form of counterinsurgency terror. In 1813 near Veracruz, when his forces encountered resistance, Colonel Ramón Monduí torched the towns of Medellín and Rancho de Tejar. Monduí expressed satisfaction at having captured rebel standards, a cannon, arms, and horses, and at leaving the insurgents and "their wretched families" without houses. While he agreed that Medellín deserved having been reduced to ashes, Calleja informed his commander: "The politics of our living together requires that you have certain consideration for the towns that obliges one to keep the buildings in provinces of small population. We do not wish to convert the country into a frightful desert and increase the evils that exist and the hatred with which measures of this nature are viewed."[33]

The implementation of counterinsurgency policies in New Spain depended upon the nature and extent of insurgent activities. Viceroy Venegas ordered army commanders to offer amnesty and pardon to those who truly eschewed violence. However, when soft persuasion and reason did not work, "extraordinary rigor," exemplary punishment, and terror became the operative policies. Summary executions of rebel officers and soldiers were common in the first few years. Given the widespread popularity of the rebellion, many royalist commanders adopted arbitrary and even cruel responses designed to bludgeon would-be insurgents into acquiescence, if not support, for the royalist cause. At Guanajuato during November 1810, Calleja imposed the draconian punishment of decimation upon a group of men accused of tearing down during the night his proclamations pardoning rebels. Failing to identify the real culprits, soldiers arrested forty men of the lower classes who happened to be in the general area where the incidents had taken place. When the prisoners could not or would not denounce those responsible for the offenses, the names of four men were drawn by lot and they were executed by firing squad.[34]

In their application of counterinsurgency programs and policies, royalist officers arriving in Mexico from the Spanish army knew a great deal about the subject firsthand from their unfortunate experiences against the French invasion and occupation armies. It is interesting that soldiers who had supported the resistance and insurgency in Spain switched roles in Mexico to introduce many of the counterinsurgency techniques they had seen used by the French. They recognized that effective counterinsurgency demanded mobility, speed, and the flexibility to pacify rebellious districts effectively. Their methods included the use of exemplary terror and of *destacamentos volantes* (flying detachments) designed to chase down and to punish guerrilla bands and the civilian populace that supported insurgency.

The *destacamento volante* set units of counterinsurgent hunters against the mobile guerrilla bands. While some isolated and mountainous provinces, such as Veracruz, became permanent foci of insurgent activity that required major military incursions to achieve any real results, flying detachments served to patrol the margins of major roads, to prevent the coalescence of insurgent bands, and to keep the guerrillas out of towns from which they drew sustenance and support. Counterinsurgency of this sort demanded enthusiasm, dedication, and constant energy from officers who had to endure difficult conditions for lengthy periods. In Mexico, the steady flow of Spanish expeditionary officers and soldiers between 1811 and 1816 stiffened locally recruited units and brought renewed vigor at times when existing counterinsurgent commanders approached a state of exhaustion. Although many historians have tended to dismiss the expeditionaries, they played a major role in keeping New Spain within the empire. Without them, independence might have come years earlier.

The first to organize flying detachments or columns was Brigadier José de la Cruz, who arrived from Spain in early November 1810. His first mission as commander of the Army of the Right was to open the strategically important road between Mexico City and Querétaro that had been cut by guerrilla bands operating out of Tula, Huichapan, and other towns. Cruz advocated the use of terror against entrenched village and district rural clans led by families such as the Villagráns and Anayas. In this region, as well as in other provinces, members of these clans acted as linking agents who articulated existing grievances and recruited support from more isolated Indian communities. With backgrounds in contraband trading and banditry, and legitimization through recognition by the major rebel leaders, these insurgents were extremely difficult to check. Despite his recent arrival in Mexico, the volatile Cruz wasted little time before he vowed to use terror and mobile counterinsurgency to obliterate opposition.[35] Rebels captured with arms in their hands were taken to towns such as Nopala and Huichapan, where they were executed before the assembled populace. Cruz informed Venegas: "Your Excellency, it is no longer possible to suffer more from this vile scum; only examples of exemplary terror will make them understand their duty."[36] Flying detachments received orders to apply a policy of "fire and blood" against any rebel village. Anyone caught with arms, unable to produce a passport, or who acted suspiciously was to be shot and the bodies were to be displayed at the places of execution.[37]

By December 1810, Cruz had formed three *destacamentos volantes* financed by a combination of donations, forced contributions, and outright confiscations. These mounted forces employed lightning speed, deception, and the cover of night to confuse the insurgents and to appear in areas where they could strike quickly and withdraw. Villages, haciendas, and ranchos located in rebel zones were stripped of all horses, arms, and weapons, even small kitchen knives. They rounded up all blacksmiths and destroyed forges that could be employed in the construction of lance points and other weapons.[38] Although the *destacamentos volantes* of 1810 were a stopgap measure to match the mobility of guerrilla warfare north of Mexico City, the concept took hold as the royalists introduced a thoroughgoing system of counterinsurgency. For most of the decade of war, regular and militia garrisons throughout New Spain operated flying detachments in cooperation with regular army formations. The major weakness of the mobile forces was that the detachment commanders often lacked intelligence data on insurgent activities. Arbitrary punishments, confiscations, and brutalities committed by counterinsurgent troops deepened bitter enmities and created many more enemies than friends. In 1811 veteran criollo officer Colonel José Antonio de Andrade reported that the enemy simply fled from any action and reformed elsewhere. The royalist troops had no idea how to identify insurgents since the campesinos dressed alike and no one gave information for fear of later reprisals.[39]

Despite these weaknesses, the flying detachments or variations on the system worked well in guerrilla insurgent zones where the population was known to be committed and excessive violence by the army posed little danger to royalist interests. In 1816, José de la Cruz operated a series of *cuerpos volantes* south of Guadalajara around the margins of Laguna de Chapala to create a tight cordon designed to prevent the Indians from supplying the rebel island fortress of Mezcala. Amnestied on numerous occasions and never repentant, Cruz described the population as "perfidious, and treacherous—using hypocrisy as their emblem."[40] Elsewhere, the creation of commandancies general in provinces of major guerrilla activity employed many characteristics of the mobile flying companies. In 1814, for example, Viceroy Calleja created a special military province under Colonel José Joaquín Márquez y Donallo, commander of the Regiment of Lobera, which embraced portions of the Intendancy of Mexico including the Llanos de Apan, Tulancingo, Pachuca, Otumba, Zempoala, Texcoco, and San Juan Teotihuacán. Small garrisons of regular infantry and dragoons were stationed in each of the towns; and the second in command, Major José Barradas, headed a mobile division based at Apan composed of the Light Infantry Regiment of San Luis, a company of Lobera, seventy-five dragoons of the Regiment of Mexico, fifty-five dragoons of the Regiment of Querétaro, and sixty mounted artillerymen with two mobile artillery pieces and a howitzer. The first mission of the mobile force was to crush insurgent congregations and to reorganize the towns. Since the residents had opted for the rebels and withheld taxes for years, they were to be heavily taxed and to provide meat, grain, and other provisions consumed by the royalist troops.[41]

As early as 1811, Félix Calleja realized that a general fragmented insurgency employing guerrilla warfare would rapidly exhaust the available regular and militia units of the royalist army. Certainly, as Abad y Queipo charged, it was premature for Calleja to declare a unilateral end to the insurgency. However, by reducing the opposition to bandits, thieves, and delinquents, he sought to gain a propaganda victory. Calleja endeavored to construct a tiered system of counterinsurgent defenses that would be based upon patriot militias organized in cities, towns, and rural districts. His Reglamento Político Militar of June 8, 1811, became one of the most important and controversial documents of the counterinsurgency. With his tiered system, Calleja hoped to regain control over the countryside, isolate and marginalize the insurgents, and harden town defenses so that the lightly armed rebels would not dare attack without artillery. As he explained to the district *subdelegados*, the army could not dispatch small forces every time a village or hacienda received a threat. The army divisions and flying detachments could not be present everywhere, and the people had to take up arms in their own defense.[42] Once this took place, the royalist army would be able to unite scattered garrisons and to concentrate forces against the major foci of insurgency.

Depending upon the districts or towns involved, Calleja's Reglamento Político Militar could be either quite successful or an abject failure. At insurgent-wracked San Miguel, Colonel Diego García Conde organized three companies of fifty men each—one of infantry and two of cavalry. During August 1811 the militiamen received daily training and appeared to exhibit a positive attitude toward "*la justa causa.*" One of the cavalry companies had some pistols and sabers, and the other two companies received lances, which were the normal weapons assigned to such units. García Conde embarked upon an ambitious project to manufacture firearms for these militias. Outside the town, the Indian communities formed two companies and contributed thirty men daily to active duty and more in emergencies.[43]

In contrast to this apparent success, at San Luis de la Paz dependent upon San Miguel, the *subdelegado*, Antonio de Flon, convened a meeting of sixty men who were to form the town militia. From their looks, all appeared to Flon as frightened and cowardly. None had arms or horses to form cavalry, and there was no money available. Later, Flon convoked a junta of the rural hacienda *mayordomos* and workers. The *mayordomos* showed up, but explained that the hacienda workers had fled "for fear of the army and the insurgents." They said that if they declared for the royalists, they would be killed by the rebels. Since they had to travel alone in the mountains, it seemed likely that they would fall into the clutches of the bands that constantly sacked the haciendas. Flon described the few rancheros who appeared as "absolutely wild men, who in general are malicious, cowardly, and rotten to the heart."[44] His general impressions notwithstanding, Flon explained the benefits of joining "*la causa buena*" and the evils of not doing so. All listened "with arms crossed and their eyes on the ground." As soon as he released them, one rode out immediately to report the contents of the junta to the rebels at Sichú. Given this state of affairs, Flon recommended against arming such elements until the army dislodged the insurgent bands in the mountains.[45]

One major criticism of Calleja's counterinsurgency plan was that he conceived a design specifically for a region of towns and large rural haciendas where there were sufficient population and financial resources to raise infantry and mounted patriot companies. Calleja called for haciendas of the first class to offer fifty militiamen; second class, thirty-five militiamen; and third class, twenty-five militiamen. In Querétaro province, for example, the haciendas were small, and none reached the status of first class. In San Luis Potosí, Calleja's model and home province, the hacienda of Jaral and other estates were vast in magnitude and contained settled populations of up to eleven thousand inhabitants. To fund fifty militiamen cost 13,000 pesos annually, twenty-five men cost 6,500 pesos, and ten men cost 2,600 pesos. Of the sixty-four haciendas of Querétaro jurisdiction, not including San Juan del Río, there were only four estates valued at 200,000 pesos that would produce approximately 10,000 pesos annually. Even the largest estates could not afford royalist companies of fifty militiamen. In his 1818 report on Querétaro province, José Miguel Barreiro concluded that recent annual sales from haciendas totaled 3,687,000 pesos, contributing a profit after expenses and taxes of only 184,350 pesos. Naturally, only part of this sum could be used for militias since a large portion went to the owners for subsistence, payments on debts, and for other obligations.[46] Barreiro pointed out that hacienda owners had also been paying the insurgents special taxes for safety and protection. However, success in the plan to establish royalist companies would allow the hacendados to terminate paying rebel taxes that drained the royalist cause.[47]

The weaknesses of Calleja's Plan Político Militar were even more evident in Veracruz province, which became a primary zone of insurgent dominance and of royalist concern. The tropical lowlands and mountainous highlands offered guerrillas every possible advantage. Yellow fever consumed European expeditionary battalions and Mexican highland regiments equally while sparing the indigenous insurgents who enjoyed inborn immunity. As viceroy, Calleja knew that Spanish expeditionaries arriving at the port suffered severe losses to tropical disease; and as an experienced commander of Mexican forces, he was fully aware of the terror generated in highlanders by mere mention of *vómito negro*. In 1813, Calleja ordered the governor of Veracruz, José de Quevedo, to implement his general counterinsurgency plan and to recruit the coastal inhabitants into patriot companies. Quevedo, like many Veracruz governors before him, resisted a defense program based upon the local population and designed to keep Europeans away from the zones of tropical disease. He wanted the commander of the Army of the South, the Conde de Castro Terreño, to station a flying division in the lowlands to keep the roads inland open and to garrison Puente del Rey.[48]

Almost all the available arable land in Veracruz province was held by absentee owners. The insurgency, fragmented as in other provinces, took on many aspects of agrarian revolution, with the landless peasants attracted to guerrilla warfare as a means to possess land. Since the inhabitants were acclimatized to yellow fever and knew the thick forests, swamps, ravines, and trackless mountains, they evaded counterinsurgency flying divisions. Calleja's Plan Político Militar demanded the proximity of

garrisons and of flying divisions in order to strengthen the ability of the
organized royalist companies to resist. While the walled city of Veracruz
contained a fairly large population, after 1812–13, the insurgents dominated the villages and countryside beyond its crumbling parapets. Even
more significant, the rural and village populations of Veracruz possessed
traditions of antigovernment activities and dedication to contraband trading. Unlike many other Mexican insurgents, they enjoyed strong maritime links to New Orleans and access to fairly high-quality arms and
munitions. After the War of 1812 between Britain and the United States,
this traffic brought significant numbers of weapons into the hands of the
Mexican rebels.

Urban defense presented innumerable challenges and problems for
counterinsurgency planners. Even the best-protected cities, such as
Querétaro, were quite porous and exposed to insurgent infiltration. Sometimes this could become extremely embarrassing and dangerous. On the
night of February 6, 1818, over one hundred insurgent horsemen rode
into Querétaro and dashed through the streets to the central palace and
square before they departed—hastened along by twenty random cannon
shots from the parapets.[49] The placement of guardhouses and barracks
had much to do with the lack of security, but fully a third of Querétaro's
population resided outside the lines of fortification, where they were exposed to rebel incursionists and robbers. At Jalapa, the majority of the
plebeian inhabitants lived outside of the precinct guarded by the city parapets. To make matters worse, the gates closed at 9:00 P.M. during summer
and at 8:00 P.M. in winter. For a significant portion of the day, the common people locked out of the town were cut off from doctors, medicines,
their confessors, and other necessities. There were small entry ports in
the gates, but nervous sentinels kept them locked; even if they were open,
the entry points were located halfway around the town from the main
residential district.[50] As in the case of Querétaro, the poor of Jalapa suffered many robberies and assaults. Army patrols lacked the frequency
and flexibility to assist civilian victims, who were often thought of as
insurgent sympathizers. Even at heavily fortified and well-defended
Puebla, rebel horsemen enjoyed the challenge of mocking urban guards
by reckless rides through the city. On February 15, 1815, at 2:30 A.M., six
insurgent horsemen caused a general alarm when they managed to bypass
the guardposts, night patrols, and other precautions to appear in the *plaza
de armas*. Finally, sentinels opened fire and the audacious visitors withdrew to a point just outside the city, where they were met by about fifty
cavalry.[51]

The protection of populous Mexico City from insurgent incursions,
spies, and plotters was a counterinsurgent's nightmare. By 1811 the city

had been divided into districts with *tenientes de policia* in charge of each. Despite severe difficulties with administration, the police authorities introduced a system of passports. There were few problems with merchants, muleteers, and transporters who obtained perpetual passports to allow them to conduct their businesses, but the regime was hard-pressed to control the innumerable Indians who came to the city irregularly with vegetables, fruit, and other produce.[52] Soldiers at the sentry posts into Mexico City often required these people to pay bribes for entry whether or not they possessed documents.[53] Within the city, crime increased dramatically during the years of war—murders, assaults, woundings in *pulquerías*, sexual crimes, thefts, robberies, drunkenness, and many other offenses. Certain that there were spies everywhere, police authorities even worried about suspicious behavior of actors who put on marionette shows and comedies. To advertise their performances, they sent drummers through the city at all hours of the day and night. Antonio Columna of the Tribunal de la Acordada worried that night comedies were a constant source of abuses and were bound to produce "evil consequences."[54]

As might be expected, the presence of a large garrison of soldiers compounded the potential for disorder. Because the regime feared illegal meetings and other gatherings that might signify insurgent plotting, all inhabitants of the capital were encouraged to report anything unusual. In April 1818 an anonymous complainant named "El Deseoso del Sosiego" reported all-night parties in a building adjoining a wineshop called La Fruta in Calle del Refugio. These events were so wild that the writer described them as a "whores and knaves market." A police raid resulted in the arrest of forty revelers—a colonel, several subaltern officers, a curate, a friar, and an assortment of civilian women and men.[55] Ordinary soldiers could not afford to spend their time in wineshops. When the *pulquerías* closed, they congregated in cemeteries or wherever they thought that they might evade the roving patrols. In May 1820, for example, at 1:00 A.M. a vigilance patrol discovered three women, a civilian male, and two drummers from the Regiment of Ordenes Militares "committing lewd acts" in the cemetery of the Bethlemite friars.[56] Although the authorities wished to uphold morals and to prevent soldiers from meeting the large numbers of prostitutes in the city, there were fears of security lapses and of threats posed by insurgent agents. Viceroy Calleja ordered the operators of inns and hostelries to submit daily lists of their guests to the *sargento mayor* of Mexico City.[57]

From the beginning of the counterinsurgency war, there was danger that in a futile struggle to combat the fragmented revolution, the royalist army would subdivide itself into impotence. Calleja's Plan Político Militar was to have given the tiered defensive system a broad rural and urban

base. Unfortunately for royalist interests, however, the insurgency endured to erode the best-guarded provincial defenses. In Veracruz province and the vast region to the south and west of Guadalajara, Valladolid,
and Mexico City, just to mention two of the permanent guerrilla foci, the
insurgents exercised complete control except during periodic sweeps by
large regular army divisions. As early as 1812, Calleja wanted to concentrate many of the dispersed garrisons into two armies of the North and
South. He worried about loss of discipline, laxity, and the development
of vices among soldiers separated from their regimental or battalion commanders.[58] The units of the Army of the Center that had crushed the first
phase of the rebellion were broken up and parceled out in companies to
garrison provinces, to provide convoy service, or to organize the various
flying detachments. Away from their regimental headquarters and command structure, companies deteriorated quickly and soldiers forgot their
discipline. Counterinsurgency was difficult when some of the best cavalry units lost their horses and equipment.[59] Even the Spanish expeditionary regiments and battalions ended up divided and dispersed in many
different locations.

Although senior officers complained bitterly about the difficulties
with military administration, recruitment, and deterioration of discipline,
Viceroy Apodaca saw no alternatives in a war against fragmented guerrilla bands spread over the surface of an enormous country.[60] In 1818,
Colonel Matías de Aguirre of the Regiment of Dragones Fieles de Potosí
informed Apodaca that he had lost touch with many detachments from
his regiment and could not report on the state of some squadrons and
companies. Men of the regiment had been mobilized in 1810 and marched
off into action, where they had remained for eight years. Their officers
were unschooled in preparing status reports and accustomed only to chas-
ing guerrilla bands.[61] Sub-Inspector General Fernando Miyares y Mancebo
noted that it was common in Mexico to have a division of one thousand
troops formed of as many as eleven different units. The results for training and discipline were "monstrous." Separated officers charged enormous debts to units that were not inspected or audited. By 1820, José de
la Cruz warned that subdivision of army units had created dangerous vulnerability that could lead to disaster.[62]

As so often occurs in counterinsurgency conflicts, the royalist army
of New Spain sacrificed its strength in efforts to hold down the country
and to chase guerrilla bands. After 1816, Spain no longer dispatched new
expeditionary battalions, leaving the Mexican royalist army without sufficient operational forces to crush the major guerrilla strongholds. Lacking continued infusions of dynamic fresh battalions to stiffen morale and
to lead offensive operations, exhaustion became a factor of increasing

significance.[63] Aware of the developing stalemate, between 1816 and 1821 Viceroy Apodaca initiated a new program to amnesty insurgents and to convince the world that the revolt was ending. While he convinced many contemporary observers and later historians that he had discovered a better means to pacify insurgency, the reality of the situation proved quite different.

Beginning in 1816, many historians have identified a lull in the independence war. Lucas Alamán described a situation in which the royalist army, backed by the hammer of effective counterinsurgency repression, restored communications and set Apodaca's amnesty machinery on the right track. With the liquidation of Javier Mina, and the destruction of a number of important rebel fortifications, Alamán declared the insurgency ended except for minor mopping-up operations against small bands in the mountainous zones of Veracruz and the region south and west of Jalisco and Michoacán.[64] More recently, Timothy Anna declared that "the restoration of royal power over New Spain was a remarkable achievement, one of the Spanish Empire's greatest victories."[65] Brian Hamnett noted that "by the end of 1819 the insurgency consisted of little more than raiding parties dedicated to the theft of cattle and horses."[66] These historians, and many others, may be described as supporting "the lull theory" of the latter stages of Mexico's independence period. Backing their interpretation were Apodaca's confident dispatches of victories, impressive lists of insurgents applying for amnesties, and effective royalist army counterinsurgency in some regions. There is no doubt that many contemporary administrators and army officers believed these indicators of victory. In fact, the apparent royalist victory was a will-o'-the-wisp illusion that was not substantiated by reality. Exhaustion after six, seven, or eight years of debilitating guerrilla war made some royalists and some rebels willing to recognize a status quo.

After 1816 there were fewer large insurgent forces remaining in the field. While Apodaca celebrated this fact, he misunderstood the real nature of the fragmented revolution. Throughout New Spain, the insurgents had broken up into smaller units that continued an autonomous existence in their regions and, in some cases, maintained loose ties with the isolated guerrilla foci. While the army sought to chase down "escaped" communities and to concentrate populations, there was simply too much territory to cover and too few soldiers. Where the royalist army managed to exert superior force, the rebels accepted amnesties, entered the provincial defense structure in their units, and waited for new opportunities. In some respects, Apodaca disregarded negative information that should have caused him to be less sanguine about the future. In 1815 the Veracruz insurgents became so strong that they were able to blockade the road between Jalapa and the port for months. One convoy languished in Jalapa for almost half a year.[67] The Consulado of Veracruz referred to "a mortal paralysis" of internal and external trade, attacking the royalist army for its military failures and repressive policies.[68] Travelers and merchants paid insurgents taxes for the right to move while the army responded with an inefficient and ineffective program of escorted convoys.[69]

Matters reached such a low state that the imperial government became extremely worried about New Spain. Severed communications and pleas from Veracruz merchants caused major changes in military planning. An expedition of almost two thousand troops, consisting of the Infantry Regiments of Ordenes Militares and Voluntarios de Navarra under Field Marshal Pascual de Liñan and Brigadier Fernando Miyares y Mancebo, ready to sail from Cádiz for Peru, was redirected by the minister of war to Veracruz. The imperial government ordered General Pablo Morillo to dispatch four thousand troops from his expeditionary army in Venezuela and the transfer of some acclimatized Mexican soldiers from Havana back to New Spain. While not all these units reached Veracruz, the imperial war ministry placed major emphasis upon opening communications between Veracruz and Mexico City and in garrisoning a defended *camino militar* that could repel the Veracruz insurgents.[70] Even with this massive pressure, the army could contain these guerrillas only temporarily. By 1818 the rebels of the fragmented bands coalesced once again to interdict commerce and to apply their system of tolls. Viceroy [Juan Ruiz de Apodaca, Conde de] Venadito had to dispatch Field Marshal Pascual de Liñan to assume the interim governorship of Veracruz, with orders to introduce a new program to establish fortified villages, to amnesty rebels, and to search out and destroy recalcitrant insurgent bands.[71]

If Veracruz province suffered a constant and bitter confrontation rather than a lengthy period of lull, the same was true in some other significant regions. In July 1818, José de la Cruz reported frequent insurgent incursions from the mountains of Guanajuato, "the seedbed of rebellion," into the districts surrounding Valladolid and Guadalajara. Similarly, the region south of Valladolid and Uruapan became the base for small bands that coalesced to raid Nueva Galicia. While they numbered only approximately 1,430 men, Cruz noted that they were "old and resolved insurgents."[72] He underscored the need for total dedication by counterinsurgent forces that had to emulate guerrilla tactics and to be ready to live in the sierras for lengthy periods. Cruz saw little use for fruitless chases that went on for fifteen or twenty days, only to end with the insurgents still on the loose. He criticized royalist commanders who believed that the countryside was pacified because they occupied a fortified town. Always quite perceptive about counterinsurgency, Cruz understood that there was not sufficient force both to pacify the regions and to contain and repress the inhabitants.[73] He was particularly upset by the fact that after years of conflict both royalists and rebels accepted a status quo and spheres of influence to permit active commercial exchanges. Army patrols in mountainous districts often encountered merchants, muleteers, and travelers from royalist zones who engaged in trade with insurgent-occupied areas.[74]

Although the royalists did manage to pacify some provinces, insurgent activities were by no means confined to isolated mountainous regions far from settled populations. In February 1816, Pedro el Negro with about fifty-five insurgents attacked the village of Nononalco near Tacuba just outside Mexico City. He went to the house of his cousin, a loyal *realista* of the Tacubaya companies, whom he robbed and hacked to death before the rebels fled.[75] On the night of May 27, 1816, mounted insurgents appeared near the royalist powder magazines at Chapultepec. The royalist garrison fired 484 cartridges before the guerrillas withdrew. This audacious attack followed a series of raids against flour mills and against the first houses at Tacubaya on the outskirts of the capital. One of these was directed against the main buildings of the Hacienda de los Morales, today a famous Mexico City restaurant in Polanco district.[76]

The fact of the matter was that there was no general lull in the ten years' war of New Spain. In 1818 at Querétaro, Brigadier [Domingo] Luaces reported that bands of two hundred to three hundred insurgents almost daily assaulted various targets, mostly against the haciendas of the district. The constant pressure exhausted and frightened the local militia companies. Luaces described a state of exhaustion that infected his command. Despite constant patrols and pursuits, he reported that the haciendas were "isolated, destroyed, sacked and ruined." The troops of Querétaro garrison had too many missions. Luaces asked for a regiment of dragoons to form flying detachments that might recover the outlying haciendas from rebel control.[77] However, efforts to recruit replacements for the Querétaro units accomplished little more than to provoke a flight of young men out of the city.[78]

Given this situation, the morale and psychological mood of the counterinsurgent army faltered. Even in the European expeditionary battalions and regiments, feelings of hopelessness and anger made the soldiers listless and amenable to desertion. Financial crisis in the general treasury and in army taxation further exacerbated the demoralization. During the so-called lull period, the viceregal government failed to make regular salary and maintenance payments to army units, leaving some in desperate financial need. In August 1818, for example, the treasury owed the Infantry Regiment of Zaragoza 14,000 pesos in back payments. The situation became so bad that officers borrowed money to help pay their men for daily provisions. Although uniforms, shoes, and equipment had deteriorated over years of hard usage, there was no money available for repairs and replacements. Some units reported that, due to their indecent nakedness, the soldiers were embarrassed to appear in public.[79] Disgruntled soldiers circulated anonymous papers and petitions criticizing their officers and demanding better treatment. On some occasions, ridiculous rumors spread through units that would have been dismissed during normal times. Desertion depleted a flying detachment north of Zacatecas when the soldiers suspected that they were being marched to Perote where they would be traded into slavery for cloth! Although the commander exhorted them to remember their oaths of loyalty and told them that they were destined only for Aguascalientes, seventy men, including some noncommissioned officers, deserted in two nights.[80]

Given these developments, the collapse of the counterinsurgency army may have appeared predictable. However, there were many other factors that accelerated the process even further. Venadito's urgent requests in 1818 for three thousand replacements from Spain to fill the depleted expeditionary battalions came to nothing. Mired in its own developing crisis, the imperial cabinet continued to delay the matter until 1821, when it was much too late to send reinforcements.[81] Insubordination and rebellion within the Spanish metropolitan army prevented the dispatch of any new units to save the disintegrating colony. Summing up the situation, the Consejo de Guerra in Madrid felt that it was impotent to act; there was no sense in sending new units to America. Without good morale, discipline, and obedience, the soldiers would desert or surrender without a fight.[82]

Spain's crisis had an even greater immediate impact upon the ability of the Mexican royalist army to maintain its tiered counterinsurgency system. While historians have recognized the significance for Mexico of the liberal revolt of Rafael Riego in January 1820, which led to the restoration of the Spanish Constitution of 1812, it was not the radicalism of the new Spanish regime that caused a backlash in conservative Mexico. The constitution permitted towns and cities throughout Mexico to cast off the crushing burden of local taxation required to support the royalist military system. After ten years of counterinsurgency, the taxes to support the army weighed unbearably upon all segments of the population. Taxes, called *arbitrios de milicias*, increased the costs of food, commercial transactions, manufactured goods, and mine output, and inflated the costs of whatever economic activities took place in a specific district or province. At the local level, juntas appointed by town *ayuntamientos* searched for new ways to tax regional and urban populations for military support. These needs included the construction of fortifications, purchases of arms, uniforms, mounts, and utensils, and the debilitating expenditures required to pay garrison troops in case the guerrillas attacked.

Throughout royalist zones, the juntas and the regional commanders surveyed the population to levy *contribuciones militares*, or wealth taxes, upon all inhabitants depending upon their total assets.[83] Over the war years, sources of funds dried up and many formerly prosperous landowners, miners, merchants, and artisans were left destitute. Some individuals who possessed estates occupied by insurgents or abandoned in war zones initiated legal proceedings to stop juntas that appraised their assets at high values and then levied taxes that had to be paid in specie. As was always the case, the poor suffered the brunt of arbitrary and violent acts by the tax collectors. In many instances, those Indians, even women, who lacked a half *real* or *real* were stripped of their "miserable rags" and left naked in the streets. The *ayuntamiento* of Miacatlán reported that some men committed suicide rather than endure the cruel treatment and threats of the tax collectors.[84] Needless to say, many more men chose life with the rebels rather than meet continuous exactions by the royalist tax collectors.

Almost spontaneously, the base level of Calleja's tiered defense structure collapsed. Through 1820, horrified regional commanders passively witnessed a process that they could not arrest. All over royalist Mexico, viceregal orders and insistence that the constitution had not altered military support taxes fell upon deaf ears.[85] Everyone argued that the constitution abolished the existing militia structure and decreed the establishment of a new national militia system. Urban and rural companies evaporated, leaving a vacuum that the royalist army simply could not fill. With the appearance of Agustín de Iturbide, a large part of the army joined his Plan de Iguala, while the remainder abandoned its garrisons and literally imploded upon Mexico City. Much of Mexico was stripped of any royalist forces based in the towns and districts to resist the many new insurgencies or regenerated insurgencies that now operated in the name of Iturbide. From Puebla, Brigadier Ciriaco de Llano felt a little ironic satisfaction when towns that had disbanded their defense forces complained to him that they had been robbed and raided by Iturbide's guerrillas.[86]

After over ten years of insurgency and counterinsurgency, independence came with shocking speed and finality. As is so often the case, the defeat of the counterinsurgent army was definitive. Iturbide's rebellion permitted a rapid shift from the stage of insurgent guerrilla bands to a conventional confrontation that ended the war. Concentration of village populations of amnestied insurgents formed excellent pools of recruits for Iturbide and new insurgent leaders. Efforts by royalist commanders, such as Pascual de Liñan, to introduce land reform programs in Veracruz province came too late to have any impact on the outcome of the war.

Corruption and loss of mission left most of the royalist army incapable of further sustained resistance. Moreover, Iturbide absorbed so much of the royalist army that the final struggle was anticlimactic. However, Iturbide's victory and the arrival of Mexican independence obscured the fact that few, if any, of the insurgents involved in the fragmented revolution achieved their goals. With changed names and slightly altered institutions, Mexico began its independent life without having solved any of the basic questions behind the struggle. These remained for the future.

Notes

1. Sobre la formación del Batallón de Voluntarios de Fernando VII de Puebla, 1810, Archivo General de la Nación, México, Ramo de Indiferente de Guerra (cited hereinafter as AGN:IG), vol. 200-A.

2. D. Manuel Abad y Queipo, obispo electo de Michoacán representa a S.M. sobre el estado de Nueva España y origen de la Revolución, México, 20 June 1815, Archivo Histórico Nacional, Madrid, Spain, Ramo de Hacienda, leg. 229-A. Abad y Queipo was in Madrid in January 1816.

3. Ibid.

4. Calleja to Viceroy Francisco Javier de Venegas, 20 August 1811, Archivo General de la Nación, México, Ramo de Operaciones de Guerra (cited hereinafter as AGN:OG), vol. 190.

5. D. Manuel Abad y Queipo . . . representa a S.M. sobre el estado de Nueva España, 1815.

6. Ibid.

7. Félix Calleja to Viceroy Venegas, San Luis Potosí, no. 2196, 21 September 1810, AGN:OG, vol. 169.

8. Calleja to Venegas, no. 2197, 28 September 1810, AGN:OG, vol. 169.

9. Calleja to Venegas, no. 33, Campo de la Pila, 9 October 1810, AGN:OG, vol. 169.

10. Intendente de San Luis Potosí, Manuel de Acevedo, to Calleja, 13 October 1810; and 17 October 1810, AGN:OG, vol. 91.

11. Calleja to Venegas, Campo de la Pila, 15 October 1810, AGN:OG, vol. 169; and Calleja to Conde de la Cadena (Manuel de Flon, Intendente de Puebla), San Luis Potosí, 2 October 1810, AGN:OG, vol. 94-A. Cadena, second in command to Calleja, marched from Puebla to Querétaro, where confusion, disorder, and fear in the city prevented him from any decisive activities.

12. Juan Antonio Riaño to Calleja, Guanajuato, 23 September 1810, AGN:OG, vol. 809.

13. Calleja to Riaño, San Luis Potosí, 24 September 1810, AGN:OG, vol. 809.

14. Riaño to Calleja, 26 September 1810, AGN:OG, vol. 809.

15. Riaño to Calleja, 27 September 1810, AGN:OG, vol. 809.

16. Riaño to Calleja, 28 September 1810, AGN:OG, vol. 809.

17. For additional detail, see Hugh M. Hamill, Jr., *The Hidalgo Revolt: Prelude to Mexican Independence* (Gainesville, 1966), 139–140; and José María Luis Mora, *México y sus revoluciones* (México, 1965), III, 37–45.

18. Jacobo María Jantos to Calleja, Venado, 26 October 1810, AGN:OG, vol. 169.

19. Cadena to Ignacio García Revollo, 30 September 1810, AGN:OG, vol. 94-A; and Cadena to Venegas, 5 October 1810, AGN:OG, vol. 94-A. Cadena was shocked by the fall of Guanajuato and the death of his brother-in-law, Juan Antonio Riaño.

20. José Alonso to Cadena, 12 October 1810; and Cadena to Venegas, 12 October 1810, AGN:OG, vol. 94-A.

21. Carlos de Urrutía to Venegas, Veracruz, 13 October 1810, AGN:OG, vol. 882.

22. Cadena to Venegas, Hacienda de la Erre, 27 October 1810, AGN:OG, vol. 882.

23. Cadena to Venegas, Villa de Lagos, 7 January 1811, AGN:OG, vol. 94-A; and Calleja to Venegas, Guanajuato, 12 August 1811, AGN:OG, vol. 190.

24. Calleja to Venegas, reservado, 29 January 1811, AGN:OG, vol. 171.

25. Calleja to Venegas, Campo de Zapotlanejo, 18 January 1811, AGN:OG, vol. 171. The estimates of royalist dead and wounded were about 150, while the insurgents were thought to have lost 6,000 to 7,000.

26. Calleja to Venegas, Guanajuato, 30 October 1811, AGN:OG, vol. 192. Also see Brian R. Hamnett, *Roots of Insurgency: Mexican Regions, 1750–1824* (Cambridge, 1986), 180–183.

27. Calleja to Venegas, 14 December 1811, AGN:OG, vol. 195.

28. Ibid.

29. Calleja to Venegas, Cañada de San Mateo, 31 December 1811, AGN:OG, vol. 195.

30. Calleja to Venegas, 20 January 1812, AGN:OG, vol. 197; and Bando de Félix Calleja, Zitácuaro, 5 January 1812, AGN:OG, vol. 165.

31. Calleja to Venegas, 6 May 1812; and Venegas to Calleja, 8 May 1812, AGN:OG, vol. 201.

32. Calleja to Ciriaco de Llano, 9 May 1812; and Llano to Calleja, Sacatepec, 10 May 1812, AGN:OG, vol. 288.

33. Intendente de Veracruz José Quevedo to Calleja, 4 April 1813; and Calleja to Quevedo, 2 May 1813, AGN:OG, vol. 692.

34. Calleja to Venegas, 23 November 1810, AGN:OG, vol. 170.

35. José de la Cruz to Venegas, 17 November 1810, AGN:OG, vol. 141.

36. Cruz to Venegas, 27 November 1810, AGN:OG, vol. 141.

37. Cruz to Venegas, 30 November 1810, AGN:OG, vol. 141.

38. Cruz to the Subdelegado of Huichapan, 6 December 1810, AGN:OG, vol. 142; and Instrucción a que deben arreglarse los Comandantes de los destacamentos volantes, December 1810, AGN:OG, vol. 142.

39. José Antonio de Andrade to Venegas, Jilotepec, 17 July 1811, AGN:OG, vol. 95.

40. Instrucciones para los comandantes de los cuerpos volantes que deben establecerse . . . para cubrir toda la orilla de la Laguna de Chapala, 1816, AGN:OG, vol. 151.

41. Calleja to José Joaquín Márquez y Donallo, 18 June 1814; and Instrucciones para el Comandante General de Llanos de Apan, 1814, AGN:OG, vol. 530. For other examples, see Brian R. Hamnett, "Royalist Counterinsurgency and the Continuity of Rebellion: Guanajuato and Michoacán, 1813–1820," *Hispanic American Historical Review* 62:1 (February 1982): 19–48.

42. Reglamento político militar que deberán observar bajo las penas que señala los pueblos, haciendas, y ranchos a quienes se comunique por las autoridades

legítimas y respectivas . . . , Aguascalientes, 8 June 1811, AGN:OG, vol. 278; and Calleja to the Alcalde of León, Ildefonso Seprién, Guanajuato, 13 August 1811, AGN:OG, vol. 177.

43. Diego García Conde to Calleja, San Miguel, 14 August 1811, AGN:OG, vol. 899.

44. Antonio de Flon to García Conde, San Luis de la Paz, 13 August 1811, AGN:OG, vol. 899.

45. Ibid.

46. A la ciudad de Querétaro le es conducente para el buen orden, José Miguel Barreiro, México, 8 August 1818, AGN:OG, vol. 511.

47. Ibid.

48. José de Quevedo to Calleja, Veracruz, 5 April 1813; and Calleja to Quevedo, 13 May 1813, AGN:OG, vol. 692.

49. Brigadier Domingo Luaces to Viceroy Apodaca, Querétaro, 4 February 1818, AGN:OG, vol. 514.

50. García Dávila to Viceroy Conde de Venadito (Apodaca), 6 July 1820, no. 72, AGN:OG, vol. 266.

51. Francisco Palacio to Brigadier José Moreno y Daoiz, Puebla, 15 February 1815; and Calleja to Moreno y Daoiz, 28 February 1815, AGN:OG, vol. 536.

52. Agustín Pomposo Fernández to Pedro de la Puente, 28 August 1811, AGN:OG, vol. 671.

53. Bando del Virrey Venegas, 5 December 1811, AGN:OG, vol. 979.

54. Antonio Columna, Tribunal de la Acordada, to Venegas, 17 August 1811, AGN:OG, vol. 673.

55. Anónimo, El deseoso del sosiego to Apodaca, 18 April 1818; and Capitán de Comisarios Antonio Acuña to Apodaca, 19 April 1818, AGN:OG, vol. 599.

56. Report of José Salazar, Compañia de Policía, 26 May 1820, AGN:OG, vol. 597.

57. José Juan Fagoaga to Calleja, 1 October 1815, AGN:OG, vol. 596.

58. Calleja to Venegas, 11 February 1812, AGN:OG, vol. 165.

59. Calleja to the Minister of War, no. 14, 5 September 1813, Archivo General Militar de Segovia (cited hereinafter as AGMS), Ramo de Ultramar, leg. 232.

60. Apodaca to Brigadier Pascual de Liñan, 1 September 1818, AGN:OG, vol. 488; and Liñan to Venadito, 3 January 1820, AGN:OG, vol. 493.

61. Liñan to Apodaca, no. 1561, 27 October 1818, AGN:OG, vol. 501.

62. Cruz to Venadito, 4 October 1820, AGN:OG, vol. 157.

63. For one interesting comparison, see Alister Horne, *A Savage War of Peace: Algeria, 1954–1962* (London, 1977).

64. Lucas Alamán, *Historia de Méjico* (México, 1969), IV, 287, 409.

65. Timothy E. Anna, *The Fall of the Royal Government in Mexico City* (Lincoln, 1978), 179. See pp. 179–187.

66. Hamnett, "Royalist Counterinsurgency and the Continuity of Rebellion," 46.

67. Consulado of Veracruz to Calleja, 13 April 1815, AGN:OG, vol. 216.

68. Consulado of Veracruz to the Secretary of State, 23 June 1815, AGN:OG, vol. 216.

69. Brigadier José de Quevedo to Calleja, 27 March 1815, AGN:OG, vol. 699.

70. Xavier Abadía to the Governor of Veracruz, Cádiz, 7 April 1815, AGN:OG, vol. 699; and Miyares y Mancebo to Abadía, Veracruz, 2 August 1815, AGMS, Ultramar, leg. 226.

71. Liñan to Venadito, 22 April 1819, AGN:OG, vol. 490.
72. Cruz to Apodaca, 18 December 1818, AGN:OG, vol. 155. For a useful regional study, see Jaime Olveda, *Gordiano Guzmán: un cacique del siglo XIX* (México, 1980), 81–82.
73. Cruz to Apodaca, 10 July 1818, AGN:OG, vol. 154.
74. Cruz to Apodaca, 26 December 1818, AGN:OG, vol. 155.
75. Sargento Mayor José Mendivil to Calleja, 22 February 1816, AGN:OG, vol. 596.
76. Mendivil to Calleja, 13 March 1816; and 22 July 1816, AGN:OG, vol. 596.
77. Luaces to Apodaca, Querétaro, 4 February 1818, AGN:OG, vol. 514.
78. Liñan to Apodaca, no. 1833, n.d., 1818, AGN:OG, vol. 486.
79. Liñan to Apodaca, no. 1032, 6 August 1818, AGN:OG, vol. 499.
80. Brigadier José Gayangos to Apodaca, 23 May 1818, AGN:OG, vol. 584.
81. José de Ymar to the Secretario de Hacienda de Indias, Palacio, 5 October 1819, Archivo General de Indias, Ramo de México, leg. 2420; and Report of the Consejo de Guerra, 1 September 1821, Madrid, AGMS, Ultramar, leg. 227.
82. Report of the Consejo de Guerra, 1 September 1821, Madrid, AGMS, Ultramar, leg. 227.
83. For the origins of the military support system, see José Moreno y Daoíz to Valleja, no. 300, Puebla, 10 March 1815, AGN:OG, vol. 536; and Christon I. Archer, "Not with a Bang but a Whimper: The Decline and Defeat of the Royalist Army of New Spain," paper presented at the Midwest Association of Latin American Studies, St. Louis, Missouri, October 1986; and "Where Did All of the Royalists Go? New Light on the Military Collapse of New Spain, 1810–1822," in Jaime E. Rodríguez O., ed., *The Mexican and the Mexican-American Experience in the Nineteenth Century* (Tempe, 1989), 23–43.
84. Ayuntamiento of Miacatlán to Presidente y vocales de la Exma. Diputacíon Provincial de México, 4 November 1820, AGN:OG, vol. 455. Many similar complaints could be listed of mistreatment directed against the poor.
85. Ayuntamiento of Jilotepec to the Intendente de México, Ramón Gutiérrez de Mazo, 8 February 1821, AGN:OG, vol. 455.
86. Llano to Venadito, no. 1292, AGN:OG, vol. 326.

3

Authoritarianism and Militarism in Ecuador

Linda Alexander Rodríguez

The new Spanish-American states inherited a tradition of militarism and military politicians as a result of the long and bloody struggle for independence. In most cases the former professional armies were either dissolved or destroyed by the irregular forces of the patriot leaders. During the post-Independence period, these armed groups resisted demobilization and expected to be rewarded for their sacrifices. After Independence the new military-political leaders often retained power by satisfying the demands of the armed groups that now constituted the armies. Those members of the armed forces who were not incorporated into the new national armed forces, or who were not accorded the rank and privileges they expected, frequently gave their support to opposition politicians who sought to topple the government.

Ecuador provides an extreme example of the political instability that characterized Latin America after Independence. Extralegal transfers of power, subsequently regularized by the adoption of a new constitution and the "election" of the leader of the victorious group, became the norm. By examining the role of the military in the political process in Ecuador, this selection demonstrates the manner in which chief executives, civilian or military, relied on armed groups to gain and retain power during the nineteenth century.

This pattern continued into the twentieth century despite the creation of a more professional officer corps. After the turn of the century, civilian politicians, who sought the support of the military in ousting their political rivals, exhorted the better-trained younger officers to save the country from corrupt politicians and older "political" officers whose actions

From *The Search for Public Policy: Regional Politics & Government Finances in Ecuador, 1830–1940* (Berkeley: University of California Press, 1985), 38–41, 46–52, 122–27, 131. ©1984 by The Regents of the University of California. Reprinted by permission of the University of California Press.

threatened the nation and the martial institution. In Ecuador, as in many other South American countries, professionalism became a rationale for military intervention in politics rather than a mechanism for depoliticizing the institution.

Although nineteenth-century Ecuador was, in theory, a constitutional republic, force became the accepted method of transferring or retaining power. All eleven constitutions promulgated in that period provided for elected officials. They also generally prohibited the reelection of a president. Political reality, however, was quite different. Ecuador has enjoyed few free elections. Indeed, elections often were held not to select a president but to ratify or legalize the power of a person who gained office through force. In such cases, elections were usually preceded by the writing of a new constitution.[1] In other instances, the government controlled elections to ensure the victory of its official candidate. In either situation, disappointed presidential contenders often violently challenged the outcome. The issue was settled temporarily when one side was defeated in battle. Such settlements, however, were always tenuous and the incumbent could expect repeated insurrections during his term of office. The use of force was not limited to military politicians: Generals Juan José Flores (1830–1834), 1839–1845), José María Urvina (1851–1856), Francisco Robles (1856–1859), and Ignacio Veintimilla (1876–1883) relied on armed might either to bring them to power or to help them retain it. But so did the leading civilian politicians. The two great nineteenth-century statesmen, Vicente Rocafuerte (1835–1839) and Gabriel García Moreno (1860–1865, 1869–1876), achieved power through armed conflict and then relied on force to remain in office.

A pattern of authoritarian politics developed in nineteenth-century Ecuador. Once in power, chief executives rapidly concluded that only a strong and unyielding authoritarian ruler could govern the country. Nothing could be accomplished if the government was preoccupied with combating subversions. Regimes abandoned the civil guarantees enumerated by the various constitutions in an effort to secure the order and stability considered necessary prerequisites for development. Liberals, conservatives, and opportunists all relied on controlled elections, press censorship, and extralegal coercion to limit the opposition. Strong leaders, whether civilian or military, reacted alike. Indeed, Rocafuerte and García Moreno proved harsher and more violent than their military counterparts.[2]

A close relationship emerged between authoritarianism and militarism during the immediate post-Independence period. The struggle for independence resulted in the formation of a large military caste that considered itself above the law.[3] In Ecuador the problem was exacerbated because the country was under martial law for several years to facilitate the liberation of Peru. Following Spain's defeat, many Gran Colombian military men returned to Ecuador. These uprooted men, who had no economic or social ties to the region, destabilized the political system. They were always ready to support a "revolution" or to back a politician who promised them rewards. After being accorded military honors, they considered themselves "liberators" entitled to privilege and rank. As such, they were unwilling to return to their former peaceful pursuits, which in most instances would have reduced them to the role of artisan or farmer. Even had they desired to abandon their military "careers," the Ecuadorian economy could not absorb them since, after Independence, the country underwent a period of severe economic depression. Thus the Venezuelans and Colombians who found themselves in Ecuador in the post-Independence period had few opportunities open to them. They found it easier to prosper through intrigue, plunder, and extortion.[4]

Not all foreign military men became predators. The ablest, those who distinguished themselves in combat or in administration, allied themselves with the Ecuadorian elite. They married into wealthy families and acquired property or became high-ranking officials in the national army.[5] Indeed, Ecuador's first president, General Juan José Flores, was a Venezuelan who had married into the Quito aristocracy. The limited peace and stability that Ecuador enjoyed in the period from 1830 to 1845 was owed in part to Flores's ability to retain the support of the foreign element that dominated the armed forces. His relationship with that group, however, ultimately provoked an anti-Flores reaction. Local politicians and national military chieftains relied on a growing xenophobia to oust Flores and exile him in 1845.[6]

Two types of armed forces—the national military and the armed guerrillas, or *montoneras*—dominated national politics until 1916, when the national army defeated the last *montonera* band. During the nineteenth century it was often difficult to differentiate between the two armed groups. The national armed forces usually gave their loyalty to the government; the guerrilla bands generally served individual strongmen, usually large landowners or former military men. If the insurgents succeeded in overthrowing the government and bringing their leader to power, they were usually rewarded with employment in the national armed forces. The defenders of the fallen government would often find themselves dismissed from the service and exiled by the victors. The cashiered officers were then available to support another political contender who might restore them to their former position and, perhaps, promote them. The cycle of rebellion became the norm because every new revolution created more "outs" who wanted to get back "in."

The history of nineteenth-century Ecuador is filled with instances of the process described above. For example, the Flores defeat in 1845 led to the dismissal of loyal officers. Many were forced into exile with Flores, while others were simply cashiered. The ousted military men seized every opportunity to overthrow the new government. As a result, President Vicente Ramón Roca (1845–1849) faced more than twenty armed insurrections during his term.[7] Although the pro-Flores group failed to topple the Roca government, it temporarily reentered politics during the administration of Diego Noboa (1850–51). After the election of 1850, the supporters of one defeated candidate, General Antonio Elizalde, rebelled against the winner, Noboa. When they failed to oust him, the new president retaliated with wholesale dismissals of officers hostile to his regime. Since Noboa's action decimated the officer corps, he attempted to rebuild the military by allowing the pro-Flores group to return and assume important positions in the armed forces. But Noboa was unable to forge an effective army in time to prevent his defeat.[8] In 1851 an ambitious political general, José María Urvina, relied on the partisans of the defeated Elizalde to help him oust Noboa. One of Urvina's first acts after gaining power was to rescind the law that permitted the pro-Flores group to return to Ecuador. A strong and distinguished general, Urvina managed to retain the support of enough military groups to maintain himself in power (1851–1856) and to elect his friend, General Francisco Robles, president in 1856.[9] Toward the end of the decade, however, an international crisis weakened the Robles government. Gabriel García Moreno, an aspiring young politician, used the opportunity to overthrow the Robles government in 1859 with the help of dissident military men, particularly the pro-Flores group.[10] This pattern of defeat, exile, rebellion, and restoration to power continued until well into the twentieth century.

The willingness of many groups to use force to attain political goals meant that national leaders, whether civil or military, had to rely on the army for support. The process gave distinct advantages to military politicians. But civilians, who formed enduring alliances with key groups in the military, also could survive. Thus authoritarianism became intertwined with militarism. The system favored strong and ruthless chief executives. Even today many Ecuadorians believe that only a "man of iron" can govern the country, but even such a man will fail if he lacks the support of the military. . . .

Although the liberals eventually developed an orderly election process, the first years of liberal domination were a period of intense conflict. They gained power in 1895, as the result of a conservative-inspired rebellion that succeeded in forcing the progressive president, Luis Cordero, to resign but that was unable to retain power. The provisional government in Quito rapidly lost control as insurrections erupted in Manabí, Latacunga, Ambato, El Oro, Los Ríos, Guayaquil, and even Quito itself. As in 1834 to 1835, 1859 to 1861, and in 1883, the country disintegrated into warring factions. Coastal liberals saw an opportunity to achieve national supremacy by inviting Eloy Alfaro to return from exile and assume command of their forces.

Alfaro had a great reputation as a liberal insurgent. A native of Manabí, he began his political career as a partisan of General Urvina. In 1864, Alfaro kidnapped a provincial governor in an abortive attempt to oust García Moreno, his first experience as a *guerrillero*. When the movement failed, Alfaro prudently fled to Panama, where he became an extremely successful businessman. Later, he used his wealth to finance liberal insurrections against conservative governments. In some instances, as in 1883 to 1884, he even led *montoneras* from Manabí and Esmeraldas against the governments of [Ignacio] Veintimilla and José Plácido Caamaño. By 1895, Alfaro had an international reputation as a soldier. Not only had he fought in the Ecuadorian civil wars, but he also had participated in similar struggles in Central America and in the Cuban Independence movement. Distinguished civilians, such as Lizardo García, Emilio Estrada, and José L. Tamayo, who would themselves later become presidents of Ecuador, invited Alfaro to lead the liberal forces in 1895.[11]

Alfaro commanded the support of other *guerrilleros*, including Leonidas Plaza, who had gained military experience in earlier insurrections. Plaza, who would eventually become president, had backed Alfaro in the abortive uprising in 1884. Like Alfaro, Plaza had escaped abroad, where he also earned an international reputation as a liberal revolutionary. After fighting in Costa Rica and El Salvador, he, along with other *guerrilleros*, returned to Ecuador to command the coastal *montoneras* that decisively defeated government troops in August 1895. Like his predecessors—Flores, Rocafuerte, Urvina, Robles, García Moreno, and Veintimilla—Alfaro first assumed power and then convoked an assembly that wrote a new constitution and elected him "constitutional" president of Ecuador in October 1896.[12]

The liberal triumph, however, did not restore peace. Alfaro's government had to quash numerous armed challenges from church-backed conservative insurgents. Ironically, the liberals controlled the conservatives more easily than the opposition that emerged from their own ranks.[13] The process of selecting a presidential successor precipitated rebellions by competing liberal aspirants.

The first crisis over the presidential succession occurred in 1900 just prior to the expiration of President Alfaro's term. The Liberal party had to select a candidate in a tense atmosphere in which gossip and press speculation heightened public apprehension. Rumors circulated that elements of the armed forces might prevent the election of a civilian. Although a number of prominent civilian liberals enjoyed widespread support, Alfaro named General Plaza the official candidate. The president apparently considered Plaza an acceptable moderate whom he could control. The other leading military contender was General Manuel A. Franco, a rabid anticlerical and radical whom Alfaro recognized he could not dominate. When Alfaro realized that he would also be unable to dominate Plaza, he withdrew his support. Plaza, however, had won the backing of the leading military men and thus reached the presidential palace despite Alfaro's opposition and Franco's rivalry. Although Plaza avoided a public break with Alfaro, the division between the two liberal leaders never healed. Their rivalry was one of the major causes of the turbulence that lasted until 1916. At times, as in the years from 1912 to 1916, the antagonism erupted into civil war. On other occasions, such as in 1906 and 1911, it merely resulted in extraconstitutional changes in government.[14]

The second crisis over the presidential succession occurred in 1904, when the breach between the Alfaro and the Plaza wings of the Liberal party had become irreconcilable. Plaza, imposing a civilian, Lizardo García, as his successor, left Ecuador to serve as ambassador in Washington. His departure set the stage for García's ouster. The Alfaro group, outraged by Plaza's choice, began slandering the new president, claiming that he was betraying the liberal cause by continuing Plaza's subversive policies. Because Plaza had encouraged conservatives to participate in his government, his rivals accused him of betraying liberalism. The charge was specious: Plaza (1901–1905) had enacted more liberal reforms than did Alfaro (1895–1901). The campaign, nonetheless, weakened the García government. Many politically astute officers lost no time in joining the Alfaro group. García attempted to save himself by recalling Plaza, but the liberal general arrived too late to prevent the president's overthrow. A military insurrection elevated Alfaro to power once more in 1906; García had been forced out after only four months in office.[15]

The 1906 revolution provides an excellent example of the way in which traditional political practices endured. Since Independence, civilian presidents remained in office only as long as military leaders supported them. Like earlier military chieftains, such as Flores, Urvina, and Veintimilla, Alfaro willingly sacrificed orderly processes to satisfy his personal ambitions. Believing himself indispensable, he was determined to retain power. Until his death in 1912, no liberal civilian president completed a term of office.[16]

Turbulence marked Alfaro's second term. After assuming power, he convoked a constituent assembly that wrote a new constitution and elected him to a second "constitutional" term (1907–1911). This, of course, was in keeping with Ecuadorian political traditions. The exercise failed to consolidate Alfaro's position; he faced growing opposition not only from conservatives but also from within his own Liberal party. Many former supporters viewed Alfaro as an opportunist who would sacrifice liberal ideals to retain power. The president reacted to the opposition by harshly suppressing dissenters, particularly the press, which had operated freely during the Plaza administration. This harassment confirmed the worst fears of Alfaro's critics, who redoubled their attacks on the government. The threat of war with Peru in 1910 briefly united the country. Once an interim settlement was negotiated, the public turned its attention to the coming presidential campaign that coincided with Plaza's return after several years abroad. The stage was set for the final confrontation between the two liberal leaders.[17]

In 1911, Alfaro supported Emilio Estrada, a leading liberal businessman from Guayaquil. As the official candidate, Estrada easily defeated his two liberal opponents, Generals Plaza and Franco. But when the president-elect declared that he would pursue an independent policy and attempted to separate himself from Alfaro, the old chieftain tried to prevent Estrada's inauguration. Alfaro accused Estrada of not taking the conservative threat seriously and demanded that the president-elect resign because he had learned that Estrada suffered from a heart condition. Alfaro acted as he did because he had no desire to relinquish power. He had used the same tactic in an unsuccessful attempt to prevent Plaza from taking office in 1901, and he also used it to justify his insurrection of 1906. Yet Alfaro himself had appointed leading conservatives to cabinet posts and to sensitive diplomatic missions. They had been sound appointments that demonstrated his political skill, but they contradicted his alleged reasons for demanding Estrada's resignation. The tactic backfired, and Alfaro was sent into exile.[18]

President Estrada's death in December 1911 unleashed a civil war that lasted five years. In Guayaquil, General Pedro Montero rebelled against the caretaker government, announcing that he opposed both the Plaza faction of the Liberal party and the conservatives. General Flavio Alfaro, Eloy Alfaro's nephew, was appointed supreme chief in Esmeraldas. The rebel leaders agreed to recall Eloy Alfaro from Panama to head the insurrection. In Quito the government appointed General Plaza, who had been Estrada's minister of finance, commander of the national armed forces. It appointed another leading liberal general, Julio Andrade, second in command. Government forces defeated the insurgents in a series of bloody battles and eventually occupied Guayaquil. Both sides were armed with the modern weapons that had been procured to meet the danger of a Peruvian invasion in 1910. Approximately nine thousand participated in the conflict: thirty-eight hundred regular troops remained loyal to the government, twenty-seven hundred regular soldiers joined the rebels, and twenty-five hundred volunteers participated on both sides. During January 1912 more than three thousand men died in the civil war. Ecuadorians were shocked by the extent of the carnage. Conspiracies, violence, and even civil war were relatively common in national politics. Major battles, however, were infrequent and seldom involved more than a few casualties. Public indignation turned against Alfaro and his supporters, who were portrayed as unprincipled opportunists willing to destroy the nation to gain their selfish ends.[19]

Although the conflict ended with an armistice that permitted the rebel leaders to go into exile, the high emotional state of the populace in Guayaquil prevented them from leaving. The public outcry to punish the rebels became so great that local officials capitulated: General Montero was tried, found guilty, and sentenced to sixteen years at hard labor—the maximum penalty under Ecuadorian law. This sentence did not pacify the outraged public. A mob attacked and brutally murdered the prisoner in the courtroom. Government officials transferred the remaining rebel leaders to the García Moreno penitentiary in Quito for safekeeping. But the capital proved as insecure as Guayaquil. Mobs burst into the prison and murdered the prisoners, including Eloy Alfaro, with a savagery that eclipsed the Guayaquil episode.[20]

During the following weeks the country lived in a state of high emotionalism and near anarchy. The army was called out to maintain order, but the situation continued to deteriorate as the new presidential elections approached. Liberals were split between supporters of Generals Plaza and Andrade. Each side believed only its candidate could save the country. In this tense situation, an unknown assailant killed General Andrade, allowing Plaza to win the election. Serious insurrections threatened his administration: pro-Alfaro and pro-Andrade dissidents accused Plaza of having plotted the death of their leaders. As a result, during the years from 1912 to 1916 the government was plagued with a series of rural guerrilla uprisings, particularly in the coastal province of Esmeraldas. Hostilities finally ended in 1916, when President Alfredo Baquerizo Moreno (1916–1920) granted a general amnesty to the rebels.[21]

The years following the liberal triumph of 1895 did not witness a change in Ecuador's political culture. Personalism remained a crucial factor. Although there were several important personalist leaders, two men—Alfaro and Plaza—dominated the first thirty years of liberal rule. Unlike Alfaro, Plaza came to believe that personalism and authoritarianism hindered Ecuador's modernization. As the arbiter of national politics between

1912 and 1925, Plaza used his influence to strengthen political institutions and to transfer presidential power peacefully from the incumbent to the victor. Despite the incessant civil strife that marred his second administration, Plaza continued the progressive policies that had characterized his first regime. He implemented reforms while respecting civil liberties, particularly the freedom of the press. This increased his stature among the public. Plaza was also the most prominent survivor of the generation of liberals that came to power in 1895.[22]

Plaza achieved unparalleled political influence in Ecuador for two reasons. First, he possessed strong ties to both the sierra and the coast. The principal economic groups in those regions believed that Plaza would protect their interests. Coastal entrepreneurs supported him because he worked to control political violence. They favored orderly government and the peaceful transfer of power because it was important for the growth and well-being of the coastal export economy. At the same time, Plaza had the backing of sierra landowners. His marriage into a highland family and his ownership of large haciendas reassured wealthy *serranos* that Plaza would not threaten their interests. The urban professional and middle classes also supported him because his progressive administration provided them with new opportunities for advancement. Plaza managed to bridge the widening gap between the traditional and modern sectors and between urban and rural groups.

The military was the second pillar of Plaza's enduring political power. During his second presidency, he promoted men loyal to him. These officers dominated the Ecuadorian army until 1925. The army played an active and crucial role in liberal politics: it not only preserved order, it also "made" elections and assured liberal victories. Plaza's authority, and the respect higher-ranking officers had for him, assured the liberal leader power.[23]

Plaza attempted to use his power to promote the institutionalization of national politics. He believed that the country would remain politically immature as long as any individual retained power. He preferred to exercise influence from behind the scenes. Plaza also believed that the office of the president was too powerful, tending to reinforce personalism and authoritarian rule. This was particularly true in a nation like Ecuador with a poorly articulated sense of civic responsibility and weak institutions. Therefore, he supported civilian presidents who would respect the powers and prerogatives the congress enjoyed under the Constitution of 1906.[24]

From 1916 to 1925 it appeared that Plaza had created an orderly transition of government. Three liberal civilians—Alfredo Baquerizo Moreno, José Tamayo, and Gonzalo Córdova—succeeded one another in controlled but peaceful elections. The congress functioned; its powers were not usurped by a powerful president. Civil liberties were generally respected. And a free and active press thrived. There were a few insurrections against the government by conservatives and disgruntled officers, but these movements were easily suppressed. It appeared that Ecuador was becoming politically mature and that its development was ensured.[25]

The liberal development program had two goals. The first sought to remove obstacles to social and economic progress, which the attacks on the church had partially accomplished. The second part of the program required positive change. The liberals acceded to power promising that an active state would foster national development. This meant public works to build the social and economic infrastructure the country needed. The state replaced the church as the principal agent providing education, health, and other social services. The emergence of an active state in Ecuador provided a new arena for regionalist struggles. Liberal rhetoric strengthened regionalist tendencies by stimulating local desires for development and prosperity. The growing power of the congress, which resulted from the Constitution of 1906 and from Plaza's policies, led to the enactment of extensive pork-barrel legislation. Nationally funded regional public works projects allowed local leaders to please their constituencies as well as deliver the votes for the national government. Liberal progress and prosperity were based on the growth of world demand for cacao, the nation's major export. Unfortunately, cacao was subject to wide fluctuations in demand and price.[26]

The advent of World War I initiated a production and marketing crisis in the cacao industry, which in turn threatened the national economy. Because the government depended on export taxes for a major part of its revenues, the decline of cacao exports had important political and economic ramifications. National and local demands for public expenditures increased at a time when the government's revenues declined. Rather than curtail public works projects, liberal governments resorted to extraordinary means of financing their programs. Normally, this meant increasing the money supply through special loans from coastal banks. These policies and the effects of the world economic slump following World War I severely disrupted the economy.[27] . . .

The combined effects of unsound liberal fiscal practices and the worsening economic crisis ended the political stability established by Plaza. The cooperation of coastal bankers with liberal governments led to widespread criticism of the banks. They were blamed for the growing inflation and, particularly, for the severe unemployment that culminated in a bloody strike in Guayaquil in 1922. The workers' actions convinced the more conservative *serranos* that social revolution was near. These events strengthened regionalism. Many highlanders viewed the progress of the coast with suspicion. Since 1895 all liberal presidents had either been *costeños* or closely identified with Guayaquil interests. The association between coastal banks and the national government convinced many highlanders that the port city dominated national politics. It was widely believed that a "corrupt coastal oligarchy" was exploiting the nation for its own selfish ends.[28] . . .

Sierra regionalists used the country's financial plight to undermine their coastal rivals. They maintained that the Ley Moratoria—inconvertibility—and the government debt to Guayaquil banks were manifestations of a successful conspiracy by port bankers to dominate Ecuadorian politics. In their view a corrupt coastal oligarchy had selfishly exploited the country. The *serranos* concentrated their criticism on the Banco Comercial y Agrícola, the government's principal banker, and its manager, Francisco Urvina Jado. They chose to ignore the national and international conditions that were the primary cause of Ecuador's economic crisis.[29]

Regional jealousies, aggravated by personal antagonisms, clouded the economic and financial debate in Ecuador. Luis N. Dillon, a highland businessman and politician, emerged as the leading critic of what he termed the corrupt relationship between Guayaquil bankers and liberal administrations. He not only shared the northern highland's antipathy toward the more prosperous coast, but his hostility was also fueled by the belief that his financial and political ambitions had been thwarted by Guayaquil bankers, particularly Urvina Jado. In 1922, Dillon had organized the Sociedad de Crédito Internacional in Quito, an institution established to issue currency in the highlands. The Sociedad had already printed and registered its notes when Urvina Jado learned that the bills had no backing. As the manager of one of the leading banks in the country, Urvina Jado considered it his responsibility to protect the nation's currency. He, therefore, complained to Minister of Finance Alfonso Larrea, who, after investigating the matter, prohibited the circulation of the Sociedad's notes.

Dillon interpreted Urvina Jado's action both as a personal attack and as an example of regional animosity. Convinced that Guayaquil bankers dominated the country's banking and currency structure, he failed to notice that Urvina Jado acted in the same fashion when the prestigious Guayaquil Banco de Descuento also attempted to circulate improperly backed bills. The banker again protested to Minister Larrea and succeeded in having the notes recalled. In both instances, Urvina Jado acted to protect the nation's currency. Dillon, nevertheless, came to loathe the manager of the Banco Comercial y Agrícola. Dillon's enmity toward the coast intensified in 1924 when he failed to receive the post of minister of finance in the Córdova government. He, as well as the highland press, accused coastal regionalists of vetoing the appointment. Although Córdova offered Dillon another portfolio, the highlander rejected it, believing that he deserved to be minister of finance since he was the manager of La Internacional, the country's largest textile factory, and because he was one of the most influential members of the highland business community.[30]

Dillon became the leading and most visible northern highland critic of the coast. Quito journalists, intellectuals, and politicians blamed a corrupt Guayaquil banking oligarchy for the country's problems. Disturbed by the ascendancy of the coast and what they perceived to be the diminishing status of Quito, the country's capital, northern highlanders charged that a small group of Guayaquil oligarchs ran the country. It was widely asserted, for example, that the president followed the orders of the manager of the Banco Comercial y Agrícola because the government owed so much money to that bank. *Serranos* interpreted the bank loans to the government as buying off the administration to retain the Ley Moratoria. They considered inconvertibility a plot by unscrupulous bankers to exploit the country, rather than a necessary measure to protect the currency. *Serranos* believed that Guayaquil bankers had vetoed Dillon's candidacy for minister of finance because the highlander opposed evil coastal practices. Dillon actively cultivated that image, speaking frequently on finances and national problems to organizations as varied as the Quito Chamber of Commerce and the military academy. Although a capitalist entrepreneur and a member of the Liberal party, he did not hesitate to ally himself with socialists and militarists to propagate his regionalist views. Indeed, he donated funds, purchased advertising, and contributed articles to *La Antorcha*, a Quito socialist paper with a strong anticoastal bias.

Northern highland intellectuals and the Quito press in general argued that the coast exploited the rest of the country, but two sierra publications, *La Antorcha* and *El Abanderado*, a military-oriented paper, were to play a key role in future events. As a socialist newspaper, *La Antorcha* published articles on socialism, but its hostility toward the "corrupt coastal plutocracy" and its demand for social reform made the paper acceptable to many *quiteños*, both civilian and military. The paper often cooperated with *El Abanderado*, a journal that had a primarily military readership, published by retired Lieutenant Colonel Victor M. Naranjo. Naranjo published articles decrying the state of the country and condemning the plutocrats who had ruled too long. He argued that the army, the government, the courts, and the universities had all been corrupted to serve the interest of a few great capitalists in Guayaquil. *El Abanderado*, however, was primarily concerned with military reform. The paper distinguished between two types of officers: the professional and the political. It called political generals, like former president Leonidas Plaza, not only a cancer on the body politic but also a major impediment to the reform and modernization of the army. The paper considered General Francisco Gómez de la Torre, inspector general of the army, who had been educated in foreign military academies, the perfect example of a professional officer. In *El Abanderado's* view, political officers concerned themselves only with promotion and spoils while professional officers considered the country and the army's interests first. The paper exhorted the young officers, the first generation to be educated in a national military academy and presumably therefore professional, to abandon the old politics and to forge a new army and a new country. *El Abanderado* promoted regionalist antipathy by continually reminding the young officers that the old political officers, like Plaza, had grown rich by permitting coastal oligarchs to despoil the country.[31]

In 1924, *La Antorcha* and *El Abanderado* cooperated in advancing their common aims. *La Antorcha*, for example, falsely asserted that the Banco Comercial y Agrícola wanted the government to sell the Galápagos Islands; *El Abanderado* supported this allegation, claiming to possess official documents that proved the charge. Similarly, the two papers collaborated to discredit Free Masonry, a movement popular among coastal businessmen but viewed with suspicion by the more conservative highlanders. The papers maintained that the Grand Lodge in Lima dominated Ecuadorian Masons, and members therefore were agents of the country's ancient enemy, Peru. These arguments aroused the fears of the young officers, most of whom were highlanders, and justified their regionalist sentiments. Starting in December 1924, the papers launched a campaign to convince the young officers that only they could save the country from the impending crisis. The papers publicized the recent military coup in Chile and praised its reforms. They also reminded the young officers that a Chilean mission had reorganized the Ecuadorian army and established the military academy where the officers had only recently studied. The conclusions were obvious; the young officers should take power, crush the corrupt coastal oligarchs, and reform the country. The articles and the exhortations of men like Dillon had the desired effect. Many young officers, writing under pseudonyms, submitted essays on national and military reform to the two papers. Their writings indicate that they blamed Guayaquil banks for the nation's problems. The fears of highlanders and, particularly, the concerns of the military men increased when President Córdova became ill and traveled to Guayaquil to recuperate. *Serranos* were convinced that the coast would dominate the president and that their interests would be forgotten.[32]

In October 1924 a group of lieutenants formed a *liga militar* in Quito to resolve the nation's crisis. Their plotting culminated in the overthrow of the Córdova government on July 9, 1925. The officers justified their actions in a twelve-point reform program, which they prepared after consultation with Luis N. Dillon, the man whom they considered Ecuador's leading economic expert. Predictably they called for the repeal of the Ley Moratoria. They arrested Francisco Urvina Jado, the manager of the Banco Comercial y Agrícola, and named Dillon to the Provisional Governing Committee that ran Ecuador after the coup. The young officers believed that they represented national, not regional, interests. Nevertheless, Urvina's death in exile and the subsequent destruction of the Banco Comercial y Agrícola symbolized the regional prejudices and economic misperceptions that triumphed in the 1925 coup.[33]. . .

The Military League, which overthrew the government of Gonzalo Córdova, included military men from all sections of the country, but the young officers in Quito and Guayaquil were its principal leaders. Although the coup began in Guayaquil on July 9, 1925, the Quito group took over the government in the capital. Without waiting for the Guayaquil representatives to arrive, they named a six-man Supreme Military Junta that in turn appointed a Provisional Governing Committee including two generals and two civilians from Quito, prominent among them Luis N. Dillon. These appointments concerned the *guayaquileños* who believed *quiteños*, hostile to the coast, had usurped control of the government. After considerable protest, one of the generals resigned and three representatives from the coast arrived to join the Provisional Governing Committee. The change did not affect the new balance of power. The coastal members received appointments to less important ministries such as education, public works, and social welfare, while highlanders filled those of interior, foreign affairs, finance, and war. Indeed, General Francisco Gómez de la Torre, minister of war, and Luis N. Dillon, minister of finance, dominated the government with the support of the young officers and the Supreme Military Junta.[34]. . .

The Supreme Military Junta, the final arbiter of Ecuadorian politics, opposed a "premature" return to constitutional government. The *costeños* in the provisional government and politically active groups in the littoral favored the prompt convocation of a constituent assembly to defend their interests. The military, mainly from the highlands, believed national reforms could not be implemented through normal political means. By naming [Isidro] Ayora, a respected physician with strong ties both to the coast and the highlands, provisional president, they forestalled elections. The Ecuadorian army probably agreed with the British minister who reported to his government that "the real solution of Ecuador would be a man of the stamp of Porfirio Díaz of Mexico to run the country with an iron hand, assisted by foreign and honest officials." The minister of the interior later defended the military's action before the 1929 constituent assembly, declaring that all who desired real change after July 9, 1925, concluded that it could only be accomplished by an honorable "dictator" who could organize and discipline the government. Parliamentary methods, he argued, could not have reformed the nation.[35]

Notes

1. Only one strong man, General Alberto Enriquez Gallo, in 1938 convoked a constitutional convention that did not "elect" him president. The following are the conventions called by *jefes supremos* to write new constitutions and to ratify their power: 1830 General Juan José Flores; 1835 Vicente Rocafuerte; 1843 General Juan José Flores; 1851 Diego Noboa; 1852 General José María Urvina; 1878 General Ignacio Veintimilla; 1883 José María Plácido Caamaño; 1897 General Eloy Alfaro; 1906 General Eloy Alfaro; 1929 Isidro Ayora; 1938 General Alberto Enríquez Gallo (not elected); 1944 José María Velasco Ibarra.

Georg Maier, "Presidential Succession in Ecuador, 1830–1970," *Journal of Inter-American Studies and World Affairs* 13:3-4 (Jul–Oct, 1971): 475–509, has a penetrating discussion of this phenomenon. The fifteen constitutions written between 1830 and 1946 are published in Ramino Borja y Borja, *Derecho constitucional ecuatoriano*, 3 vols. (Madrid: Ediciones Cultura Hispánica, 1950), III, 105–699.

2. Richard Pattee, *Gabriel García Moreno y el Ecuador de su tiempo* (México: Editorial Jus, 1944), 87–89; Jacinto Jijón y Caamaño, *Política conservadora*, 2 vols. (Riobamba: La Buena Prensa de Chimborazo, 1929), I, 273–289; Vicente Rocafuerte to Juan José Flores, Quito, April 27, 1836, in Jaime E. Rodríguez O., *Estudios sobre Vicente Rocafuerte* (Guayaquil: Archivo Histórico del Guayas, 1975), 256–257.

3. On this point see Tulio Halpering Donghi, *The Aftermath of Revolution in Latin America* (New York: Harper and Row, 1973), 1–43. According to Rocafuerte: "Our revolutions . . . have resulted from the military spirit, which, contrary to all political theory, General Bolívar established." Rocafuerte to Francisco de Paula Santander, November 30, 1834, in Rodríguez, *Estudios*, 189.

4. Luis Robalino Dávila, *Orígenes del Ecuador de Hoy*, 7 vols. (Puebla: Editorial Cajica, 1967), III, 480. See also David Bushnell, *The Santander Regime* (Newark: University of Delaware Press, 1954).

5. The best-known foreign military men who settled in Ecuador include: Marshal Antonio José de Sucre (Venezuelan); General Juan José Flores (Venezuelan); General Isidoro Barriga (Colombian); Colonel Francisco Tamaríz (Spanish); Colonel Bernardo Daste (French); Colonel Ricardo Wright (English); Colonel Juan Illingworth (English).

6. The best study of Flores is Robalino Dávila's first volume of his *Orígenes del Ecuador* entitled *Nacimiento y primeros años de la República*.

7. Abraham Eraso, *La Provincia de Bolívar en 1834* (Quito: n.p., n.d.); Robalino Dávila, *Orígenes del Ecuador*, III, 67–69.

8. Robalino Dávila, *Orígenes del Ecuador*, III, 194–218; Julio Tobar Donoso, *Monografías históricas* (Quito: Editorial Ecuatoriana, 1937), 99–255.

9. Robalino Dávila, *Orígenes del Ecuador*, III, 294–305, 355–393.

10. Ibid., III, 395–466; IV, 169–298; Eraso, *La Provincia de Bolívar*, 49–50.

11. Robalino Dávila, *Orígenes del Ecuador*, VII, pt. 1, 21–41, 63–73.

12. J. Gonzalo Orellana, *Resumen histórico del Ecuador*, 2 vols. (Quito: Editorial Fray Jodoco Ricke, 1948), I, 55–57; Robalino Dávila, *Orígenes del Ecuador*, VII, pt. 1, 77–111, 274–275; VII, pt. 2, 582; Jorge Pérez Concha, *Eloy Alfaro* (Quito: Talleres Gráficos de Educación, 1942), 129–133; *El Telégrafo*, no. 15415 (April 23, 1928); Ecuador, Ministro de Guerra, *Informe, 1913*.

13. Pérez Concha, *Eloy Alfaro*, 201–204, 222–225, 245–255; Robalino Dávila, *Orígenes del Ecuador*, VII, pt. 2, 659–690.

14. *El Comercio*, no. 7354 (February 13, 1926); *El Telégrafo*, no. 15415 (April 23, 1928); Robalino Dávila, *Orígenes del Ecuador*, VII, pt. 2, 619–650.

15. Luis Larrea Alba, *La Campaña de 1906* (Quito: Editorial Cyma, 1962), is the best study of the causes and consequences of the 1906 insurrection. See also Robalino Dávila, *Orígenes del Ecuador*, VIII, 18–41.

16. Larrea Alba, *La Campaña de 1906*, 123–127; Ecuador, Ministro de Guerra, *Informe, 1913*, 34–37.

17. Ecuador, Ministro de lo Interior, *Informe, 1908*, iii–iv; M. de Lambert to secretary of state, Quito, July 17, 1925, National Archives (hereafter NA), Record Group (hereafter R.G.) 84, 822.00/604; Larrea Alba, *La Campaña de 1906*, 128–173.

18. Francisco Güarderas, *El Viejo de Montecristi* (Puebla: Editorial Cajica, 1965), 421–450; Ecuador, Ministro de lo Interior, *Informe, 1912*, iii–iv; Robalino Dávila, *Orígenes del Ecuador*, VIII, 390–490.

19. Ecuador, Ministro de Guerra, *Informe, 1913*, 27–45; Robalino Dávila, *Orígenes del Ecuador*, VIII, 491–584, 594–611.

20. Güarderas, *El Viejo*, 421–450; Ecuador, Ministro de lo Interior, *Informe, 1912*, v–vii; Ecuador, Ministro de Guerra, *Informe, 1913*, 27; Robalino Dávila, *Orígenes del Ecuador*, VIII, 611–680; *La Prensa* (Quito), January 16, 1912; *La Constitución* (Quito), January 17, 1912; *El Grito del pueblo ecuatoriano* (Guayaquil), January 24, 1912.

21. Ecuador, Ministro de Guerra, *Informe, 1913*, 30–33; *1919*, 4; *El Comercio*, no. 7161 (August 3, 1925); Ecuador, Ministro de lo Interior, *Informe, 1915*, v–xi, xv; *1916*, v–viii; Roberto Andrade, *¡Sangre! ¿Quien la derramó? Historia de los últimos crímenes cometidos en la nación del Ecuador* (Quito: Imprenta Antigua de *El Quiteño Libre*, 1912), is an anti-Plaza attack. Segundo L. Moreno discusses the Esmeraldas campaign in *La Campaña de Esmeraldas de 1913–1916 encabezada por el Coronel Graduado Don Carlos Concha Torres* (Cuenca: Tipografía Universidad, 1939).

22. Ecuador, Ministro de lo Interior, *Informe, 1915*, v–ix, xv, xxxvi, lii, lxx; *1916*, v–x, xiv–xv. For a brief discussion of Plaza's two administrations see Julio C. Troncoso, *Odio y sangre* (Quito: Editorial Fray Jodoco Ricke, 1958), 63–70.

23. Ecuador, Ministro de Guerra, *Informe, 1913*, 54–70; Charles Hartman to secretary of state, January 1, 1920, NA, 822.00/471; R. M. de Lambert to secretary of state, Quito, July 17, 1925, NA, 822.00/604; G. A. Bading to secretary of state, Quito, April 20, 1925, NA, 822.00/582; *El Telégrafo*, no. 15730 (March 3, 1929); Ildefonso Mendoza, "La Revolución de Julio," *El Comercio*, no. 9033

(September 17, 1930); no. 9065 (September 19, 1930); *La Antorcha* (Quito), no. 4 (April 11, 1925).

24. R. M. de Lambert to secretary of state, Quito, July 17, 1925, NA, 822.00/604; G. A. Bading to secretary of state, Quito, April 20, 1925, NA, 822.00/582; Memorandum from Division of Latin American Affairs, Department of State, to Dr. Rowe, Washington, D.C., May 28, 1920, NA, 822.00/485; Orellana, *Resumen histórico,* I, 84–86.

25. Charles Hartman to secretary of state, Quito, June 6, 1919, NA, 822.00/459; July 22, 1919, NA, 822.00/462; January 1, 1920, NA, 822.00/471; January 11, 1920, NA, 822.00/469; January 15, 1920, NA, 822.00/470; *El Telégrafo,* no. 14386 (July 9, 1925); A. M. Tweedy to J. H. Stablès, Quito, May 21, 1918, NA, 822.00/453; G. A. Bading to secretary of state, Quito, June 25, 1924, NA, 822.00/549; March 31, 1925, NA, 822.00/579; April 20, 1925, NA, 822.00/582; February 27, 1924, NA, 822.00/536; R. C. Michell to Foreign Office, Quito, February 28, 1924, British Foreign Office (hereafter FO) 371/79541, A2194/373/54.

26. *El Comercio* (August 21, 1921); Ildefonso Mendoza, "La Revolución de Julio y sus actores," *El Comercio,* no. 9066 (September 19, 1930); Ecuador, Ministro de Hacienda, *Informe, 1922,* 9–15, 31–32; *1923,* 8–10, 13–17, 28; *1921,* v; *1916,* x–xi.

27. Frederic W. Goding to secretary of state, Guayaquil, November 9, 1920, NA, R.G. 84; Harold W. Deane to secretary of state, Quito, March 31, 1922, NA, 822.00/505; Frederic W. Goding to secretary of state, Quito, November 29, 1921, NA, 822.51/340; R. C. Michell to Foreign Office, Quito, January 30, 1925, FO 371/10619, A 1229/1229/54; *El Comercio,* no. 7363 (February 22, 1926); no. 7459 (May 29, 1926); "Mensaje especial que el Señor Presidente de la República envía al Congreso Nacional," August 10, 1930, in Ecuador, Ministro de Hacienda, *Informe, 1930, Anexo,* 356–365; Ministro del Tesoro, "Informe, June 12, 1931," in Ecuador, Ministro de Hacienda, *Boletín,* no. 38, 96–97 (hereafter cited as Ecuador, Ministro del Tesoro, "Informe, June 12, 1931").

28. Luis N. Dillon, *La crisis económico-financiera del Ecuador* (Quito: Editorial Artes Gráficas, 1927), 24–26, 36–37; *La Antorcha,* no. 1 (November 16, 1924); no. 2 (November 23, 1924); *El Abanderado* (Quito), no. 9 (January 19, 1925). The cacao crisis and the 1922 strike are discussed in Lois Weinman, "Ecuador and Cacao: Domestic Response to the Boom-Collapse Monoexport Cycle" (Ph.D. diss., University of California, Los Angeles, 1970). Joaquin Gallegos Lara recounts the events leading to the November 15, 1922, tragedy in his novel, *Cruces sobre el agua* (Guayaquil: Casa de la Cultura Ecuatoriana, 1946). See also Ecuador, Ministro de Hacienda, *Informe, 1921,* xxxi–xxxii.

29. For a history of banking in Ecuador see Julio Estrada Ycaza, *Los bancos del siglo XIX* (Guayaquil: Archivo Histórico del Guayas, 1976).

30. Víctor Emilio Estrada, *El momento económico en el Ecuador* (Guayaquil: Litografía e Imprenta la Reforma Jacinto Jouvin Arce e Hijos, 1950), 37; *El Guante,* no. 5353 (May 29, 1925); *El Comercio,* no. 7095; R. M. de Lambert to secretary of state, Quito, July 17, 1925, NA, 822.00/604.

31. *La Antorcha,* año 1, no. 1 (November 16, 1924); año 1, no. 2 (November 23, 1924); Leonardo N. Muñoz, "Interview" (Quito: December 3, 1971); *El Abanderado,* año 1, no. 4 (December 15, 1924); año 1, no. 3 (December 8, 1924); año 1, no. 10 (January 26, 1925); año 1, no. 9 (January 19, 1925); Luis A. Rodríguez, "Interview" (Quito: March 26, 1972); Luis A. Rodríguez, "Mis recuerdos," 25, in Luis A. Rodríguez papers in the possession of Jaime E. Rodríguez O. (Los Angeles); *El Comercio,* no. 7095 (May 29, 1925).

32. *La Antorcha*, año 1, no. 6 (November 16, 1924); año 1, no. 8 (December 31, 1924); año 1, no. 12 (January 31, 1925); año 1, no. 13 (February 7, 1925); año 1, no. 16 (February 28, 1925); año 2, no. 2 (March 30, 1925); *El Abanderado*, año 1, no. 15 (March 2, 1925); Rodríguez, "Mis recuerdos," 30.

33. For a detailed discussion of the formation of the *liga militar* and the coup of July 9, 1925, see Linda A. Rodríguez, "The Liberal Crisis and the Revolution of 1925 in Ecuador" (Master's thesis, University of Texas, Austin, 1972). *El Telégrafo*, no. 14391 (July 12, 1925); no. 14399 (July 19, 1925); no. 14389 (July 11, 1925); no. 14394 (July 14, 1925); *El Ejército Nacional*, año 4, no. 26 (1925).

34. Rodríguez, "The Liberal Crisis," 106–114.

35. R. C. Michell to Foreign Office, Quito, December 31, 1923, FO 371/9542, A895/895/54; Ecuador, Ministro de lo Interior, *Informe, 1926–1928*, 5–6.

4

The War of the Pacific

William F. Sater

During the nineteenth century, boundary disputes and competing territo-
rial claims frequently disrupted normal relations between the nations of
Latin America. The potential for armed conflict was heightened when dis-
putes encompassed territories with important economic resources. Do-
mestic press coverage of border incidents and treaty violations often
inflamed public opinion, putting pressure on governments to defend their
nation's honor and territorial integrity against rapacious sister repub-
lics. Nationalist fervor precipitated six major wars in South America. These
struggles drained national treasuries, destabilized governments, and ex-
posed weaknesses within both victorious and vanquished armed forces.

The War of the Pacific (1879–1884) was one of the major intraregional
conflicts of the nineteenth century. For the second time since Indepen-
dence, Chile fought against Peru and Bolivia, both to resolve territorial
disputes and to enhance its regional dominance. The southern nation de-
feated its northern rivals and stripped them of nitrate-rich territories in
the Atacama Desert. As William Sater demonstrates, Chile achieved vic-
tory despite a critical press and growing public disenchantment with the
government.

The so-called War of the Pacific, which erupted in 1879, was a conflict between Chile on the one side, and Peru and Bolivia on the other. In simple terms Chile was an energetic, economically expanding nation that coveted the great mineral treasures, particularly in nitrates, found in the coastal provinces of

From *The Heroic Image in Chile: Arturo Prat, Secular Saint* (Berkeley: University of California Press, 1973), 34–47, 176–80. ©1973 by The Regents of the University of California. Reprinted by permission of the University of California Press.

> her neighbors, Bolivia and Peru. Irresistibly tempted
> by these underdeveloped and sparsely occupied ar-
> eas, Chile took advantage of the customary political
> anarchy in the Republics to take the provinces by a
> war of conquest.
> —JOHN LLOYD MECHAM, *A Survey of United States-
> Latin American Relations* (1965)

I

Bolivia precipitated the War of the Pacific when it imposed higher taxes on the Chilean-owned nitrate companies operating in the Atacama Desert. Since colonial times the Atacama had been considered worthless until the discovery first of guano and then of nitrates made this area extremely valuable. Suddenly, Bolivia and Chile laid claim to this previously neglected strip of desert, and for years each nation engaged in fruitless negotiations hoping to have its jurisdiction recognized. In 1874, Chile signed an agreement relinquishing its rights to the disputed terri-tory in return for which Bolivia agreed not to increase the taxes on the Chilean Compañía de Salitre y Ferrocarriles for twenty-five years. Al-though the Atacama officially became part of Bolivia, most Chileans still considered the area morally theirs, since the majority of its population and economic enterprises were owned by their countrymen, and resented the fact that their compatriots had to live under the uncertain rule of Bolivia.[1]

Following on the heels of the Argentine crisis, the increase in taxes antagonized the already touchy Chileans who considered the Bolivian action not only arbitrary but also insulting to Chile's national honor. For this reason, when [President Aníbal] Pinto demonstrated a willingness to parley with the Bolivians, a substantial portion of the press objected. Bolivia, the journals complained, had never contributed to the develop-ment of the Atacama, and now it was using the issue of taxation as a pretext for the eventual expropriation of Chilean property.[2]

The Chilean press demanded that Pinto protect the nation's honor and enforce its treaty rights.[3] A public meeting even advocated the use of force to defend the nationally owned industries.[4] In February 1879, Pinto ordered his troops to occupy the littoral, basing his action on the concept of "revindication," a doctrine that claimed Chile was entitled to repos-sess its former territory on the grounds that, by raising the taxes, Bolivia had voided its 1874 treaty with Chile. Although this action led to a Boliv-ian declaration of war, the Chilean press almost unanimously supported the president's decision.[5]

Chile had other enemies besides Bolivia. Some feared that Argentina and Peru might possibly intervene.[6] This anxiety, at least that regarding Peru, was not illusory, for within a week after the seizure of Antofagasta, Chilean newspapers, noting that pro-Bolivian demonstrations were taking place in Lima, began to express doubts about their northern neighbor's neutrality.[7] Peru, in the meantime, sent a diplomatic mission to Chile to mediate between the two disputing nations. Although the Chilean government officially welcomed it, many newspapers doubted that it would be effective: Bolivia did not appear disposed to arbitration, and Peruvian demands for the withdrawal of Chilean troops from the littoral were unacceptable.[8] According to many Chileans, the return of the disputed territory would expose their compatriots in the north to the caprice of the Bolivian government's reprisals.[9]

While the Peruvian mission remained in Chile, the local newspapers continued to reprint the increasingly hostile statements being made by the Lima press.[10] The Chileans considered these editorials unjust. They denied that Chile had any imperialistic designs and sought to reassure the Peruvians that the occupation of the Atacama would ultimately benefit them, because industry in the disputed area would prosper more under Chilean than Bolivian administration.[11]

The Chilean press noted, however, that the Peruvians were arming their fleet and reinforcing their garrison at Iquique. Both the papers and the Congress asked the government to clarify the significance of these actions and their possible repercussions.[12] While some newspapers were willing to interpret the Peruvian moves as purely defensive acts against a possible Bolivian violation of its territorial integrity, they did not explain why Peru was readying its fleet when Bolivia had no navy, or why Peru was sending weapons to Bolivia.[13]

Within a few weeks, many believed that a Peruvian declaration of war against Chile was imminent and that Peru's diplomatic mission was merely a subterfuge to gain time.[14] Some claimed that Peru and Bolivia had signed a secret military alliance, an allegation both the press and the Congress wanted the Pinto government either to confirm or deny.[15] Before March ended, however, few, if any, doubted that such a treaty existed. On the contrary, most of the Chilean press argued that it was Peru that had encouraged the Bolivians to raise the taxes on the Chilean-owned nitrate company. The press theorized that the Peruvians had promised the Bolivians a favorable trade treaty in return for which the Bolivians would raise the taxes on the Chilean mines. The Bolivians, never expecting the Chilean company to pay the taxes, had planned to use the company's refusal as a pretext for expropriating its holdings, knowing that the Chilean government, already embroiled in a border dispute with Argentina, could not retaliate. The Fierro-Sarretea Treaty with Argentina, however, saved Chile, for it no longer had to worry about its eastern border. Bolivia, unfortunately, had committed itself and was past the point of no return.[16]

The final rupture in Chilean-Peruvian relations was almost anticlimactic and occurred when the Chilean government demanded to know whether there was a secret treaty between Peru and Bolivia, and, if so, whether Peru would remain neutral in case of war. When Peru replied that it could not declare its neutrality because of its 1873 alliance with Bolivia, Pinto, with congressional support, declared war on April 5, 1879.

II

Chile was seriously unprepared for war. The government, for reasons of economy, had drastically reduced its military expenditures and scaled down the size of the armed forces. The Chilean military could muster only twenty-four hundred troops, most of whom were protecting its southern border against the Indians. The National Guard, often considered at best a tool of political repression and at worst a useless extravagance, had also been gutted; by 1879, it numbered but 7,161 men, a 70 percent reduction over the previous year.[17]

The regular army's units were not only under strength, they were badly equipped with old Comblain rifles and American carbines, with little additional matériel should the army have to expand. The National Guard was in even worse condition, because its infantry units used the obsolete Minié rifle, which had a tendency to explode when fired, while the cavalry did not even have firearms, only lances and sabers. Only a few of the reserve artillery units possessed fieldpieces, but these were almost useless, because they were made of bronze. In essence the National Guard was militarily unimportant; it could not even clothe or arm its own members, let alone provide a trained reserve to supplement the regular troops.[18]

It is extremely difficult to evaluate the military potential of the Allies. As the years have elapsed, the Bolivian and Peruvian historians have often exaggerated Chile's strength and underestimated their own nation's military prowess in order to excuse the Allied defeat.[19] Although there is some agreement on the size of Peru's National Guard—approximately sixty-five thousand men—various historians have estimated the strength of that nation's army at anywhere from two thousand to seven thousand. Despite the discrepancy, it can be ascertained that the Peruvian army could muster at least 5,789 men at the beginning of the war. Like the Chileans, the Peruvians also had tried to reform their army by sending military missions to Europe to study new methods and to acquire weapons. These plans never came to fruition, however, because of financial problems. Again like Chile, Peru equipped its troops with a variety of weapons, relying mostly on the Casteñon rifle, a modified version of the Chassepot, and possessed a few artillery units, most of which were inadequately equipped.[20]

Bolivia's prewar military strength is also something of a mystery. Although the peacetime army numbered between twelve hundred and twenty-three hundred men, the nation also had a large National Guard of some fifty-four thousand, which was increased by mobilizing all unmarried men between the ages of sixteen and forty once war began.[21] The Bolivian army's equipment consisted of a bizarre assortment of different weapons of varying calibers and nationalities, although it received substantial numbers of new and modern weapons from Peru and Argentina.[22]

Whatever their material deficiencies, the Allied armies still outnumbered their enemy by more than two to one, a fact of which the Chileans were uncomfortably aware.[23] While some of the Chilean press might sarcastically describe the average Bolivian soldier as an illiterate Indian, they still feared him. The enemy, it was observed, was strong, well armed, and dedicated. Even before Peru's entry into the war, various Chilean news journals were already disturbed about fighting just Bolivia and cautioned the nation not to be too impetuous or optimistic;[24] Peru's involvement in the struggle increased these fears.[25]

Like the army, the Chilean navy had also suffered from economy measures. By 1879, one transport and a corvette had been sold, while two other warships, the *Covadonga* and the *Esmeralda*, were disarmed. The active fleet consisted of six vessels: the two ironclads, *Blanco Encalada* and the *Cochrane*; the corvettes, *Chacabuco, Magallanes*, and *O'Higgins*; and the transport, *Toltén*. Not all of the fleet, however, was battle ready. The *O'Higgins* and the *Chacabuco* required such extensive repairs on their boilers that one naval officer recommended that they be used only as sailing ships. The *Blanco Encalada* needed its armor repaired; and its bottom, like that of the majority of the fleet, was so fouled that its speed was reduced by almost one half. Of the entire squadron, the director of arsenals considered only the ironclads, the *Magallanes*, and the *Toltén* seaworthy.[26]

Additional problems plagued the navy as well. The fleet did not possess sufficient transports, making logistic support difficult. The navy also lacked both junior officers and able-bodied seamen because the government had closed the Naval Academy and the School of Mariners in 1876. For this reason, some of the ships were so understrength when the war began that Chile had to hire foreigners to man its fleet. Perhaps Luis Uribe, a survivor of Iquique and later an admiral, was correct when he subsequently declared that Chile triumphed in the War of the Pacific only because Peru was the more disorganized.[27]

The mainstay of Peru's navy was its two ironclads: the monitor *Huáscar* and the frigate *Independencia*. There were also two other ironclads, but these were so old that they had been relegated to coastal defense. Peruvian historians have claimed that Peru's navy was more decrepit than its army. Manuel Vegas and Geraldo Arosemena stated that the fleet had not participated in firing exercises for over five years. They also alleged that a substantial number of ships had been either disarmed or dismantled when the war began.[28] According to [Mariano] Paz Soldán, only the *Pilcomayo* was really seaworthy, while supposedly the rest of the squadron was in varying stages of decay.[29]

These later judgments do not agree with the reports of various contemporary observers. In 1878 the Peruvian government declared its fleet was the "best organized and disciplined of all the Pacific States."[30] While this might be dismissed as propaganda, in that same year the Ministerio de Marina pronounced the *Huáscar* in perfect condition.[31] In March 1879, two Peruvian newspapers were pleased to report that the *Manco Capac*, the *Huáscar*, the *Independencia*, and the *Unión* were ready for combat.[32] These remarks tend to indicate that Peru's fleet was a worthy adversary for the Chileans. Indeed, one might wonder if they had not taken on more than they could handle.

Both sides were aware of their respective deficiencies and tried to augment their naval strength by purchasing additional vessels. Peru sought to acquire an ironclad from Italy, hoping to sail it immediately to Callao. The Chilean government tried to block these transactions, and even considered ambushing any newly purchased Peruvian ship as it entered the Strait of Magellan.[33] Throughout the war, each nation waged a diplomatic struggle to deprive the other of munitions and supplies from abroad. Peru once hired an English torpedo expert, a former Royal Navy officer, to act as an instructor, but the Chileans successfully prevented him and his torpedoes from reaching the enemy. The Peruvians had similar luck when they stopped a shipment of torpedo boats, labeled farm machinery, from reaching Chile.[34]

In addition to these two avowed enemies, Chile faced the threat of Argentine intervention. Argentine naval vessels, operating out of Peruvian ports or launching an attack from the Atlantic, in conjunction with the Peruvians from the north, would have caught the Chilean navy in a vise.[35] The Chilean fleet, therefore, had to win some initial victory to demonstrate to its eastern neighbor that its intervention would be foolhardy.

III

Apparently, it was the lack of a clearly defined strategic objective, not material deficiencies, that prevented Chile from winning this necessary victory. Although there was general agreement that naval superiority was a prerequisite to the conquest of Peru, there was a crucial and costly difference of opinion on how to achieve this needed maritime supremacy. The president and his advisers had favored an immediate attack on Callao, hoping to destroy or immobilize the Peruvian fleet, after which the Chileans could then launch an attack against Lima, thus capturing Peru's political and military nerve center while bypassing its garrisons in the south.[36]

The commander of the Chilean squadron, Admiral Juan Williams Rebolledo, did not agree with his superiors. He claimed that the fleet was unable to launch an attack against Callao because it was too dangerous. He further argued that the navy did not possess the necessary logistic support to sustain a blockade so far from its base of operations. As an alternative, Williams proposed to blockade Iquique, which he did on April 5, 1879. The admiral believed that this action, which would deprive Peru of its nitrate revenue, in conjunction with additional attacks on the Peruvian coast, would force the enemy to abandon his fortified port and come south to attack the Chileans.[37] This essentially passive strategy miscarried, however, for it permitted the Peruvian fleet to arm its capital ships and to fortify both Callao and Arica, an important port to the south.[38] In addition, the Peruvian naval commander, Miguel Grau, capitalized on the Chilean inertia by harassing its lines of communication, knowing full well that as long as the Chilean fleet remained off-balance, Peru was safe from invasion.

Four contests marked Williams's tenure as fleet commander: Chipana, which was inconclusive; the assault on Callao, which was a farce; the blockade of Iquique, which was useless; and the capture of the *Rimac*, which was a disaster. Chipana occurred within the first weeks of the war, on April 15, 1879, when two Peruvian ships attacked the *Magallanes*. The battle was really only a brief skirmish because the Peruvians had to give up the pursuit when one of their ships blew a boiler. Despite the unheroic quality of the contest, both sides glorified the encounter—the Chileans for having escaped, and the Peruvians for having forced the enemy to retreat.[39] Except for the occasional bombardment of an undefended nitrate dock, it was not until mid-May that the Chilean fleet took any decisive action. Until then, it steamed off Iquique wasting precious coal, its crew riddled by scurvy and demoralized by inactivity.[40]

Suddenly, on May 16, without informing either his president, the minister of the navy, or his own officers about his destination, Williams embarked on his ill-fated attack on Callao. As noted earlier, his expedition was hardly a masterpiece of planning or execution. During the trip north, Williams managed to lose his fleet collier. He further handicapped the expedition by including in the attack force vessels whose slow speed substantially inhibited the entire convoy's rate of progress. Finally, the admiral failed to deploy some of his ships to reconnoiter ahead. Had he done so on the evening of May 19, he might have intercepted the southward-bound Peruvian fleet, thus averting the disaster of Iquique.[41] Having botched his earlier attack on Callao, thereby fulfilling his own prophecy that such a mission was impossible, Williams reverted to his old stratagem of reinstating the sterile blockade of Iquique.

Although the loss of the *Independencia* drastically altered the naval balance of power in Chile's favor, both Williams and Grau ignored this fact, the first out of obstinacy, the second out of a sense of desperation. The Peruvian fleet continued to attack Chilean shipping and coastal cities, and even occupied Punta Arenas, a port more than three thousand miles south of Lima. In the meantime Williams moped off Iquique waiting for a glimpse of his enemy and perhaps secretly glad that he did not appear. Occasionally the admiral made some half-hearted attempt to capture the *Huáscar*, but each time he failed. This should have been expected: because he had refused to allow his ships' bottoms to be cleaned or their engines to be repaired, Williams's squadron was no match for the speed of the "Ghost of the Pacific."[42] In a fit of pique the admiral vented his frustrations by shelling more nitrate docks and once even bombarding the defenseless city of Iquique, claiming that the enemy had the effrontery to launch a torpedo attack against him.[43]

As might be expected, those who worked with Williams described him as a difficult individual. Independent to a fault, he rarely consulted with the president, let alone with his army counterpart or his subordinates.[44] He appeared to despise General [Justo] Arteaga, the commander of the army expeditionary forces, and refused to coordinate his efforts with those of the military.[45] The admiral often behaved erratically, frequently countermanding his orders for no apparent reason.[46] Terrified of torpedoes (a reasonable fear, but one inconsistent with his profession), Williams imagined them everywhere, and refused to anchor for the night unless assured he was safe.[47] This fearless mariner also suffered from ill health, supposedly syphilitic in origin, and used this as a threat to resign from command knowing that the government dared not replace him because the admiral was far too popular with the fleet.[48] Williams, moreover, enjoyed the protection of the Conservative party, which was considering running him as its candidate for the presidency in 1881.[49] Any move against him by Pinto, therefore, would have embroiled the president in political infighting, something he wished to avoid because he already had enough foreign enemies.

While Williams was vacillating, the army had been training and equipping its personnel. The weeks of inactivity became difficult to endure, and many soldiers deserted because of material shortages and poor pay. Condemned to wait upon the navy's pleasure, their officers complained about Williams's conduct of the operations.[50] Various high-ranking government officials shared the army's disdain of the admiral, accusing him of not actively pursuing the Peruvian fleet.[51] Plans were afoot to ease Williams from authority, political consequences be damned, when the capture of the *Rimac* finally forced him from command. The loss of the *Rimac*, a transport carrying men and equipment to the north, precipitated a government crisis and eventually led to the collapse of the ministry of Antonio Varas. His successor replaced Williams with the younger and more dynamic Galvarino Riveros. The new commander ordered his ships cleaned and repaired and, after dividing the fleet into two divisions, each built around one of the ironclads, began to search for the *Huáscar*.

On October 8, one task force sighted the *Huáscar* and the *Unión* sailing north. As the outnumbered enemy fled, the second Chilean squadron blocked its escape route. The *Unión*, capitalizing on its speed, outdistanced the Chileans. The *Huáscar*, however, turned to face its six pursuers off Punta Angamos. Within seventy minutes the Peruvian ship, an abattoir, struck its colors. Grau and the majority of his officers and men were dead, and with them perished Peru's chance of winning the war. Shortly after this battle the Chilean army invaded the Peruvian province of Tarapacá. By January 1881, Lima, the jewel of the old Viceroyalty, was in Chilean hands. The war was to linger on for a few years more before the diplomats finished what the generals had begun. In 1883, Peru ceded Tarapacá to Chile and gave it temporary control over the provinces of Tacna and Arica. Bolivia, which did not sign an armistice agreement until 1884, suffered the most, losing its coastal provinces and its outlet to the sea. Isolated in the altiplano, it was to continue to harass Chile in hopes of regaining its lost territory. For Chile the happy conclusion of the war, however, tended to obscure the difficulties of the early days of the struggle. . . .

IV

When war was declared, the entire nation pledged its support to the Pinto government.[52] *El Ferrocarril* informed the public that the hour of sacrifice had arrived and that Chile demanded that each should fulfill his duty.[53] In a pastoral letter, the bishop of Concepción stressed the need for "abnegation, valor, and above all, obedience to duty, even unto death." Chile, he noted, had always abided by the motto of living with honor or dying with glory, and he expected this tradition to be honored.[54] La Serena's bishop reiterated these demands and ordered his clergy to preach that it was glorious to die when the motherland was in danger.[55]

It was not only the people who were to bear the burden. The press included the government in the need for sacrifice, enjoining it to be vigilant in equipping the soldiers and resourceful in directing the war effort and leading the nation. Pinto and his ministers were warned that they too must sacrifice to be examples of "unblemished patriotism, sacrificing everything, even their personal comfort," to capture glory.[56] If the government fulfilled its duties, if it led Chile to victory, then it would be a "strong government . . . beloved . . . a government which the people of Chile and their representatives would forgive many failures."[57] The president was warned, however, that the nation would not tolerate any act that would besmirch the nation's honor; Chile demanded nothing less than victory from its leaders.[58]

The initial outburst of euphoric patriotic unity was short-lived, and the Chilean press soon found substantial reasons for being discontented with Pinto. Initially the public complained about the government's failure to forestall an Allied attack by establishing defensive positions in the north. Later it was the blockade of Iquique that excited the critics, who claimed this stratagem was ineffective because it allowed the enemy to reinforce its southern garrisons at will and prevented the fleet's being used to best advantage.[59] Some of the press noted that while the fleet waited outside Iquique, the entire Chilean coastline was defenseless. The critics supported this allegation by citing the example of Chipana where, as a result of the government's mishandling, disaster had almost befallen the Chileans—a fate, it noted, that had been avoided only because of the intervention of Divine Providence and the skill of the *Magallanes*'s captain. The press, like the public, was unaware that it was Williams, not the president, who was the author of the blockade and instead blamed it on "the faint hearted and cowardly spirit . . . in the Moneda [Chile's presidential palace]."[60]

The sinking of the *Independencia* quite naturally encouraged the press to be more voluble in its complaints about continuing the blockade. After all, Chile had won naval supremacy and should assert it to best advantage. When it did not—when the blockade was reinstituted—the protests became more shrill. The government was accused of being both incompetent and deaf to the pleas for action, and of conducting the war without a "design, plan, or overall strategy."[61] While the government waited, the Peruvians continued to fortify their cities, causing one source to wonder if the administration was waiting until the enemy was prepared before attacking.[62] When Peruvian arms shipments from Panama reached Callao unhindered, the government was congratulated for being so vigilant.[63] It was particularly galling that the Peruvian navy, supposedly inferior in ships and men, was still on the offensive. As it raided the Chilean littoral, some sarcastically recommended that the Chileans should copy Peruvian naval tactics.[64]

Throughout June and July the cries for an offensive filled the nation. The army, immobile since the seizure of Antofagasta, became demoralized. Recruits, who at the outbreak of the war rushed to enlist, now deserted with alacrity on seeing that those entrusted with waging the war were failing in their duty.[65] The civilians became equally dissatisfied. The average citizen, it was reported, on encountering a friend in the street, no longer inquired after his companion's health, but on the progress of the war.[66] The public's attitude toward the government became increasingly hostile as newspapers fanned the fears of an anxious and frustrated people. The press blamed the government for not providing sufficient food, clothing, and ammunition for the troops; for permitting incompetent officers to remain in command; for playing partisan politics.[67] These errors, along with the failure to seize the initiative, disenchanted the people, who were described as being caught up in an "atmosphere of impatience, of disgust and restrained fury . . . owing to the inertia and confusion . . . of the directors of the war."[68]

The nation, it was asserted, had sacrificed for the war, giving freely of its money, its blood, and its youth.[69] It was not with the people that the fault lay, but with the government, characterized as a "monopoly of blunders,"[70] and the ally of a criminally complacent and self-seeking Congress, which had plunged Chile into a pit of despair.[71] Nowhere, lamented one paper, was there a leader, for if there were "a strong heart, a clear eye, and a vigorous arm in the Moneda, the war would have been over by May."[72]

The lack of confidence in the executive and legislative branches of the government made some yearn for the return of a [Diego] Portales.[73] One anonymous citizen even suggested turning the nation over to a dictator who would rule for the duration of the war.[74] More significant were the threats that the people would act violently unless the government demonstrated its ability to lead. *Las Novedades* described the public's mood as being quite amenable to "popular action" and remarked that it would be very "easy to raise twenty or thirty thousand men to answer the cry of the motherland wounded by treachery."[75]

The *Rimac*'s capture seemed to be the final blow. Seized without firing a shot in its own defense, its flag still flying, the vessel was incorporated into the Peruvian navy; and its crew and passengers, a crack cavalry unit, were interned. When the news reached Santiago, crowds gathered before the Congress building calling for the ministers to resign. That same evening, mobs chanted, "Death to the traitors," in front of the Moneda. Rioting ensued, and troops responded to the rocks of the crowd with bullets, wounding and killing many.[76] The public's protest had been in vain, for, according to one newspaper, Pinto "in an excess of foresight and . . . cowardice . . . had fled to Viña del Mar."[77]

Although the press generally disapproved of the rioting, fearing that it might indirectly aid the enemy, it nonetheless sympathized with the people and considered the demonstrations a logical consequence of the government's incompetence, corruption, preoccupation with partisan politics, and outright treachery.[78] More rioting was predicted, even rebellion, unless the president and his government acceded to the public's demands for an aggressive war.[79] One paper was less optimistic over the prospect of Pinto's completing his term of office and pointedly reminded him that [Bernardo] O'Higgins had abdicated rather than precipitate a civil war.[80]

The public, unaware that it was Williams and not Pinto who had stalemated the war, turned on the president, the Congress, indeed, the entire Chilean political establishment. The failures of the war were never attributed to the Chilean people, only to their leaders, who supposedly were incapable of comprehending the meaning of patriotism. The press stated that it was not in the Moneda or the Congress where patriotism existed, but in the north, with the army and navy. A populist movement began, which attacked the moral bankruptcy of almost the entire Chilean ruling class. The public unfavorably compared the present war leaders with those who had led Chile in its fight for independence and its later struggle against Peru in 1838.[81]

What the nation needed to do, it was claimed, was release this spirit, the spirit of the true Chile. The motherland cried out for patriotism, "not the patriotism of music, pomp, and song . . . but the patriotism of Montesquieu . . . a love of country greater than the love of self," a "pure patriotism abnegating, vehement, sincere, which knows how to sacrifice, and actually sacrifices all for the enrichment, the brilliance, the prosperity and the triumph of the motherland."[82]

Notes

1. *El Ferrocarril*, March 15, 1879; *El Mercurio*, February 15, 25, 1879; *Los Tiempos*, February 18, 1879; *El Independiente*, February 14, 1879.

2. *El Ferrocarril*, January 21, March 22, 1879; *Los Tiempos*, January 16, February 16, 1879; *La Patria*, January 21, February 11, 1879; *El Independiente*, February 11, 14, 1879.

3. *El Ferrocarril*, February 12, 1879; *El Mensajero del Pueblo*, March 8, 1879; *Los Tiempos*, January 22, 1879; *La Discusión*, February 9, 1879.

4. *El Ferrocarril*, February 14, 1879.

5. *El Mercurio*, February 25, 1879; *Los Tiempos*, February 18, 1879; *El Diario de Avisos*, February 13, 1879; *La Revista del Sur*, February 20, 1879.

6. *Los Tiempos*, February 9, 1879; *Las Novedades*, February 10, 1879; *La Patria*, February 26, 27, March 1, 1879; *El Diario de Avisos*, February 20, 22, 1879.

7. *El Ferrocarril*, February 23, 1879; *El Independiente*, March 11, 12, 1879; *La Patria*, February 28, 1879.

8. *El Independiente*, March 4, 1879.

9. *Los Tiempos*, February 19, 1879.

10. *El Estandarte Católico*, March 1, 4, 1879; *El Ferrocarril*, March 1, 1879; *El Independiente*, March 6, 1879.

11. *El Ferrocarril*, March 8, 9, 1879; *El Independiente*, March 8, 1879.

12. *El Independiente*, March 13, 18, 1879; *El Ferrocarril*, March 18, 1879; *La Patria*, March 12, 1879; *Senado, sesiones secretas*, March 24, 1879, p. 7.

13. *Los Tiempos*, March 11, 1879; *La Patria*, February 28, 1879.

14. *El Mercurio*, February 28, March 1, 1879; *El Estandarte Católico*, March 11, 1879; *Las Noticias* (Talca), March 14, 1879.

15. *El Estandarte Católico*, March 1, 1879; *La Patria*, February 28, March 4, 1879; *El Mercurio*, February 25, March 1, 1879; *El Independiente*, March 13, 23, 1879; *El Ferrocarril*, March 20, 1879; *Las Noticias*, March 7, 1879; *Diputados, sesiones estraordinarias*, March 27, 1879, p. 716; *Diputados, sesiones secretas*, March 29, 1879, p. 113; *Senado, sesiones secretas*, March 24, 1879, pp. 7–9.

16. *El Mensajero del Pueblo*, March 22, 1879; *El Ferrocarril*, March 26, 27, 28, 1879; *El Independiente*, April 4, 1879; *El Estandarte Católico*, March 29, 31, 1879.

17. *Resumen de la hacienda pública desde 1833 hasta 1914*, p. 47; *Memoria de Guerra i Marina presentada al Congreso Nacional de 1876* (Santiago: Imprenta Nacional, 1876), pp. ix, xxi; *Memoria de Guerra de 1877*, pp. xi, xvii; *Memoria de Guerra de 1878*, pp. xii, 100.

18. Carlos Grez, "La supuesta preparación de Chile para la Guerra del Pacífico," *Boletín de la Academia Chilena de la Historia*, III (1935), 138–139; Emilio Körner and J. Boonen Rivera, *Estudios sobre historia militar* (Santiago: Imprenta Cervantes, 1887), II, 292; *Memoria de Guerra de 1878*, Anexo no. 3, pp. 101–102.

19. Mariano Paz Soldán, *Narración histórica de la guerra de Chile contra Perú y Bolivia* (Buenos Aires: Imprenta y Librería de Mayo, 1884), pp. 106–115; Carlos Dellepiane, *Historia militar del Perú* (Buenos Aires: Círculo Militar, 1941), II, 66, 75; M. Fernando Wilde Cavero, *Historia militar de Bolivia* (La Paz, 1963), pp. 137–142, 145–146; J. C. Clavero, "Perú, Bolivia i Chile sus departamentos, población, . . . en 1879," in Pascual Ahumada Moreno, *Guerra del Pacífico* (Valparaíso: Imprenta del Progreso, 1884), I, 146; Körner and Rivera, *Estudios sobre historia militar*, II, 294–295; Francisco A. Machuca, *Las cuatro campañas de la Guerra del Pacífico* (Valparaíso: Imprenta Victoria, 1926), I, 95.

20. Clavero, "Perú, Bolivia, i Chile," p. 146; Paz Soldán, *Narración histórica*, p. 109; Dellepiane, *Historia militar del Perú*, II, 66, 75, 79; Körner and Rivera,

Estudios sobre historia militar, II, 294–295; Perú, *Memoria del ramo de guerra presentado al Congreso ordinario de 1878 por el Ministerio de Guerra y Marina* (Lima: Imprenta del Estado, 1878), I, 3–6.

21. Clavero, "Perú, Bolivia, i Chile," p. 146; Wilde, *Historia militar de Bolivia*, pp. 145–146; Edmundo H. Civiti Bernasconi, *Guerra del Pacífico (1879–1883)* (Buenos Aires: Circulo Militar, 1946), I, 119, 121; Machuca, *Las cuatro campañas*, I, 37.

22. Agustín Blanco to Ministerio, May 1, 1879; Quiñones to Ministerio, April 17, 1879, in Ahumada, *Guerra del Pacífico*, II, 16–18.

23. Körner and Rivera, *Estudios sobre historia militar*, II, 290, 294–295; Indalicio Téllez, *Historia de Chile—Historia militar* (Balcells i Cía., 1925), I, 151–154.

24. *El Estandarte Católico*, March 8, 20, 1879; *El Mercurio*, March 1, 21, 1879; *The Chilian Times*, May 3, 1879; *El Constituyente*, March 7, 1879; *El Independiente*, March 5, 19, 20, 1879; *El Correo de La Serena* (La Serena), February 22, 25, March 20, 1879; *El Ferrocarril*, February 25, March 5, 1879.

25. *El Correo de Quillota* (Quillota), April 14, May 1, 1879; *The Chilian Times*, March 10, 1879; *El Mercurio*, April 6, 1879; *Las Noticias*, April 3, 1879; *El Independiente*, March 19, 20, 1879.

26. Alejandro García Castelblanco, *Estudio crítico de las operaciones navales de Chile* (Santiago: Imprenta de la Armada, 1929), p. 154; Ramón Vidal Gormaz, "Memoria del comandante de arsenales," *Memoria de Guerra*, 1878, p. 241; *Memoria de Guerra*, 1878, pp. 221, 232–233; Luis Uribe Orrego, *Los combates navales en la Guerra del Pacífico* (Valparaíso: Imprenta de "La Patria," 1886), p. 11.

27. Uribe, *Los combates navales*, pp. 9–11.

28. Manuel Vegas G., *Historia de la marina de guerra del Perú* (Lima: Imprenta "Lux" de E. L. Castro, 1929), pp. 179–180; Geraldo Arosemena Garland, *El contraalmirante Miguel Grau* (Lima: San Martí y Compañía, 1946), p. 72.

29. Paz Soldán, *Narración histórica*, pp. 107–108.

30. "La Perou en 1878. Notice historique et statistique (publicación final hecha con motivo de la esposición universal de París)," quoted in Diego Barros Arana, *Obras Completas*, vol. XVI, *La Guerra del Pacífico* (Santiago: Imprenta, Litografía, Encuadernación Barcelona, 1914), p. 72.

31. Perú, *Memoria . . . de marina*, II, 8–9, 13.

32. *La Opinión Nacional* (Lima), March 14, 1879; *El Comercio* (Lima), March 14, 1879, in Ahumada, *Guerra del Pacífico*, I, 548.

33. Rafael Sotomayor to Aníbal Pinto, April 7, 1879, "Correspondencia de don Rafael Sotomayor a don Aníbal Pinto sobre la Guerra del Pacífico," *Revista Chilena*, XV (1922), 182 (hereafter cited as *CRS*); Rafael Vial to Antonio Varas, March 15, 1879, *Correspondencia de don Antonio Varas sobre la Guerra del Pacífico* (Santiago: Imprenta Universitaria, 1918), pp. 18–19 (hereafter cited as *Varas*).

34. Alberto Blest Gana to Marquis of Salisbury, June 28, 1879; Marquis of Salisbury to Alberto Blest Gana, July 6, 1879; Treasury Chambers—Draft Treasury, July 14, 1879, in Great Britain, Public Record Office, *Foreign Office 16 (Chile)*, vol. 204.

35. Domingo Santa María to José Victorino Lastarria, May 20, 1879, "Cartas de don Domingo Santa María a José Victorino Lastarria," *Revista Chilena*, VI

(1918), 250; Rafael Sotomayor to Aníbal Pinto, May 12, 1879, *Correspondencia de Pinto*, vol. I.

Peru attempted to obtain aid from Argentina. See the letters of the Peruvian Minister to Argentina and Irigoyen, March 26, 1879, and May 7, 1879, in José M. Echeñique Gandarillas, "La declaración de guerra del 5 de abril de 1879," *Revista Chilena*, XI (1927), 76.

36. Letter of Rafael Sotomayor to Aníbal Pinto, May 5, 12, 1879, *Correspondencia de Pinto*, vol. I; Gonzalo Bulnes, *Guerra del Pacífico* (Valparaíso: Sociedad Imprenta y Litografía Universo, 1911), I, 180, 191–197.

37. Juan Williams Rebolledo, *Operaciones de la escuadra chilena mientras estuvo a las órdenes del contra-almirante Williams Rebolledo* (Valparaíso: Imprenta Progreso, 1882), pp. 20–21; letter of Rafael Sotomayor to Antonio Varas, April 21, 1879, in *Varas*, pp. 49–50; letter to Rafael Sotomayor to Aníbal Pinto, May 5, 1879, in *Correspondencia de Pinto*, vol. I.

38. Arturo Cuevas, *Estudio estratéjico sobre la campaña marítima de la Guerra del Pacífico* (Valparaíso: Talleres tipográficos de la Armada, 1901), pp. 17–21; García, *Estudio crítico*, pp. 163–164.

39. *El Ferrocarril*, April 27, 1879; *El Independiente*, April 19, 1879; letter of Rafael Sotomayor to Aníbal Pinto, April 27, 1879, *CRS*, 192.

40. Letter of Rafael Vial to Antonio Varas, May 9, 1879, in *Varas*, p. 76; Williams Rebolledo, *Operaciones de la escuadra*, p. 33.

41. Cuevas, *Estudio estratéjico*, p. 43; García, *Estudio crítico*, 160.

42. For the campaign of the Huáscar see M. Melitón Carvajal, "Reseña de la campaña del Huáscar contra Chile en 1879," *Revista Chilena*, XV (1922), 87.

43. Letter of Domingo Santa María to Antonio Varas, July 20, 1879, in *Varas*, p. 191.

44. Domingo Santa María to Aníbal Pinto, June 25, 1879, *Fondos Varios*, vol. 416; letter of Rafael Sotomayor to Antonio Varas, June 16, 1879, in *Varas*, p. 148.

45. Letter of Rafael Sotomayor to Aníbal Pinto, June 7, 1879, *Correspondencia de Pinto*, vol. I; letter of José Alfonso to Aníbal Pinto, May 23, 1879, *Fondos Varios*, vol. 414; letter of Rafael Sotomayor to Antonio Varas, June 5, 1879, in *Varas*, p. 129.

46. Letter of Domingo Santa María to Aníbal Pinto, June 25, July 26, 1879, *Fondos Varios*, vol. 416.

47. Letter of Domingo Santa María to Antonio Varas, July 20, 1879, in *Varas*, p. 190; letter of José Alfonso to Aníbal Pinto, August 1, 1879, *Fondos Varios*, vol. 414.

48. Letters of Rafael Sotomayor to Aníbal Pinto, May 12, June 4, 1879, *Correspondencia de Pinto*, vol. I.

49. Letter of Domingo Santa María to Aníbal Pinto, June 25, 1879, *Fondos Varios*, vol. 416.

50. Letter of Justo Arteaga A. to Aníbal Pinto, May 16, 24, June 6, 1879, *Fondos Varios*, vol. 415; letter of José Alfonso to Aníbal Pinto, June 13, 1879, *Fondos Varios*, vol. 414; letter of Domingo Santa María to Aníbal Pinto, June 25, 1879, *Fondos Varios*, vol. 416; letter of Roberto Souper to Cornelio Saavedra, June 4, 1879, *Fondos Varios*, vol. 559.

51. Letter of Domingo Santa María to Aníbal Pinto, June 24, 1879, *Fondos Varios*, vol. 416; letter of Rafael Sotomayor to Aníbal Pinto, June 4, 1879, *Correspondencia de Pinto*, vol. I.

52. *El Ferrocarril*, April 15, 1879; *La Patria*, April 23, 1879; *El Independiente*, April 15, 1879.

53. *El Ferrocarril*, April 9, 1879.

54. Pastoral del Ilustrísimo Obispo de la Concepción José Hipólito Salas, *Boletín de la Guerra del Pacífico*, May 2, 1879.

55. Pastoral del Ilustrísimo Obispo de La Serena, José Manuel Orrego, *Boletín de la Guerra del Pacífico*, May 2, 1879.

56. *El Estandarte Católico*, March 28, 1879; *La Patria*, March 22, April 4, 1879.

57. *El Independiente*, March 2, 1879.

58. Ibid., April 9, 1879.

59. *La Patria*, April 5, 9, 1879.

60. Ibid., April 16, 1879.

61. *El Independiente*, June 12, 1879.

62. *El Centinela* (San Carlos), June 19, 1879.

63. *El Mensajero del Pueblo*, July 26, 1879.

64. *El Independiente*, July 22, 1879.

65. *La Patria*, July 19, 1879.

66. *El Nuevo Ferrocarril*, July 21, 1879.

67. *El Independiente*, June 7, July 11, 1879; *La Patria*, July 26, 1879.

68. *El Independiente*, July 11, 1879.

69. *La Patria*, August 1, 1879.

70. *El Nuevo Ferrocarril*, July 21, 1879.

71. *El Centinela*, July 12, 1879; *La Patria*, August 12, 23, 1879; *El Mercurio*, June 20, 1879.

72. *La Patria*, July 10, 1879.

73. *El Correo de Quillota*, June 29, July 24, 1879; *El Mercurio*, July 15, 1879.

74. X. [pseud.], *La patria está en peligro* (1879), pp. 4–5.

75. *Las Novedades*, May 28, 1879; *La Opinión* (Talca), July 31, 1879.

76. *Los Tiempos*, July 31, August 1, 1879.

77. *El Independiente*, July 31, 1879.

78. *El Mercurio*, July 31, August 1, 1879; *El Nuevo Ferrocarril*, August 11, 18, September 15, 1879; *La Patria*, August 1, 1879; *El Independiente*, August 2, 1879; *La Discusión*, September 4, 1879.

79. *La Revista del Sur*, August 7, 1879; *El Mercurio*, August 1, 13, 1879.

80. *El Mercurio*, July 31, 1879; *Las Noticias*, August 1, 1879.

81. *El Mercurio*, August 22, 1879; *El Independiente*, August 1, 1879; *La Patria*, August 2, 1879; *La Discusión*, September 4, 1879.

82. *La Patria*, August 2, 1879.

5

The South American Military Tradition: Preprofessional Armies in Argentina, Chile, Peru, and Brazil

Frederick M. Nunn

During the nineteenth century most Latin American countries experienced periods of political upheaval and widespread civil war. Armed groups, whether composed of regular soldiers or ad hoc armies, contributed substantially to the political instability of the era. Understandably, both governments and military leaders periodically sought to convert the irregular forces, which often dominated their nations' militaries, into professional, institutionalized, and modern organizations. To accomplish their goals, they emphasized formal military education and obtained European advisers to assist in reforming and training their forces.

In the latter part of the nineteenth century, Chile, Peru, Brazil, and Argentina intensified their efforts to improve military education and modernize institutional structures by enlisting the aid of French and German military advisers. Two factors stimulated military reform: external threats and the drive for national integration. Unresolved territorial disputes and conflicting geopolitical strategies ensured that military preparedness remained a domestic priority; these South American countries had engaged in intraregional wars that highlighted the weaknesses of their armed forces and underscored the importance of a strong national defense.

On the domestic level, national leaders viewed the creation of a modern professional military as critical to the consolidation of civilian political authority. Ironically, in the absence of strong and effective civilian

From *Yesterday's Soldiers: European Military Professionalism in South America, 1890–1940* (Lincoln: University of Nebraska Press, 1983), 44–69, 305–10. ©1983 by the University of Nebraska Press. Reprinted by permission of the University of Nebraska Press.

institutions, the modernization of the armed forces in these countries fre-
quently thrust the military into politics.

B y the time the French and German officers arrived in South America
[in the late nineteenth century], European officers had served for
years in the Ottoman Empire and Japan, launching Turks and Japanese
toward military modernity. The success with which European military
professionalism was transmitted can be assessed in two ways. Obviously
the Japanese learned some of their lessons well, for their artillery and
infantry performed well against the Russians in 1904–1906. Still, it would
be less than candid to say Japanese successes were strictly the result of
Jacob Clemens Meckel's teachings or emulation of great general staff
techniques. The Russian Empire was a military shambles, and its navy
was no less a pathetic imitation of a modern fighting unit than its army.
The fact remains, however, that Japan owed much in the way of organization, techniques, tactics, and strategy, though not spirit, tradition, and post-
Meiji fervor, to the Europeans.

The Ottoman Empire stands as an example of little reward for much
effort. The work of Goltz Pasha and the Liman von Sanders mission did
not achieve their purposes.[1] True, the Turks under Abdul Hamid II did
ally with the Central Powers in their time of need; German foreign policy
followed military missions in other cases, too. This alliance, however,
proved worthless in the military sense, about as worthless as, say, Peru's
nineteenth-century ties with Bolivia. But there were some results anent
the inculcation of a military ethos. The Young Turk movement, arguably
in its inception a medical corps movement, was in the greater sense a
result of frustrated professionals seeing themselves out of step with the
state, nation, and society about them. Political action and the rise of the
military caste, modern-style, in post-1900 Turkey and Japan—"neo-
Janizaries" and "neo-samurai"—came as results of European values su-
perimposed on exotic (to Europe) reality.

Reality in South America included both commitment to the martial
spirit and the need for national defense. On their arrival in Buenos Aires
and Santiago, Lima, and Rio de Janeiro, the French and Germans found
raw material, its quality variable and its availability not always guaranteed. Existing military organizations presented challenges, and not all
South Americans welcomed their new mentors.

Argentines trace their military institutional history as far back as 1810,
when the Escuela de Matemáticas in Buenos Aires trained some engineers to lead twenty-four hundred veteran militiamen, and see their martial heritage beginning with the expulsion of the British invasion force of
1806 by creole militiamen led by Juan Lavalleja. Military education was

not even sporadic during most of the nineteenth century, not even codi-fied until 1864, when President Bartolomé Mitre attempted to arrange for cadets at the Escuela de Artes y Oficios to study at St. Cyr [in France]. His successor, Domingo Sarmiento, founded the Colegio Militar in 1869 and ordered the procurement of foreign instructors.[2] Aside from these good intentions there was little action, and until 1880 provincial militias were more significant than the national army—a portent of army compatibility with strong, centralized government in Argentina (and elsewhere).

Several events and some national issues of import encouraged Ar-gentine leaders of the post-Rosas era to undertake the modernization of the army. The 1864–1870 war with Paraguay, in which Argentina, Brazil, and Uruguay struggled for six years to defeat the "South American Prussia" (some might prefer Macedon), convinced both Mitre and Sarmiento that Argentina needed to assure its new-found integrity and sovereignty. Co-ordination of the war effort was difficult; cooperation among the prov-inces was tenuous.[3] Paraguay proved a resolute little country, and Brazil was not the most amiable of allies.

Over the nineteenth century the presence of Brazil as a rival on the Atlantic and in the River Plate basin also indicated a need for national defense; indeed, the Argentine-Brazilian rivalry is a dominant theme in the entire history of military professionalization on the Atlantic coast of South America. During the 1829–1852 Rosas era (and even earlier) the two powers had clashed repeatedly over influence in the Banda Oriental. This Argentine-Brazilian rivalry is merely an extension of the older Luso-Hispanic conflict over access to the La Plata estuary and the Paraná River route to the continental hinterland. Until the commencement of hostili-ties between Chile and the Andean allies in 1879, the latter hoped for Argentine participation on their side. But the long-standing dispute be-tween Buenos Aires and Santiago over Argentine-claimed, Chilean-settled Patagonia came to an end. Satisfied with the acquisition of territory via peaceful means, Argentina did not go to war, and a southern frontier opened for expansion in the Río Negro-Río Colorado areas.

But not before "the conquest of the desert." When President Nicolás Avellaneda selected General Julio A. Roca to succeed Dr. Adolfo Alsina as war minister in 1878, the government's policy toward the few remain-ing indigenous hostiles in the south changed radically. Alsina had relied on frontier garrisons, treaties, and patrols along the Río Negro line, fea-tures that made this aspect of Argentine expansion comparable with that of the United States prior to 1876 and the Little Big Horn debacle. Gen-eral Roca had commanded a garrison in southern Córdoba province and was experienced in Indian fighting; he immediately pressed for an offen-sive sweep south, and the rest is history.[4] By the end of 1879 the Río

Negro line was pacified and communications with Patagonia by land
assured. Within a year, Roca was president and the army had a champion
in office. The desert campaign (concentrated efforts in the Chaco, along
the northern Andean frontier and Patagonia, had been undertaken since
1870) proved the value of a federal army superior to provincial militias.

In 1875 the army received roughly 18 percent of the national budget,
in 1880 just over 41 percent, thereafter just under 14 percent until 1895,
and under 10 percent of budgetary expenditures until 1914.[5] Actual peso
amounts increased every year, despite percentage variations, and amounted
to roughly one third of education expenditures. At the end of the century
the army had sixteen hundred officers and six thousand men, and in 1914
eighteen hundred officers and twenty-two thousand men; obligatory military service made the difference in size.[6] Roca introduced general staff
organization in 1884, during his first presidency, although the staff system had functioned in rudimentary fashion since 1861; the Escuela Superior de Guerra, founded in 1900, provided the talent for staff service. Both
necessary ingredients of a modern military organization became functional realities only after the arrival of German officers in 1899.

Between Mitre's and Sarmiento's "era of good intentions" and the
promulgation of obligatory service, general staff regulations, and codes
lay a good deal of slow, hard work by Argentines and Germans alike. The
troubled history of the Colegio Militar (Palermo), later named Colegio
Militar San Martín, ceased only under Sarmiento, for Mitre's plan to send
cadets to St. Cyr was shelved when the war with Paraguay broke out.
Sarmiento's decree of September 7, 1868, and subsequent legislation in
October, then still another decree in 1870, finally got the Colegio Militar
on firm ground, at least organizationally and fiscally. Three years later
one Captain Otto Rose took up his duties as artillery instructor.[7]

In the last decades of the century Argentine cadets studied in their
three years at the Colegio mathematics, military history and geography,
military law, cartography, languages, tactics, marksmanship, and fenc-
ing. There was little pure or applied science in the curriculum. Three cadets graduated in 1873, no more than thirteen a year for the next decade,
thirty-five in 1884, and no more than 159 in any year until 1915.[8] Until
the arrival of the Germans, graduation from the Colegio was not a prerequisite for a commission. Manuals were Spanish translations of French
works or original Spanish works in use since midcentury. Admission to
the Colegio was open to healthy, literate males between the ages of fourteen and eighteen. Three years of study led to the rank of sublieutenant
and five to the initial rank of second lieutenant until 1884, when the top-
ranking students in each *promoción* were accorded that rank on graduation. In 1888 the government incorporated the national guard into the

army, giving Argentina a poorly trained and roughly equipped reserve force on paper of sixty-five thousand men ranging in age from seventeen to fifty years.[9] Eleven years later great changes took place.

The failure of Argentina to develop a military organization commensurate with its political system ought to be seen in terms of the development of that system. Until 1852, Argentina was a collection of provinces, a loose federation beholden to the strongman of Buenos Aires province, Juan Manuel de Rosas. Then, after his fall and exile, the federal system established by the Constitution of 1853 allowed provinces to retain their own armies as militias. National defense had been associated only temporarily with foreign threats or adventures. Despite the fact that both Mitre and Sarmiento were aware of the need for a national army, it took a military man as president (Roca, 1880–1886) and the formal establishment of a sovereign federal government to place the national army in a position at least theoretically superior to that of gaucho- and peasant-manned militia units.

Roca's first presidency, during which he established the so-called *unicato*—presidential domination of the executive branch—set the stage for the suppression of the old federalism and the erection of provincially dominated centralism under executives beholden to specific provincial political interests. This was the arrangement that dominated Argentine government and politics until the triumph of the Radicals in 1916. Roca's policy of arming his army well and of imitating the staff system for organizational and planning purposes did more than place the army in a theoretically superior position; these measures gave him the power to exert his will over recalcitrant provincial bosses and opposition politicians. By the 1890s the army had become a political creature, subject to the whims of the chief executive. Roca's return to the Casa Rosada in 1898 provided a second stage in the emergence of the modern Argentine army as a political interest group.

Between the Roca presidencies the army became involved actively in politics. The revolt of June 26–29, 1890, involving Leandro Alem, the Radicals, and General Manuel J. Campos, then the 1893–94 mutiny in Corrientes, were symptomatic of the times and alarming enough to persuade Roca and his right-hand man General Pablo Riccheri to seek German assistance in the professionalization, and removal from partisan politics, of the army.

So did the example directly west of the Andes, where, by 1900, Roca and Riccheri thought Chileans were planning war. If the association of national defense consciousness and strong, centralized government with strong, efficient military organization is valid (it is a tenet of South

American military ideology today), Chile stands as an example of advanced military status in the nineteenth century. For Chilean leaders were ever wary both of their northern Andean neighbors and of Argentina to the east.

War created and maintained the Republic of Chile. Chileans fought for their own independence and Peru's. They fought Indians in the south; they fought each other in the 1820s; and while Conservative party leader General Joaquín Prieto and his éminence grise, Diego Portales, fashioned the political system that dominated Chile until 1891, they fought Peruvians and Bolivians. They fought them twice: between 1836 and 1839, again between 1879 and 1884, when simultaneously their southern forces finally pacified the warlike Araucanians. Chile, like Argentina, increased its national territory and protected it with armed force.

There had been a military school of sorts in Chile since 1817. It functioned intermittently between the ouster of Supreme Director Bernardo O'Higgins in 1823 and the triumph of the Prieto-led Conservatives seven years later. Portales reopened the Escuela and put it on a sound footing financially. The government reversed policies of earlier years and recruited only from members of known Conservative or nonpartisan families. By the end of the decade the professional officer class was an armed extension of the Basque-Castilian aristocracy. As this oligarchy began to show signs of strain, there were examples of conspiracy and political activity by officers (1851, 1859), but on both occasions it was civilians who initiated conspiracies.[10] A further buffer between the army and exponents of partisan issues was the presence of a militia, forerunner of the national police, that had responsibility for routine maintenance of internal order.

Like the Brazilians and Peruvians, Chilean military historians routinely see their subject as continuous, dating from colonial times (sometimes even precolonial). The fusion of Araucanian and Spaniard, aborigine and Iberian, defender and conqueror, created a "race of warriors," they argue.[11] This is not the case with their Argentine counterparts; it is comparable to Peruvian and Brazilian military historiography, in which lip service to aboriginal contributions to institutional development has been paid.[12] Where resistance by civilized aborigines was either organized or protracted, the South Americans have seen fit to absorb that resistance as part of their self-justification and martial spirit. What civilian writers of all genres see as quaint and folkloric, or decadent and inferior, Chileans, Brazilians, and Peruvians in uniform have noted as a sign of national vitality and strength—on paper, at least.

Chile emerged from the War of the Pacific as the leading power on the Pacific coast of South America. By the time Argentina had violently subdued its Indian inhabitants and was still resolving its internal controversy over the relationship of capital city to province and nation, Chile had defeated Bolivia and Peru and occupied the City of the Kings [Lima], once Spain's proudest South American city. In the euphoria of victory Chilean leaders were not blind, however. The army had a wealth of tradition, whether contrived of the stuff that went into Alonso de Ercilla y Zúñiga's *La araucana* or fashioned from the less than thrilling reality of Maipú and Lircay, Yungay, Chorrillos and Miraflores, or the Araucanian campaigns.[13] There is no question as to the backlog of experience drawn upon by Chilean commanders, whether forcing their way north toward Lima or pushing back the Indians along the southern frontier. The discipline of the army was outwardly solid; its links to the ruling elite were still intact, even if strained by the infusion of new blood during the War of the Pacific, when so many officers lost their lives.

Therefore, President Domingo Santa María, at the urging of high-ranking officers, instructed Guillermo Matta, head of Chile's diplomatic mission in Germany, to seek out a qualified instructor. Flushed with their foreign victories at sea, on the desert, and in the foothills of the Andes, yet mindful of obvious shortcomings in organization, matériel, and morale, Chileans turned to the victors of Sedan and conquerors of Paris, those masters of modern warfare collectively known as the Prussian Army. Chile thus set the standard to which her neighbors would march toward military modernity in the decades to come. Only in the case of Peru would foreign instructors have comparable authority and influence over a South American army. Nowhere would they have the direct command functions they would have in Chile.

Matta found his man, or thought he had. Jacob Clemens Meckel came with high recommendations, but he chose to go to Japan instead. He became a legend there.[14] The second name on Matta's short list was that of Captain Emil Körner, a Saxon commoner who had served with distinction in the Franco-Prussian War. An agreement was made and a contract drawn up; a new era began. Emil Körner would become a legend in Chile.

Chile had nearly twenty-five thousand men under arms, equipped for the most part with outdated French and German rifles and Krupp field-pieces, when the war with Peru and Bolivia ended. A sharp reduction in size followed, so that when Körner arrived there were no more than six thousand men in uniform and a militia of perhaps six thousand more.[15] The army received no more than 10 percent of the federal budget. The Escuela Militar, on solid ground since the 1830s, produced about fifty junior lieutenants a year; there were not a thousand qualified officers, and though many had leadership experience from the recent war, they had little formal training. Those who had graduated from the Escuela studied tactics and strategy, military history, basic physics and chemistry, mathematics, and technical subjects of a military nature. Chileans were better fighters than theoreticians. Most of the younger officers looked forward to the arrival of this unknown Saxon captain; many of their superiors were skeptical of his ability to improve an army that had defeated Peru and Bolivia.

Four years before some Argentine officers conspired with Leandro Alem's Civic Union of Youth, then, Körner inaugurated the first courses in Chile's Académia de Guerra. Chile was clearly the military leader of the entire continent. The kind of difficulties that retarded development of a national, professional army in Argentina were no longer inhibitive to a coordinated Chilean military or defense policy when Körner took up his duties. For the time being the political system was stable. There was little pressure from outside the ruling class for systematic change. No provincial clique contested for power with the energy of the "Córdoba Clique" in Argentina; no provincial militia rivaled the national army.

Both countries undertook military professionalization because of the awareness of potential threats to national security. Both had triumphed in recent wars and had put a finish to aboriginal foes within national boundaries. In Argentina there may have been more of a sense of political expediency, that is, a necessity to do something in order to preclude military-political involvements despite the presence of Roca as champion. Military involvement in the incidents of the 1890s lends some weight to such a hypothesis. In Chile the political interests of the army officer corps were determined by the 1891 civil war, then by the inculcation of Prussian values from the bottom of the officer corps up. Obviously by 1890 there were rifts within the corps of both countries, or there would not have been collusion in the Radical-inspired movements of the 1890s in Buenos Aires and Corrientes nor a division of sentiment in the 1891 revolt against [President José Manuel] Balmaceda across the cordillera. From the beginning, therefore, civilian political issues of some magnitude influenced the process of professionalization in Germany's client states. This was equally true in the French client states, Peru and Brazil, diplomatic and military rivals, respectively, of Chile and Argentina.

Peru smarted from its war losses of the 1880s. For the second time in barely a half-century, Peru had fallen to Chile, her Bolivian alliances had done her no good, and her prospects for the future had dimmed. The government was discredited and the army and navy reduced to pathetic imitations of defense forces. The introspective and pessimistic nature of Peruvian social and political thought stems, in part, directly from the country's collapse in 1879–80, the occupation of Lima by Chilean forces, and the victor's demands solemnized in the 1883 Treaty of Ancón. The

loss of Tacna, Arica, and Tarapacá deprived Peru of rich copper and nitrate deposits that might have contributed to economic growth. The Tacna-
Arica dispute was not settled until 1929 (and festers on, owing to
Bolivian-Chilean-Peruvian disputes over access for the Bolivians to the
sea). Tacna-Arica was to Chile and Peru—and Bolivia also—what Alsace-
Lorraine was to France and Germany, for a quarter of a century concomi-
tantly, then for a decade beyond World War I. Of the four countries
considered in these pages, Peru had the least to work with in the effort to
create a modern army.

It is difficult to take seriously Peruvian tracing of their military history to pre-Columbian times, but Peruvians do just that: to an alleged
training school near Cuzco for *Incanato* nobles. From that point forward,
peninsulars and creoles dominate official histories. Education of Euro-
Peruvians for military service dates from the eighteenth century, when
creole militia officers were supposed to study mathematics if they expected to serve in artillery units.[16] Spaniards routinely studied mathematics for artillery service (from 1715 on in Barcelona), and there were courses
from 1764 on in Havana, making Viceroy [Manuel de] Amat's urging of
mathematics on creole aspirants seem less prejudicial or out of line than
one might think.[17] Military education in the national period began in 1823
with a short-lived academy opened by President José María Riva Agüero,
where theory was heavily emphasized; then again in 1826 with the founding of the Colegio Militar Andrés de Santa Cruz, located in an abandoned
convent in the San Felipe district of Lima.[18] In 1830, President Agustín
Gamarra decreed the opening of the Escuela Militar. The Escuela lasted
for four years, then closed from 1834 to 1851. All of these were located
in Lima proper; none had adequate funding. Riva Agüero's administration did not last long enough to provide any kind of continuity, nor did
that of Santa Cruz. The Escuela Militar de Chorrillos dated from a decree
of January 7, 1850, emitted by President Ramón Castilla, Peru's midcentury soldier-politician. Marshal Castilla wanted the existing facilities
(such as they were) removed from the political life of the capital, so he
moved military education in toto from a building on Calle Espíritu Santo
to the summer barracks in rural (now suburban) Chorrillos, south of the
capital on a bluff near the sea. It successively recessed in 1854, functioned again from 1859 to 1867 (despite the 1862–1866 conflict with
Spain), then recessed during the War of the Pacific. By that time most
of the three-year program's courses were held in Lima again, where
cadets studied mathematics, geography, languages, drill exercises, and
marksmanship. [Nicolás de] Piérola began the reform program with the
hiring of French instructors and the relocation of the school in Chorrillos—
still outside the city, but beginning to blend with suburban Miraflores.

When he did so, military training in Peru was in a sorry state. The on-again, off-again postwar programs, which included a course for noncommissioned officers inaugurated by President Andrés Cáceres in 1888, were held in antiquated barracks. Navy and army cadets shared classes, and the turnover of instructors was rapid, owing to political interference. An estimated four hundred students attended these classes, many of which existed on paper only; funding was undependable and facilities were obviously primitive. Military presidents—Gamarra, Castilla, Cáceres—had made most of the plans. Gamarra even hired a German, one Major Karl Pauli, to teach in Peru and publicly advocated civics classes for conscripts. Civilian politicians—the Civilistas, then Piérola—showed more interest in proper finance, facilities, and faculty. They saw education as a means of weaning men in uniform from political aspirations.

When the reform program began, the Peruvian army had distinctive racial characteristics. All the troops were Indians or *cholos*. The vast majority of officers were Euro-Peruvians, still known as creoles, and they came from Lima or the other, smaller urban centers. *Clases* (noncoms) were of peasant stock, *cholos*, and a few Indians. Some took courses with officer cadets, and these *clases*—or *niños*, as they were called condescendingly—were highly regarded for their valor in the war with Chile. From the beginning of Peru's modern era, the officer class in Peru has included men from throughout the country of both European and mixed origin, giving rise to the ceaseless claims that the army is the "nation in microcosm."[19] The historical ability of noncommissioned officers, representative of the lower classes and racially mixed, to rise to officer status, though rarely to high rank, is more pronounced throughout the national period in Peru than in Argentina, Brazil, or Chile (or, for that matter, Bolivia). Indeed, some sources allude to *cabitos* (from *cabo*, corporal) moving into the officer class from the 1820s forward.[20] At the close of the century the army was equipped with Winchester rifles, Krupp or Schneider-Creuzot fieldpieces, and, as one astute observer noted, "some bayonets that were functional."[21]

The War of the Pacific had done greater damage to military education schemes, for the Lima-Chorrillos area was the scene of battles and occupation between 1880 and 1883. Thus, even before Piérola took action, Gamarra and others had seen clearly the formulation of defense policy and isolation of the army from politics as one and the same process. Peruvian officialdom's first French mentor put it tersely: "As soon as the Chileans left, army leaders realized that professional preparation, the training of officers and non-commissioned officers, was the first step toward the reconstitution of the exhausted and nearly defenseless national organism."[22] Post-1884 war ministers Colonels Javier de Osma and Justiniano

Borgoño had urged the funding and staffing of military schools, but political conflict and economic limitations simply precluded action until Piérola's ascendance in the 1890s.

Peru had maintained approximately fifty-five hundred men under arms prior to the war, and kept a six-thousand-man peacetime force afterwards. On paper 4,250 were volunteer career soldiers and 1,750 were conscripts or one-year enlistees.[23] Until the arrival of Paul Clément, Peru's was decidedly a paper army.

Only with the reestablishment of internal order would continued support for a professional officer corps be forthcoming. In the 1890s binding of the army to maintenance of stability, therefore, was a necessity, but not a foregone conclusion. The forging of the Civilista-Democrat coalition by Piérola, and its duration until 1908, then the rise of [Juan] Leguía, proved critical to harmonious military-civilian relations. Inculcation of French colonial military theory only drew the first *afrancesados* away from ruling forces, however, for during the first decade of this century junior officers began to see their country in a decidedly different way than did most of their superiors.

Meanwhile, far across the continent, the Brazilian army had toppled a monarchy, created a republic, helped promulgate a constitution, and lost its credibility on internal battlefields and in the political arena—all within a decade. Victorious years before against Paraguay, Brazilians had shared the gains of victory with their erstwhile Argentine allies. Inept politically, they now shared the ignominy of political ineptitude with their confreres from Peru. Traditionally removed from politics, until the 1880s, at least, they had a past characterized by respectability similar to that of the Chileans.

The very vastness of Brazil and the continuation of the Brazilian monarchy after independence conspired to inhibit a political army. Titled officers were but a uniformed nobility in the best tradition of nineteenth-century Europe. The national army was really little more than a collection of provincial units, recruited, staffed, and trained apart. Until the Paraguayan War, Brazil had never mobilized on a large scale, and it showed. Local landowners had bands of fighting men, private armies that could put the nationals to shame.

Independence, moreover, did not even provide the army with either a glorious tradition or the makings of one in order to justify its importance or existence. Separation from a weakened Portugal was achieved in 1822 with minimal violence: a few skirmishes with recalcitrant pro-Portuguese units of the colonial forces and Lord Cochrane's investiture of Salvador da Bahia. When Emperor Pedro I attempted to hold the Cisplatine

Province (Brazil's name for Uruguay) in 1826–27—neither the first nor the last unfortunate involvement in that country—he used German, and even some Irish, mercenaries, not his Brazilian troops. This was a blow to the latter's pride, alienated them from the monarch, and contributed to his downfall in 1831. Separatist movements during the 1831–1840 regency and following the restoration of the monarchy did little to either endear Pedro II to the army or provide the latter with prestige or influence. Not until 1864 and a new Platine-Paraná Basin imbroglio was national defense seriously considered on a grand scale, and only then did anything resembling a "military point of view" exist in Brazil. As with the Chileans, victorious Brazilian officers would use victory to justify improvement of their lot.

Prince Regent João (João VI, 1816–1822) founded an Acádemia Real Militar in Rio de Janeiro in 1810 for the purpose of improving organization and ordnance.[24] The Academia functioned intermittently throughout the Dominion period and into Pedro I's reign. Ideally the Acádemia availed qualified young men of a six-year course: two years of preparatory and four of professional training, expanded to eight years in 1815. Poor funding, the uncertain situation of the Regency period, and regional revolts precluded the early postindependence emergence of a true officer class.[25] During these years Brazil had more in common with Argentina and Peru than with Chile.

In 1852 an infantry and cavalry training center opened in Pôrto Alegre, capital of Rio Grande do Sul, where separatist sentiment ran strong. Chartered in 1851, it specialized in the two branches of training only, lending a gaucho touch to foot and horse soldiers. Three years later the Acádemia Militar San Pedro opened its doors, and the Escola de Aplicação in Rio for advanced training of officers also opened. In another three years Rio boasted the Escola Central Militar and a preparatory school as well.[26] However much activity there appears to have been at midcentury, officer training was not standardized, nor even considered all that necessary. Classes were irregular, schedules were highly flexible, and no cohesive corps of graduates emerged from military schools.

During the War of the Triple Alliance several training centers turned out officers rapidly in Pôrto Alegre, Rio, and Fortaleza. After the war, officer training continued in haphazard fashion, with schools in Rio—a preparatory school in Realengo and the Escola Militar in Praia Vermelha—and a school at Rio Pardo in Rio Grande do Sul. By the time the empire fell in 1889 the majority of officers had come either out of the Paraguayan War or from the institutions in Pôrto Alegre or Realengo-Praia Vermelha. Early in this century, at the prodding of career officers like Hermes da Fonseca, there still were programs designated as Escolas de Aplicação for artillery and engineers and artillery and infantry, and a general military course and staff training in Rio Grande do Sul, as well as a staff school, the Escola de Estado Maior do Exército, and the Praia Vermelha center in Rio. On the eve of World War I, Praia Vermelha was Brazil's best-equipped and best-funded military educational institution.

Regionalism was still a factor. Each state had its own *colónia* at Praia Vermelha, composed either of alumni of the state military preparatory schools or of those who entered the cadet corps from civilian *colégios*. The Escola reflected state political issues as well as state loyalties. There were frequent suspensions of classes, such as one during the 1904–5 mutiny caused by the involvement of cadets in protest against compulsory smallpox vaccination.[27] Compounding political and regional influences on the formation of a military mentality was the lack of a highly specialized professional curriculum. An inordinate amount of time (as compared to that allotted in Argentina, Chile, and Peru) was given over to pure science, political and social thought, and philosophy. If the impact of Positivism—attributed to the proselytizing tendencies of Lieutenant Colonel Benjamin Constant Botelho de Magalhães, a mathematics instructor at Praia Vermelha, and subsequently first war minister of the Republic—has been exaggerated, the effect of loosely structured liberal arts courses and the lack of strictly professional courses on politically and regionally minded cadets should not be dismissed. Benjamin [Constant] even questioned the true vocation of most cadets, alleging that many entered the officer corps, as others entered the clergy, in order to gain a free education and a secure career.[28]

An army that numbered sixteen thousand men and officers in 1865 grew quickly to sixty-seven thousand by 1866 but contracted sharply afterward. It was no more capable of sustaining a protracted campaign than it had been during the war with Paraguay. The army barely kept pace with changes in doctrine, strategy, and tactics. In the wake of confrontation in the South American heartland the army found itself in an ironic situation: the victors were forgotten. Pedro, no friend of the military, did not yield to the arguments of generals nor to those of the army's champion, Luis Alves de Lima e Silva, Duke of Caxias, that the empire needed an army capable of defending it at any time. Brazil's most significant military figure of the past century, Caxias held the country together during the 1831–1840 regency. He was an able war minister (1855–1857, 1861, and 1875–76), was in the field during the Paraguayan war, and carried the army's case to Pedro. He was also a noble, close to the emperor and only informally speaking a professional army officer. He may have been the army's champion, but he was also the emperor's man. Between 1870 and his death in 1880 the army was buffeted by the rough and troubled politics of the late Empire.[29] Caxias did much to protect the institution but did little to satisfy those who wanted to professionalize the officer corps along European lines.

From 1880 to 1889 the army became embroiled in a series of political questions, as Liberals maneuvered with their military link, Viscount Pelotas [José Antônio Corrêa da Camara] and Conservatives countered with theirs, Marshal [Deodoro da] Fonseca. Abolition, Republicanism, Positivism, the upgrading of military capabilities, and the dignity, inviolability, and professional nature of the institutions, as well as regional issues, were subjects of cadet discussions. In the 1880s some Brazilian officers may have seen a political stance similar to that of their Spanish American brethren as necessary to the cause of modernization. The Brazilians searched for an identity. Their role as founders of the Republic did not result in a political stance, nor did it result in rewards commensurate with what officers thought was their due. It merely perpetuated the *questão militar*: just how politically involved could military men be? Before the fall of the Empire the question centered on the right to speak out on political, social, and economic questions. With the Empire's demise, active officers were excluded from elective office, but the armed forces exercised the *podor moderador*, formerly the emperor's moderative power of intervention. Thus the military did gain a sense of collective legitimacy for a stance; corporate self-interest—already evident in Marshal Deodoro's 1889 defiance of the emperor—was existent, but there was little substance to it.[30]

A good part of the officer corps in 1889 was composed of nonaristocrats and there was a sizable "military family" contingent. A few officers were of Negro origin. Spread thin, assigned duties in the interior military colonies, and denied a modern system of rail transport comparable to that in rival Argentina (a product of economic expansion more than of military planning based on the lessons of the Franco-Prussian War), the army was armed with French Comblain rifles and Krupp artillery pieces. Outdated Portuguese field manuals remained in use until 1913. Cadets specialized in branch training (when they could get it) and learned little of the other branches of the service. Attempts to centralize training were shunted aside, as was the obligatory service code, first introduced in 1874. Recruits were of Negro and mixed background, and 70 percent were illiterate. As one specialist wrote, what came of all this were "isolated efforts, lost opportunities, measures that did not reach the point of execution. On the other hand, the intellectual level of the corps improved, they . . . were still heterogenous, composed of educated or scientific[ally educated] officers and uneducated doltish [ones]."[31] Such was the institution that had toppled an empire.

Military modernization in Brazil came only during the Republican era, and only after the army had been persuaded to retire from active participation in politics. Entrapped for five years (1889–1894) and humbled by the disastrous 1896–97 Canudos campaigns, the army emerged less than lustrous from its "chest to chest" confrontation with civilian political life.[32] What Benjamin Constant and his activist cadre had hoped for—a quick thrust against the Empire and a retirement to the barracks—had ended up as a disaster. Early in this century, years before the arrival of the French, Marshal Hermes [da Fonseca] began the groundwork on which the likes of Maurice Gamelin and Charles Huntzinger would try to build a modern officer corps. When they did, the Brazilian army numbered nearly thirty thousand men. The rise from sixteen thousand to sixty-seven thousand in 1865–66 was followed by reductions to nineteen thousand in 1871, fifteen thousand in 1880, and thirteen thousand in 1889—the low point in many ways for officers and emperor alike, and the point where the state *forças públicas* became more powerful than the national army.[33] From 1889 forward, the army had only one way to go, but it was a long, slow climb up.

In the last decade of the nineteenth century, the armed forces of Argentina, Brazil, Chile, and Peru confronted politics in different ways, but the confrontations resulted in comparable reactions. Each of the armies had undergone the rudiments of professionalization; each had officers in important staff or command positions who understood, at least, the need for modernization of equipment. In three of the armies there was a core of junior officers who already considered themselves either underprivileged or superior to their commanders, or both. Only in Peru was there no clear rift within the officer corps during the first decade of this century. Each army had its champion—or soon would have.

Argentines, whether sympathetic to the newborn Radical party or not, knew that Julio Roca believed in a modern, well-equipped, and well-trained fighting force. With the passing of the Empire, Brazilian officers found that their champion, Marshal Deodoro, could do little in the chaos following Pedro's abdication. Benjamin Constant attempted to initiate a reform scheme while he was in the war ministry, but failed. After the establishment of civilian rule in 1894 and the Canudos disasters of 1896–97, the army was reduced to observer status and shown to be a white elephant, and not until the outspoken Marshal Hermes took up the cause could the damage be repaired.

When the dust settled following the Chilean Civil War of 1891, Emil Körner found himself in a superb position to carry out Prussianization. Balmacedista officers were purged from the rolls, and those who had received commissions in 1891 were kept on with Körner-trained junior grades and the older veterans of the War of the Pacific. The officer corps was a divided lot: Germanophile juniors, grizzled veterans of the Peruvian campaign, and the 1891 volunteers. This division and the fact that the army's most articulate champion was a foreigner (albeit very popular in Chile) influenced the development of military-civilian relations as much as domestic tribulations in Argentina and Brazil influenced development there. The 1890s, as noted, proved salutary to the modernization of Peru's officer corps and its army. Fiscal health, the multiracial composition of officialdom, the abilities of Piérola, and the coming of Colonel Clément precluded the early development of divisions within the nascent officer corps.

It is clear that civil conflict has had much to do historically with political action by South American men in uniform. Not until what have been called the "institutional *golpes*" of the 1960s and 1970s has civil conflict resulted in widespread military-imposed and -administered alternatives with long-range goals in mind. Early in this century, just as the modern, professional armies took form, officers were as vulnerable to outside influences as were the governments they served. Thus the Civic Union of Youth and its spawn, the Radical party, made inroads into the Argentine officer corps precisely as professionalization got under way. The experiences of the 1890s induced Brazilian officers to realize just what the results of political activity could be. The crisis of 1891 in Chile and the ensuing parliamentary system did the same for Chilean officers. In Peru the great differences between the words and the actions of political leaders led to the strikingly early and sophisticated elaboration of an army officers' "point of view."

None of the armies discussed here, with the qualified exception of Chile's, had a consistent tradition of professional preparation by 1890. This may have retarded the ability to seize an initiative in the 1890s—provided anyone had been inclined to do so. Economic growth in Argentina and Peru and the dramatic nature of political revolutions in Brazil and Chile may have conspired to temporarily strengthen civilian political leadership. Hence there may be a cause-and-effect link between moderation in the civilian sector—moderate economic growth, moderate expansion of the elite and of the politically articulate population, moderate social change brought about by wider distribution of economic opportunity—and moderation of the military profession's thinking. . . .

Obviously something resembling a military point of view can be discerned at any time in these countries about the middle of the nineteenth century: efficient government and proper training and equipping of the armed forces. But as long as no one involved them in anything but the traditional responsibilities of national defense, officers did not menace the essence of things political; participation was on partisan and personal, not professional, grounds. But when the Brazilians were ordered out of barracks and posts to supervise the capture and return of escaped slaves (after having seen the fighting capabilities of ex-slaves in the 1864–1870 war), or to smash the Canudos rebels; when Peruvians and Chileans struggled to make soldiers out of illiterate *cholos*, Indians, and *rotos* (after having witnessed troop-training methods in France and Germany); and when Argentines were subjected to the manipulations of post-Roca political leaders, then the shaping of a formal, defined ethos did take place. In sum, the establishment of professional officer corps in South America based on European models and the incessant aping of those models led officers to adopt beliefs and value systems that differed from those of the society about them. This would not have happened without specialized training and resultant expertise, a defined defense role, and professional attitudes based on internal regulation, norms, and practices that set armies apart from civilian sectors.

It is clear that Argentina, Brazil, Chile, and Peru adopted European military systems for two prime reasons based on necessity and a third reason based on desire. The prime reasons were to isolate the army and ensure civilian control of government. Argentine and Peruvian, and later Brazilian, leaders saw the need to mollify officers, to co-opt them, and to keep them happy and occupied in the barracks. Activity there, on the parade ground, and on study trips would allow civilians a free hand to run national affairs. This was particularly attractive when the allure of foreign capital and the expansion of extractive industries, agriculture, stock raising, and mining opened a new era. Chilean leaders saw less need for isolating the army and navy from politics, though the issue would come to the fore well into the professionalization process. In Chile the prime reason for modernization was the desire to maintain defense capabilities. In Argentina, Brazil, and Peru this was of some importance as well.

A glance at the map of South America gives visual evidence of defense concerns. South America has been a geopolitician's paradise and a source of international conflict since colonial times. Leaving aside details of the frontier, squabbles involving Spain and Portugal, it is sufficient to repeat that Argentine-Brazilian rivalries derive from colonial disputes in the Platine and Paraná basins. Paraguay, Uruguay, and much of modern Bolivia were under the jurisdiction of Buenos Aires in the late eighteenth century; their independence from *porteño* control was a jolt to the new Argentine government. Brazil's interests in the upper Paraná, Uruguay, and Paraguay basins, and the occupation of Uruguay (known as the Cisplatine Province from 1816 to 1827), were early signs of geopolitical rivalry in the area. Argentine and Brazilian policy since the last decade of the nineteenth century hinges on power politics in the Platine-Paraná zone, access to the Platine heartland, and a power balance on the Atlantic coast. Historically it stands to reason that what impedes the armed forces from fulfilling the dictates of their policies cannot be tolerated.

America's Alsace-Lorraine was merely the late nineteenth-century, temporary resolution of a similar power rivalry on the Pacific coast. Like the War of the Triple Alliance, the War of the Pacific was partially the result of colonial-era issues colliding with mutual antipathy, fear, and distrust. Chile was a breakaway extremity of the Viceroyalty of Peru, and maintained its independence and expanded its territory by force of arms. As with Argentina and Brazil, Pacific coast military policy hinged on maritime and territorial power conflicts and continued tenuous relations compounded by the mediterranean status of Bolivia.

By the end of the century, as Robert Burr has noted, there was a functional balance-of-power relationship in South America.[34] Indeed, Theodore Mannequin helped point out the European qualities of South American power politics as early as 1866, politics based on the territorial interests of Argentina, Brazil, Chile, and Peru, on Argentina's imperialistic nature, on Atlantic-Pacific trade rivalries, on Brazil's "disputed conquests" achieved by treaty, and on the emergence of the (as yet informal) Brazil-Chile and Argentina-Peru axes.[35] If diplomacy was highly derivative of European international relations, it should not seem odd that defense policy was equally derivative. This derivation, in conjunction with the characteristics of indigenous society, politics, economics, and culture, produced a Europeanized military caste in a quasi-Europeanized setting. Hopes that this would result in a Europeanized military-civilian relationship, albeit an idealized one, were high, doubtless, but they had the substance of misguided wishful thinking and nothing more. In South America, a wedge between military and civilian institutions was being driven into place.

By the 1890s the Europeans were barely aware of South American military activity. They knew of the Triple Alliance and the war that bore its name, and of the War of the Pacific too. They could follow the upheavals of 1889, 1890, and 1891 in Brazil, Argentina, and Chile with great interest. News of London's financial coup in Lima traveled far, rapidly. Although Germans were aware of Körner's work in Chile, they were far more interested in Colmar von der Goltz's in Turkey, building his "bridge between Central Europe and Asia" ([Helmuth von] Moltke was less than enthusiastic), and Meckel's work in Japan. They were far more concerned with Germany's latest colonial ventures in Togo, Cameroon,

Tanganyika, and Southwest Africa. Germans were hardly enthusiastic about the abilities of Latins to absorb military expertise. [Friedrich von] Bernhardi, author of "the book that caused the war," observed tersely that, after all, being an amalgam of Gothic and Mediterranean, they were inferior to racially pure Germans.[36]

Likewise the French, even after Clément arrived in Peru, became more deeply interested in imperial adventures in Indochina, Madagascar, and North Africa, ventures of greater import to military-civilian relations and international affairs. The French appeared to be proof of Guglielmo Ferrero's comment of 1898 that "French colonial policy signifies that the age of great military undertakings is now ever past in Europe. It therefore strives to perpetuate the glory of arms in Asia and Africa."[37] Appearances are ever deceiving. It was too soon, perhaps, for reflection on the presence of Europeans in South America, too soon, probably, to ascertain just what this could mean beyond extrapolation from conclusions like that made in 1903 by Paul Jaillet: "It is totally logical that the role of the army will not be the same as long as the colonies-to-be are situated in different climates and latitudes."[38]

At the beginning of the age of professionalization in South America, the French and Germans had large armies composed of volunteers and career soldiers. In 1889 the French army numbered nearly 490,000, and Germany had slightly fewer, just under 470,000. Both could count on two million men in case of mobilization for war. France regularly had a larger number of men under arms until the end of the century. Her defense-oriented doctrines and colonial theories appealed to Peruvians. Just as obviously the Prussian offense-oriented order of battle and doctrine were a great attraction to more aggressive-minded Argentines and Chileans.[39] The advantages of small fighting forces led by professional officers expressed in *Das Volk in Waffen* were obvious to all South Americans, for none of the four continental powers could ever hope to put in the field an army comparable to that of France or Germany.

Whereas the Germans who went abroad were innocents when it came to politics, French officers were attuned to political life Republican-style. Their Latin pupils reflected these peculiarities, more so when social distinctions in the French and German officer corps became significant and when German politics became enmeshed in social questions early in this century. By that time South Americans could respond both to [Thomas] Bugeaud's declaration of 1832 to the Chamber of Deputies that "French bayonets only thirst for the blood of the stranger . . . in the sense that they only desire to fight against the enemies of France, but they also are always ready to fight the factions," and to Goltz's dictum of 1899: "States which are weak from a military point of view, and which are surrounded by stronger neighbors invite war, and if they neglect their military organizations from false motives, they court this danger by their own supineness."[40]

Troubled armies, those in need of refurbishing, resuscitation, or discipline, looked to armies that had proved themselves capable and resilient—but that were no less conscious of their associations with state, nation, and society. What little interest the Europeans had in their clients-to-be can be found in the pages of professional journals, and consists primarily of news items and correspondence from America.

Chile, since it was the first South American country to adopt a European military system, received the most regular coverage. Körner's plans to send outstanding Chilean cadets to study at the Kriegsakademie and the previous year's military parade in Santiago received notice early in 1890 in Germany's major military journal, *Militär Wochenblatt*, and in 1892 the *Revue Militaire de l'Étranger* noted for its French readers that Körner's congressional forces had utilized Krupp artillery in their victory over Balmaceda.[41] The article drew attention also to the mobility of the rebel forces as contrasted with the lack of mobility on the part of the loyalists. Firepower, strategic control of both the nitrate provinces and the sea, and the lack of adequate land transportation to facilitate a loyalist campaign in the north figured in the news from the Pacific. The German counterpart of the *Revue Militaire de l'Étranger*, the *Internationale Revue über die Gesammten Armeen und Flotten*, revealed with pride the accomplishments of the Körner mission as of the mid-1890s. Chilean officers, the dispatch noted, were better disciplined than any South American counterparts; they were hardworking and conscientious. Discipline, broken in 1891, had been restored by the Saxon "missionary," but Chilean officers, though warmly appreciated and universally praised by civilians, "still had a long way to go before achieving the social standing enjoyed by Germans."[42] *Neue Militärische Blätter* carried a strictly professional appraisal of Körner's wartime feats.[43]

Despite her upheaval, commercial significance, and strategic position anent Brazil, Argentina drew slightly less attention than Chile. In a *Militär Wochenblatt* essay of 1890, the writer claimed that a real revolution would have occurred if the army had not remained loyal to the government, perhaps giving more credit to the Civic Union of Youth than was its due. The army's "unity, concentration, and discipline" had saved Argentina from anarchy.[44] The theme of the military as balanced against upheaval was a constant in German literature. The next appearance of news from Argentina in the pages of the *Wochenblatt*, nearly a decade later, was a mere snippet of news about the duties of Colonel Alfred Arent, new director of the Escuela Superior de Guerra, and about German and

French officers serving in other South American countries.[45] Interest in the Latin world was slow building until after the turn of the century. Brazil fared more poorly, Peru not at all, prior to 1900. A brief note in the *Revue Militaire de l'Étranger* gave some statistics on the Brazilian Army in 1890.[46]

Such was the extent of officially published knowledge of the armies of South America's leading countries at the dawn of the age of professionalization. Travelers' accounts, newspaper coverage, and the like provided military men with most of their information on South America. Classified materials, it must be supposed, were little better in content and sophistication. With the turn of the century, though, the quantity and quality of coverage improved, for by then not only was there more interest and contact, but the great enterprise of the German and French "martial missionaries" had begun in Argentina, Chile, and Peru. Brazil as well soon showed signs of interest in establishing ties with the Kaiser's army. South America, then, came face to face with European military professionalism.

Notes

1. See Walter Goerlitz, *History of the German General Staff, 1657–1945*, trans. Brian Battershaw (New York: Frederick A. Prager, 1965), p. 97.

2. Augusto A. Maligne, *Historia militar de la república argentina durante el siglo 1810 a 1910* (Buenos Aires: La Nación, 1910), p. 154; República Argentina, *Reseña histórica del colegio militar, 1810–1910* (Buenos Aires: Imprenta del Colegio Militar, 1927), pp. 9–13.

3. See Ramón J. Carcano, *Guerra del Paraguay*, 3 vols. (Buenos Aires: n.p., 1939–41), for a detailed treatment of Argentina's involvement in the war. Charles J. Kolinski's *Independence or Death: The Story of the Paraguayan War* (Gainesville: University of Florida Press, 1965) presents the Paraguayan point of view. Pelham Box, *The Origins of the Paraguayan War* (Urbana: University of Illinois Press, 1929), is also valuable, especially for treatment of Brazilian motives.

4. See J. del Viso, "La conquista del desierto," *Revista Militar* (May 1934), pp. 917–57.

5. República Argentina, *Memorial del departamento de guerra presentado al honorable congreso nacional correspondiente al año 1925–1926* (Buenos Aires: Departamento de Guerra, 1926), pp. xi–xxii.

6. República Argentina, *Monografía histórica del estado mayor del ejercito argentino* (Buenos Aires: Estado Major General del Ejército, n.d.), pp. 53–128, passim.

7. *Reseña histórica del colegio militar*, p. 13.

8. Ibid., p. 23.

9. See Augusto G. Rodríguez, *Reseña histórica del ejército argentino (1862–1930)* (Buenos Aires: Secretaría de Guerra, 1964), p. 95.

10. See Frederick M. Nunn, *The Military in Chilean History: Essays on Civil-Military Relations, 1810–1973* (Albuquerque: University of New Mexico Press, 1976), pp. 53–59.

11. The best examples are: Comité de Historia del Estado Mayor del Ejército de Chile, *Historia militar de Chile*, 3 vols. (Santiago: Estado Mayor General del Ejército, 1969), I, 7–86; Alberto Polloni, *Las fuerzas armadas de Chile en la vida nacional: Compendio cívico-militar* (Santiago: Editorial Andrés Bello, 1972), passim; Agustín Toro Dávila, *Síntesis histórico-militar de Chile* (Santiago; Editorial Universitaria, 1976), pp. 2–48; Indalicio Téllez Cárcamo, *Historia militar de Chile* (Santiago: Instituto Geográfico Militar, 1925), passim; and José M. Barceló Lira, "La evolución del ejército desde la ocupación del territorio araucano (1859–1879) hasta nuestros días," *Memorial del Ejército de Chile* (March–April 1935), pp. 199–218. Needless to say, these works are all by army officers. See also Gerardo Zúñiga Montúfar's *El ejército de Chile: Impresiones y apuntes* (Santiago: Imprenta Universo, 1904). This is a perceptive appraisal by a Costa Rican major studying in Chile.

12. See Nelson Werneck Sodré, *História Militar do Brasil*, 2nd ed. (Rio de Janeiro: Civilização Brasileira, 1968), pp. 33–45.

13. For example:

> Chile my scene; a fertile land remote,
> Hard by the border of antarctic seas,
> Home of a stiff-necked people, wed to arms.
> Renowned in war, by neighbor nations feared;
> Whose hot distempered blood alike revels
> At rule domestic and at stranger yoke.
> No king among themselves they own, nor e'er
> Have bowed the knee to foreign conqueror.
> —*La araucana* (1569), canto I, stanza 6

14. See Ernst Presseisen, *Before Aggression: Europeans Prepare the Japanese Army* (Tucson: Arizona University Press, 1965), passim.

15. Nunn, *The Military in Chilean History*, 70–71.

16. For example, consult Carlos Ríos Pagaza, *Historia de la escuela militar* (Lima: Centro de Instrucción Militar, 1962), passim; Estado Mayor General del Ejército del Perú, 5a Sección, *Monografia histórica del ejército peruano* (Lima: Estado Mayor General del Ejército, 1930); and Carlos Dellepiane, *Historia militar del Perú*, 2 vols. (Buenos Aires: Círculo Militar, 1941). Vol. 1 of the last-cited work deals with the preindependence period and the decades up to 1879. José Zárate Lescano, in his "Consideraciones sobre la historia integral del ejército peruano," *Revista Militar del Perú* (January–February 1969), pp. 48–57, argued that a Peruvian military spirit can be traced to ca. A.D. 900; hereafter cited as *RMP*.

17. This is treated in Leon G. Campbell's *The Military and Society in Colonial Peru, 1750–1810* (Philadelphia: American Philosophical Society, 1978).

18. The most useful material on early military education in Peru can be found in Ríos Pagaza, *Historia de la escuela militar*; Felipe de la Barra, *La escuela militar y su papel profesional y social* (Chorrillos: Imprenta de la Escuela Militar, 1939); Paul Clément, ed., *La escuela militar en el XXV aniversario de su fundación, 1898–1923* (Lima: Empresa Tipográfica La Unión, 1924); and, in English, Lyle N. McAlister, "Peru," in McAlister, Anthony P. Maingot, and Robert A. Potash, *The Military in Latin American Socio-Political Evolution*

(Washington: American Institutes for Research, 1970), pp. 21–83. This last is an indispensable source for the comparative study of institutional development of the armies of Argentina (by Potash), Colombia (by Maingot), and Peru and Mexico (by McAlister), emphasizing the late nineteenth and the twentieth centuries.

19. Edgardo Mercado Jarrín emphasized that this is especially true of post-1940 graduating classes (*promociones*) in his seminal "El ejército de hoy y su proyección en nuestra sociedad en período de transición (1940–1965)," *RMP* (November–December 1964), pp. 1–21. See the discussion of this essay and other important Peruvian military literature in Nunn, "Professional Militarism in Twentieth Century Peru: Historical and Theoretical Background to the *Golpe de Estado* of 1968," *Hispanic American Historical Review* 59, no. 3 (August 1979), pp. 391–417. The theory that the officer corps had spoken for the middle classes and selected regional interests was advanced by James Petras and Nelson Rimensnyder in "The Military and the Modernization of Peru," in Petras, ed., *Politics and Social Structure in Latin America* (New York: Fawcett Books, 1970), pp. 130–158.

20. Carlos A. Miñano M., *Las misiones militares francesas en el Perú* (Lima: n.p., 1959), p. 5; Clément, *La escuela militar,* p. 15. Jehoval Motta, in his *Formação do Oficial do Exército: Currículos e Regímes na Académia Militar, 1810–1944* (Rio de Janeiro: Editôra Artes Gráficas, 1976), makes the same point for Brazil.

21. Clément, *La escuela militar,* p. 17.

22. Ibid., p. 18.

23. Celso Zuleta, "Historia militar del Perú," *Boletín del Ministerio de Guerra y Marina* (January 15, 1905), pp. 167–74. This was the forerunner to the *Revista Militar del Perú.* See as well the editorial, "Breve reseña histórica del ejército peruano," *RMP* (March–April 1967), pp. 32–41.

24. *Annuário da Escola Militar, 1914* (Praia Vermelha: Escola Militar, 1915), pp. 9–58, contains information on nineteenth-century Brazilian military education.

25. See "A Escola Militar: Síntese Histórica da sua Fundação e Evolução," *Revista Militar Brasileira* (January–March 1942), pp. 13–70, hereafter cited as *RMB.* The entire issue was devoted to the Escola Militar.

26. A good deal of the following discussion is based on information in João Baptista Magalhães, *A Evolução Militar do Brasil: Anotações para a História* (Rio de Janeiro: Biblioteca do Exército, 1958); Francisco de Paula Ciadade, "Da Missão Militar Franceza ãos Nossos Dias," *RMB* (July–December 1954), pp. 131–86; and Sodré's *História Militar.* See also Sodré's useful essay, "História Militar Brasileira," *RMB* (June–December 1944), pp. 355–66.

27. See Robert Nachman's "Positivism and Revolution in Brazil's First Republic."

28. Benjamin Constant Botelho de Magalhães, cited in Heitor Lyra, *História da Queda do Império,* 2 vols. (São Paulo: Companhia Editôra Nacional, 1964). See esp. I, 75–79, 414–18.

29. See Theodorico Lopes and Gentil Torres, *Ministros de guerra do Brasil, 1808–1850,* 4th ed. (Rio de Janeiro: Borsoi, 1946), for data on Caxias. William S. Dudley's "Professionalization and Politicization" and "Institutional Sources of Discontent" are invaluable for information on politics and the army in the latter stages of the Empire.

30. Documented conclusions on this issue can be found in Lyra, *Historia de Queda do Império*, pp. 77–94; Magalhães, *A Evolução Militar*, esp. pp. 310–35; and Sodré, *História Militar do Brasil*, pp. 130–62.

31. Paula Ciadade, "Da Missão Militar Franceza ãos Nossos Dias," p. 319.

32. Cunha's *Rebellion in the Backlands* remains the best, most readable account of the Canudos campaign. It was Caxias himself who said: "Let us march shoulder to shoulder, not chest to chest." Cited in L. Correia Lima, "Pela pátria, pelo exército," *A Defeza Nacional* (April 1970), p. 148.

33. Magalhães, *A Evolução Militar*, 312.

34. Robert N. Burr, *By Reason or Force: Chile and the Balancing of Power in South America, 1830–1905* (Berkeley and Los Angeles: University of California Press, 1965), pp. 1–11.

35. Th. Mannequin, ed. and trans., *Antagonisme et solidarité des états orientaux et des états occidentaux de l'Amérique du Sud* (Paris: Dentú, 1866), passim. Nearly forty years later, comments made by C. H. Sherril of the U.S. mission in Buenos Aires confirmed the outside world's convictions about Argentina's pacific ways and Brazil's aggressive policy of territorial aggrandizement at the expense of limitrophe states. Sherril to Knox, Deparment of State Files, 835.00/95, July 20, 1910.

36. Friedrich von Bernhardi, *Kriegsbuch (The Customs of War)*, trans. J. Ellis Barker (London: Wm. Dawson and Sons, Ltd., 1914), pp. 33–34. The English edition bore the subtitle cited herein on its cover. "General A.," in *Les Réformes dans l'armée française: Comparaison entre cette armée et l'armée allemande* (Paris: Libraire Militaire de L. Baudoin et Cie., 1897), made it clear that any army unable to withstand a campaign during a European winter, or similar conditions, did not merit consideration as a true army.

37. Guglielmo Ferrero, *Militarism (Il Militarismo)* (London: Wardlock and Co., Ltd., 1902), p. 223.

38. Paul Jaillet, *Essai historique et critique sur le colonisation militaire* (Paris: V. Giard et E. Brière, 1903), p. 17.

39. [Marshal] Joffre wrote that a newly formed army, a "young army" in his words, naturally favored offensive doctrines. It succumbed to what he called the "mystique of the offensive." *Memoirs*, trans. T. Bentley Mott, 2 vols. (London: Geoffrey Bees, 1932).

40. H. D'Ildeville, *Memoirs of Marshal Bugeaud: From His Private Correspondence and Memoirs*, trans. Charlotte M. Vonge, 2 vols. (London: Hurst and Blackett, 1884), I, 322; Goltz, *The Conduct of War: A Short Treatise on Its Most Important Branches and Guiding Rules*, trans. F. G. Leverson (London: Kegan Paul, 1899), pp. 2–43.

41. E. K. [Emil Körner], "Militärische Nachrichten aus Chile," *Militär Wochenblatt* (January 11, 1890), pp. 117–19, hereafter cited as *MW*; "La Dernière campagne au Chile," *Revue Militaire de l'Étranger* (April 1892), pp. 304–30 (hereafter cited as *RME*).

42. "Die deutschen Offiziere in Chile," *Internationale Revue über die Gesammten Armeen und Flotten* (March 1897), pp. 491–97.

43. "Der Krieg in Chile," *Neue Militärische Blätter* (March 1893), pp. 215–25.

44. "Die Revolution in Buenos Aires," *MW* (November 18, 1890), pp. 2836–41.

45. "Vier fremde Militärkommissionen," *MW* (August 19, 1899), p. 1842.

46. "L'Armée brasilienne," *RME* (March 1893), pp. 278–79.

6

The Armed Forces and Industrialists in Modern Brazil: The Drive for Military Autonomy, 1889–1945

Stanley E. Hilton

As the larger states of Latin America have industrialized, they have focused on producing at home products of great importance to the country. Weapons have naturally fallen into this category. Indeed, the expansion of weapons' manufacturing has become an important symbol of modernization in several nations, particularly among the largest South American countries—Argentina, Brazil, and Chile.

Brazil has emerged as South America's dominant military power and the region's major manufacturer and exporter of armaments. Its military-industrial development strategy reflects a long-standing belief that national security and industrial self-sufficiency are inexorably linked. Twentieth-century global and regional instability and the ongoing rivalry with Argentina heightened Brazil's preoccupation with defending its national interests in a hostile world.

Military and civilian planners viewed reliance on foreign suppliers for armaments as a fundamental obstacle to the development of an adequate defense. Since military self-sufficiency could not be achieved without broad-based industrialization, the armed forces supported government incentives to foster private industrial development and national defense industries utilizing Brazilian materials. The country's emerging military-industrial development strategy forged strong ties between civilian industrialists and the armed forces. By the 1950s the goals of national development and military autonomy had merged.

From *Hispanic American Historical Review* 62, no. 4 (November 1982): 629–73. ©1982 by Duke University Press. Reprinted by permission of the publisher.

Defense analysts in the late 1970s were increasingly impressed by a surprising phenomenon in the international arms sector: the emergence of Brazil as not only the leading manufacturer of war matériel in the Third World, but a significant exporter of hardware as well. "Clearly Brazil is rapidly joining the big league producers," one observer aptly commented.[1] The creation of a "military-industrial complex," one of the striking offshoots of Brazil's remarkable economic development in recent times, was not accidental. Financial considerations naturally were instrumental in the drive for general industrial self-sufficiency that has been a major component of Brazilian national strategy for fifty years, but that drive, along with its complementary campaign for arms autonomy, has deep roots in elite perceptions of national needs and in Brazil's experiences with arms dependence during the turbulent first half of the century. The Old Republic (1889–1930) was an important period in the evolution of Brazil's military-industrial sector primarily because of the formation then of a body of elite opinion that advocated reduced dependence in matters of national security. The real "takeoff," however, came during the Getúlio Vargas era (1930–1954) when modernization of the armed forces became one of the government's priority goals. Sharing fully the preoccupation of the generals and admirals with Brazil's vulnerabilities in a lawless world, Vargas and his civilian counselors, as well as military leaders, were keenly aware of the critical importance of enhancing national capacity to meet the ominous demands of the era—and the official consensus was that effective military strength required an industrial base that was as independent as possible.

The need for an expanded and more efficient defense establishment became progressively clear to Brazilian strategists as the country moved into the twentieth century. Indeed, as cracks in the structure of European peace began to appear at the turn of the century, disquiet slowly spread in elite circles, especially in view of the disturbing colonial thrust of great power politics.[2] The outbreak of war in 1914 justified the pessimism of Brazilian analysts. Reverberations of the conflict quickly reached Brazil and, after Washington's declaration of war and attacks on Brazilian ships by German submarines, Rio de Janeiro also joined the Allied cause. Defeat of the Central Powers did not bring the peace to Europe that many predicted; on the contrary, the Versailles settlement generated new instability, and throughout the 1920s Brazilian observers attentively studied European tensions. "The threat of war continues to hang permanently overhead," wrote one admiral from Paris in 1925.[3]

A constant source of preoccupation to Brazilian policymakers was the unsettled state of South American politics. Early in the century, for example, [Palacio] Itamaraty worried justifiably about the possibility of war between Argentina and Chile; then in 1905 and again in 1910, civil strife in Paraguay induced Rio de Janeiro to send a flotilla to the area to protect its interests; and during the same period, rebels from Uruguay crossed the Brazilian border, inviting countermeasures and provoking fears in Itamaraty that civil war there might cause a "general conflagration" in the Southern Cone.[4] Boundary disputes with adjacent countries often led to severe tensions.[5] Enduring friction between Chile and its Andean neighbors, and, more important, the animosity that prevailed between Bolivia and Paraguay throughout the 1920s as a result of their competing claims to the Chaco kept Brazilian leaders on frequent alert.[6]

Underlying the whole problem of continental instability was Brazil's historic rivalry with Argentina. Brazil's victory in the arbitration of the Missions dispute in 1895 set the stage for a marked revival of tensions in the twentieth century. The two adversaries engaged in an intense naval race in the early 1900s and border alarms were common. Senator Ruy Barbosa in 1908 warned President Afonso Pena that Argentina might attack without warning, and the two countries in fact approached the brink of war that year.[7] Hostility subsided temporarily as European peace disintegrated, but the two governments then followed divergent policies and, as Brazil entered the Allied camp, its leaders kept a troubled eye on Argentina's rearmament, its perceived expansionist tendencies, and its alleged pro-German sympathies.[8] The first postwar decade saw a recrudescence of antagonisms. All Brazilian defense plans centered on the possibility of Argentine aggression, and in the face of expanding *porteño* military budgets and politicoeconomic maneuvering in neighboring countries, Brazilian strategists became convinced that the country could suddenly find itself at war.[9]

Given the instability of the international environment, it was obvious to Brazilian planners that the country's defensive capacity might at any moment be challenged. How efficient were national capabilities? Dramatic episodes in the mid-1890s provided a disquieting answer. First, civil war in Rio Grande do Sul, accompanied by a month-long naval revolt in Rio de Janeiro, during which foreign warships proceeded peremptorily vis-à-vis both government and rebels, was a source of keen embarrassment. Equally humiliating was the Canudos affair in 1897, when it took government troops four attempts over a one-year period and cost five thousand lives to crush a band of rebellious backlands fanatics in Bahia. During the conflict, federal commanders faced staggering logistical problems, and President Prudente de Morais was forced to appeal to state authorities for aid.[10] Capabilities improved little over the next decade. On agreeing to serve as minister of war in Pena's administration, General Hermes da Fonseca candidly admonished him in 1906 that conditions in the army were "woeful," while a sympathetic federal congressman went further, complaining that the armed forces were "sadly unequipped to defend the nation against any enemy, even a 3rd or fourth-class power." The Baron of Rio Branco, Brazil's Bismarckian foreign minister (1902–1912), was gloomily blunt: "As for the state of our defenses, it is the most regrettable possible," he confided. Successive presidents in the prewar period cautioned Congress about the deficiencies of the armed forces, whose shortcomings were underscored by events during the World War I era. Naval commanders, who customarily concentrated attention on the threat from the south, now had to consider possible challenges in the north, where they found shocking conditions at base facilities. At home the army faced a Canudos-like test in 1914–15 in Santa Catarina-Paraná, where repeated expeditions failed to disperse another band of religious fanatics, who were subdued, finally, by a division of six thousand troops.[11]

By the end of World War I the discontent within the officer corps over the material plight of the armed forces was nearly universal. "From North to South rain telegrams about the precarious situation of the units," Finance Minister João P. Calógeras told the president-elect in 1918. The complaint of General Augusto Tasso Fragoso, head of the army's Diretoria de Material Bélico (DMB), regarding artillery was typical. "You can't imagine how backward we are in this respect; it's a disgrace!" he wrote a few months after the Armistice in Europe. Indeed, the task ahead, Calógeras said frankly to President Epitácio Pessoa on assuming the portfolio of war in 1919, was to "*create* the Army."[12] During the ensuing decade, military planners made frequent comparative studies of Brazilian and Argentine strength and invariably found Brazil wanting, a realistic judgment that foreign experts shared.[13] The army's unspectacular campaign against another rebel column that wandered the backlands for two years in the middle of the decade was simply one more reminder of national military weakness.[14]

The permanent sense of uneasiness within the ranks of those responsible for national strategy and defense over the country's military inadequacy led them to place primary emphasis on the question of matériel. The absence of a domestic industrial base meant that the armed forces were locked into dependence on foreign suppliers. Contracts for the naval program of 1904–1907 went to British and Italian builders, and the only new vessel acquired after 1914 was a submarine, purchased from Italy in 1927. With regard to munitions, the fleet, meanwhile, was, in the words of the minister of navy in 1920, merely a "tributary of England." The army, too, was almost totally dependent upon imports—in 1900 it even ordered carrier pigeons from Belgium. Germany was the major prewar source of hardware. Beginning in 1892 the Krupp firm became the "undisputed" supplier of cannon, while by the turn of the century the Deutschen Waffen-und-Munitionsfabriken in Berlin, which controlled the marketing of Mauser arms, had "practically a monopoly" on the sale of carbines to Brazil, and sister companies provided various other articles. Indeed, during the 1890s, "Brazilian military reviews looked like German arms displays."[15] After Fonseca's visit to Germany in 1908 and the subsequent dispatch of junior officers there—the future "young Turks"—to serve with German regiments, Rio de Janeiro placed orders for Luger pistols, bought several hundred thousand Mauser rifles, awarded additional contracts to Krupp, and bought gunpowder and optical equipment from other German firms.[16] The Madsen company in Denmark supplied automatic weapons, and much of the canvas used to make personal field equipment came from British mills.[17] The elimination of German firms from the postwar arms trade, coupled with the presence of a French Military Mission (FMM) in Brazil after 1918, made France the source of most of the modest purchases of mortars, machine guns, artillery, and used armored cars in the 1920s.[18] France, furthermore, thanks to an aviation mission in Brazil, also furnished the planes, engines, and machine guns for the army's fledgling air corps, while the navy purchased aircraft from the United States, Britain, and Italy.[19]

The disadvantages of dependence were painfully obvious to national strategists. The cost of foreign hardware, for one thing, often seemed exorbitant; certainly the requirements in foreign exchange exceeded Brazil's means at various junctures. A lack of exchange, in fact, plagued administrations throughout the era. Declining revenues in the early 1900s made it difficult for proponents of a bigger army and navy to insist on greater defense expenditures. President-elect Pena and his financial advisers in 1905, for example, worried about future financing of the naval modernization program then under way, especially in view of the economy-minded Congress. During his ensuing administration, problems mounted: foreign creditors were disgruntled because Rio de Janeiro was spending money on the armed forces, work on the army's new powder factory was hampered by delays in making payments to contractors and workers, funds for a new naval arsenal were short, Fonseca angrily submitted his resignation because the army's budget for 1909 was slashed, and there were no funds for the emergency acquisition of ships that Rio Branco urged.[20] The government ultimately had to rescind a contract for one battleship because of its limited foreign exchange, a problem that became increasingly acute in following years. Early in World War I, after having to resort to a new funding loan, the minister of finance was forced to promise the House of Rothschild that "every nerve will be strained in every department so as to bring about the strictest economy and retrenchments," creating a situation in which, to the disgust of Minister of War José Caetano de Faria, the administration had to scrape up "almost nickel by nickel" the money to meet basic obligations.[21]

In the 1920s the financial crisis worsened. Pressed by the military, Pessoa championed a greater defense effort, agreeing to a sizable order for French artillery and urging Congress, in vain, to vote credits for a naval arsenal. His successor, Artur Bernardes (1922–1926), also wanted to bolster the armed forces, but the government's financial situation, he confided to a former minister of navy, was "much more grave than we supposed." The navy ultimately was compelled to scrap a building program, while the army had to nullify its largest artillery contract and abandon other aspects of its modernization plans. After examining the state of the treasury, Bernardes's successor, Washington Luis (1926–1930), told Tasso Fragoso, now head of the Estado-Maior do Exército (EME), or army general staff, that the "tanks are empty" and that he consequently had to "close the taps."[22]

Brazilian officials found additional cause for disgruntlement in the aggressive sales methods frequently used by foreign agents who, in their zeal to edge out rivals, allegedly were not above "adulterating" the facts about their products.[23] Certainly competition among arms exporters was keen and Brazil sometimes did receive inferior articles. Ships hastily ordered from the United States during the naval revolt in 1893, for example, were said to be in pathetic condition. At the turn of the century, the Ministry of War bought almost 750,000 Mauser cartridges that turned out to be defective; smokeless powder that arrived for its Krupp artillery also proved unsuitable and had to be exchanged. Military technicians in 1906 discovered an "extremely high percentage" of cracked shells among a consignment for testing weapons, and in 1911 tests conducted on 145,000 recently purchased Mauser rifles showed the barrels to be structurally weak, which led to two years' delay in securing and adapting new barrels from Germany.[24] Shipments of equipment, moreover, occasionally reached Brazil incomplete or in improper sequence, which meant further delays in achieving operational status. There were also cases in which foreign companies failed to meet production schedules or in which shipments to Brazil went astray.[25] The need to import gunpowder revealed another drawback in obtaining matériel from external sources: stocks often deteriorated in Brazil's warm climate before they could be used. In the case of a wartime order placed by the navy with British suppliers, the powder arrived only after a lengthy delay and had been so "crudely manufactured" that its active life was considerably shortened.[26] Then, too, there were sometimes disheartening difficulties in obtaining the necessary ammunition for arms previously purchased.[27]

A fundamental disadvantage of dependence on foreign manufacturers was that the flow of matériel was governed by the interests or needs of supplier countries and therefore was vulnerable to events over which Brazil had no control. This became unhappily evident when war broke out in Europe and the British blockade disrupted the contracts with Krupp and other German firms to which Rio de Janeiro had paid large sums in advance.[28] Unable to acquire weaponry in Europe, Brazil gave contracts to suppliers in the neutral United States, but when the latter mobilized for war in 1917, Washington informed Rio de Janeiro that its arms would have to be reserved for U.S. troops. Brazilian authorities ran into the same problem with a naval purchasing program that had to be shelved because no Western country would sell vessels. Brazil's own break with the Central Powers naturally led to the nullification of remaining contracts with German companies, and in 1920 the government itself was trying to find a way to obtain the prewar Krupp matériel it had ordered, which included items indispensable to the proper functioning of some weapons that had arrived years before.[29] International politics, that is, the defeat of Germany, largely accounted for Brazil's decision to contract the FMM, an idea that had been criticized because it might lead to the adoption of French equipment and thus to a further mélange of matériel. The mixing of weapons, in fact, had already become a problem; in some cases it occurred within the same unit.[30] With the temporary eclipse of Brazil's traditional German suppliers, that very thing happened. Plans for modernization of the fleet, on the other hand, ran afoul of the disarmament movement in the 1920s. In 1924, for example, the State Department, for broader policy reasons of its own and with total disregard for Brazil's strategic concerns, threatened to withdraw Washington's naval mission contracted two years earlier if Rio de Janeiro proceeded with a naval buildup.[31] The disarmament debates in Europe under the aegis of the League of Nations also seemed to jeopardize efforts to import armaments, since proposals frequently contained limitations on private sales to foreign governments. Brazilian delegates saw in such schemes the hands of stronger countries that wanted to maintain military superiority over weaker nations.[32]

The alternative to dependency was autonomy—this was an axiom affirmed with regularity by top-ranking military and civilian authorities after the turn of the century. The minister of war in 1903, for instance, urged the development of munitions production because it would make the armed forces "entirely independent" from overseas markets and eliminate "obstacles and difficulties" in obtaining supplies. Pena told Congress the same thing in 1908, and General Fonseca, as minister of war and then as president (1910–1914), repeatedly stressed the importance of expanding domestic military manufactures in order to "free ourselves from foreign markets" and "thus achieve the independence we need in a matter related so intimately to our security." Wartime leaders saw in the European conflict stark proof of the need for greater military-industrial autonomy. Spokesmen for the EME were emphatic in 1917: "We need to manufacture our explosives and powders, our rifles and machine guns; cast our cannon and battleships; build our vessels, our airplanes and dirigibles, our submarines and minesweepers; make our canned goods and fodder; weave our cloth, [and produce our] gear and utensils, from the raw material to the delicate finishing touch."[33] The lessons of the war were not lost on later leaders. Military industries had to be organized, said President Delfim Moreira in 1919, "whatever the sacrifices required." Military commanders in the 1920s understandably pressed for greater industrial autonomy, and their pleas found strong resonance in executive circles. For Bernardes in 1926, "if we do not produce our own war materials, freeing ourselves from the foreign market, our national defense will always be precarious."[34]

Some progress was made during the period in expanding military production, but the problem was complex. Government defense establishments were few in number, poorly organized, ill-equipped, and deficiently manned. When Brazil entered the century, there were army arsenals in Rio de Janeiro, Pôrto Alegre and Cuiabá, naval arsenals in the federal capital, Belém, and Mato Grosso, and three munitions plants—one in Realengo, a suburb of the capital, for cartridges; one at Estrela, in the state of Rio de Janeiro, for manufacturing powder; and a moribund powder plant in Mato Grosso. The immediate task, as military experts saw it, was to achieve greater autonomy in the production of munitions, which meant that Realengo was a primary target of modernization efforts. The government purchased a considerable amount of machinery from Germany in the early 1900s, but the lack of technicians hindered operations. Production rose from a half-million finished cartridges in 1900 to six million in 1914, but this was a far cry from the projected level of forty-five million a year.[35] General Caetano de Faria, who was responsible for creating the DMB in 1915, pressed for larger budgetary allotments in order to expand Realengo's activities to include the manufacture of artillery munitions, but little was accomplished in that sense, except to contract European technicians to help impose organization.[36]

The results of the endeavor to intensify and diversify work at the army arsenals were also uneven. An early decision was taken to build a new Arsenal de Guerra in Rio de Janeiro (AGRJ), and Krupp received most of the contracts for machinery and equipment, which were delivered in 1900 along with the "entire metallic structure" of the new buildings. Over the next few years considerable expansion of the physical plant took place and machinery was installed, but the problem of skilled labor again impeded progress. Fonseca ordered additional machinery in 1911, but the European crisis disrupted deliveries. One small triumph that a pleased wartime chief executive did report was that the AGRJ had started making many of the iron articles for the cavalry that formerly had been imported.[37]

As for naval repair and construction, the major need was a modern arsenal to replace the scattered ramshackle installations known collectively as the Arsenal da Marinha do Rio Janeiro (AMRJ). Discussion of the subject began in 1890, but the financial squeeze and a division of opinion over the ideal location for new facilities caused seemingly interminable delays.[38] Finally, in 1910, the government awarded a contract to a French company to build what became known as the Arsenal da Marinha da Ilha das Cobras (AMIC), but perennial financial problems and then the war led to abandonment of the project. A consortium of British shipbuilders submitted a proposal in 1918 for an arsenal that would produce "war matériel of all descriptions," and official interest sharpened. The new arsenal, Pessoa told Congress optimistically, repeating his minister of navy, would "liberate the country . . . from foreign tutelage." By the early 1920s, after several years of neglect, the government had to start over. The British group, joined by Bethlehem Steel, presented the only proposal judged viable in public bidding, but engineering doubts and what seemed excessive costs led the administration to give a contract to a São Paulo firm in 1922. Even so, it took Congress another four years to vote funds for the project.[39]

The principal achievement in the federal sector during the Old Republic, aside from launching work on the AMIC, was the establishment of a modern powder factory, but here, too, the results were spotty. Underlying the project was the desirability of producing a more powerful, "double-base" powder, that is, one that contained nitroglycerine, for more effective use of artillery shells. The government in the early 1900s purchased three farms near the small town of Piquete in the state of São Paulo and there built a dam and hydroelectric plant to power the future factory. The Du Pont Company in the United States supplied all the machinery and technical assistance, and in 1908 the project was completed. For good measure, Piquete was equipped to manufacture "simple-base" powder as well, a fortuitous decision since the high command subsequently opted to continue using such powder in the army's fieldpieces, which meant that much of the new machinery went unused.[40] After taking over the Ministry of War in 1919, Calógeras, who saw in Piquete a means of freeing the armed forces from their "bondage," had additional facilities erected there for the production of trotyl (TNT) and also revived the idea of making double-base powder, placing orders in Europe for new machinery, a program continued by his successor, General Fernando Setembrino de Carvalho.[41]

The nationalization of all stages of production was not yet the official crusade that it would be after 1930, but government leaders during the Old Republic became increasingly committed to that goal. [President Wenceslau] Bras proudly announced in 1918, for example, that the troops were now using purely domestic ingredients in several items of personal equipment. Navy spokesmen in the mid-1920s called for a survey of the military possibilities of national raw materials in order to stimulate their development, and Captain Thiers Fleming, head of Bras's Gabinete Militar during the war and now the navy's ordnance chief, was particularly active in trying to promote autonomous munitions production.[42] One important aspect of the Piquete project was that it was designed originally to make explosives from purely domestic raw materials. Du Pont had insisted, however, on using U.S. cotton, potassium nitrate, and pyrite for the trials, and thereafter the army continued to import those items. The war-generated supply crisis underscored the dangers of such dependence, though, so army specialists began sounding the need to substitute imports. Captain Egydio Castro e Silva, one of the army engineers responsible for building Piquete, gave a series of lectures to the Clube Militar in 1916 on the theme of nationalization of defense production that attracted the attention of his superiors, and when Calógeras assumed the portfolio of war, he drafted Castro e Silva, now a major on duty with the EME, to serve on his personal staff as an industrial expert. Beginning late in 1919, after a local firm offered to supply pyrite to Piquete, the major stumped energetically on behalf of eliminating unnecessary imports. Brazil's vulnerability to a blockade, he argued in 1920, made it vital that defense plants be as autonomous as possible. Calógeras, who as a congressman twenty years earlier had advocated the establishment of an explosives factory that used "exclusively national resources," was easily convinced and issued orders to Piquete to use not only domestic pyrite, but cotton as well.[43]

Frequently voices were raised in favor of developing metallurgical industries, especially iron and steel, in order to enhance national security through a greater range of defense manufactures. Early in the century there were only two small steel mills in Brazil, clearly an inadequate base for a military-industrial sector of any consequence. Calógeras was an early advocate of expanded steel production, and the Chamber of Deputies in 1907 justified the idea of government loans to a company that would organize a large-scale steel plant on the grounds of the "imperious necessity of emancipating the country militarily." Fonseca's trip to Germany converted him to the cause, and Castro e Silva became an influential disciple, arguing that not only military industries but the general economy demanded the processing of the country's coal and iron ore. Since autonomous naval construction was impossible without similar metallurgical self-sufficiency, navy spokesmen were firm champions of steel development, particularly in view of the lessons of World War I.[44]

As a result of wartime restrictions, interest in steel manufacture heightened. Although unenthusiastic about official industrial activity, General Caetano de Faria, to cut costs, decided to revive and transform an obsolete government foundry at Ipanema, in São Paulo, that had been shut down in 1896. He put Major Antonio Mendes Teixeira, a metallurgical expert, in charge of the project and sent him to the United States in search of modern steel-making equipment in 1917. The following year Congress approved the "Wenceslau Bras Law," which authorized the government to make loans to private companies to develop or increase steel production, and three firms obtained such aid.[45] By the end of the war, increasing sectors of the elite had come to share the high command's concern over the fact that the absence of domestic steel capacity left Brazil's defense plants helpless "tributaries" of foreign markets. Both Pessoa and Bernardes sought to spur steel manufacture. "Without it," Pessoa declared, "our arsenals and factories will never have a life of their own nor can we be assured of an efficient defense." Bernardes became famous for his xenophobic advocacy of national steel enterprise—"the first condition for our economic autonomy," he said. During both their administrations the 1918 law was renewed; in 1923 it was modified to permit profit guarantees for a firm that agreed to make steel rails and the "war matériel that the government may need." It was during Pessoa's government that Percival Farquhar's Itabira Iron Ore Company received its controversial and ill-fated concession to export ore and build a steel mill. The contract, finally approved by Congress during the Luis administration, obligated the future plant to produce "special steels for the government's war and naval arsenals." The Belgo-Mineira Steel Company was also launched in the early 1920s, and military planners made studies of the possibility of establishing a huge "military port" in Angra dos Reis that would include a mill that could make steel for ships, cannon, and shells.[46]

One critical question addressed during the Old Republic was that of the proper relationship between the public and private sectors. The Chamber of Deputies, on authorizing loans for steel production in 1907, opined that state control was "incompatible" with healthy development of that branch of industry, and Fonseca, the following year, speaking in broad terms, was likewise unequivocal: "The State, as an industrialist, should undertake no action except to fill gaps left by private industry; [and] never compete with it." The general, consequently, was in favor of turning over to civilian manufacturers the production of as many military supplies as possible since they could do so "with economic advantage." General Pedro Ivo Henriques, director of the AGRJ, concurred, arguing in 1912 that by sharing the manufacture of war matériel with private industry in peacetime, the government would be facilitating the task of possible emergency mobilization. In his talks to the Clube Militar, Castro e Silva made essentially the same point. Nationalize defense production, yes, he said, in the sense of reducing dependence on foreign markets, but leave it as much as possible to the private sector, where a valuable pool of specialized labor would be formed and the bureaucratic inertia of public enterprise could be avoided. Ideally, he declared, the army's role would be limited to that of technical supervision. As long as private capital displayed "ineptitude or fear," however, he thought the state should take the initiative. Calógeras agreed that the burden of military production should rest on the civilian sector, but he cautioned against excessive subsidization of private manufacturers. "The only thing that we can and should do is stimulate their production by guaranteeing a market," he wrote privately. And like his military colleagues, he saw in peacetime government-industry collaboration a "preliminary rehearsal for industrial mobilization." Calógeras's lack of enthusiasm for official industrial endeavors probably explains why, as minister of war, he jettisoned the Ipanema project.[47]

Naval authorities echoed army spokesmen in arguing in favor of civilian predominance in defense production. At the turn of the century, Captain Duarte Bacellar lectured at the Escola Naval to President Manoel de Campos Salles and other high officials on the need for official incentives for private metallurgical establishments, and through the press he sought to spread the same message. Fleming, before the war, also spoke out on behalf of government assistance to private industry in the fields of steel and naval construction, and in the 1920s he urged official aid for the creation of private munitions factories. The "industrial state," he said, had to be avoided because it brought "inconveniences and disadvantages of all kinds." Admiral Alexandrino Alencar, the minister of navy, reached the same conclusion in 1924. Brazil, he remonstrated, should follow the lead of such countries as the United States, Great Britain, Germany, and Italy, which left defense production to the private sector. State monopolies, he declared, stifled initiative, whereas profit-minded civilian manufacturers sought to improve their products through research. All the army should do, he concluded, was exercise technical control over its contracts.[48]

The extent of civilian participation in defense work is not clear. Since the backbone of manufacturing activity during the era was the textile sector, logically the major civilian role would be that of supplying clothing,

bedding, and the like. The minister of war reported in 1900 that, when he
opened public bidding for a contract to furnish uniforms, there had been a
"huge" number of respondents. But in addition, there was a vast array of
light manufactures that the armed forces obtained from local industry. In
the early 1900s, for example, the army bought shoes, dishes, building
materials, and paper from domestic companies. The navy, for its part,
was doing business on the eve of World War I with more than sixty firms,
excluding shipbuilders, that provided scores of products, from acids, inks,
and soap to carbon paper and wire. Early in the war Captain Estevão Leitão
de Carvalho, a "young Turk" and member of General Caetano de Faria's
staff, persuaded footwear manufacturers to make special boots for the
army modeled on those worn by German troops. By the 1920s the military was acquiring, besides those items, myriad other articles, among them
iron beds, nails, canvas, khaki, silverware, glass, and rain gear.[49]

The owner of the Usina Esperança, one of the two prewar steel mills,
failed to secure official assistance for his proposal to expand his operations to include the manufacture of projectiles,[50] but the Bras administration did later award a contract to a small plant that managed to supply
several hundred tons of iron to the army before going bankrupt. During
Calógeras's tenure as minister, moreover, he and Castro e Silva devised a
sizable building program that was farmed out largely to the construction
firm owned by Roberto Simonsen. Simonsen ultimately built more than
forty barracks and several hospitals and depots, relying on various civilian suppliers (and the United States) for materials.[51] Fleming used his
authority as head of the navy's Diretoria de Armamento during this period to establish ground-breaking contacts with industrialists interested
in possible contracts for artillery projectiles. Of greater practical significance was the navy's cooperation with private shipyards. Already at the
turn of the century it had given contracts for the assembly or construction
of smaller vessels because of the reduced cost of civilian work and also,
according to the navy minister, in order to encourage the industry. The
leading private yard was Lage & Irmãos, later the Companhia Nacional
de Navegação Costeira (CNNC), which continued to receive contracts in
ensuing years. As a result of a plea by the CNNC in 1915, the government
eliminated import duties on naval construction materials, and subsequently
it established a system of cash prizes for ships built domestically. Having
pressed several Lage vessels into government service during the war, the
Bras administration persuaded Congress in 1918 to help defray the cost
of new facilities for the CNNC, whose defense work continued throughout the 1920s.[52] The aviation industry, of course, was in its infant stage
everywhere, so it was apparently not until the late 1920s that serious discussion of the feasibility of domestic production began. In mid-1927 the

FMM urged the establishment of a plant to build airplanes designed to use French engines, and the army's air director pushed the idea, suggesting that the high command try to interest civilian entrepreneurs.[53]

In the broad view of the evolution of Brazil's military-industrial complex, the Old Republic looms as a key period not so much because of the statistics of production (which are not available) and actual material achievements, but because of the emergence then of a growing realization of the need for greater defense modernization and autonomy. It was also during that period that important questions about defense production were first raised and answers supplied that, by and large, would satisfy ensuing generations. That more was not accomplished was the result primarily of factors beyond government control. The takeoff in military production and military-civilian industrial cooperation had to await increased centralization of political authority, the onset of true industrialization, and the recruitment of broader sectors of the political and industrial elites to the cause of military autonomy, developments that would occur under the stimulus of depression and war during the Vargas era.

The intensified official campaign to develop a national industrial-military capacity after 1930 was a function in large part of elite perceptions of the somber challenges of the period. The aggressive behavior of Japan in Asia, Italy in Africa, and Germany in Europe posed, in the eyes of both military and civilian leaders, an implicit threat to Brazil, and instability in South America, where war raged between Bolivia and Paraguay for three years, was an immediate and grave menace. Brazilian analysts attributed to historic adversary Argentina major responsibility for that conflict, which they regarded as part of a systematic encirclement policy on the part of Buenos Aires that was intended to weaken Brazil politically and economically. At the same time, Argentina's energetic military buildup was cause for special disquiet.[54]

Brazil's own capabilities remained extremely limited and military spokesmen worried constantly about the armed forces' lack of equipment and weaponry. "We are disarmed and Argentina's military superiority over us is incontestable," exclaimed Chief of Staff Tasso Fragoso in 1931. The civil war the following year laid bare the military's logistical weaknesses, and throughout the remainder of the decade the high command sounded a constant alert about the lack of preparedness, a phenomenon stressed by foreign experts as well. Minister of War Eurico Dutra summed up the pervasive disgruntlement in 1938 when he labeled the army "a painful fiction."[55] If the army was ill-equipped for combat, the navy was virtually useless. Comparative analyses of Brazilian and Argentine strength left policymakers bitterly pessimistic. The nation's maritime defense, warned the Estado-Maior da Armada (EMA) in 1931, rested "almost exclusively" on the two prewar battleships since the rest of the units simply had "no value." The maneuvers of 1935 revealed the pathetic condition of most of the fleet, leading Admiral Henrique Guilhem, the minister of navy, to warn Vargas in 1936 that it was "no longer a factor of combat."[56]

The need for matériel of all kinds was patent, but the options remained limited. The first priority, because of the speed of execution and domestic industrial weakness, was to place orders abroad, but national experience in this regard continued to be frustrating. The navy met with irritating rebuffs in 1931 and 1932 when it sought aid from the U.S. and British governments, and a new naval program in 1933–34 met with similar problems. The State Department actively discouraged U.S. shipbuilders from bidding for contracts, arguing that Brazil's expenditures might spur a naval race in South America and would reduce the amount of money available to that country for "necessary purposes." The attitude of European governments was less paternalistic, but difficulties arose when Brazil's financial situation forced it to insist on barter-like (compensation) arrangements that would allow it to pay for ships essentially with raw materials, which brought negotiations back to square one.[57]

Washington's attitude seemed to change in 1935 when certain officials, including Franklin Roosevelt, gave repeated assurances that Brazil would be able to purchase soon-to-be-decommissioned cruisers. Early in 1936, however, Argentine authorities got wind of the negotiations, and their protests, coupled with the worsening European situation, led Washington to renege on its pledges to Brazil, causing a resentful Vargas government to sound London about acquiring destroyers and to close contracts with Italian builders for three submarines.[58] The final humiliation in naval negotiations with the United States came in 1937 when, after proposing to lease six aged destroyers to Brazil, the Roosevelt administration once more backed down because of an outcry from Buenos Aires. Disillusioned Brazilian authorities immediately opened talks with European suppliers, signing contracts at the end of 1937 for the construction of three destroyers in England. But here, too, the disadvantages of dependence were made painfully clear: less than three weeks after the outbreak of World War II, the Foreign Office informed Itamaraty that the British government had requisitioned the destroyers.[59]

The army's experience with dependence during the period was likewise frustrating. The São Paulo revolt in 1932 forced army leaders to scramble to acquire munitions and hardware abroad. The French government, bowing to public pressure, refused to honor a contract for ammunition, while the State Department delayed delivery of airplanes in order to avoid "embarrassing incidents," such as the bombing of towns. In all, Rio de Janeiro placed orders in eight countries, but did not take delivery of the vast bulk of the matériel until the fighting was over.[60] Efforts to acquire artillery during the general era were similarly disappointing. Financial problems caused lengthy delays in negotiations and it was not until 1937 that the first contract for field artillery was signed with Krupp, which agreed to deal on a compensation basis. The following year Krupp received a major contract for delivery of approximately nine hundred pieces of artillery over six years, but once again Brazilian plans ran afoul of foreign troubles: Berlin in 1940 requisitioned important segments of the orders, while the British blockade hindered, and ultimately prevented, shipments of other consignments for which Rio de Janeiro had made advance payments.[61]

The primary reason that Brazilian interest in German arms remained keen after war had spread across Europe was that there were no alternative suppliers. Washington, despite its heavy pressure on Rio de Janeiro after 1939 to participate effectively in its hemispheric defense program and despite firm promises from Roosevelt himself that it would help equip Brazil's armed forces, failed to provide effective assistance until 1942. All that the War Department offered in 1939–40 were small British-made mobile guns of World War I vintage that had never been fired, for which there was neither ammunition nor ballistic information available, and which U.S. ordnance experts admitted were earmarked to be "cut up and sold as junk."[62] So desperate was Brazil's situation that Rio de Janeiro nonetheless ordered nearly a hundred of the cannon. It then took Washington over a year to deliver them and it was not until late 1942 that Brazil succeeded in obtaining six thousand rounds of ammunition from England. Aside from these weapons, the only modern matériel sent to Brazil by the United States before Pearl Harbor consisted of "a few searchlights and a token shipment of automotive equipment and light tanks."[63]

Brazilian leaders made no secret of their resentment at being led down what Chief of Staff Pedro de Góes Monteiro called a "trail of promises" during 1940–41—the ambassador in Washington complained in "scathing" terms to the State Department at one point in 1940—and in 1942, after breaking relations with the Axis in January, their disgruntlement heightened. Dutra not only complained to Vargas, but vented his irritation within the officer corps as well.[64] Eventually, after a fitful start in which the State Department worked hard to overcome the reluctance of harried War Department planners, U.S. aid finally started to flow, albeit slowly and not in the quantities desired by Brazilian authorities, who found themselves forced into the war in August by German submarine attacks.[65]

What made arms dependence all the more unpalatable was the knowledge that Brazil's defense supplies were governed by the interests of other governments and could be jeopardized by events beyond its control. The

Italo-Ethiopian crisis combined with a desire on Washington's part to appease Argentina, for example, had blocked the transfer of U.S. ships in the mid-1930s. The European war then had interrupted the delivery of ships and cannon. And the very existence of arms negotiations with Washington after 1939 was primarily a function of U.S. and not Brazilian strategic concerns; that is, the sudden U.S. interest in Brazilian defense stemmed from preoccupation with the northeastern bulge, which Washington judged vulnerable to Nazi machinations aimed at the United States, whereas the chief threat to Brazil, in the eyes of planners in Rio de Janeiro, came from Argentina.[66] Washington's anxiety about the Axis challenge in Brazil became even more dramatic after Pearl Harbor, which was the motive for the renewed commitment to arm Brazil. But what would happen if the U.S. priorities changed? When Allied forces landed in North Africa in November 1942, virtually eliminating the remote possibility of an Axis intrusion into the Northeast, Brazil's bargaining power plummeted. Leitão de Carvalho, now a general and Brazil's senior military negotiator in Washington, quickly alerted Vargas to probable difficulties in obtaining hardware as a consequence, setting in motion a process of discussion that culminated in a proposal by Rio de Janeiro early in 1943 to prepare an expeditionary force for possible service in Europe—all as a means of ensuring continued deliveries of U.S. arms to bolster defenses vis-à-vis Argentina.[67] Rio de Janeiro, in other words, was compelled to undertake a major policy demarche, one that it had not planned to make, because of its dependence upon a foreign power for the means of national defense.[68]

Despite that gambit, Brazil's participation in the war obviously was incidental to victory. Late in 1943, U.S. military spokesmen cautioned that the demands of more urgent theaters would have to be satisfied before Brazil's, a possibility that once more generated alarm in Rio de Janeiro. Again, Brazil's defense preparations apparently were jeopardized by external factors beyond national control. Fortunately, in this case, Washington's growing interest in a postwar aviation agreement, and especially sudden disquiet in the United States over a revolution in Bolivia seemingly effected with the connivance of Buenos Aires, sustained deliveries to Brazil.[69] That assistance, however, failed to meet Brazilian expectations. In April 1944, Vargas wrote personally to Roosevelt reminding him of Argentine obstructionism and asking for extensive naval aid, but Roosevelt's reply two months later was that the "strategic situation" did not permit transferral of the ships. The lesson again was clear: Brazil's rearmament program remained at the whim of foreign strategic concerns. The end of the war in Europe drove the point home when Washington informed Rio de Janeiro that Lend-Lease assistance could be continued only to those allies at war with Japan, a warning that obligated Vargas to go through the farce of declaring war on that country in June 1945 in the vain hope of maintaining the flow of U.S. equipment.[70]

The commonsense conclusion that Brazilian leaders drew from their experience with arms dependence after 1930 was that national security demanded greater military-industrial autonomy. The Vargas government consequently launched a determined and remarkably successful campaign for general industrialization in which security considerations played an important role.[71] With specific regard to defense production, Vargas, two months after taking power, promised military leaders that his regime would make "the greatest efforts" to develop war industries, and in ensuing years the need to do so became gospel in policy-making circles.[72] Because of the economic crisis the accomplishments of the 1930s were modest, but a significant start was made. Early in 1931 a special military commission, headed by (Captain) Sylvio Raulino de Oliveira, was set up to survey the country's metallurgical establishments in order to determine which might be able to furnish items to the armed forces, a move that helped to define needs and possibilities. The Pirelli affiliate in São Paulo, for example, displayed an interest in military contracts for electrical and rubber articles, while the Belgo-Mineira reported that, with the proper equipment and government financial assistance, it could manufacture cannon and machine guns.[73]

Later that same year Vargas created the Comissão Nacional Siderúrgica (CNS), or National Steel Commission, a mixed civilian-military body under the jurisdiction of the Ministry of War, to examine the export and industrial possibilities of Brazil's iron ore resources. Oliveira and his colleague on the metallurgical commission, (Captain) Edmundo Macedo Soares e Silva, represented the army on the CNS, whose members also included Calógeras and a naval officer. One immediate accomplishment of the CNS was to persuade Vargas to ban the exportation of scrap metals. Used steel, especially in the form of discarded rails, would be excellent raw material for artillery shells, Macedo Soares explained. The military experts felt no sense of urgency regarding implantation of the so-called *grande siderurgia*. Asked for an opinion about the possible revision of Farquhar's contract, they argued emphatically that the questions of ore exports and steel should be separated. The only defense requirement that might be made of a steel concessionaire, said the CNS, after consulting the EME and EMA, would be steel for naval construction. Indeed, said the CNS in February 1932, the eight mills then operating could produce all the low-technology steel that was needed; the only impediment was a lack of markets. The high command was thus more interested in protecting and expanding existing mills than in creating a new complex. The Belgo-Mineira could meet the present requirements of army factories, wrote General Benedito Silveira, head of the EME in 1934, and long-range general military needs should be carefully gauged and then farmed out "as much as possible" to existing plants.[74]

In addition to the metallurgical and steel commissions, Vargas early in 1932 established another to study the feasibility of installing an aircraft plant in Brazil, but its work was interrupted by the São Paulo revolt that year. The civil war forced the central authorities to make an emergency industrial effort that required great improvisation,[75] at the same time that it left government leaders all the more determined to strive for more military-industrial self-sufficiency. At the end of the conflict, new machinery was ordered from Germany to equip federal plants to make ammunition, rifle barrels, and artillery shells, and in May 1933 a special military commission sailed for Europe to make additional purchases and study war industries there. Late that same year, Vargas, explaining that a "military-industrial complex" (*parque*) would, besides its defense functions, serve as a stimulus to steel production and to "subsidiary civilian industries," decreed the establishment of three new federal war plants. At the same time the aircraft study group, urged on by the EME, resumed its work.[76]

When Góes Monteiro, the most outspoken critic of national military weakness, assumed the portfolio of war in January 1934, one of his first acts was to instruct the commission in Europe to hasten the purchase of machinery for the new federal factories. What the government really needed, he officially told Vargas twice in March, was a national policy of autonomous defense production, and by the middle of the year his staff had devised an army reorganization scheme designed, in the twisted English of the U.S. military attaché, to "make Brazil as nearly self-sufficient for war materials as could be had." To help finance the plan, Góes Monteiro's friend General Pantaleão Pessoa, head of the Casa Militar, urged in vain the establishment of a special military fund through increased consumer taxes, remonstrating that development of defense industries was an "imperious necessity."[77] The difficulties of financing a rearmament program, of course, were what led at this time to barter negotiations with potential European suppliers.[78]

Within severe budget constraints, the government intensified its military-industrial program in subsequent years. Army plants, using new machinery from Germany, produced artillery shells, bombs, rifle barrels and parts, explosives, fuses, signal rockets, and gas masks in increasing quantities. The army's air branch organized an assembly plant that by the late 1930s was turning out small numbers of planes of Brazilian design that used U.S. engines.[79] Most of the army's public share—secret credits were also involved—of the five-year plan that Vargas promulgated in

January 1939 was earmarked for defense plants.[80] The navy during this period had moved to end the hiatus in national construction since the empire by laying the keel of a monitor at the recently completed AMIC in June 1936. A year later, armed with blueprints obtained from Washington and secret credits, the Ministry of Navy began assembly of three destroyers—work enormously handicapped by a lack of skilled laborers. Over the next two years not only the monitor but six minesweepers as well were launched. Since shipbuilding played the major role in the navy's long-range program, 60 percent of its share of the five-year plan was destined for the two arsenals in Rio de Janeiro, the AMIC and the old naval yard. By the end of the decade, furthermore, the navy had completed at the Galeão air base assembly of more than a score of Fokk-Wolf training planes, which it had started in 1936 with German technical assistance and engines.[81]

Plans for an aircraft factory matured during this period as a project of the Ministry of Transportation, headed by Colonel João Mendonça Lima. Military experts decided that it would be best to place the undertaking in the hands of private industry. They selected the future site of the plant—Lagoa Santa, a backwater village located on a small lake in Minas Gerais—and in September 1938 opened public bidding. According to government terms, the contractor would have to use Brazilian materials whenever possible, give priority to official orders, and allow military and federal civilian personnel to serve apprenticeships in the factory. The only bidder was Construções Aeronáuticas, a Franco-Brazilian company in Rio de Janeiro, whose offer was accepted in September 1939.[82]

During the 1930s the army made significant progress toward eliminating one of the critical bottlenecks in military production: the absence of technicians. Late in 1930 it established its Escola Técnica, where many of the specialists who later staffed factories and industrial laboratories were trained. Aside from courses in metallurgy, chemistry, electricity, armaments, and the like, the Escola brought in guest lecturers—(Major) Macedo Soares spoke there on "Industrial Mobilization" in 1937—and provided field experience, that is, visits to, and apprenticeships in, civilian firms. Since the equipment and technology for defense plants had to be imported, Dutra decided in mid-1937 to create military commissions in the major arms-exporting countries whose primary tasks included arranging technical courses or apprenticeships in foreign industries for Brazilian officers. On the eve of World War II, the high command gave priority in its technical training program to engineers who specialized in armaments, chemistry, and metallurgy.[83]

During the years that preceded the war, military planners defined an industrial policy that, without major modification, would remain Brazil's approach in ensuing decades. The critical concept and goal underlying the program was "nationalization," by which they meant not only domestic manufacture of an increasing range of articles, but all possible utilization of national raw materials or semifinished components. In 1933 the minister of war decreed that the use of imported raw materials in army plants was "definitively prohibited" except in cases of "manifest impossibility." A "Study Committee for the Use of National Raw Materials" was set up under Oliveira to determine such cases, and thereafter army planners with increasing success pushed consumption of domestic resources. The DMB was especially anxious about such critical industrial materials as copper, lead, aluminum, and zinc, urging their production "at any price" in order to reduce imports. The relevant war plants during the mid-1930s began using locally produced acids, lubricating oils, and low-grade steel.[84] In the campaign for nationalization, the high command had in Vargas not only a firm ally but a watchdog on the alert for lapses.[85] The constitution that he announced late in 1937 to launch the Estado Novo contained an article calling for the "progressive nationalization" of all industries deemed "basic or essential to the nation's economic or military defense," and the terms of the subsequent bidding for the Lagoa Santa project reflected the government's general intentions. In the spring of 1939, as the European situation worsened, Dutra instructed General Sylvio Portella, head of the DMB, to make an all-out effort to increase the use of Brazilian products, and Portella passed the word along to the directors of war plants. In dealing with civilian manufacturers, Portella added, preference should be given to those that utilized national ingredients.[86]

Military leaders during the 1930s studied carefully the question of the relationship between the state and private industry in the area of national defense and, in general, they reached the same conclusions that colleagues had during the Old Republic. Góes Monteiro's plans in 1934 for "industrial mobilization" and the vital allied issue of metallurgical production prompted emphatic arguments that industrial activity was best reserved to the private sector, with the military logically assuming the role of technical superviser in the case of defense contracts. Dutra, then head of the air branch, vigorously championed the integration of civilian manufacturers into defense work, arguing, with regard to the future airplane factory, that if it could not count on domestic industrial support, it would be of little interest to national defense. Oswaldo Aranha, as minister of finance (1931–1934), had supported the new government war plants, but he was "radically opposed" to federal production of aircraft, artillery, machine guns, and the like. "Private industry, having guaranteed consumption, [and] with small initial favors, can and should manufacture all this and with great advantages," he told a receptive Góes Monteiro in

1935. For General Pessoa, chief of staff that year, continued government initiative was necessary in the first stage of creating an industrial defense establishment, especially in areas of little appeal for private companies and in order to form a reservoir of technical skills. As he commented to Vargas, the state had to "take the lead and prepare officers and workers capable of adapting and utilizing private industry in time of war."[87] The high command logically opposed the idea of an official steel company, advocating instead that, when the time came to set up a large-scale complex, the government have a controlling interest.[88]

To help determine what might be obtained from industry, military planners not only surveyed metallurgical installations early in the decade, but the Ministry of War also ordered the creation of a confidential register of all firms that made munitions, explosives, and arms. The army air branch, to define "air industrial mobilization" possibilities, sent questionnaires to more than twenty-six hundred companies in 1934, and by the end of the decade its new "industrial mobilization section" maintained files on some thirty-five hundred establishments, while the navy's Diretoria de Armamento kept similar track of manufacturers in a position to handle defense work for the fleet.[89] By the outbreak of war in Europe, army leaders divided industries into two broad categories: those that turned out only war supplies, and those that produced, or could produce, for both civilian and military consumption. The latter group, which included "especially all basic industries," was to be left "entirely in the hands of the civilians," although military technicians would be at the disposal of both classes of industry. The armed forces actually would prefer to leave all production to the civilian sector, Portella explained, admonishing his subordinates to take all steps to share armaments technology with private manufacturers. Aside from furnishing technical information, machines, and even engineers, the army supported cooperative firms with contracts and it endorsed their applications for tax exemptions and federal loans. The statutes of the Banco do Brasil, in fact, were modified in April 1939 to permit it to underwrite the establishment of private factories that were judged necessary for national defense by the EME or EMA and were approved by Vargas.[90]

A wide range of companies collaborated with the armed forces during the 1930s. When civil war broke out in 1932, military authorities, lacking virtually everything in sufficient quantities, hastily appealed to the private sector for myriad articles, from clothing to bombs. So intense was the need and the cooperation that the EME recommended creation of an emergency "technical organ especially designed to supervise industrial mobilization." Manufacturers on the Paulista side were mobilized by the Federação das Indústrias do Estado de São Paulo (FIESP), under the leadership of Simonsen, and made a prodigious effort to supply the rebel troops with everything from uniforms to makeshift armored cars, a promising sign of military industrial potential. During Góes Monteiro's sixteen months as minister of war, the high command actively sought to encourage firms whose activities were endorsed by the raw materials committee. A report by (Major) Oliveira's metallurgical study group in 1934 pointed out that civilian industry could furnish the steel for rifle barrels and artillery shells, and, with the army's technical aid and contracts, laminated nonferrous metals. In the latter regard, the committee specifically had in mind the Matarazzo organization in São Paulo, which had indicated an ability to provide laminated aluminum, copper, tin, lead, and zinc. At the same time, Dutra's air branch gave orders to civilian manufacturers for tools, fuses, and parts; later, as minister, he awarded contracts to various suppliers, among them a manufacturer of tires and steel wheels, a steel producer, and a recently founded electrochemical company in Rio de Janeiro that used strictly national raw materials and not only received army contracts, but had its request in 1938 for a government loan endorsed by the EME and the Conselho de Segurança Nacional.[91] Throughout the period the Ministry of War facilitated the importation of chemicals, acids, fuses, and other products by firms that made explosives, matches, and similar items.[92] For their part, naval authorities originally wanted to farm out the construction of minesweepers to private yards, but found none in a position to do so on acceptable terms. Nonetheless, Admiral Guilhem advised Vargas early in 1940, the private sector was furnishing "a great variety" of products to the navy, and São Paulo manufacturers were going to supply all the electrical material for the destroyers the navy was then building.[93]

By 1940 civilian industries collaborating with the military included the electrochemical company in Rio de Janeiro and one in Rio Grande do Sul that furnished copper items; a firm in Minas Gerais that supplied aluminum; the Laminação Nacional de Metais, a Paulista enterprise controlled by the Matarazzo interests that made semimanufactured articles and parts; the Belgo-Mineira and another mill in Minas Gerais that were selling over a hundred tons of steel a month to the army; the Companhia Nitro-Química Brasileira (CNQB), which made cellulose and was studying, with army technicians, the possible establishment of a factory to produce synthetic nitric acid: two gaucho plants that manufactured items for weapons and munitions; four companies in São Paulo that had army contracts to supply the first nationally made machine tools; the Nansen firm in Belo Horizonte and one in São Paulo that made precision parts; a

Paulista munitions plant; textile mills in Santa Caterina; Pirelli, which had a near monopoly of the manufacture of electrical transmission materials and which supplied the armed forces "on a larger scale"; and the Mesbla corporation, organized that year under U.S. license and with military contracts, Brazil's first parachute factory.[94]

The spread of war across Europe gave powerful impetus to developmentalism in Brazil, and this perforce had increasing military dimensions. War-created restrictions and possibilities now forged a broader alliance between the private sector and the military. Simonsen, speaking for the FIESP, suggested more intense cooperation in mid-1940, sparking the interest of the EME and leading to a nationwide survey of industrial facilities and stocks of raw materials by the Conselho Federal de Comércio Exterior to determine mobilization possibilities.[95] "Buy domestic" was the admonition from the Ministry of War and the Conselho de Segurança Nacional to other ministries in 1941, while army spokesmen made specific appeals to industry for defense production and Portella's DMB strove to help cooperative manufacturers secure critical raw materials from the United States.[96] Following Pearl Harbor, the pressure from the high command on civilian administrators for expanded war production was continuous, and in 1942 Vargas decreed a series of measures designed to discipline the economy according to military requirements. As Góes Monteiro put it at a meeting of generals in September, the government had to increase industrial output "everywhere and by all means."[97]

Military assistance to private firms during the war followed prewar guidelines, with the additional benefits of draft exemptions for workers and more intense technical aid.[98] The CNQB, through the army's influence, obtained special freight rates, tax exemptions, a Banco do Brasil loan, and a contract for guncotton. Later in the war the army worked out an arrangement with the CNQB, whose majority stockholder was the Klabin family in São Paulo, for the establishment of a trotyl plant and vigorously defended the project against the argument of Finance Minister Artur Souza Costa that it would be best to create a state monopoly of munitions production.[99] In another instance, the Ministry of War offered one Roland Laraque a contract to establish an arms and machinery factory. The contract, ratified by the Conselho de Segurança Nacional, obligated him to maintain a workers' training school, allow army apprentices to work in the factory, and import only items not available in the domestic market; in return, he was to enjoy exemption from import duties and would have guaranteed government orders during a sixteen-year period.[100] In other cases the army championed loans for chrome, zinc, copper, and aluminum plants, and pushed long-term contracts for artillery shells with a Paulista firm to which it rented U.S. Lend-Lease machinery, for detonators and shell casings with the Nansen company, and for grenade casings with a steel mill.[101] To replace its antiquated Hotchkiss automatic weapons, the army in 1943 devised a plan for the manufacture of Madsen machine guns by Laminação Nacional de Metais.[102] During the same period the Ministry of War, interested in binoculars and range finders, threw full weight behind a civilian engineer named Décio Vasconcellos, who first landed a contract to make telescopes and then elaborated, with military support, plans to set up an optical instruments factory.[103]

The Lagoa Santa project had possessed military dimensions from the very beginning. The contract between the Ministry of Transportation and Construções Aeronáuticas, signed in 1940 for the building of the Fábrica Nacional de Aviões (FNA) was a fifteen-year cost-plus arrangement. The government guaranteed the company a 15 percent profit on its orders and granted it the standard exemptions from sales and import taxes. After its creation in January 1941, the Air Ministry placed an officer in charge at Lagoa Santa and used special credits to speed up construction. The plan was to start assembling and gradually manufacture, under license with the North American Aviation Corporation, single-engine primary trainers beginning late in 1943. Supply shortages in the United States, political problems,[104] and financial difficulties caused delays, but by the end of the war the FNA had started to turn out planes for the Air Ministry, which had increased its orders and made advance payments in order to help the company.[105]

Activity in federal war plants was substantial, as output reached an all-time high in 1942 and then increased another 60 percent the next year.[106] The high command became involved in several new federal or federally controlled projects, most actively of course in those that promised some tangible military benefits within a relatively short period. The famous Volta Redonda steel enterprise, in part a Ministry of Transportation undertaking, was not an immediate priority of military leaders, but they supported it. Army technicians, such as Macedo Soares, were involved in early negotiations with Washington for loans, equipment, and technical assistance, and (Colonel) Oliveira, who also took part in those negotiations, was invited in 1942 to become vice president of the Companhia Siderúrgica Nacional, a mixed enterprise organized to execute the project. "The purchase of its equipment," the colonel wrote to Vargas, "is for the country's economic defense what that of armaments is for its military [defense.]."[107] Plans for a national engine factory, the Fábrica Nacional de Motores (FNM), bore fruit during the war, despite difficulties in importing U.S. equipment. Colonel Antonio Guedes Muniz, an army engineer, was the driving force behind the project, which belonged to the Ministry of Transportation and was designed to turn out Curtiss-Wright engines.[108]

Late in the war the high command's major industrial goal was the acquisition of complete arms factories from the United States, a possibility raised by Brazilian negotiators in Washington in 1943. Dutra and his advisers wanted to avoid further direct state undertakings, if possible, so they sounded civilian firms about running any such factories and the response was positive. The Conselho de Segurança Nacional was enthusiastic about the venture, judging it a "very rare" opportunity to reduce dependence on "problematical" foreign suppliers. Once again the Ministry of Finance suggested that the projected factories might better be run as "state or parastate" enterprises, but Vargas backed the military.[109] The plan was included the following year in joint negotiations with Washington for weapons standardization, but then U.S. interest in the scheme dissipated with the end of the war.[110]

Elite perceptions of external challenges and national needs changed little in the period of renewed international instability generated by the collapse of Germany and Japan in 1945. The world, Foreign Minister João Neves da Fontoura wrote in 1946, "is mad, with few possibilities of cure." The Cold War, with its manifold repercussions around the globe, was an ominous development. "We are going through a period similar to that which preceded Munich," warned Aranha from his new post at the United Nations in 1947, voicing a widespread conviction in Brazilian policy-making circles.[111] Military leaders during the Dutra presidency (1946–1950) attentively followed East-West antagonisms and feared another general conflagration; at least, they sensed, the West was in for a protracted siege. The outbreak of war in Korea in 1950 only deepened their pessimism.[112] Within the hemisphere the historic threat from La Plata assumed a sharper profile as the Juan Perón regime aggressively sought to forge a neutralist bloc of Spanish-speaking countries as a counterweight to Brazilian and U.S. influence. Especially disturbing were Argentina's military preparations, including the continued expansion of defense industries.[113] If the threat remained clear, so did the necessary response: just as in the crisis-laden prewar years, Brazil had to beef up its armed forces and modernize its equipment.[114]

The national experience with arms dependence also did not change in the postwar era, much to the disgruntlement of Brazilian leaders. Negotiations with the North Americans in 1944–45 had raised hopes, but Lend-Lease aid quickly dried up. By December 1945 the new navy minister was complaining that Washington's attitude had "modified the situation completely," while a Ministry of War spokesman cautioned the U.S.

embassy that resentment was festering within the high command over the delay in executing rearmament commitments, a sign that Washington was "inclined to treat Brazil as a small brother, rather than an important nation pledged to full military cooperation." As the State Department and Congress successfully fought against a program of postwar military aid to Latin America, Brazilian dissatisfaction heightened. While Argentina was expanding its military potential, Minister of War Canrobert Pereira da Costa groused in 1947, Brazil was still waiting for matériel "solemnly promised" by Washington more than two years before.[115]

The Korean crisis laid bare once more the various disadvantages of dependence. The high command hoped to capitalize on U.S. insistence on emergency hemispheric mobilization to transform Brazil, with Washington's aid, into the "second great industrial center" of the Americas, one that could supply finished goods "to ourselves and to our allies, including the United States." The Estado-Maior das Forças Armadas, a postwar creation then headed by Góes Monteiro, foresaw expanded production of not only steel, textiles, chemicals, machinery, and nonferrous metals, but a wide range of arms and munitions as well. All three services elaborated specific industrial requests: the air force wanted raw materials and semimanufactured items in order to continue building planes at Lagoa Santa and Galeão, and it sought machinery to enable the FNM to turn out "vital parts" for airplane engines and combat cars; the army hoped to acquire equipment, loans, and technology to develop nonferrous metals and increase production of arms and munitions; and the navy placed priority on equipment to make cannon, torpedoes, depth charges, mines, and electronic apparatuses.[116] U.S. mobilization, however, made acquisition of materials for war plants both problematical and expensive, if not impossible.[117] Hardware, too, especially on a preferential basis, was difficult to secure. In one revealing episode, it took a direct complaint to President Harry Truman to close a contract for two used cruisers promised before the Korean conflict began; even so, actual delivery was made only after much greater delay and cost than originally projected because of the war-generated demands on U.S. repair yards.[118] None of the plans formulated by Navy Minister Renato Guillobel (1951–1954) to purchase ships from the United States proved feasible, a fact that led him at one point to threaten not to renew the contract of the U.S. Naval Mission. As for the army, its difficulties in obtaining matériel were compounded by Rio de Janeiro's refusal to contribute troops for the UN effort in Korea.[119]

Dissatisfaction with dependence on the United States in the postwar period led to intensified efforts to diversify sources of supply, as well as to expand domestic military production. The army in 1947 opened negotiations with Bofors, the Swedish armaments firm, for artillery, subsequently placing orders, and later it prodded the government about trying to obtain Krupp arms to fulfill the prewar contracts. During Vargas's second presidency, after unsatisfactory discussions with Washington, the air force in 1952–53 purchased sixty jet fighters from Great Britain on a compensation basis, with cotton the item of exchange. And Admiral Guillobel, in his frustration over financial difficulties and fruitless pleading with U.S. authorities, acquired landing craft and transport vessels in compensation transactions with Holland and Japan, and he ordered warships from France.[120]

The real goal, however, remained the achievement of greater military-industrial autonomy, an oft-heard theme of postwar elite commentaries. The admonition by General João Amorim e Mello, secretary general of the Conselho de Segurança Nacional in 1949, that steps be taken to remove all obstacles to national industrialization reflected military priorities.[121] The central idea behind the establishment of the Escola Superior de Guerra (ESG) that year was that industrialization was the key to national security. "Consequently," recalled General Idálio Sardenberg, one of the organizers of the ESG, "the country needed to create the means by which it could manufacture its weapons in the future." The goal of the ESG, which became the most influential articulator of the ideology of development, was to inculcate, particularly among civilian elites, the doctrine that national security and industrialization were inseparable. In other words, the message that the ESG sought to transmit to political and business circles was, as Sardenberg put it: "We need to have national arms and we want you to help us in this regard. We believe that, freeing ourselves from the importation of arms, we will be a country with greater international authority."[122] That conviction, of course, underlay the decision to give priority to industrial cooperation in talks with Washington regarding mobilization to meet the Korean crisis.[123] "What we want and aspire to," Minister of War Newton Estillac Leal publicly explained in 1952, "is a Brazil that with its own means satisfies its defense needs." Vargas, the following year, candidly said that his development program had "security" as one of its main objectives and that the Conselho de Segurança Nacional "continuously" studied the "civilian," that is, industrial, aspects of that linkage.[124]

The strategy of military-industrial development in the postwar period followed closely the guidelines established earlier. It now became rigid policy of the services, for example, before placing orders abroad or authorizing the importation of war-related materials by private firms or police agencies, to try to locate a suitable domestic product.[125] Because much of Brazil's hardware was U.S. made or, in the case of the navy and air force, constructed in Brazil with U.S. materials, and because some machinery and industrial raw materials were not available inside the country, they were not always successful,[126] but the point is that domestic industry had priority in the armed forces' procurement policies. Technical expertise was a central ingredient in military self-sufficiency; the army, consequently, strove to improve its technical training program, creating specialized courses in war matériel, for example, and it sent larger numbers of engineers to Europe and the United States.[127] The Ministry of War at the same time imported European technicians and engineers for its defense plants. "Although the state should not be the main producer of war matériel," Pereira da Costa wrote in justification, ". . . to the state falls the study of prototypes and the analysis of the effects of weapons and their modifications, using . . . its factories as laboratories for experimental industrial production."[128] An important postwar endeavor was the establishment of the Marambaia weapons-testing center, an "essential element" of a military-industrial sector, said Góes Monteiro, who, as minister of war in 1946, also created a new Departamento Técnico e de Produção do Exército (DTPE) to oversee defense production.[129]

Efforts to cut technological corners were not always successful. The high command's keen interest in importing from Germany, France, and the United States complete factories for making arms, steel, and military vehicles, for instance, brought no immediate results, probably because army leaders could find no civilian entrepreneurs willing to face the responsibility and risks in assuming ownership, as Pereira da Costa insisted.[130] To avoid "our remaining tributaries of the North American market," the army hoped to obtain "a few" munitions plants from the United States, but the State Department's reluctance and postwar inflation forced a reduction of the scope of the program to machinery for a single plant and also delayed the undertaking until the early 1950s.[131] An army plan in 1949 to purchase thirty thousand semiautomatic Belgian rifles did clear the Conselho de Segurança Nacional and the Ministry of Finance without great difficulty because the proposed contract called for the cession of patents, blueprints, and machine tools to permit local manufacture.[132] The high command attached special significance to the contract with Bofors for antiaircraft guns because it included a similar provision and thus would make it possible, Pereira da Costa exulted in 1947, for the army to "create" a national cannon industry. The contract also allowed Brazilian army officers to undergo technical training in Bofors plants in Sweden. The AGRJ early in 1954 turned out the first cannon and by the end of that year "three great industrial establishments" were working on the initial order of fifty guns.[133]

Naval planners during the postwar years concentrated first on finishing construction of six destroyers begun earlier by the Lage yard. Several smaller vessels were also built in the "new" Arsenal da Marinha, a fusion of the AMIC and the old arsenal, and by 1950 the high command had formulated plans for torpedo and artillery factories,[134] the latter becoming a pet project of Guillobel, who negotiated with Bofors for the arming of the corvettes purchased from Holland and for the cession of patents so that future artillery could be manufactured in Brazil. The transfer of technology, in fact, became a cardinal principle in Guillobel's negotiations with foreign suppliers. The contracts for corvettes and landing craft awarded to Japanese and Dutch firms required standardization of motors and the opening of a branch factory for the manufacture of spare parts, while the agreement for French warships stipulated that half the vessels would be assembled in Brazil and that all of them would be armed with Bofors guns.[135] As for the Air Ministry, its major endeavors were establishment of the Parque Aeronáutico in São Paulo and construction of the Centro Técnico da Aeronáutica in São José dos Campos (São Paulo), which, according to the 1946 project, would include "great laboratories for the development of industries in general" and which was completed in 1953.[136]

The armed forces continued to figure prominently in mixed ventures such as the Companhia Siderúrgica Nacional, where various army engineers were assigned and which (General) Oliveira eventually headed.[137] The FNM, under a plan devised by (General) Muniz, was transformed in the late 1940s into a mixed company with the state controlling a majority of the shares. While continuing to do repair work on aircraft engines, the FNM began converting to the production of agricultural machinery, truck motors, and automotive parts. Then, with an army colonel as president of the company and another colonel and admiral on the board of directors, it signed a contract with Alfa-Romeo for the assembly and gradual manufacture of trucks, in increasing stages of nationalization beginning in 1952. The first year, with equipment and technical assistance from the Italian corporation, the FNM turned out a thousand trucks. In mid-1953, furthermore, it signed a contract with an Italian consortium led by Fiat for the manufacture of tractors.[138] The interest of the military in petroleum development has been assessed, but it is worthy of note here that the president of the Conselho Nacional de Petróleo was an army colonel.[139]

Civilian manufacturers benefited substantially from the assistance or interest of the armed forces during the first postwar decade. Contacts between the military and industry were continuously broadened. In view of the widespread international instability, the high command intensified its now permanent study of the mobilization and conversion potential of private industry, extending significantly its statistical coverage in 1950.[140] Military and industrial representatives worked closely together on various agencies and councils involved in promoting general economic development, such as the Conselho Federal de Comércio Exterior, directed by General Anápio Gomes in the late 1940s, the Joint Brazil-United States Development Commission (1950–1953), the ESG, of course, and the Comissão de Desenvolvimento Industrial (CDI), established in 1951. Colonel and soon-to-be-general Carlos Berenhauser Júnior was president of the CDI's subcommittee charged with stimulating "nonexistent or insufficient" industries, a group whose members included (General) Macedo Soares and that actively encouraged import substitution.[141] It was a subcommittee headed by Commander Lúcio Meira that drew up the plan in 1952 for creating an automobile industry by imposing progressive restrictions on imports of automotive parts and banning after July 1953 the importation of complete vehicles.[142]

Admiral Guillobel, both as director of the AMIC during the Dutra presidency and subsequently as minister, insisted as a matter of policy on leaving manufacturing activities to civilian firms. In the 1950s he pressed for and obtained a special Naval Fund, which in part was intended to stimulate industry through naval procurement. The Fund was never as large as the navy desired, but Guillobel and his subordinates assiduously cultivated closer ties with the private sector, opening a purchasing office in São Paulo and holding personal meetings and discussions with industrial representatives.[143] The Air Ministry continued to support the Lagoa Santa plant with contracts in the postwar period, and it also granted orders for light planes to a new company set up in São Paulo.[144]

The Ministry of War, working through its new Diretoria de Fabricação (Department of Manufacturing), a division of the DTPE, naturally intensified its efforts to integrate key elements of the private sector into its industrial program. "The cooperation of private industry is gaining daily in importance and becoming increasingly more necessary," Pereira da Costa commented to Dutra early in 1949.[145] In one case, the high command pushed through a Banco do Brasil loan for a Paulista machinery firm that had agreed during the war to set up a plant for the manufacture of artillery casings, made advance payments on orders, insisted in 1948 on a multiyear contract for the company, and, in effect, kept it afloat in the early 1950s despite its general financial weakness and the strong opposition of the Banco do Brasil.[146] Another São Paulo enterprise that had established a small branch for producing grenade casings received successive contracts as well as army backing for import tax exemptions and cargo space on federal railroads.[147] Engineer Décio Vasconcellos, destined to be a pioneer in the optical instruments field, landed a ten-year contract for binoculars at the end of the war. The Ministry of War also smoothed the way for him to bring over Italian and German technicians, while General Pereira da Costa personally wrote to the governor of São Paulo in support of Vasconcellos's bid for state financing and intervened to facilitate importation of equipment for the firm. By 1950, Vasconcellos had supplied more than eighteen thousand sets of binoculars to the army and was employing two hundred fifty technicians. When he asked the government to increase its orders, the EME argued that it was a "patriotic duty" to assist him.[148]

During this same period the Ministry of War, among other steps to aid individual establishments, urged sales tax exemptions for its orders with ammunition companies;[149] worked out a plan with the CNQB for the expanded production of caustic soda and synthetic nitric acid;[150] supported another firm engaged in a similar venture by giving it contracts, ensuring that it received scarce fuel oil, and endorsing its import of materials;[151] purchased electrical items from Pirelli;[152] placed repeated orders with Nansen for grenades;[153] provided technical assistance to a company that wanted to start manufacturing industrial explosives, and gave contracts to several others for fuses, shells, grenades, and arms;[154] licensed myriad firms all over the country, including Matarazzo, to import special industrial raw materials;[155] pressed Itamaraty and the Ministry of Labor for work permits and visas for European technicians destined for private industry;[156] and offered general encouragement to producers of aluminum, steel, special textiles, and glass.[157]

Some of the above-mentioned and similar measures encouraged, and others were a result of, the formulation by the EME of a broad plan late in the Dutra administration for civilian manufacture of war matériel. The matter was urgent from a military standpoint, said the EME, and would bring general "economic advantages" in the form of reduced dependence. Both the Ministry of Finance and the Conselho de Segurança Nacional, which late in 1949 had called for general measures of support for industries "of interest to national security," blessed the plan early in 1950.[158] Details of the program are not known, but its execution required funds, and correspondence among the high command, the Ministry of Finance, and Vargas reveals constant budgetary problems. Indeed, early in 1954, Minister of War Cyro Espírito Santo Cardoso pleaded for the creation of a Special National Defense Fund to overcome the difficulties in meeting the army's needs. Vargas at this time reported that private firms had received military contracts the previous year totaling more than 56 million cruzeiros, but budgetary impediments still threatened manufacture of war items in ensuing months, at least in the quantities sought by army leaders. Vargas's last minister of war complained strongly in June about cuts in army allocations and warned that the "rhythm" of defense production inevitably would be lessened.[159]

By the end of the Vargas era something important clearly had occurred in the military-industrial sector during the preceding quarter of a century. Before the Revolution of 1930, Brazil neither built nor assembled airplanes, naval construction was exceedingly limited, and its few arms and munitions plants were poorly equipped, inadequately manned, and their range of activities severely circumscribed, focusing primarily on small-arms cartridges and weapons repair. The role of the private sector in defense production was minimal, and was limited to light manufactures and low-technology items. Under the impact of grave international challenges in the 1930s and 1940s, however, national leaders gave systematic emphasis to industrial "mobilization" as a means of strengthening the country against external threat. The supreme goal of autonomy was a distant one, but at every hand they sought to reduce dependence on overseas arms' markets whose interests, history had demonstrated, often diverged from Brazil's. The collaboration of private industry was judged vital to a modern system of national defense; indeed, military authorities throughout the first half of the century were firmly opposed, both as a matter of principle and on practical grounds, to extensive state industrial activity. That was why, especially after 1930, military authorities, while expanding the output of indispensable federal plants, energetically strove to attract an increasing variety of private firms to defense work through contracts, loan endorsements, tax favors, and technical assistance. Directly responsible for defense tasks, the high command logically stressed industrial projects with more immediate military application. In Vargas's case, a long-range vision of economic greatness conditioned his policies and allocation of resources, but he was also acutely sensitive to the urgent necessity of defense production and in that regard he and his military counselors marched shoulder-to-shoulder. By the mid-1950s an array of civilian factories was cooperating with the armed forces, and projects such as the automotive industry were under way that would open up new dimensions for military production. Clearly the experience of World War II and the manifold threats posed by the Cold War had convinced increasing segments of the elite that it was necessary to give an industrial character to national preparedness. The Vargas era was thus crucial to the definition of the concept of "security and development," Brazil's national motto since the 1950s.

Notes

1. David Harvey, "Latin America and North American Arms," *Defense & Foreign Affairs Digest*, 7 (1979), 16.

2. Joaquim Nabuco to D. Alves Ribeiro, Nov. 6, 1899; Nabuco to Nilo Peçanha, Oct. 15, 1906, Arquivo Nacional (hereinafter cited as AN), Rio, Joaquim Nabuco Papers; Brazilian Minister (Washington) to Ministério das Relações Exteriores (hereinafter cited as MRE), Jan. 31, May 18, 1900, Palácio Itamaraty (Rio), Arquivo Histórico do Itamaraty (hereinafter cited as AHI); Brazilian Minister (Montevideo) to Baron of Rio Branco, Nov. 27, 1902; Nabuco to Rio Branco, Sept. 2, 1902, Jan. 18, 1908, AHI, Rio Branco Papers; Federal Deputy Laurindo Pita, speech, June 7, 1904, in Julio Noronha, *Programa Naval de 1904* (Rio, 1950), p. 155; Gen. Pedro Ivo Henriques, *Os Arsenaes de Guerra da República* (Rio, 1912), p. 11; Lt. Col. Augusto Villeroy, memo, July 20, 1908, Ministério da Guerra (hereinafter cited as MG), Rio, Arquivo do Exército (hereinafter cited as AEX); Ambassador Domicio da Gama (Washington) to João P. Calógeras, Nov. 23, 1911; Gama to Hermes da Fonseca, Dec. 29, 1911, Instituto Histórico Geográfico e Brasileiro (hereinafter cited as IHGB), Rio, Domicio da Gama Papers (hereinafter cited as Gama Papers).

3. Percy A. Martin, *Latin America and the War* (Baltimore, 1925), pp. 30–106; Thomas E. Skidmore, *Black into White: Race and Nationality in Brazilian Thought* (New York, 1974), pp. 149–161; Adm. Carlos Souza e Silva to MRE, Apr. 21, 1925, AHI; Stanley E. Hilton, "Brazil and the Post-Versailles World: Elite Images and Foreign Policy Strategy, 1919–1929," *Journal of Latin American Studies* (hereinafter cited as *JLAS*), 12 (Nov. 1980), 342–344.

4. MRE to Brazilian minister (Santiago), Nov. 22, 1901, AHI; Brazil, Cámara dos Deputados, *Mensagens Presidenciaes* (hereinafter cited as *Mensagens*), 4 vols. (Rio, 1912–22), I, 364, II, 19; Rio Branco to Minister of War (hereinafter cited as MW), Mar. 9, 1906, AEX; Afonso M. Pena to Fonseca, June 24, 1908, AN, Afonso M. Pena Papers (hereinafter cited as AMP); Rio Branco to José Carlos Rodrigues, Aug. 21, 1908, IHGB, José Carlos Rodrigues Papers (hereinafter cited as JCR); Rio Branco to Pena, Dec. 11, 1908, AN, Afonso Pena Jr. Papers (hereinafter cited as APJ).

5. Minister of Navy (hereinafter cited as MN) to Rio Branco, Mar. 12, 1904; Rio Branco to MN, May 2, 1904, Mar. 11, July 27, 1905, AHI; Rio Branco to MW, Feb. 8, 1908, AEX; E. Bradford Burns, *The Unwritten Alliance: Rio Branco and Brazilian-American Relations* (New York, 1966), pp. 40–49.

6. MRE circular, Aug. 23, Dec. 10, 1927, AHI; Hilton, "Brazil and the Post-Versailles World," 346.

7. Seward Livermore, "Battleship Diplomacy in South America, 1905–1925," *Journal of Modern History*, 16 (Mar. 1944), 31–45; Fonseca to Pena, Feb. 22, 1908, AMP; Ruy Barbosa to Pena, May 7, 1908, AMP; Burns, *Unwritten Alliance*, pp. 143, 185.

8. Estado-Maior da Armada (hereinafter cited as EMA) to MN, May 28, 1915, Ministério da Marinha (hereinafter cited as MM), Rio, Arquivo da Marinha (hereinafter cited as AM); Brazilian Military Attaché (Buenos Aires) to Estado-Maior do Exército (hereinafter cited as EME), Oct. 2, 1917, Oct. 12, 1918, AEX; Souza e Silva, memo, Nov. 10, 1917, Museu da República (Rio), Nilo Peçanha Papers (hereinafter cited as NP); Souza e Silva, memo ("A Situação Sul-Americana"), Aug. 1918, AHI.

9. Souza e Silva to MN Raul Soares, Aug. 10, 1920, Centro de Pesquisa e Documentação de História Contemporânea (hereinafter cited as CPDHC), Rio, Raul Soares Papers (hereinafter cited as RS); United States Military Attaché (Rio) to War Department (hereinafter cited as WD), May 23, 1922, July 30, 1925, Na-

tional Archives (hereinafter cited as NA), Washington, Record Group (hereinafter cited as RG) 165, Records of the WD General Staff, docs. 2657-K-13, 2006-6-1; Gen. Nestor Passos to Artur Bernardes, Aug. 6, 1926, APJ; Hilton, "Brazil and the Post-Versailles World," 348–350.

10. Frederick M. Nunn, "Military Professionalism and Professional Militarism in Brazil, 1870–1970: Historical Perspective and Political Implications," *JLAS*, 4 (May 1972), 33; Gen. Miguel Girard to Prudente de Morais, July 22, July 24, 1897; Gov. M. F. de Campos Salles (São Paulo) to Morais, July 28, 1897; Gen. Artur Andrade Guimarães to MW, Aug. 5, 1897, IHGB, Prudente de Morais Papers. See, too, Raimundo de Menezes, *Vida e Obra de Campos Salles* (São Paulo, 1977), pp. 136–137; Celis Debes, *Campos Salles: Perfil de um Estadista* (São Paulo, 1977), pp. 71–72; Tristão de Alencar Araripe, *Expedições Militares contra Canudos: Seu Aspecto Marcial* (Rio, 1960), p. 221.

11. Fonseca to Pena, Oct. 12, 1906; Rodolfo Paixão to Pena, Dec. 9, 1907, AMP; Rio Branco to Gama, Dec. 15, 1908, Gama Papers; *Mensagens*, I, 284–285, 339, 362–363; Commander, Division of the North, to EMA, Apr. 5, 1918; EMA to MN, June 22, 1918, AM. On the campaign in the south, see José Maria Bello, *A History of Modern Brazil 1889–1964*, trans. by James L. Taylor (Stanford, 1966), p. 224.

12. Calógeras, *Problemas de Administração: Relatório Confidencial Apresentado em 1918 ao Conselheiro Rodrigues Alves* [. . .], 2d ed. (São Paulo, 1938), p. 119; Augusto Tasso Fragoso to Military Attaché Alfredo Malan (Paris), Mar. 10, 1919, in Tristão de Alencar Araripe, *Tasso Fragoso: Um Pouco de Historia do Nosso Exército* (Rio, 1960), p. 481; Calógeras to Epitácio Pessoa, Jan. 4, 1922, IHGB, Epitácio Pessoa Papers (hereinafter cited as EP). Cf. Souza e Silva to Soares, Apr. 2, 1920, RS; MG, *Relatório Apresentado ao Presidente da República* [. . .] *1920* (Rio, 1920), p. 28. For additional insights into the military's effectiveness during this general period, see Frank D. McCann, Jr., "The Nation in Arms: Obligatory Military Service during the Old Republic," in Dauril Alden and Warren Dean, eds., *Essays Concerning the Socioeconomic History of Brazil and Portuguese India* (Gainesville, 1977), pp. 211–243.

13. Hilton, "Brazil and the Post-Versailles World," 346–347.

14. The story is told in Neil Macaulay, *The Prestes Column: Revolution in Brazil* (New York, 1974). As the campaign dragged on, one general expressed the fear that the idea of federal military inadequacy was "taking root in the public mind." Passos to Bernardes, Aug. 6, 1926, APJ. For a field commander's lament about material deficiencies, see Gen. Alvaro Mariante to MW Fernando Setembrino de Carvalho, May 19, 1926, AEX.

15. MM, *Relatório* [. . .] *1906* (Rio, 1906), p. 5; Brassey, *The Naval Annual 1909* (Portsmouth, 1909), p. 39; Brassey, *The Naval Annual 1914* (Portsmouth, 1914), p. 58; MM, *Relatório* [. . .] *1920*, p. 27; MG, *Relatório* [. . .] *1901* (Rio, 1901), pp. 152–153; Gerhard Brunn, *Deutschland und Brasilien 1889–1914* (Cologne, 1971), pp. 265–266.

16. Hermes da Fonseca Filho, *Marechal Hermes* (Rio, 1961), pp. 75–79; MW to Brazilian Military Commission in Europe, Feb. 17, Apr. 10, Apr. 29, 1909, June 10, 1911, AEX; Calógeras to MRE, May 31, 1920, AHI; memo ("Stellungnahme der Fried. Krupp . . ."), n.d. [1938], NA, Department of State (hereinafter cited as DS), Microfilmed Records of the German Foreign Ministry (hereinafter cited as RGFM), roll 229, frame 194559; Gerhard Brunn, "Deutscher Einfluss und deutsche Interessen in der Professionalisierung einiger lateinamerikanischer

Armeen vor dem 1. Weltkrieg (1885–1914)," *Jahrbuch für Geschichte von Staat, Wirtschaft und Gesellschaft Lateinamerikas*, 6 (1969), 332, 334.

17. MW to Minister of Finance (hereinafter cited as MF), Jan. 11, Mar. 2, May 5, June 15, 1916; Calógeras to Diretor de Contabilidade (MG), Oct. 31, 1919, AEX; Col. Anápio Gomes, "O Problema do Equipamento," *Revista de Intendência*, 16 (Jan.–Feb. 1942), 5.

18. Calógeras to Brazilian Military Commission in Europe, Jan. 3, 1922, AEX; Pantaleão da Silva Pessoa, *Reminiscências e Imposições de uma Vida, 1885–1965* (Rio, 1972), p. 54.

19. Calógeras to Brazilian Military Commission in Europe, Jan. 23, 1920; Passos to EME, May 17, 1927, AEX; Nelson Lavanère-Wanderley, *História da Força Aérea Brasileira*, 2d ed. (Rio, 1975), pp. 33, 60, 67, 78, 99.

20. MF to Pena, Nov. 18, Dec. 7, 1905; Calógeras to Pena, Nov. 29, 1905; Pena to Senator João Pinheiro da Silva, Dec. 11, 1905; Pena to David Campista, Aug. 3, 1908, May 5, 1909; Brazilian Chargé (Paris) to Pena, Oct. 30, 1908; Sen. Arnolfo Azeredo to Pena, Aug. 12, 1908; Pena to MN, Nov. 11, 1908; Fonseca to Pena, Nov. 15, 1908, AMP; Rio Branco to Gama, Dec. 15, 1908, Gama Papers.

21. United States Naval Attaché (Rio) to Office of Naval Intelligence, Apr. 12, 1923, RG 59, General Records of the DS, doc. 832.34/177; Rothschild & Sons to Rodrigues, Jan. 12, 1915, JCR; José Caetano de Faria to Setembrino de Carvalho, Jan. 29, 1915, CPDHC, Fernando Setembrino de Carvalho Papers (hereinafter cited as FSC). On the financial crisis of the 1920s, see Annibal Villela and Wilson Suzigan, *Política do Governo e Crescimento da Economia Brasileira, 1889–1945* (Rio, 1973), p. 155.

22. E. Pessoa, "Os Trabalhos da Ilha das Cobras," *Jornal do Comércio* (Rio), Apr. 16, 1933; Bernardes to Setembrino de Carvalho, Oct. 27, 1922, FSC; Bernardes to Soares, Nov. 23, 1922, RS; Artur Bernardes, *Mensagem Apresentada ao Congresso Nacional* [. . .] *1925* (Rio, 1925), pp. 99–100; Gen. Hastimphilo de Moura (Diretoria de Material Bélico [hereinafter cited as DMB]) to MW, Feb. 1, 1924, AEX; Setembrino de Carvalho, *Memórias: Dados para a História do Brasil* (Rio, 1950), pp. 262–263; Tasso Fragoso, "A Revolução de 1930," in Araripe, *Tasso Fragoso*, p. 525.

23. Capt. Pargas Rodrigues, "Matériel de Artilharia Francez e Alemão," *A Defesa Nacional* (hereinafter cited as *ADN*), I (Jan. 1910), 117.

24. Murilo Ribeiro Lopes, *Rui Barbosa e a Marinha* (Rio, 1953), pp. 120–121; MG, *Relatório* [. . .] *1900* (Rio, 1900), pp. 57–58; Comissão Técnica Militar, memo, Apr. 28, 1906, NP; *ADN*, I (Feb. 10, 1914), 165; *ADN*, I (Mar. 10, 1914), 206.

25. Egydio Castro e Silva, *As Indústrias Militares em Nosso País: Conferências no Clube Militar em 1916* (Rio, 1940), p. 86; MW to Brazilian Military Commission in Europe, May 11, 1909, June 10, 1921, AEX.

26. *Mensagens*, III, 294; MM, *Relatório* [. . .] *1920*, p. 27.

27. This happened, for example, in the case of two battleships sent to the United States for refurbishing at the end of World War I, where small cannon were installed, but once the initial stock of projectiles had been fired, it proved impossible, despite lengthy negotiations, to obtain more, which forced the navy to seek suppliers in Europe. In another instance, a U.S. firm sold torpedoes to the navy in 1923, but none of them was test-fired for more than two years because the company failed to deliver the explosive charge. Secretary of Navy to DS, June 29, 1928, RG 59, 832.34/207.

28. Foreign Minister (hereinafter cited as FM) to MW, Jan. 28, 1915, AEX; MG, *Relatório* [. . .] *1916* (Rio, 1916), p. 9; MG, *Relatório* [. . .] *1917* (Rio, 1917), pp. 12–13.

29. U.S. Chargé (Rio) to DS, Apr. 13, 1917; Secretary of War to DS, July 30, 1917; DS to U.S. Chargé (Rio), Aug. 8, 1917, RG 59, 832.24/8, 20; Lt. Col. Alípio Gama (Comissáo Militar Brasileira de Estudos e Compras nos Estados Unidos), "Primeiro Relatório Parcial [. . .] Julho de 1918" (typewritten), AEX; MW to FM Peçanha, Jan. 4, Nov. 4, 1918, NP; Calógeras to Brazilian Military Commission in Europe, Mar. 22, Mar. 23, Apr. 25, 1921, AEX; Calógeras to MRE, May 31, 1920; MRE to Brazilian embassy (Paris), June 25, 1920, AHI.

30. *ADN*, I (May 10, 1914), 241–242; *ADN*, 2 (Oct. 10, 1914), 31.

31. DS, *Foreign Relations of the United States 1924*, 2 vols. (Washington, D.C., 1939), I, 323–326 (hereinafter cited as *FRUS*, year).

32. MN to FM, Apr. 20, 1922; Admiral José Penido (Paris) to MRE, July 15, 1922; Souza e Silva to FM Felix Pacheco, Apr. 15, 1924, Mar. 4, 1925; Pacheco to Ambassador Afrânio de Melo Franco (Geneva), June 13, 1925, AHI; unsigned memo ("Opinião Naval Brasileira sobre a Limitação de Armamentos"), n.d. [1926], Felix Pacheco Papers (private), Rio; Estevão Leitão de Carvalho, *Memórias de um Soldado Legalista* (Rio, 1962), II, 144–145.

33. MG, *Relatório* [. . .] *1903* (Rio, 1903), p. 7; *Mensagens*, I, 619, II, 32, 371, III, 37, 135, 292, 477, 485; MG, *Relatório* [. . .] *1915* (Rio, 1915), p. 13; MG, *Relatório* [. . .] *1916*, p. 9; MG, *Relatório* [. . .] *1917*, p. 13; *Boletim Mensal do Estado Maior do Exército*, II (Jan.–Feb. 1917), 7.

34. *Mensagens*, IV, 77, 188, 314, 443; Col. Francisco Moraes (Intendente da Guerra), "Relatório Apresentado ao Diretor de Administração da Guerra [. . .] no Anno de 1919" (mimeo), AEX; Capt. Artur Pamphiro, "Indústria Militar," *ADN*, 10 (Feb. 10, 1923), 551–552; Setembrino de Carvalho, *Memórias*, p. 242; Souza e Silva to MRE, Apr. 15, 1924, AHI; MM, *Relatório* [. . .] *1924* (Rio, 1924), pp. 9–10, 53–54; MM, *Relatório* [. . .] *1925* (Rio, 1925), pp. 48–50; Bernardes, *Mensagem* [. . .] *1926* (Rio, 1926), p. 152.

35. João P. Magalhães, *A Evolução Militar do Brasil* (Rio, 1958), pp. 336–337; *Mensagens*, I, 515; Egydio Castro e Silva, *A Margem do Ministério Calógeras* (Rio, 1962), pp. 181–182; Castro e Silva, *Indústrias Militares*, pp. 83–87; MG, *Relatório* [. . .] *1901*, p. 233; *ADN*, I (May 10, 1914), 258–259, (Aug. 10, 1914), 366.

36. Estevão Leitão de Carvalho, *Discursos, Conferências e Outros Escritos* (Rio, 1965), pp. 207, 210; *Mensagens*, II, 371.

37. MG, *Relatório* [. . .] *1901*, pp. 153, 178; *Mensagens*, I, 284, 338, 516; MG, *Relatório* [. . .] *1911* (Rio, 1911), p. 88; Castro e Silva, *Ministério Calógeras*, pp. 186–187; *Mensagens*, III, 477.

38. MM, *Relatório* [. . .] *1900* (Rio, 1900), p. 63; Thiers Fleming, *A Mudança do Arsenal de Marinha do Rio de Janeiro* (Rio, 1914), pp. 13–22, 129–168; Afonso Arinos de Melo Franco, *Rodrigues Alves: Apogeu e Decleinio do Presidencialismo*, 2 vols. (Rio, 1973), II, 486–488.

39. Thiers Fleming, *O Novo Arsenal de Marinha na Ilha das Cobras* (São Paulo, 1927), pp. 21, 30; memo ("Proposta dos Snrs. Armstrong, Whitworth and Co. Ltd. e Vickers Ltd."), May 22, 1918; British minister to Peçanha, June 18, 1918, NP; *Mensagens*, IV, 314; Fleming to Soares, Jan. 17, 1920; Souza e Silva to Soares, June 23, 1920, RS; Presidential Secretary to E. Pessoa, Feb. 9, Apr. 1, 1921, EP; Pessoa, "Os Trabalhos da Ilha das Cobras."

40. MG, *Relatório* [. . .] *1903*, p. 7; *Mensagens*, I, 514; MG, *Relatório* [. . .] *1907* (Rio, 1907), p. 13; MG, *Relatório* [. . .] *1916*, p. 10; Castro e Silva, *Ministério Calógeras*, pp. 30–32.

41. Calógeras, *Problemas de Administração*, p. 66; Calógeras to Col. José Leite de Castro (Paris), Mar. 6, 1922, AEX; *Mensagens*, IV, 629; Thiers Fleming, *Carvão, Munições e Navios* (Rio, 1927), p. 49.

42. *Mensagens*, III, 477; MM, *Relatório* [. . .] *1924*, p. 9; Fleming, *Carvão*, passim.

43. MG to MF, Feb. 17, June 3, 1916; Calógeras to Delegado do Tesouro Brasileiro (London), Jan. 31, Mar. 20, 1920, AEX; Castro e Silva, *Ministério Calógeras*, pp. 147–174; Castro e Silva, *Indústrias Militares*; Calógeras to Pena, July 29, 1899, AMP; MG (Calógeras), *Relatório* [. . .] *1920*, p. 52; Calógeras to E. Pessoa, n.d. [1922], *Mensagens*, IV, 629.

44. Calógeras to Pena, Nov. 1, 1906, Apr. 2, 1907, Aug. 8, 1908, AMP; Cámara dos Deputados, [Resolution] N. 197–1907, NP; Fonseca Filho, *Marechal Hermes*, pp. 189–190; Castro e Silva, *Indústrias Militares*, pp. 53–54; Capt. Duarte Huet de Bascellar, lecture ("Indústria de Guerra e Marinha de Guerra"), Escola Naval, May 28, 1902, in Duarte Huet de Bacellar, *Problemas Navais* (Rio, 1952), p. 38; MM, *Relatório* [. . .] *1904*, p. 19 (annex); MM, *Relatório* [. . .] *1917* (Rio, 1917), p. 4; MM, *Relatório* [. . .] *1918* (Rio, 1918), pp. 24, 26.

45. Lt. Col. Democrito Silva to Fonseca, Dec. 14, 1908; Antonio Mendes Teixeira to Leite de Castro, Mar. 17, 1931, AEX; Fleming, *Carvão*, p. 70.

46. MG, *Relatório* [. . .] *1919*, pp. 33–40; Elysio de Carvalho, *Brasil Potência Mundial* (Rio, 1919), p. 5; *Mensagens*, III, 37, 477, IV, 78, 188; Bernardes, *Mensagem* [. . .] *1926*, p. 152; Law 4632, Jan. 6, 1923, *Coleção das Leis* [. . .] *do Brasil de 1923*, 2 vols. (Rio, 1924), I, 36;" Memorial Apresentado pela Itabira à Comissão Militar de Estudos Metalúrgicos," n.d. [1931]; Teixeira, memo ("Ante-Projeto de uma Usina Siderúrgica em Angra dos Reis"), Dec. 11, 1922, AEX. For a survey of steel development during the period, see Humberto Bastos, *A Conquista Siderúrgica no Brasil* (São Paulo, 1959), pp. 101–129. On Percival Farquhar and the Itabira project, see Charles A. Gauld, *The Last Titan, Percival Farquhar* (Stanford, 1964).

47. Cámara dos Deputados, [Resolution] N. 197–1907, NP; MG (Fonseca), *Relatório* [. . .] *1908* (Rio, 1908), p. 89; Henriques, *Os Arsenaes de Guerra*, pp. 5–10; Castro e Silva, *Indústrias Militares*, pp. 125–127; Calógeras, *Problemas de Administração*, pp. 98–101; Teixeira, "Ante-Projeto." Editorialists for the nationalist military review *ADN*, launched by the "young Turks" before the war, energetically opposed state industrial activity in the 1920s, arguing instead that public authorities, in the case of defense-related manufactures, should make "judicious concessions" to private entrepreneurs. "Necessidades Industriais da Defesa Nacional—A Indústria Civil e Militar e os Arsenaes de Guerra," *ADN*, 10 (Apr. 10, 1923), 570–571.

48. Bacellar, "Indústria Siderúrgica e Marinha de Guerra," p. 38; Bacellar, "O Novo Arsenal de Marinha," *Jornal de Comércio*, Feb. 24, 1906, in ibid., p. 43; Fleming to [?] Marques, Apr. 12, 1912, in Fleming, *A Marinha de Guerra em 1912* (Rio, 1954), p. 17; Fleming, *Carvão*, p. 54; MM, *Relatório* [. . .] *1924*, pp. 54–57.

49. MG, *Relatório* [. . .] *1900*, p. 54; MW to MF, June 2, June 8, June 12, 1893, AEX; MM, *Relatório* [. . .] *1913* (Rio, 1913), pp. 59–69 (annex); Leitão de

Carvalho, *Memórias*, I, 202; memo ("Cópia da Demonstração Enviada ao Congresso Nacional"), Sept. 12, 1921, EP.

50. J. J. de Queiroz Júnior (Usina Esperança), memo, July 10, 1909, NP. Among other things, Queiroz Júnior asked for prepaid orders, customs favors, and free transportation on federal railroads.

51. *Mensagens*, III, 477; Calógeras to Diretor de Contabilidade (MG), Dec. 18, 1919, Jan. 6, Feb. 26, 1920, AEX; Castro e Silva, *Ministério Calógeras*, pp. 89–115; Roberto Simonsen, *A Construção dos Quarteis para o Exército* (São Paulo, 1931).

52. Fleming, *Carvão*, pp. 76–78, 97–98, 106–107; MM, *Relatório* [. . .] *1900*, p. 65; Henrique Lage to MF, May 5, 1921, EP.

53. Mission Militaire Française, "Rapport au sujet de l'aviation: Programme de matériel et organisation de la fabrication nationale" (typewritten), June 28, 1927; Mariante (Diretoria de Aviação) to MW, June 22, Aug. 2, Oct. 15, 1928; EME to MW, Feb. 23, 1929, AN, Pedro de Góes Monteiro Papers (hereinafter cited as PGM).

54. Brazilian Naval Attaché (Buenos Aires) to EMA, May 12, June 3, 1936, AM; Brazilian Ambassador (Buenos Aires) to MRE, July 28, 1936, Mar. 9, 1939; Brazilian Ambassador (Berlin) to MRE, May 19, 1936, Aug. 14, 1937, May 7, 1938, MRE to MG, Feb. 25, 1932, July 31, 1937, Mar. 3, 1938, AHI. Elite perceptions of general international conditions in the 1930s are documented in Stanley E. Hilton, *Brazil and the Great Powers, 1930–1939: The Politics of Trade Rivalry* (Austin, 1975), pp. 5–15.

55. Tasso Fragoso to MW, Oct. 29, 1931, IHGB, José Carlos de Macedo Soares Papers (hereinafter cited as JCMS); MW to MF Oswaldo Aranha, Dec. 12, 1932, CPDHC, Oswaldo Aranha Papers (hereinafter cited as OA); Gen. Pedro de Góes Monteiro to Getúlio Vargas, Aug. 29, 1934; Gen. João Gomes Ribeiro to Góes Monteiro, Oct. 29, 1935, PGM; Gen. Eurico Dutra to MF Artur Souza Costa, Feb. 10, 1938, CPDHC, Artur Souza Costa Papers (hereinafter cited as ASC). See, too, Hilton, *Brazil and the Great Powers*, pp. 111–121.

56. Admiral Augusto Souza e Silva to FM Afrânio de Melo Franco, Jan. 7, 1931, Biblioteca Nacional (Rio), Afrânio de Melo Franco Papers (hereinafter cited as AMF); EMA to MN, Oct. 29, 1931, JCMS; MM (Henrique Guilhem), "Relatório [. . .] 1936" (typewritten), n.d. [Jan. 8, 1937], AN, Coleção Presidência da República (hereinafter cited as PR).

57. EMA to MN, Nov. 6, 1931, JCMS; MN to MRE, Nov. 24, 1931; Brazilian Ambassador (Washington) to MRE, Dec. 1, 1931; Brazilian Ambassador (London) to MRE, Dec. 23, 1931, Dec. 30, 1932, AHI; United States Ambassador (Rio) to DS, Dec. 1, 1931; DS to United States Ambassador (Rio), Dec. 1, 1931; DS memoranda, Dec. 6, 1933, Mar. 15, Aug. 15, 1934, RG 59, 832.24/213, 236; Public Records Office (London), Records of the Foreign Office (hereinafter cited as RFO), docs. A1417/979/6, AH064/979/6, A7797/979/6, A1658/267/6; J. Samuel White & Co. to Souza Costa, Sept. 19, 1934, ASC; Stanley E. Hilton, "Military Influence on Brazilian Economic Policy, 1930–1945: A Different View," *Hispanic American Historical Review* (hereinafter cited as *HAHR*), 53 (Feb. 1973), 78–80.

58. Aranha (Washington) to Vargas, Jan. 18, May 3, May 28, 1935, Jan. 10, Feb. 27, 1936, CPDHC, Getúlio Vargas Papers (hereinafter cited as GV); Ambassador Alexander Weddell (Buenos Aires) to DS, Mar. 18, Mar. 20, 1936, RG 59,

832.24/264, 265; Weddell to Secretary of State Cordell Hull, Mar. 20, 1936; Undersecretary of State Sumner Welles to Hull, Mar. 31, 1936, Library of Congress, Cordell Hull Papers, box 38, folder 88; Welles to Franklin D. Roosevelt, Mar. 25, 1936, Franklin D. Roosevelt Library (Hyde Park), Franklin D. Roosevelt Papers (hereinafter cited as FDR), Official File 366; Aranha to Vargas, May 27, 1936, OA; Ambassador Hugh Gibson (Rio) to Welles, July 17, 1936, Hoover Institution (Stanford), Hugh Gibson Papers, box 48, Welles folder; EMA to Guilhem, June 17, 1936, AM; MRE to Brazilian Ambassador (London), Sept. 3, 1936, AHI; British Naval Attaché (Rio) to Director of Naval Intelligence (London), Oct. 28, 1936, RFO 371, A987/251/6. On the Italian contract, see Hilton, "Military Influence," 89–90.

59. Aranha to Vargas, July 19, 1936; Vargas to Aranha, July 21, Aug. 6, 1936, GV; Macedo Soares to Vargas, Jan. 26, 1937; Welles to Macedo Soares, Feb. 10, 1937, JCMS; Souza Costa to Aranha, Aug. 18, 1937, OA; Brazilian Ambassador (Berlin) to Auswärtiges Amt, Aug. 12, 1937, RGFM 229/194511; MM, "Relatório [. . .] 1937–1938–1939" (typewritten), AM; British Ambassador to MRE, Sept. 18, 1939, AHI. The general outlines of the destroyers episode of 1937 are traced in Bryce Wood, "External Restraints on the Good Neighbor Policy," *Inter-American Economic Affairs*, 16 (Autumn 1962), 3–24.

60. EME to MW, July 12, 1932, AEX; MW to Aranha, July 21, July 31, 1932; Aranha to Banco do Brasil (hereinafter cited as BB), July 27, Aug. 10, Aug. 18, Aug. 25, Sept. 3, 1932, OA; MW to FM, July 23, July 28, Aug. 16, Aug. 25, AEX; DS memo, Sept. 7, 1932, RG 59, 832.248/64; United States Military Attaché (Rio) to WD, Feb. 2, 1933, Jan. 1, 1934, RG 59, 832.24/78, 87.

61. Hilton, *Brazil and the Great Powers*, pp. 118–129, 186–190; German Ambassador to FM Aranha, Apr. 11, 1940, AHI; Aranha to Vargas, Jan. 2, 1941, OA; Dutra, "Boletim Especial Secreto," n.d. [Jan. 1941], GV; British Ambassador to Aranha, Dec. 6, Dec. 15, 1940, AHI. According to Dutra, Brazil took delivery of only one eighth of the 1938 contract, yet it made payments valued at 35 percent more than the matériel received. Souza Costa to Vargas, Aug. 1943, PR. On the British blockade and German arms shipments to Brazil, see Frank D. McCann, Jr., *The Brazilian-American Alliance, 1937–1945* (Princeton, 1973).

62. Aranha to Vargas, Feb. 14, 1939; Monteiro to Vargas, July 7, 1939; George C. Marshall to Góes Monteiro, Oct. 5, 1939, GV; Lt. Col. Lehman Miller to Lt. Col. [?] Buchman, Sept. 11, 1939, George C. Marshall Institute (Lexington, Va.), George C. Marshall Papers, box 58, folder 13; Herbert Feis (DS) to Welles and Hull, Oct. 30, 1939, RG 59, 832.24/180; Ordnance Office (WD) to Assistant Chief of Staff, Feb. 14, 1940, RG 165, 309-T-25.

63. Stetson Conn and Byron Fairchild, *The Framework of Hemisphere Defense* (Washington, D.C., 1960), pp. 268, 271, 302.

64. Góes Monteiro to Dutra, Nov. 13, 1940, MG (Rio), Arquivo do EME (hereinafter cited as AEME); DS memo, Aug. 27, 1940, RG 59, Office of American Republics Affairs, Brazil Memoranda, vol. 3; Góes Monteiro to Dutra, Aug. 28, 1940; Dutra to Vargas, Nov. 20, 1940, Feb. 25, 1942, AEME; Miller to Lt. Col. Arthur Wilson (WD), quoted in Wilson to Marshall, May 12, 1941, Marshall Papers, 58/14; MG (Dutra), "Boletim Especial Secreto n. 10," Mar. 23, 1942, OA.

65. Dutra to Souza Costa, Mar. 24, 1942, AEME; Air Minister Pedro Salgado Filho to Ambassador Jefferson Caffery, Oct. 27, 1942; Salgado Filho to Adm. Jonas Ingram, Oct. 29, 1942, AN, Pedro Salgado Filho Papers (hereinafter cited as PSF).

66. The closest thing to a national war plan that Brazil possessed· was one elaborated in 1937–38 and predicated on a surprise attack by Argentina, and from the beginning of politicomilitary negotiations with Washington in 1939, Brazilian army leaders insisted on their concept of strategic priorities. Aranha, wartime foreign minister, candidly told Caffery in mid-1941 that his major worry was that Argentina might attack Brazil if the latter openly sided with the United States against Germany. Hilton, "Military Influence," 88; Stanley E. Hilton, "Brazilian Diplomacy and the Washington-Rio de Janeiro 'Axis' during the World War II Era," *HAHR*, 59 (May 1979), 211; Caffery to DS, July 16, 1941, RG 59, 810.20 Defense/1329.

67. L. Carvalho to Vargas, Nov. 27, 1942; L. Carvalho to Aranha, Dec. 23, 1942, Jan. 27, 1943; Dutra, memo, Jan. 6, 1943 (with Vargas notation); Vargas to L. Carvalho, Mar. 29, 1943; L. Carvalho, "Relatório dos Trabalhos da Delegação do Brasil à Comissão Mista de Defesa Brasil-Estados Unidos" (typewritten), June 1943; Dutra to L. Carvalho, July 17, 1943, IHGB, Estevão Leitão de Carvalho Papers (hereinafter cited as ELC). See, too, L. Carvalho's *A Serviço do Brasil na Segunda Guerra Mundial* (Rio, 1952), passim.

68. The expeditionary force, true, would bring postwar political benefits, but at the time there was little enthusiasm at the policy-making level for the venture. See, for example, Salgado Filho to Gen. Eduardo Gomes, Oct. 6, 1943, PSF; Góes Monteiro to Dutra, Dec. 10, 1943, ELC.

69. Carvalho to Dutra, Nov. 20, 1943; Carvalho to Aranha, Feb. 15, 1944, ELC; Hull to Roosevelt, Jan. 18, 1944; Roosevelt to Hull, Jan. 12, Jan. 14, 1944, *FRUS, 1944*, 7 vols. (Washington, D.C., 1965–67), VII, 567–569.

70. Vargas to Roosevelt, Apr. 13, 1944; Roosevelt to Vargas, June 8, 1944; Vargas to FM Pedro Leão Velloso, May 26, June 5, 1945; Leão Velloso to Vargas, May 30, 1945, GV.

71. Stanley E. Hilton, "Vargas and Brazilian Economic Development, 1930–1945: A Reappraisal of His Attitude Toward Industrialization and Planning," *Journal of Economic History*, 35 (Dec. 1975), 758, 769–771.

72. Getúlio Vargas, *A Nova Política do Brasil*, 11 vols. (Rio, 1938–45), I, 85. For commentaries on the need for defense-related industries, see P. Pessoa, memo, n.d. [Oct. 1932]; P. Pessoa to Vargas, Feb. 17, 1934, Pantaleão Pessoa Papers (private), Rio; Aranha to Vargas, Mar. 25, 1933, GV; Góes Monteiro, interviews, *O Jornal* (Rio), Nov. 5, 1933, *Jornal do Comércio*, Jan. 20, 1934; Góes Monteiro to Vargas, Jan. [?], 1934, GV; Góes Monteiro to Vargas, Mar. 9, Mar. 12, 1934, PGM; EME to MW, Nov. 3, 1933, PR; Gen. João Castro Júnior (DMB) to MW, Feb. 5, 1935, AEX; Souza Costa, lecture ("Mobilização e Finanças de Guerra"), EME, Oct. 23, 1937, ASC.

73. MG, Departamento de Pessoal, *Boletin do Exército*, 19 (Jan. 25, 1931), 158; Pirelli S.A./Companhia Nacional de Condutores Elétricos, "Resposta ao Questionário da Comissão Militar de Estudos Metalúrgicos," n.d. [1931]; [Belgo-Mineira], memo ("Matériel de Guerre"), n.d. [1931], AEX.

74. Edmundo Macedo Soares e Silva to MW, Aug. 31, 1931; Comissão Nacional Siderúrgica, memo, Feb. 11, 1932; Comissão Nacional Siderúrgica to Monteiro, Mar. 2, 1934, AEX; Gen. Benedito Silveira (EME) to Góes Monteiro, Mar. 21, 1934, PGM.

75. Capt. Victor Carvalho e Silva, memo, Jan. 26, 1932, PR; EME to DMB, July 23, Aug. 29, 1932; DMB, bulletin, Aug. 3, 1932; MW to Minister of Transportation, Oct. 13, 1932, AEX.

76. MW to Aranha, Sept. 27, 1932; DMB to Haupt & Cia., Oct. 13, 1932, OA; MW to FM, May 24, 1933, AHI.

77. Góes Monteiro to Comissão Militar Brasileira na Europa, Jan. 18, 1934; Góes Monteiro to Vargas, Mar. 9, Mar. 12, 1934, PGM; U.S. Military Attaché (Rio) to WD, June 2, 1936, RG 165, 2724-K-5/3; P. Pessoa notebook, P. Pessoa Papers; Pessoa, *Reminiscências*, pp. 159–160.

78. J. Samuel White Co. to Souza Costa, Sept. 19, 1934, ASC; German Minister (Rio) to Auswärtiges Amt, Jan. 14, Jan. 28, 1935, RGFM 4465/226276, 226287; Comissão de Estudos para a Instalação de uma Fábrica de Aviões (hereinafter cited as CEIFA) to FM, MN, MW, Feb. 18, 1935, JCMS.

79. U.S. Military Attaché (Rio) to WD, Mar. 17, June 2, 1936, RG 165, 2006-142/4, 2724-K-5/3; MG, *Relatório* [. . .] *1938* (Rio, 1938), p. 72; MG, *Relatório Apresentado* [. . .] *pelo* [. . .] *Diretor da Aeronáutica do Exército, 1939* (Rio, 1940), pp. 7–8, 11–12, 28.

80. Dutra to Vargas, n.d. [Jan.–Feb. 1939], PR; Hilton, "Military Influence," 93–94.

81. MM, "Relatório [. . .] 1936"; MM, "Relatório [. . .] 1937–1938–1939," AM; United States Navy Department to United States Naval Mission (Rio), Nov. 11, 1935, NA, RG 80, L11-7/E712; Brazilian Chargé (Washington) to MRE, Apr. 16, 1937, AHI; Souza Costa to Vargas, May [?] 1939, PR.

82. MG, Diretor de Aviação (Dutra), "Relatório Anual 1934" (typewritten), AEX; CEIFA to FM, MN, MW, Feb. 18, 1935, JCMS; U.S. Military Attaché (Rio) to WD, Oct. 21, 1936, Dec. 27, 1938, RG 59, 832.248/145, 170; Ministério da Viação e Obras Públicas, *Concorrência Pública para o Estabelecimento de uma Fábrica de Aviões* (Rio, 1938); Caffery to DS, June 2, Sept. 22, 1939, RG 59, 832.248/196, 205.

83. MG, Inspetoria Geral do Ensino, "Relatório Sumário do Ano de 1937" (mimeo), annexed to Gen. Pedro Cavalcanti de Albuquerque to Dutra, Mar. 17, 1938; Dutra to Director, Departamento de Pessoal (MG), July 28, 1937; DMB, Boletim 190 (Aug. 14, 1939), AEX.

84. *Boletim do Exército*, n. 30 (May 31, 1933), p. 1148; MG, *Relatório* [. . .] *1936*, pp. 92–93; U.S. Military Attaché (Rio) to WD, June 2, 1936, RG 165, 2724-K-5/3; MG, *Relatório* [. . .] *1940, Secreto*, AEME.

85. See, for example, Souza Costa to MW, Mar. 30, 1935, June 22, 1936, ASC.

86. Article 144, *Constituição dos Estados Unidos do Brasil, 1937* (Rio, 1937), p. 39; DMB, Boletim 85 (Apr. 11, 1939), AEX.

87. MN to Vargas, Nov. 17, 1932, OA; Góes Monteiro to Vargas, Mar. 12, 1934 (with enclosure), PGM; MG, Diretor de Aviação (Dutra), "Relatório Anual 1934"; Aranha to Góes Monteiro, Mar. 29, 1935; Góes Monteiro to Aranha, June 5, 1935, OA; P. Pessoa to Vargas, Oct. 3, 1935, GV.

88. Silveira to Góes Monteiro, Mar. 21, 1934, PGM; MM, *Relatório* [. . .] *1935*, p. 2.

89. MW to DMB, Dec. 2, 1932, AEX; MG, Diretor de Aviação (Dutra), "Relatório Anual 1934"; MG, *Relatório* [. . .] *pelo* [. . .] *Diretor da Aeronáutica, 1939*, p. 12; MM, "Relatório [. . .] 1937–1938–1939."

90. Sylvio Raulino de Oliveira, memo, July 5, 1940, AN, records of the Conselho Federal de Comércio Exterior (hereinafter cited as CFCE), box 81, file 1060; "Crédito Agrícola e Industrial," *O Observador Econômico e Financeiro*, 5 (Dec. 1940), 135.

91. Comissão de Compras (MG) to Diretor de Intendência (MG), Sept. 7, 1932; EME to DMB, Aug. 26, 1932, AEX; Clovis de Oliveira, *A Indústria e o Movimento Constitucionalista de 1932* (São Paulo, 1956); Góes Monteiro to Companhia Nickel do Brasil, May 28, 1934; Góes Monteiro to Vargas, June 7, 1934; Comissão Militar de Estudos Metalúrgicos, memo ("Necessidades Imediatas do Exército"), n.d. (annexed to Góes Monteiro to Vargas, Mar. 12, 1934), AEX; MG, Diretor de Aviação (Dutra), "Relatório Anual 1934"; Souza Costa to Dutra, Oct. 23, 1937, ASC; Companhia Eletro-Química Fluminense to Vargas, Apr. 27, 1938; Companhia Eletro-Química Fluminense, memo, Jan. 18, 1939, OA.

92. See, for example, MW to FM, Jan. 21, Feb. 26, 1932, Jan. 6, Jan. 12, 1938, Jan. 13, Jan. 27, 1939, AEX.

93. MM, "Relatório [. . .] 1937–1938–1939."

94. Oliveira, memo, July 5, 1940, CFCE 81/1060; Capt. Arnaud Veloso, "Fardamento e Equipamento," *Revista de Intendência*, 16 (Sept.–Oct. 1942), 628; memo ("A Pirelli S.A. em Face do Decreto n. 4166"), May 22, 1943, OA; Caffery to DS, Aug. 28, 1940, RG 59, 832.24/248.

95. Oliveira, memo, July 5, 1940, CFCE 81/1060; Conselho Federal de Comércio Exterior, memo, July 5, 1940; Conselho Federal de Comércio Exterior to Monteiro, Sept. 10, 1940, CFCE 82/1060.

96. Conselho de Segurança Nacional (hereinafter cited as CSN), circular to ministries, July 29, 1941, PR; *O Estado de São Paulo*, July 18, 1941; Gen. Sylvio Portella (DMB) to Aranha, Apr. 29, 1941, AHI.

97. Dutra to Souza Costa, Dec. 11, 1941, Mar. 24, 1942; Dutra to Vargas, Feb. 22, Feb. 25, 1942, AEME; MG (Gabinete), memoranda, Mar. 19, July 9, Sept. 5, 1942; EME, minutes, Sept. 21, 1942, AEX.

98. MG (Gabinete), memoranda, Apr. 30, Nov. 6, 1941; Dutra to Vargas, Jan. 21, 1942; Dutra to CSN, May 26, 1943; Dutra, Aviso 219, Jan. 27, 1944, AEX.

99. U.S. Vice-Consul (São Paulo) to DS, Jan. 27, 1940; Caffery to DS, Mar. 8, 1940, RG 59, 832.24/198, 204; Souza Costa to Vargas, Jan. [?], July [?], 1943, PR; MG (Gabinete), memoranda, Feb. 3, June 6, 1944, Jan. 4, 1945, AEX.

100. Souza Costa to Vargas, May [?], Sept. [?], 1941, PR; MG (Gabinete), memoranda, May 29, Aug. 6, Dec. 11, 1941, AEX.

101. Souza Costa to Vargas, Jan. [?], May [?], 1942, June [?], 1943, PR; Dutra to Vargas, Dec. 2, 1943, AHI; MF to Dutra, Nov. [?], 1946, PR.

102. Welles to Secretary Henry Stimson, Apr. 28, 1943; Stimson to Welles, May 8, 1943, RG 59, 832.24/1578; Souza Costa to Vargas, June [?], Oct. [?], 1944, PR.

103. MG (Gabinete), memoranda, Dec. 23, 1943, June 1, 1944, Mar. 3, 1945, AEX; Souza Costa to Vargas, Apr. [?], Dec. [?], 1944, PR.

104. René Couzinet, founder of Construções Aeronáuticas, was on the State Department's list of undesirable aliens and was finally forced to turn his holdings over to a Matarazzo-controlled company. Welles, memo, Oct. 19, 1942; DS memo, Dec. 30, 1942, RG 59, 832.24/448, 460; Couzinet to Salgado Filho, Dec. 10, 1942, PSF.

105. "Fábrica Nacional de Aviões," *O Observador Econômico e Financeiro*, 7 (June 1942), 27–28; Souza Costa to Vargas, Feb. [?], 1942, PR; Col. Vasco Alves Secco (Washington) to Salgado Filho, Nov. 17, 1942, PSF; Marshall to L. Carvalho, Dec. 12, 1942, ELC; Lavanère-Wanderley, *História da Força Aérea*, p. 331.

106. Dutra to Vargas, Mar. 18, 1942; Dutra, Portaria 5862, Jan. 4, 1944, AEX; Dutra to Souza Costa, Apr. 12, 1944, AEME.

107. Soares e Silva to Minister of Transportation João Mendonça Lima, July 26, 1941; Soares e Silva to Export-Import Bank, Oct. 16, 1941, PR; Oliveira to Vargas, Oct. 24, 1942, GV.

108. Antonio Guedes Muniz to Salgado Filho, Feb. 19, 1941, PSF; Muniz to Mendonça Lima, July 12, Sept. 19, Oct. 3, 1941, PR; DS memoranda, Dec. 28, 1943, Jan. 21, 1944; Hull to Caffery, Apr. 18, 1944, RG 59, 832.248/295, 496, 498A; Souza Costa to Vargas, Jan. [?], 1945, PR.

109. CSN to Vargas, Feb. 27, 1943; Souza Costa to Vargas, Aug. [18], 1943, PR.

110. CSN to Vargas, July 20, 1944, Apr. 17, 1945; Souza Costa to Vargas, Oct. 26, 1944, PR; Gen. Alvaro Fiuza de Castro to Joint United States-Brazil Military Commission, Nov. 27, 1944; Air Ministry memo, Jan. 22, 1945; Salgado Filho et al., memo ("Missões e Planos da Força Aérea Brasileira"), Apr. 12, 1945, PSF.

111. João Neves da Fontoura to Góes Monteiro, Aug. 9, 1946, PGM; Aranha to FM Raul Fernandes, Sept. 25, 1947, OA. For similar commentaries, see Fernandes to Aranha, Nov. 16, 1947, OA; Hildebrando Acioly (MRE) to Aranha, Oct. 8, 1947, Hildebrando Acioly Papers (private), Rio; MF to Dutra, Mar. 9, 1948, PR.

112. See, for example, Military Attaché (Gen.) Angelo Mendes Moraes (Paris) to Góes Monteiro, Jan. 29, Feb. 12, Apr. 20, 1946, PGM; Monteiro to EME, Mar. 11, 1946, AEX; Gen. Alcio Souto to Dutra, Sept. 2, 1946, PR; Gen. Oswaldo Cordeiro de Farias, speech, *O Jornal*, May 19, 1949; Lt. Col. J. H. Garcia, "A Outra Guerra," *ADN*, 37 (May 1950), 95–96; Gen. A. Castro Nascimento, "A Preparação para a Guerra," *ADN*, 37 (June 1950), 5–14; Gen. Aurélio de Lyra Tavares, *O Brasil de Minha Geração*, 2 vols. (Rio, 1976–77), I, 241–246, 259–260.

113. Military Attaché Cordeiro de Farias (Buenos Aires) to Góes Monteiro, Mar. 21, May 21, June, 24, 1946; Góes Monteiro to Cordeiro de Farias, Mar. 21, July 10, 1946, PGM; MW Canrobert Pereira da Costa to Dutra, Feb. 5, 1947, PR; Castro Arnon de Mello, "Situação Político-Militar da Argentina e suas Relações com o Brasil" (typewritten), Dec. 22, 1948, Biblioteca Nacional.

114. MN to President José Linhares, Dec. 2, 1945; MN to Dutra, Mar. 15, 1946, PR; Gen. Juarez Távora, *Uma Vida e Muitas Lutas: Memórias*, 3 vols. (Rio, 1973–76), II, 206; MW to Aranha, Feb. 24, 1947, OA; Acioly to Aranha, Mar. 13, 1947, Acioly Papers.

115. MN to Linhares, Dec. 2, 1945, PR; U.S. Chargé (Rio) to DS, Dec. 28, 1945, *FRUS, 1945*, 9 vols. (Washington, D.C., 1967–69), IX, 620–621; Pereira da Costa to Dutra, Feb. 5, 1947, PR. For further details, see Stanley E. Hilton, "The United States, Brazil, and the Cold War, 1945–1960: End of the Special Relationship," *Journal of American History*, 68 (Dec. 1981), 601–602.

116. Góes Monteiro to Vargas, Mar. 7, 1951; Góes Monteiro to EME, Mar. 20, 1951, AEX.

117. MW to Dutra, Nov. 22, 1950; MF to Dutra, Nov. 24, 1950, July 25, Sept. 19, 1951, PR.

118. MF to Dutra, Nov. 17, 1950, Aug. 1, Aug. 13, Aug. 22, Oct. 17, 1951, PR; Góes Monteiro to EMA, July 30, 1951, PGM.

119. Renato de Almeida Guillobel, *Memórias* (Rio, 1973), pp. 541–543; Góes Monteiro (Washington) to EME, Aug. 3, Sept. 20, Sept. 29, 1951, PGM. Góes Monteiro was in Washington to conduct negotiations for military cooperation vis-à-vis the Korean crisis. See Hilton, "The United States, Brazil, and the Cold War," 611.

120. DS memo, Oct. 24, 1945, RG 59, Office of American Republics Affairs, Brazil Memoranda, vol. 10; MW to Departamento Técnico e de Produção do Exército (hereinafter cited as DTPE), Dec. 16, 1949, AEX; CSN to Dutra, Sept. 26, June 22, 1950; MF to Dutra, Aug. 19, 1949, PR; London *Times*, Oct. 29, Nov. 14, 1952, Feb. 11, 1953; Guillobel, *Memórias*, p. 362; MM, *Relatório da Comissão Fiscal da Construção de Navios no Japão* (Rio, 1973), pp. 1–2.

121. Gen. João Amorim e Mello (CSN) to Dutra, Feb. 15, 1949, PR. For elite emphasis on the need to industrialize, see Cristovam Dantas, "A Despensa da Europa," *O Jornal* July 18, 1946; Lt. Col. Carlos Berenhauser, Jr., "Mentalidade Industrial," *Boletim do Círculo de Técnicos Militares*, 9 (June 1947), 80; MW to Dutra, Jan. 8, 1949, AEX; editorial, *Correio da Manhã* (Rio), Mar. 9, 1949; editorial, *O Jornal*, May 26, 1949; Valentim Bouças to Dutra, Apr. 4, 1948, PR; MN Sylvio de Noronha, *Cinco Anos de Governo* (Rio, 1951), p. 8; Lyra Tavares, *O Brasil de Minha Geração*, I, 266–272, 283.

122. Idálio Sardenberg, interview, Apr. 27, 1980, in Lourenço Dantas, ed., *A História Vivida*, 2 vols. (São Paulo, 1980–81), II, 362–364. See, too, Gen. Augusto Fragoso, "A Escola Superior de Guerra," *Problemas Brasileiros*, 88 (Dec. 1970), 19–34.

123. Hilton, "The United States, Brazil, and the Cold War," 611–612.

124. Newton Estillac Leal, speech, *Jornal do Comércio*, Jan. 6, 1952; Getúlio Vargas, *O Governo Trabalhista do Brasil*, 4 vols. (Rio, 1952–69), III, 302.

125. See, for example, MG to Secretário de Segurança Pública (São Paulo), Jan. 13, 1947; MG to Conselho Federal de Comércio Exterior, Feb. 10, 1947; MG to BB, Dec. 6, 1949; MG to Tribunal de Contas, Dec. 20, 1949; MG to Superintendência da Moeda e do Crédito, June 7, 1954, AEX.

126. Noronha, *Cinco Anos de Governo*, p. 4; MW to FM, May 13, 1947; MW to Dutra, Aug. 18, Sept. 8, 1948, Apr. 26, July 5, Nov. 8, 1950; MG to BB, June 25, 1951; MG to Diretoria de Fabricação do Exército, Jan. 2, Feb. 5, 1952, AEX; MN to Dutra, Mar. 5, 1950; MF to Dutra, June 2, 1950; Min. of Air to Vargas, May 11, 1951; MW to Vargas, Sept. 9, 1953, Jan. 27, 1954, PR.

127. MW, Aviso 246, Mar. 19, 1948; MW to DTPE, Jan. 3, 1947; MW to Dutra, Jan. 8, 1949; MW to FM, Jan. 10, Aug. 27, 1947, Aug. 16, 1950, AEX.

128. MW (Pereira da Costa) to Dutra, Dec. 4, 1946, AEX; *Coleção das Leis de 1948* (Rio, 1949), V, 131; MW to Min. of Labor, Feb. 28, 1950; MW to Chief, Estado-Maior das Forças Armadas, Feb. 3, Mar. 8, 1950, AEX.

129. Góes Monteiro to Linhares, Oct. 31, 1945; MW to Dutra, Jan. 8, 1949; MG to Câmara dos Deputados, Sept. 3, 1951, AEX; MG, *Regulamento do Departamento Técnico e de Produção do Exército* (Rio, 1946).

130. MW to FM, Jan. 11, 1947; MW to Dutra, Sept. 22, 1948; MG to DTPE, Apr. 12, 1949, AEX.

131. MF to Linhares, Oct. [?], Nov. 16, 1945, PR; MW to Dutra, June 7, 1947, Apr. 19, 1950, AEX; MF to Dutra, Dec. 1, Dec. 22, 1949, Aug. 11, 1950, PR; MG to Presidential Secretary, July 10, 1951, AEX; MW to Vargas, Jan. 28, 1953, PR; *ADN*, 40 (Sept. 1953), 131.

132. MF to Dutra, Dec. 29, 1949; MW to Dutra, Jan. 18, 1950, PR.

133. MW to Dutra, Aug. 27, 1947, AEX; CSN to Dutra, Sept. 26, 1947, PR; MG to Delagação do Tesouro Brasileiro (New York), Nov. 1, 1947; *O Estado de São Paulo*, Jan. 27, 1954; MG to BB, Nov. 18, 1954, AEX.

134. MF to Dutra, Jan. [?], Mar. 15, 1946, June 9, Aug. 25, 1950, PR; Noronha, *Cinco Anos de Governo*, p. 4.

135. Guillobel, *Memórias*, pp. 304, 308.

136. MF to Dutra, May [?], June 14, 1946, Nov. 11, 1950; Dutra to Air Minister, Aug. 27, 1946, PR; São José dos Campos, *O Centro Técnico da Aeronáutica: Informações Gerais* (São José dos Campos), 1953.

137. MW to CSN, May 13, 1947, AEX.

138. MF to Dutra, Aug. [?], 1946, Sept. 15, 1948, Oct. 27, 1949; Muniz to Dutra, Apr. 2, 1947, PR; U.S. Embassy (Rio) to DS, Oct. 4, 1949, RG 59, 832.24/10-449; *ADN*, 40 (Jan. 1953), 137; Banco Nacional de Desenvolvimento Econômico, Grupo Misto de Estudos, memo, Feb. 15, 1953, OA; *ADN*, 40 (Oct. 1952), 154, (Sept. 1953), 131–132.

139. John D. Wirth, *The Politics of Brazilian Development, 1930–1954* (Stanford, 1969), pp. 161–183; Peter S. Smith, *Oil and Politics in Modern Brazil* (Toronto, 1976), pp. 49–74.

140. MW to Dutra, Jan. 22, 1947; MW, Nota Circular no. 18 (to Regional Commanders), Feb. 22, 1950, AEX.

141. Comissão de Desenvolvimento Industrial (hereinafter cited as CDI), "Relatório de 1952" (mimeo), OA.

142. Ibid.; *ADN*, 40 (Nov. 1952), 175, (Dec. 1952), 138.

143. Guillobel, *Memórias*, p. 307; Guillobel to Vargas, Mar. 19, Apr. 15, 1953, PR; Vargas, *Mensagem ao Congresso Nacional* [. . .] *1953* (Rio, 1953), pp. 45–48; *O Estado de São Paulo*, Jan. 27, Apr. 29, 1954.

144. MF to Dutra, July 12, 1946; CSN to Dutra, Aug. 30, 1948, PR; Lavanère-Wanderley, *História da Força Aérea Brasileira*, pp. 333–334; *ADN*, 40 (Sept. 1953), 131.

145. MW to Dutra, Jan. 8, 1949, AEX.

146. MF to Dutra, Apr. [?], 1946, June 24, 1948, CSN to Dutra, Oct. 14, 1948, PR; MW to Dutra, Feb. 4, Sept. 22, 1948, Jan. 19, 1949, May 24, Dec. 8, 1950; MG to BB, Oct. 24, Nov. 10, Nov. 17, 1950, AEX; BB, memo, n.d. [Feb. 1954], OA.

147. MW to Dutra, Aug. 15, 1946; MG to Estrada de Ferro Central do Brasil, Nov. 9, 1950, AEX; MF to Dutra, Nov. [?], 1946, Aug. 5, 1948, PR.

148. MF to Dutra, Sept. [?], 1946, PR; MW to FM, Dec. 26, 1946, June 22, 1949; Pereira da Costa to Governor of São Paulo, Aug. 9, 1947; MW to MF, May 26, 1948; MW to Dutra, Dec. 13, 1950, AEX; MF to Dutra, Dec. 12, 1951, PR.

149. MF to Linhares, Dec. [?], 1945; MF to Dutra, Feb. [?], 1946, PR.

150. MF to Dutra, Aug. 27, 1948, PR.

151. MG to MRE, Dec. 31, 1946, Mar. 9, 1948, Dec. 2, 1949, Dec. 5, 1950; MW to Conselho Nacional de Petróleo, Jan. 30, 1948, AEX.

152. MG to Companhia Industrial Brasileira Pirelli, Mar. 28, 1950, AEX.

153. MG (Gabinete), memo, Aug. 24, 1949; MW to Dutra, Mar. 31, May 10, July 26, Aug. 2, 1950, AEX.

154. MF to Dutra, Sept. 22, 1948, May 13, 1949; MF to Vargas, Feb. 21, 1951, PR.

155. See, for example, MG to MRE, Dec. 13, 1946, Jan. 15, 1947, Mar. 12, 1948, Dec. 2, 1949, June 28, 1950, AEX.

156. MW to FM, Sept. 15, 1947, Feb. 26, 1951; MW to Minister of Labor, Mar. 10, 1949, Apr. 19, 1950, AEX.

157. MW to DTPE, Apr. 18, July 16, 1947; MG to Companhia Textil Agro-Industrial, Jan. 14, 1949; MG to Otica Milando, Feb. 4, 1950; MG to BB, May 6, 1954, AEX.

158. CSN to Dutra, Sept. 8, Sept. 27, 1949; MF to Dutra, Mar. 16, Oct. 11, 1950, PR.

159. MW to Vargas, Feb. 18, June 22, 1954; MF to Vargas, Apr. 14, 1954, PR; Vargas, *Mensagem ao Congresso Nacional* [. . .] *1954* (Rio, 1954), p. 49.

7

Caudillismo and Institutional Change: Manuel Odría and the Peruvian Armed Forces, 1948–1956

Daniel M. Masterson

The process by which caudillos were eliminated and institutional military authority established has been long and arduous in many Latin American countries. Within the political sphere, that process has been paralleled by a shift away from governments dominated by individual military men to regimes based on corporate power. While a few nations such as Chile managed that change relatively easily, the experiences of states such as Bolivia and Paraguay are more typical of the region. For the armed forces the issue has been compounded by the debility of the civil institutions and processes. As a result, the "better"-trained military men have tended to "assume" the responsibility for the nation's well-being.

The reform of the Peruvian armed forces during the Odría administration (1948–1956) provides an opportunity to examine the complex and, at times, contradictory nature of professionalization and institutional change. New institutions for advanced military training played an important role in the development of a corporate identity and in the formation of an ideology that stressed the central role of the armed forces in national development. Since Peru, like a number of other Latin American nations, had weak civil institutions, the military's new self-confidence and expanded vision of national security became the justification for a new generation of officers to intervene in politics under the guise of assuming responsibility for the welfare of the nation.

From *The Americas* 40, no. 4 (1984): 479–89. Reprinted by permission.

A braham Lowenthal, in characterizing the Peruvian military government of General Juan Velasco Alvarado, cautioned that the regime
was not a "typical caudillo" venture but rather an essentially "institutional" effort.[1] His caveat is certainly justified when one considers that
Peru was dominated until recent decades by such modern era military
chieftains as Luis M. Sánchez Cerro, Oscar R. Benavides, and Manuel A.
Odría. Yet when General Odría seized control of Peru on October 27,
1948, the Peruvian army was striving desperately for increased professionalism. In order to retain the army's support, the caudillo was thus
compelled to enact institutional reforms that made the officer class more
conscious of its modernizing mission and, ironically, far less tolerant of
Odría's personalism. This study will analyze the military policies of the
Odría regime in order to explain the changing outlook of the Peruvian
armed forces during the caudillo's eight-year rule.

Before beginning this analysis, a brief review of the Peruvian military's troubled process of professionalization in the half century before
Odría's *golpe de estado* will help place this discussion in a clearer perspective. This review will especially emphasize the intense rivalry between
the armed forces and Peru's strongest civilian political institution, the
Alianza Popular Revolucionaria Americana, or APRA party.

Although French army advisers laid the foundation for Peruvian military professionalism during this century's early years, their dictum that
"the officer may think what he wishes but more than anything he must
obey," was all too often ignored by the Peruvian army officer corps in the
decades before Odría.[2] These years saw Peru produce better-trained and
more highly educated men in uniform but they also witnessed intense
civil-military strife that divided the officer corps, damaged its self-
image, and diverted its attention from a "nation-building" role that one
officer in 1933 asserted would "tie the country together."[3]

Understandably, military men before World War II rarely mentioned
these problems while they portrayed the army in their service journals as
the "most noble symbol of the nation."[4] In truth, however, battlefield de-
feats and repeated military conspiracies reflected the army's low morale,
poor discipline, and lack of corporate solidarity.

These difficulties were mitigated somewhat by Peru's smashing defeat of Ecuadorian army units in the 1941 border war, but even in the
aftermath of this convincing victory junior army officers openly challenged their commanders' professionalism. Specifically, these critics accused their superiors of exploiting their commands for political gain. In a
series of manifestos distributed throughout the army in early 1945 a militant cadre of junior army officers attacked their institution's leadership.
One of these flyers read: "A few generals who have benefited from the

government are not the army, they are not even a part of it. Rather they are a few individuals and nothing more. They do not have the weight of opinion of the officer corps behind them because they lack professional prestige which they have lost through their dedication to politics."[5]

Marshal Benavides and the much-decorated hero of the Ecuador campaign, General Eloy G. Ureta, were unquestionably the targets of this criticism. As both jockeyed for political support in their respective bids for the presidency in 1945, the army was forced to choose sides, and this prompted the younger officers to protest that only "defeated and decadent nations" were then ruled by military men. Benavides and Ureta were implored to emulate the examples of [John J.] Pershing, [Ferdinand] Foch, and [Douglas] MacArthur, who, in the eyes of the army militants, had not exploited their military prestige for political gain.[6]

The victory of a civilian, José Luis Bustamante y Rivero, in 1945 did not lessen armed forces discord. Indeed, the next three years witnessed even more intense military strife stemming mainly from APRA efforts to suborn army senior officers as well as soldiers and sailors of the line. These tactics resulted in the bloody Callao naval mutiny of October 3, 1948. But, in a broader context, they reflected the consistent pattern of plotting, intrigue, and rebellion that characterized APRA-military relations in the sixteen years following the even more violent Trujillo rebellion of 1932.

Ever since the Trujillo revolt of July 1932, which cost the lives of approximately fifty military and police personnel and over one thousand civilians, army men and *Apristas* have supposedly hated each other with an enduring passion.[7] Unquestionably, the years between the Trujillo and the Callao insurrections were the most violent of this century. This era saw Sánchez Cerro's death at the hand of an *Aprista* assassin and the imprisonment, deportation, and execution of party members by the hundreds as a result of their conflicts with the military establishment. Yet despite these clashes, sizable numbers of military men rejected institutional loyalties and conspired with APRA for a wide variety of social, political, and personal motives. This consistent trend of APRA-military intrigue drove many loyal officers to seek the party's destruction. But these efforts were answered by staunch *Aprista* resistance quite often supported by military dissidents who distrusted or actively opposed the policies of their anti-APRA superiors. Thus, while APRA remained an actively militant force in Peruvian politics, it undermined military discipline and thereby impeded professionalism. Furthermore, *Aprista* subversion allowed caudillos such as Sánchez Cerro, Benavides, and, most particularly, Odría to employ the anti-Aprismo battle cry as their principal tactic for gaining power.[8]

When the sailors of five warships mutinied in Callao harbor on October 3, 1948, in an attempt to ignite a broad-based revolution, their actions provoked a crisis that shattered armed forces morale and set the stage for Odría's *golpe de estado*. Following the abortive revolt, hundreds of officers and enlisted men were imprisoned or expelled from the armed forces. Within the navy alone more than eight hundred were interrogated and two hundred subsequently jailed. Loyal junior officers, while acknowledging their institution's disgrace, blamed the navy's "poor leadership" for the mutiny. These disenchanted younger officers called for a total navy reorganization from top to bottom: to be carried out, not by their own discredited senior officers, but rather by officers of the U.S. naval mission. This did not happen, but continued unrest within the navy soon compelled its high command to implement reforms aimed at assuring the allegiance of a badly shaken institution.[9]

Without question, the events of October 3 provoked the worst armed forces crisis of this century. On the other hand, Callao also brought about APRA's demise as a revolutionary force. After the mutiny the party was in shambles. Its militant rank and file, having planned and instigated the revolt, bitterly accused the party leadership of "cowardice" and "treason" for denying the rebels support once the revolt had begun. *Aprista* chiefs in turn charged what they termed "young hotheads" with "treacherous" acts leading to the party's persecution.[10] Odría's suppression of APRA after 1948 unquestionably blunted its revolutionary potential. With the party leadership either imprisoned or scattered in exile, few military or civilian dissidents expected APRA to seriously challenge the caudillo. Nonetheless, the party leadership's inaction in the midst of the Callao fiasco brought discredit to APRA's once militant image. Meeting in Guatemala in 1952, *Aprista* radicals acknowledged this, claiming the party had lost "a large part of its continental prestige, especially its right to be the genuine representative of the working class and the peasantry" when party chiefs denied APRA's involvement in the mutiny.[11] Clearly, Callao convinced party chief Victor Raúl Haya de la Torre that revolution was no longer the path to power. Thus, when APRA abandoned the activist arena, the greatest threat to armed forces corporate unity ended.

Armed forces commanders during the last weeks of October 1948 could not foresee this. Consequently, they urged tough authoritarian measures aimed at crippling APRA. Odría, who for years had vigorously attacked Aprismo and promised to smash the party that he claimed had "poisoned the minds and sickened the hearts of the Peruvian people," was thus able to seize power in a traditional, bloodless *golpe de estado*.[12]

Although Odría patterned his so-called Restoration Movement of Arequipa after Sánchez Cerro's *golpe* of 1930, he little resembled the impetuous and undisciplined *cholo* who seized control of Peru as a mere lieutenant colonel. In contrast, Odría boasted impeccable "professional credentials." His impressive record as a military educator and administrator at the Chorrillos Military Academy and the Superior War College was complemented by his skillful command of the army's First Light Division in the 1941 Ecuadorian campaign. After his battlefield victories, Odría's career steadily progressed until he was named Bustamante's minister of government in 1947.[13] Soon thereafter, one prophetic observer commented that "the President has taken upon himself a dangerous counselor and perhaps his master."[14] Like the senior commanders criticized by army militants in the early 1940s, Odría's "professionalism" had obviously not muted a growing political ambition. Callao thus afforded this tough-minded officer the chance to exploit both his significant personal prestige and his well-known, violent anti-Aprismo feelings to achieve what Manuel González Prada caustically characterized as the ultimate rank of a successful Peruvian military man.

Odría entered the National Palace, however, only after some key armed forces leaders acquiesced because they were unwilling to shed army blood in defense of the weak and discredited Bustamante regime. Other officers resented Odría's exploitation of the armed forces' demoralized condition in order to gain power. Consequently, the caudillo faced the stiff challenge of mollifying a restive officer corps that demanded long-overdue institutional reform as a price for its continued support.[15]

During the first years of his regime, Odría tried to placate his fellow officers by employing the time-honored methods of past military strongmen. He granted generous military pay increases with the greatest salary hikes going to the army's junior officers. Modern hospital facilities and low-cost housing were also constructed for armed forces personnel while at the same time the government purchased large quantities of surplus arms and relatively sophisticated naval vessels and aircraft from the United States and Great Britain. But these measures failed to satisfy progressive elements within the officer corps who were still haunted by the Callao revolt and troubled by the uneven quality of military education and training. They exerted pressure on Odría through their spokesman on the army's General Staff and Superior Council for the initiation of badly overdue internal military reforms and the expansion of specialized postacademy education.[16]

Peru's politically charged promotion and military justice process had traditionally aroused intense discord and provoked many of the civil-military conspiracies that divided the officer corps in the years after 1930. Realizing this and responding to the pressure from army leaders who sought a more merit-oriented institution, Odría enacted a series of administrative reforms after 1951 that clarified previously ambiguous promotion criteria, modernized a dated military justice system, and stipulated more precise terms governing discipline and retirement. A 1955 law establishing universal criteria for Peru's three armed services in these areas created the first comprehensive body of military law and laid the groundwork for the creation of a long-delayed armed forces joint command in 1957.[17] While it cannot be said that these measures entirely prevented partisan politicking within the officer corps, they did unquestionably promote a greater respect for more rational military regulations, and this fostered greater institutional cohesion.

Even more important than these reforms were the advances made in military education. Ever since the founding of the Center for Higher Military Studies (Centro de Altos Estudios Militares, CAEM) in 1950 and the less well-known Center of Military Instruction (Centro de Instrucción Militar, CIMP) one year earlier, Peruvian military officers have come to be recognized as the most highly schooled in Latin America. This fact, above all else, explains the increased corporate self-confidence and heightened sense of professional mission manifested by military men as they emerged from the Odría years. For example, the CAEM's first director, General José del Carmen Marín, boasted during the Center's early years: "When we [the Peruvian military] have a solid school system, nobody will be able to stop us."[18]

Much of the research analyzing Peru's "new military professionalism" has properly emphasized the influence of the CAEM. Yet many observers have isolated this institution from the long process of the military's professional development. As early as 1904 articles appearing in Peruvian military journals urged the army to pursue more energetically its social mission and nation-building potential. By the 1930s some senior officers were calling for a higher military studies center that would integrate the army's modernizing impulse into a comprehensive national defense doctrine.[19] Although this theme was frequently repeated after it was underscored by the border conflict with Ecuador and the total war lessons of World War II, because of civil-military strife and related armed forces factionalism its expression was generally confined to the pages of the army's service journals and general staff reports.

Soon after Odría seized power, however, intellectually active officers led by Generals Marín, Juan Mendoza Rodríguez, Nicolas Lindley López, and Marcial Romero Pardo campaigned actively for the creation of a higher military studies center and their efforts finally came to fruition when the CAEM opened in 1950.[20] Although Odría originally sought to isolate politically unreliable officers at the CAEM, under the astute leadership of General Marín and his successor, General Romero Pardo, the Center soon became a prized assignment for armed forces officers destined for high command posts.[21]

The CAEM's original charter charged it with defining a national war doctrine and incorporating its basic principles into the training of armed forces officers with high command potential. In addition, CAEM students were directed to study fundamental questions of national defense and their relation to basic national problems as a part of a highly specialized one-year program of technical and social science education.[22] In an address delivered at the CAEM's opening, General Marín effectively character-ized the Center's intended mission: "In the final analysis the armed forces will always be the principal agent for national defense. But the potential for the military to realize its full strength in wartime is directly depen-dent upon the full exploitation of the nation's human and material resources. It is thus necessary for us to study analytically the concept of national defense in order to be able to relate national potential to military preparedness."[23]

In short, this perspective held that a weak and underdeveloped Peru was extremely vulnerable to internal subversion and insurgency as well as external military threats. National development and security thus became closely interwoven concepts and the CAEM's slogan, "There is no defense without development," aptly characterized the Center's pro-fessional credo.

Although it emphasized the armed forces' social action mission, it would be inaccurate to regard the CAEM's doctrine as evidence of the military's radicalization after 1950. Odría was certainly no radical developmentalist; yet in 1952 even he employed CAEM-style rhetoric in characterizing the army as "a model of efficiency and solidarity which is of primordial importance in promoting Peru's progress and develop-ment."[24] Similarly, while looking back at the CAEM's first years during a 1962 conversation with the U.S. ambassador, Peru's rigidly conservative navy minister, Admiral Guillermo Tirado Lamb, insisted that the military had then become more clearly aware of what he termed its "dominant role as a disciplined and intellectually prepared force" destined to find solutions to the problems of underdevelopment.[25] Furthermore, it should be remembered that contemporary CAEM-like institutions in Brazil and Argentina espoused similar doctrines, but later military regimes adopted policies far different from those initiated in Peru after 1956.

If the CAEM did not draw the officer corps leftward during the Odría regime, it did more precisely define a common military ideology that jus-tified the armed forces' role as Peru's primary development agent. Addi-tionally, it increased the military's capacity for independent political action by enhancing its professional self-image. As late as 1946 army officers felt it necessary to deny that the army was unproductive.[26] But after 1950, as a result of a more sophisticated military educational system and Peru's shortage of skilled civilian technocrats, military men of all political tendencies regarded their institution, in the words of one prominent officer, as Peru's "permanent vehicle for modernization."[27] As the Odría dictatorship wore on, this perception led the officer corps to withdraw its support for the caudillo, whose regime by 1955 was generally perceived as overly oppressive, corrupt, and limited in vision.

From the beginning of his regime, Odría encountered opposition from officers who deeply resented his use of the army primarily as an instrument of political repression. In late 1948 officers from eight army garrisons throughout Peru condemned what they termed the government's "policies of persecution and death."[28] These attacks were renewed in July 1949, when army opponents, insisting that their views were shared by the rank and file, authored a manifesto declaring Odría had "profaned the name of the armed forces" and made the army a "painful spectacle to the Peruvian people."[29] Outspoken critics could be found even within the army's general staff. Colonel Miguel Monteza, deputy chief of staff in 1950, confided to the U.S. military attaché that the army's involvement in the enforcement of the Internal Security Law, which imposed virtual martial law during most of Odría's rule, had bred a "solid foundation of dissatisfaction within the army."[30]

While Odría was able to withstand increasing challenges from army opponents until his decision to retire in 1956, it is clear that senior commanders as well as their traditionally more militant junior colleagues increasingly sought to disassociate the armed forces from the caudillo. In February, the army commander at Iquitos typified this when he "pronounced" against the government. While appealing for support from other garrisons, the rebel general charged that Odría planned to use the armed forces "as an instrument of terror against the people" in continuing his dictatorship. In a radio address immediately preceding the surrender of his quixotic movement, General [Marcial] Merinos [Pereyra] defended his actions, claiming his uprising's principal objective was the establishment of a "clearer understanding with the Peruvian people regarding the intentions of the armed forces."[31]

The army's decision not to support the dissident general's movement did not signify its lack of sympathy with his objectives. By 1956 few military men were willing to back the discredited Odría beyond the limits of the presidential term to which he was elected without opposition in 1950. Soldiers who considered the increasingly isolated strongman "too old hat for Peru" and who deplored their widely held image as the "watchdogs of the oligarchy" now exerted significant influence within the army.[32]

More confident of their abilities and more prone to regard themselves as a patriotic and technically sophisticated elite, these officers now sought a more comprehensive and positive mission for the armed forces.

As has been noted, the military reforms undertaken under Odría served as the lens that brought this professional perspective into sharper focus. This clearer vision soon led Peru's men in uniform to reject the old-style caudillo politics of the past for a mission characterized two decades later by General Juan Velasco Alvarado as "nationalist, independent, and humanist."[33] Lest we dismiss the legacy of caudillismo too quickly, however, it should be recognized that when the "Revolutionary Government of the Armed Forces" began faltering badly, Velasco himself was eased from power by fellow officers who attacked his "personalism" and "caudillo tendencies."[34]

Notes

1. Abraham F. Lowenthal, ed., *The Peruvian Experiment: Continuity and Change Under Military Rule* (Princeton: Princeton University Press, 1975), p. 3.

2. Major Carlos Echazú, "La disciplina militar," *Boletín del Ministerio de Guerra y Marina* (December 1914), pp. 1451–1455; cited in Frederick M. Nunn, "Professional Militarism in Twentieth-Century Peru: Historical and Theoretical Background to the *Golpe de Estado* of 1968," *Hispanic American Historical Review* 59:3 (August 1979), 408 (hereafter cited as *HAHR*).

3. Lieutenant Colonel Manuel Morla Concha, "Función social del ejército en la organización de la nacionalidad," *Revista Militar del Perú* (October 1933), pp. 843–872 passim (hereafter cited as *RMP*). For a detailed account of the civil-military rivalries of this period see my unpublished Ph.D. dissertation, "The Peruvian Armed Forces in Transition, 1939–1963: The Impact of National Politics and Changing Professional Perspectives," Michigan State University, 1976. Victor Villanueva Valencia, *Ejército Peruano: del caudillaje anárquico al militarismo reformista* (Lima: Juan Mejia Baca, 1973), is also very useful.

4. General Federico Hurtado, "El ministro de guerra se dirige a la ciudadanía," *RMP* (March 1938), pp. i–xxii; cited in Nunn, "Professional Militarism in Twentieth-Century Peru," *HAHR* 59:3 (August 1979), 404.

5. U.S. Ambassador John Campbell White to the Secretary of State, February 2, 1945, National Archives, Record Group 59, 823.00/2-245 (hereafter cited as NA, RG).

6. Comité Revolucionaria de Oficiales del Ejército, "Carta abierta al General Eloy G. Ureta," Colección de Volantes, Biblioteca Nacional del Perú (Lima), 1945 folder (hereafter cited as CV-BNP).

7. Useful accounts of the Trujillo revolt are Rogger Mercado, *La Revolución de Trujillo* (Lima: Fondo de Cultura Popular, 1976); Guillermo Thorndike, *El año de la barbarie, Perú 1932* (Lima: Nueva Americana, 1969), pp. 186–187; and Victor Villanueva, *El Aprá en busca del poder* (Lima: Editorial Horizonte, 1975), pp. 95–113.

8. See my "Soldiers, Sailors and Apristas: Conspiracy and Power Politics in Peru, 1932–1948," in *The Underside of Latin American History*, John F. Bratzel

and Daniel M. Masterson, eds. (East Lansing: Center for Latin American Studies, Michigan State University, 1976).

9. G-2 Report No. 536711, February 10, 1949, U.S. Military Attaché to Department of the Army; and *La Prensa*, October 30, 1948.

10. Victor Villanueva, *La sublevación aprista del 48: tragedía de un pueblo y un partido* (4th ed., Lima: Editorial Milla Batres, 1973), passim.

11. Victor Cardenas, Laureano Checa, Hector Guevara, and Orestes Romero Toldeo, *El Apra y la revolución, Tesis para un replanteamiento revolucionario* (Buenos Aires, 1952), pp. 5–9.

12. *La Prensa*, October 31, 1948, p. 1.

13. Unsigned, "El General de Brigada D. Manuel A. Odría, Presidente de la Junta Militar del Gobierno," *RMP* (October 1948), pp. v–viii.

14. U.S. Ambassador Prentice Cooper to Sec. of State, October 30, 1947, NA, RG 59, 823.00/10-3047.

15. Most air force senior officers and the Inspector General of the Army, General Federico Hurtado, opposed Odría's *golpe* but they were "outvoted" by army senior officers, including the commander of Lima's Second Infantry Division, General Zenón Noriega. G-2 Report No. 507002, November 4, 1948, U.S. Military Attaché to Department of the Army, NA, RG 319.

16. Victor Villanueva, *El CAEM y la revolución de la fuerza armada* (Lima: Instituto de Estudios Peruanos, 1973), pp. 28–33; G-2 Report No. 667591, May 17, 1950, U.S. Military Attaché to Department of the Army, NA, RG 319.

17. See Perú, Ministerio de Guerra, *Ordenes Generales del Ejército*, March 11, 1949, p. 71, and *Legislación militar del Perú*, July 2, 1956, p. 11, in the Centro de Estudios Histórico-Militares (hereafter cited as CEHM).

18. Quoted in Carlos A. Astiz and José Z. Garcia, "The Peruvian Military: Achievement Orientation, Training and Political Tendencies," *Western Political Quarterly* XXV:4 (Deember 1972), 672.

19. See Nunn, "Professional Militarism in Twentieth-Century Peru," and General Juan Mendoza R., "El ejército peruano en el siglo XX," in José Paraja Paz-Soldan, ed., *Visión del Perú en el siglo XX* (Lima: Ediciones Liberia Stadium, 1962), pp. 293–349.

20. Generals Marín and Romero Pardo served as the first two directors of the CAEM; Mendoza Rodríguez and Lindley López held the positions of minister of education and director of the Center of Military Instruction, respectively.

21. For a discussion of Odría's efforts to use the CAEM as a "junkyard" for his political opponents see Villanueva, *El CAEM*, pp. 40–41, and G-2 Report No. 642900, March 3, 1950, U.S. Military Attaché to Department of the Army, NA, RG 319.

22. Authorization for the Center's creation was included in the *Ley Organicio del Ejército* in *Legislación militar del Peru,* CEHM, July 14, 1950.

23. Villanueva, *El CAEM*, pp. 41–42.

24. General Manuel A. Odría, *Principios y postulados del movimiento restaurador de Arequipa: Extractos de discursos y mensajes del General Don Manuel A. Odría* (Lima, 1956), pp. 202–204.

25. Admiral Tirado made this statement to U.S. Ambassador James I. Loeb in 1962. Personal interview with Loeb, Cabin John, Maryland, December 17, 1973 (hereafter cited as Loeb interview).

26. See Lieutenant Colonel Cesar A. Pando Esgusquiza, "El ejército, Es enproductivo?" *RMP* (August 1946), pp. 371–387.

27. Colonel Edgardo Mercado Jarrín, "El ejército de hoy y un proyección de nuestra sociedad en periodo de transición, 1940–1965," *RMP* (November–December 1964), p. 1.

28. "A los señores y oficiales de los Institutos Armados." This manifesto was signed by officers from the army garrisons at Cuzco, Arequipa, Piura, Lambayeque, Puno, Iquitos, and Huancayo, CV-BNP, 1948.

29. "Manifesto a los institutos armados y el pueblo del Perú," CV-BNP, July 1949.

30. G-2 Report No. 642900, March 3, 1950, U.S. Military Attaché to Department of the Army, NA, RG 319.

31. The *Peruvian Times*, February 17, 1956, p. 2.

32. These two statements were attributed to General Julio Doig Sanchez and General Juan Bossio Collas, respectively. General Doig made his statement to U.S. military personnel in Washington while serving as Peru's military attaché in 1962. General Bossio reportedly linked the armed forces to the oligarchy while serving as minister of government in the same year. Loeb interview.

33. Velasco characterized the military government's program in these words while announcing the "Plan Inca" during a national television address in July 1974.

34. See my "Peru's New Leader," *The Christian Century*, XCII: 40 (December 1975), 1112–1114.

8

The Military and Development

Peter Calvert and Susan Calvert

Many Latin American countries experienced severe economic and social dislocations during the 1960s and 1970s. Faced with crises that, in their view, threatened national security, a group of well-educated military leaders, who believed that they were better prepared than their civilian counterparts to govern, assumed control of their nations. The new military regimes were characterized by two features that distinguish them from past military interventions: their long duration and, in several cases, their extreme brutality.

Military regimes in Argentina, Bolivia, Brazil, Peru, Chile, Ecuador, Guatemala, Honduras, El Salvador, and Panama sought to promote national security through the eradication of leftist political groups and the promotion of economic development. Despite the great differences in size, population, wealth, and level of development of their countries, the leaders of the armed forces of the region shared a belief that they were the ones best prepared to modernize their nations. Their policies, which the authors refer to as "military developmentalism," were based on the assumption that an authoritarian government constituted a precondition for economic development and internal peace.

While some military governments contributed to economic growth, as in the case of Chile, others, such as those in Peru and Panama, left chaos and conflict in their wake. In all instances, the Draconian measures employed by the military to stifle dissent undermined civilian political institutions and engendered endemic violence. The nonmilitary regimes that followed have proved unable to hold the armed forces accountable for their actions. Relations between them and the military have remained "delicate."

From *Latin America in the Twentieth Century* (London: Macmillan Press, 1990), 118–51. ©1990 by Macmillan Press. Reprinted by permission of Macmillan Press and St. Martin's Press.

Argentina after Perón

The ousting of [Juan] Perón in September 1955, known by anti-Peronistas as the Liberating Revolution, was followed by a brief period of Catholic Nationalist military government, which sought to re-integrate Peronism into Argentine politics. The replacement soon afterward of General [Eduardo] Lonardi by General [Pedro] Aramburu as president, however, expressed the underlying dominance of hard-line anti-Peronists. They sought to demobilize labor and to keep it demobilized. Peronist resistance (*la resistencia*) to incursions into areas in which labor had gained under Perón was impressive, but behind it the nature of industrialization itself was changing from the mid-1950s in a manner that would in itself reduce the influence of organized labor. Foreign involvement in the economy encouraged by the internationalist orientation of the Aramburu government further enhanced the power of capital as against labor, as medium-sized manufacturing enterprises increasingly yielded to big business.

This process continued under the Radical government of Arturo Frondizi, who, despite making overtures to Peronism, presided over the acceleration of the demobilization of rank-and-file labor and the growth of union bureaucracy, features that were to last until the end of the 1960s and would be supportive of the institution of direct military rule in 1966. The three civilian governments of the later 1950s and early 1960s were marked by political and economic crises, and survived at the discretion of the military, which itself experienced political infighting that probably delayed the return to military rule. A stagnating economy with relatively slow growth, compared to the great economic successes temporarily being registered elsewhere in Latin America, massive budget deficits, and economic drift based on an absence of purpose reflected Argentina's lack of a clear identity. Inflation, unemployment, and flight of capital all co-existed with political problems primarily associated with the persistence of Peronism. Yet they also expressed the underlying disunity of the fragmented party system. By June 1966, with organized labor divided, pressures from business interests rising, and compromise between competing military factions temporarily achieved, General Juan Carlos Onganía assumed power in a bloodless coup against the ineffectual civilian government of the Radical, Dr. Arturo Illia, a coup that supporters termed "the Argentine Revolution."

Onganía dissolved Congress and the provincial legislatures. The Supreme Court ceased to operate. All political parties were suspended. Police powers as well as military ones were enhanced in the political sphere, and political arrests occurred as individual rights were disregarded.

State violence increased, especially in the purging of the universities to eliminate the student base of Peronism. Manifestations of youthful "decadence" were given military treatment; soldiers patrolled the streets, administering compulsory haircuts to young men whose hair, in the generally prevailing fashion, was deemed too long. In the economic sphere, on the other hand, the watchword was "rationalization," resulting in the further opening of Argentina to foreign capital penetration. Measures taken under this head included reductions in overmanning of public utilities, removal of rent and price controls but control of wages and salaries, and a credit squeeze that hit nationally owned, small- to medium-sized enterprises particularly hard. Thus the Onganía regime succeeded in alienating many members of the middle class, whether salaried or self-employed, and not just organized labor. Labor resistance became more apparent toward the end of the decade. More seriously, so did the activities of guerrilla groups, and not only Onganía but the continuance of military rule itself was challenged by an increasing number of assassinations of union leaders and of military officers by the Montoneros (Peronist guerrillas). The beginning of the end of military rule, however, was marked explicitly by a popular rising in Córdoba in 1969. Although the origins of the rebellion seem minor now, a rise in student refectory prices bringing the student population of the city onto the streets and a change in Saturday working (the abolition of a full day's pay for a half day's work termed the "English Saturday" in Argentina) having the same effect among car workers, the city was beyond the control of the military authorities for some hours. Known as the Cordobazo (the blow of Córdoba), the rising was suppressed by force, but key elements in the Army took note and sought to control the forces of change.

Hence, Onganía was replaced in 1970 by General [Roberto] Levingston, a man so unknown to the general public that his photograph had to be displayed to show them what he looked like. He was a front for the senior General [Alejandro] Lanusse, who assumed power in his own right the following year. He did so to oversee what he had come to realize was inevitable, the restoration of civilian government and the eventual return of Perón from almost two decades of exile in Madrid. Perón himself being prevented by residence qualifications from standing as a candidate, in March 1973 a left-wing Peronist, Dr. Héctor Cámpora, won the presidential elections. Within months, with Lanusse safely out of the way after a curious apology to the people of Argentina for his unconstitutional behavior, Cámpora in turn (reluctantly, it is said) stood down in favor of his leader. Perón returned by air on June 20, but the triumph his supporters had planned turned to disaster as rival factions fired on one another and there were many deaths, the road from Ezeiza International Airport being strewn with their bodies. The plane carrying Perón had been diverted else-where. Though in September of that year Perón was elected with some 61 percent of the popular vote, it was already ominously clear that the violence unleashed was going to be too much for him to control.

Guerrilla action was escalating when Perón's death on July 1, 1974, removed the last vestiges of control. His successor was his vice president and third wife, María Estela Martínez de Perón, known as Isabel, whom he had met when she was a dancer in Panama and had hired to type his political testament, *Force Is the Reason of Beasts*. Inexperienced as she was in practical politics, Isabel, as her husband had done some years be-fore, soon fell under the influence of an éminence grise, José López Rega, a mystic and, it was said, a sorcerer (as witness his nickname, El Brujo), who moved the administration sharply to the right. From his Ministry of Social Welfare, López Rega controlled a paramilitary organization, the right-wing Argentine Anti-Communist Alliance (AAA), which provided "death squads" for the elimination of "terrorists" and was to provide the infrastructure and the ideological justification for the military to do the same in due course.

By March 1976 the economic incompetence of the Peronist govern-ment, especially its half-hearted attempts to appease in turn various sectoral demands, had led to hyperinflation. Worse still from a purely economic point of view, increasing alienation accelerated the use of bomb-ings, kidnappings, and murders against businessmen and business targets, especially foreign-owned companies. Terrorist attacks and para-military shootings became generalized and added to the chaos and dis-order. Arguments continue about which came first: leftist subversion or rightist violence. It does not really matter, since the overall effect was the same. Economic chaos and political disorder therefore formed both the cause and the justification for the seizure and detention of Mrs. Perón and the installation of a new military government under the austere commander-in-chief of the Army, General Jorge Videla.

Isabel Perón was seized as she left the Casa Rosada (the presidential office building at the northern end of the Plaza de Mayo in Buenos Aires) to return to the presidential residence in the pleasant suburb of Olivos. Initially she was imprisoned in the south of the country before being re-turned under house arrest to the *quinta* she had shared with her late hus-band in the southern suburb of San Vicente. There she remained until her release in 1981, when she went into exile in Madrid. During her exile and through the early period of democratic government under the Radicals she remained titular head of the Peronist movement. The realization that her occasional presence in Argentina cost the Peronists thousands of potential supporters in reminding the electorate of the chaos over which her government had presided belatedly led in 1986 to her being replaced as leader of the movement.

The 1976 regime, like the 1966–1973 one, but unlike previous Argentine military governments, saw itself as holding power for the foreseeable future. It was not to be a transitional arrangement that would presage the election of a new, more acceptable civilian government, but a permanent one, which would stay in place to preside over nothing less than the total reorganization of civil society to expunge communism and other features deemed contrary to the Western way of life. This Process of National Reorganization (usually known simply as "the Process") was to penetrate all aspects of Argentine society, beginning in the schools and universities. Teachers were once more purged, subversive (and not-so-subversive) books were burned, artists were proscribed and driven into exile, formal political channels were closed down, and, most notoriously, a wholesale counterterror was unleashed on all suspected of being left-wing or having left-wing sympathies. Estimates of the number who perished in the first two years of what became known as "the Dirty War" (la Guerra Sucia) fluctuated wildly at the time, but it is now known that some nine thousand were killed and it is all but certain that the real figure was over fifteen thousand. Many of those who were rounded up, tortured, and "disappeared," it is certain, had no left-wing credentials. Friends and relations, seized on suspicion, also died, some children on the argument that since their elder brothers and sisters were suspects, they too in time would grow up into "subversives." Women were seized, raped, and tortured only because they were attractive, and the babies of some of the "disappeared" were taken from their mothers at birth and given to military families.

The justification of this horror was that it would end subversion and make Argentina economically strong. However, the economic policies of the regime were disastrous and led to corruption on a scale even greater than anything that had gone before. Corruption was not confined to the looting of the property of "subversives" and their families, nor to the labeling as "subversive" of individuals whose property was desired, but it permeated all the economic dealings of the regime. As the economy was opened up to foreign capital, loans were sought for grandiose developmental schemes, and a substantial proportion of these funds disappeared into the pockets of both civilian contractors and their military contacts. The peso was deliberately allowed to become overvalued. This made the foreign loans seem cheap in the short term, but it also encouraged consumer imports and a frantic spending spree. At the first sign of trouble, then, domestic capital took fright and fled abroad to more secure financial markets.

By 1980 the Dirty War had been "won," but the economic crisis deepened and began to lead to bankruptcies. Videla, as promised, handed over power at the end of a five-year term to General [Roberto] Viola (1981), who was regarded as more moderate. But within months he in turn was displaced in a putsch by the hard-liner General [Leopoldo] Galtieri, who once in control of the junta engineered his own succession to the presidency in December 1981 without, however, relinquishing command of the Army. Continuing economic problems at home, the reassertion of the influence of organized labor in large public demonstrations, and divisions in the officer corps, now that any threat of subversion appeared to have been ended, had given Galtieri the opportunity to ally himself with fiercely nationalist elements in the Navy and Air Force. The invasion of the Falkland Islands (Islas Malvinas) in April 1982, and the subsequent defeat of Argentina by the British Task Force, brought about a more clear-cut abdication of power by the Argentine armed forces than was experienced in other Latin American countries. A period of transition during which the military destroyed evidence of their crimes and sought guarantees of their personal safety and that of the military institution preceded an open, honest, and relatively peaceful election that returned the Radicals to power and Dr. Raúl Alfonsín to the presidency.

Military Rule in Bolivia

For Bolivia, 1964 marked the reassertion of direct military rule after the protracted period of MNR [Movimiento Nacional Revolucionario] government. An attempt at the assassination of General René Barrientos Ortuño, who had fought with Air Force elements on the side of the MNR rebels in 1952, encouraged the popular acclaim of this earthy, charismatic figure and led President [Victor] Paz Estenssoro reluctantly to field him as his vice presidential candidate for the 1964 elections. Paz retained power because the opposition parties boycotted these elections, but in November fell prey instead to the personal ambitions of his vice president, who led the coup against the MNR regime. For two years Barrientos ruled as joint president with a colleague, General Alfredo Ovando Candía; in 1966 he was elected in his own right.

Barrientos's popularity stemmed at least in part from the fact that he was the first president of Bolivia to speak Quechua, the mother tongue of many of its inhabitants. He also inherited the clientelist network established by the MNR and made many tours of the country distributing largesse in the form of footballs, bicycles, and other material goods. His regime was personalist, corrupt, and chaotic, exhibiting the style associated with the traditional caudillo. His was not a tight institutional dictatorship of the kind set up in Brazil in 1964 and two years later in Argentina. The Barrientos regime was in foreign affairs pro-United States, pro-foreign capital, and anti-Communist, but it did not develop the ideology of the national security state. The armed forces were expanded and their political role greatly enhanced, but collectively they never achieved even the level of unity associated with military interventions of the 1960s and 1970s elsewhere in Latin America. Repression was unsophisticated and arbitrary. Factionalism within the military institution was contained in the short term by co-opting key factional leaders into government. Barrientos succeeded in retaining peasant support, though fewer people benefited from the redistribution of land than under the previous regime. His government was most criticized abroad because it was, as might have been expected, hostile to organized labor and to the political Left. As early as 1965, Barrientos imposed a state of siege and used troops to dismantle the miners' militias and to occupy the mines. Escalating state violence was also the order of the day against the increasing activity of guerrilla groups, notably that led in person by Che Guevara.

The death of Barrientos in 1969, when the helicopter he was piloting flew into power lines, led to a brief vice presidential succession followed by a disparate series of corrupt and unstable military governments interspersed with brief civilian interludes. Despite the common institutional base of the military governments, they covered a wide spectrum of ideological positions. General Ovando, who served on his own briefly as president (1969–70), was a moderate reformist in the tradition established by the MNR. He was succeeded after a violent contest for power between rival military factions by General Juan José Torres González, whose radical ideology led him to seek Soviet aid, attack the United States, and mobilize organized labor. In so doing he stirred up centrist as well as right-wing civilian opposition and alienated many of his brother officers, preparing the way for the bloody coup that brought Colonel Hugo Banzer Suárez to power.

Banzer's own attempted coup earlier in the year had failed, and its leader was imprisoned. The collapse of the Torres government in August 1971, however, led to his release. He proclaimed himself president and embarked on a further wave of violence against the political Left, especially students, who at that time were particularly suspect. While civilian opposition was suppressed, opposition within the military was contained. Banzer had the support of Brazil and, behind it, of the United States, following the Nixon-Kissinger policy of so-called benign neglect. Further, some domestic civilian elements were behind him, most importantly among the agroindustrial sector, and some political factions, notably that of Paz himself. MNR supporters were given seats in Banzer's cabinet in coalition with the right-wing Falange Socialista Boliviana (FSB).

Banzer had in fact been rapidly promoted under the MNR regime, becoming a full colonel at the age of thirty-five. He was still only forty-four when he became president. His relative youth and his U.S. military training were reflected in the ideological character of his government, which had much more in common with the "bureaucratic-authoritarian" regimes of Brazil and Argentina than the regime of his predecessor, Barrientos, though this was because of the heavy and growing influence of Brazil, and Bolivia moved away from previously close relations with Argentina. Military rule was seen as a long-term necessity to be accompanied by depoliticization of the masses and modernization of the economy, especially by the expansion of education and the construction of roads. Although Soviet aid was retained, Banzer sought and obtained increased U.S. financial assistance and opened up the Bolivian economy further to foreign capitalist penetration.

Massive devaluations of the peso in accordance with IMF [International Monetary Fund] requirements and removal of subsidies on basic goods and services led to high inflation and huge increases in the cost of living. Demonstrations were repressed and ugly stories of peasant massacres began to circulate. In November 1974 civilian elements were dismissed from the government and Paz was exiled. Economic problems were increasing; repression accelerated the development of internal opposition, including that of the church. National strikes in 1976 led the government to close the universities and made it clear that the successful repression of labor was no longer possible. President [Jimmy] Carter's election in the United States added pressure on the question of human rights. In 1978, after the longest period in office of any Bolivian leader since Independence, Banzer held elections and so lost the power that on three occasions he has tried to regain by election. The elections were won by a civilian coalition called Democratic and Popular Unity (UDP), which again included Paz's breakaway faction of the MNR. General Juan Pereda Asbún, whom Banzer had placed in charge of the repressive Department of Political Order, annulled the elections and assumed office himself. Immediately he faced internal unrest and U.S. pressure, which increased until a left-wing coup of junior officers displaced him. The Army commander, General David Padilla Arancibia, became president, supported by the Left, with the stated intention of returning power to the civilians and allowing the military to return to the barracks. Bolivia's was the first of the military developmentalist regimes to decide to do so, but unfortunately it was not immediately to be successful.

Indecisive elections in July 1979 resulted in almost equal votes for the two old rivals of the MNR: Dr. [Hernán] Siles Zuazo and Dr. Paz Estenssoro. Congress too was divided and established instead an interim government under the president of the Senate, Walter Guevara Arze. Deeply suspect because of the role he was believed to have played in conveying the text of his namesake Che Guevara's diaries to Havana, Guevara lacked support both in Congress and among the Army, and presided over a deepening political and economic crisis. Public unrest again met fierce military repression. Another coup led to the two-week presidency of Colonel Alberto Natusch Busch, under whom soldiers ran amok in La Paz and as many Bolivians died in this brief military interregnum as in the whole seven years of General Banzer. In face of popular resistance, military commanders again allowed Congress to restore civilian government under interim rule of the MNR president of the Chamber of Deputies, Dr. Lidia Gueiler Tejada.

Dr. Gueiler, the second woman in the world (after Isabel Perón) to be chosen as an executive president, was an able leader who in happier times might have done very well. Instead she was faced with the same problem as her predecessors, a corrupt Army deeply enmeshed in politics and unwilling to surrender its valuable personal and institutional privileges. In April 1980 she tried to break out of this constraint when she replaced the Army commander with her cousin, General Luís García Meza. The following month the UDP again led in indecisive elections and Siles was chosen as prospective president after tough congressional bargaining. But he was not to assume the office just yet. In June, Dr. Gueiler survived a crude abortive coup through her prudence in locking her bedroom door and thus delaying the military conspirators long enough to allow her to telephone for help. The following month, García Meza intervened, with the advice and encouragement of the Argentine Army, to prevent the succession of Siles. Political arrests and the exile of Siles were only the preludes to a regime even more repressive and economically disastrous than its predecessors, if fortunately short-lived. Those lucky enough to be released after being interrogated as suspected subversives by the García Meza regime reported to human rights organizations their identification of many of the officers involved in the repressive process as Argentines. Again the characteristic use of *che* gave their national origins away. Labor leaders were tortured and killed, but passive resistance among workers was strong and divisions among the Bolivian officer corps were widened. With military encouragement, the growing of coca and the smuggling of cocaine was transformed into an illegal industry so widespread that it was impossible to eradicate and so vast that its turnover was believed to exceed that of the legal economy. Hence, the United States and other countries refused to recognize it, U.S. opposition to the regime being based more, it seemed, on its opposition to narcotics than its desire to promote human rights.

A military junta under General Celso Torrelio Villa displaced García Meza in August 1981, but in turn yielded power to the Army chief of staff, who proved no more competent to deal with gathering economic catastrophe. Finally, the discrediting of military government in Argentina helped precipitate the move back to civilian government, and in near desperation elections were brought forward and Siles inaugurated in October 1982. At last he was again to have the chance to show what he could do to put matters right. The problem was that for many years it had been too late, and in the meanwhile he had changed. In 1986, wholly discredited by economic failure, he was replaced in a free election by Dr. Paz.

The Brazilian Revolution

Following [Getúlio] Vargas's suicide a series of brief constitutional, but nonelected, presidents flitted across the stage before new elections took place. At one point, the situation became so chaotic that two separate military factions dispatched tanks to the presidential palace. One of the factions was held back by the traffic. When they found their rivals already in possession, as John Gunther recalls in his *Inside South America*, "the enemy crews then proceeded to play football together, using their tanks to mark the goals."

In 1956, Dr. Juscelino de Oliveira Kubitschek, who had won the elections rather unconvincingly on behalf of a coalition comprising the Labor party and the Social Democratic party, assumed the presidency with João Goulart ("Jango") as his vice president despite military opposition to Goulart, whom they regarded as a dangerous left-winger. Kubitschek, born of Czech stock in Minas Gerais, and a medical doctor by training, was an unusual combination of dreamer and practical man. His most notable achievement in office was to fulfill a century-old dream and transfer the capital four hundred miles inland to a new city, Brasília, planned and built on a virgin site in the state of Goias. The new city, designed by architects Lúcio Costa and Oscar Niemeyer, in the shape of an arrow pointing toward the Brazilian interior, symbolizes the opening up of the heartland of the nation. Characteristically they did not design the houses of the people who were to live there; that was left to private enterprise. Kubitschek also built up the national car industry, but this further advance on the economic front was overshadowed by the high spending and corruption for which he was formally charged in 1964. It has been said of Kubitschek that he promised "fifty years' progress in five" but delivered forty years' inflation in four.

The 1960 elections returned to the presidency another extraordinary character, the dynamic reforming governor of São Paulo, Jânio Quadros, his emblem a broom with which he would clean up government. João Goulart was again returned to the vice presidency as representative of the Labor party, on a separate ticket from the coalition of Social Democrats backing Quadros. Hence when after less than a year in office Quadros unexpectedly resigned in a fit of pique, he plunged the country into crisis. The Army resisted the succession of Goulart, and the president of the Chamber of Deputies became interim president while a formula was worked out allowing Goulart to take the presidency only after the constitution had been amended to create a new office of prime minister and so reduce presidential powers. At a time of ideological polarization within Brazil, and following the Cuban Revolution, Goulart was associated more clearly with the political Left than perhaps his actions warranted. Like his brother-in-law, Leonel Brizola, then governor of Rio Grande do Sul, Goulart was a nationalist and opposed U.S. intervention in Brazil. He made promises of reforms, including agrarian reform, but was constrained in what he could do by the economic circumstances in which he had to operate.

Brazil's development problems in the early 1960s remained much the same despite Kubitschek's expenditure on grand schemes. The interior was still underdeveloped; the nation lacked the essential infrastructure of roads and railways. Only some 5 percent of potential arable land was under cultivation. Thus despite its massive economic potential, especially in terms of hydroelectric power and mineral and agricultural production, Brazilian gross national product per head of population was low. Likewise, in human terms, social problems were immense. More than half of the population was under the age of sixteen, about half were illiterate, housing conditions in the *favelas* (shantytowns) around the major cities were appalling, and the infant mortality rate remained colossal, this last reflecting the inadequacy of health services and the poor standard of public sanitation and water supply as well as the poverty of the population. Goulart's presidency came at a time when increasing political and economic demands in consequence of the rapidly growing population coincided with a short recession. Between 1956 and 1963 the economy had grown at an annual rate of between 7 and 9 percent, at the cost of accelerating inflation. When the recession came, inflation continued to rise, touching 1,200 percent per annum.

Declining support for the civilian regime was a natural consequence of falling income and the accompanying industrial unrest. Respect for political leaders was already low—as a gesture of contempt for the government in the local elections of 1962 many *paulistas* (inhabitants of São Paulo) cast their votes for Cacareco, a favorite hippopotamus in the local zoo. Nevertheless, the following year Goulart was able to muster enough votes in a plebiscite to throw off the shackles the armed forces had fastened on him and to recover the presidential powers lost in 1961. But Goulart's incompetence contributed to the worsening economic situation, not to say crisis, of 1963–64. The cost of living continued to spiral, the government deficit to widen. As capital left the country, U.S. aid to Brazil was cut. The economic crisis was paralleled in the instability of government personnel and in Goulart's increasing inability to get Congress to agree to his proposals.

In September 1963 there took place in the new capital, Brasília, a revolt by several hundred NCOs and enlisted men in all three services. The president of the Chamber of Deputies was among the hostages taken by the rebels. Though the revolt was quickly suppressed, considerable fear was generated among right-wing politicians recognizing their own vulnerability and senior officers concerned to maintain military discipline. Goulart did not condemn the revolt and thus fed rightist fears that he would use the military for his own purposes at some future date. When in October Goulart asked Congress to approve the imposition of a state of siege to contain the wave of industrial unrest and political violence sweeping the nation, Congress refused and Goulart withdrew the request. The violence continued, and many senior military officers began to believe that not only was military discipline threatened, but public order had actually broken down. In March 1964, Goulart brought matters to a head with a mass rally at which he decreed the nationalization of some private oil refineries, the expropriation of some underutilized land, as well as the enfranchisement of illiterates. Brizola, then still a relatively youthful firebrand, also made a rousing speech in which he threatened the dissolution of Congress if it did not ratify these decrees. This was the signal the armed forces had been waiting for. Public opposition, already high, increased further with women marching in protest against Goulart's policies, which they claimed were an attack on God and on the family. Senior officers, noting the president's clumsy attempt to win support among the Navy by giving them an aircraft carrier, were confirmed in their view that he and his brother-in-law were stirring up insubordination in the ranks. Matters came to a head in 1964, when a military revolt broke out in Minas Gerais in protest at the presence of what were vaguely referred to as "Communists" in the government. The governor of the state supported the revolt, and Goulart ordered troops to put it down. In the confusion that followed, it soon became clear that Goulart had in fact lost control of the Army and that key elements of it had moved over to support the rebels.

The coup that followed, subsequently termed "the Brazilian Revolution," brought the Army chief of staff, General (later Marshal) Humberto Castello Branco, to the presidency. An honest man, a hero of the wartime Expeditionary Force, and, within limits, a constitutionalist, he allowed Congress to "elect" him initially to finish Goulart's term, and later to extend that term to 1967. The new government received the immediate good wishes of the Johnson administration in the United States and in due course the restoration of U.S. aid. The independent foreign policy of the early 1960s gave way to an unashamedly and uncritically pro-Western stance, which would lead Brazil the following year to support U.S. intervention in the Dominican Republic. But the purpose of the high-ranking military officers of the Higher War School (Escola Superior de Guerra, ESG) who had planned for such a takeover was not simply to depose a president, but to reconstruct Brazilian society, and the stresses soon showed. Though Congress continued to meet, the constitutionalism of the new regime was only formal and was ignored whenever it happened to be convenient. Most left-wing politicians were deprived of their political rights for a long period of years, and the number of political prisoners and exiles continued to mount as a series of purges occurred throughout the first year. Most ominously, within three months of the military coming to power, a new and formidable secret police organization was created. Responsible only to the president, the new organization, euphemistically termed the Servicio Nacional de Informações (SNI), was given a free hand in all matters of national security both internal and external. Not surprisingly it soon grew out of the control of the hard-liners of the ESG who had set it up. In the meanwhile, the military attempt to restore order inevitably meant a further concentration of power in the hands of the federal government, and from the outset the states lost much of their autonomy. Then after the Social Democratic/Labor party alliance did well in the elections of 1965, pressure from hard-liners within the government mounted and Castello Branco, despite his constitutional inclinations, became increasingly authoritarian. Existing political parties were abolished, elections were to be indirect only, and presidential authority was enhanced to include such powers as the power to annul elections. Realizing that the complete suppression of opinion could be dangerous, however, in 1966 two new parties were brought into existence: the pro-government Aliança Renovadora Nacional (ARENA), and a small legal opposition party, the Brazilian Democratic Movement (MDB).

The new regime's economic policy was stabilizing in the short term and inflation was reduced. But the new regime had taken power with the intention of holding on to it long enough to make Brazil economically strong and able to hold its own in the outside world, and inevitably this had other important economic effects. Taxation was reformed and public expenditure cut in most areas. Where state spending was increased, as, for example, in education, it was done in a fashion that increased rather than decreased inequality, since the additional funds were devoted mainly to the expansion of secondary and higher education in accord with the national plan to produce more skilled managers. The unequal distribution of income that characterized the period after 1964, moreover, had the conscious purpose of creating the kind of domestic market needed to encourage further economic growth in manufactured goods such as consumer durables. However, by 1967 little had been achieved. Brazil still had the largest foreign debt in the world. Nine tenths of its foreign exchange earnings were still derived from agriculture, but since Goulart's measures had been revoked, land utilization was as inefficient as ever and food was still being imported. Industrial development was down and unemployment was up.

The choice of General Artur Costa e Silva to succeed Castello Branco in 1967 represented a further victory for the hard-liners. Costa e Silva had played a leading part in the coup of 1964. Under the combined influence of the unrest of 1968 and the outbreak of urban terrorism in South America, the regime took a sharp turn to the right. In November 1968 what Brazilians term an internal coup took place as the government assumed total control. The Fifth Institutional Act swept away the remaining vestiges of constitutional government and installed a frankly authoritarian regime, under which the SNI, the military intelligence organization which it had superseded, and other competing intelligence agencies sought out, tortured, and occasionally assassinated real or suspected terrorists. When Costa e Silva died suddenly in 1969 his figurehead civilian vice president was not allowed to succeed him and his policies were continued by General Emilio Garrastasú Médici, the former head of the SNI, who served as president for a five-year term from 1969 to 1974.

When Médici left office the urban guerrilla threat, which had never been very serious, had been eliminated and repression had eased off. Meanwhile, between 1967 and 1974 Brazil had experienced its "economic miracle," achieving average growth rates of between 11 and 13 percent per annum. The miracle was, however, more apparent than real, for three reasons. The rates of growth were not really much greater than those achieved under the despised civilian regimes before 1964, yet they had been achieved at a much higher social cost in terms of deprivation and inequality. Brazil was still exporting only 5 percent of its manufacturing output, and by 1974, in response to the "first oil shock," the slowdown had begun. Worst of all, as oil prices tripled overnight, Brazil was in the almost uniquely uncomfortable position of having no sources of oil of its own.

For the rest of the decade, therefore, successive military regimes tried to grapple with these unpalatable facts while using the declining threat from the revolutionary Left as an excuse for a very gradual process of "decompression" (*distensão*). From a position of strength, the armed forces would slowly retreat to barracks over a period of many years, while retaining their ability to control the people and institutions they left behind, a process of liberalization but not of democratization. In practice the process proved much harder to control than they had imagined, as they had not reckoned with the irrepressible Brazilian urge for change. Both General Ernesto Geisel (1974–1979) and his successor, General João Baptista Figueiredo (1979–1984), found themselves caught between civilians pressing for faster liberalization and hard-line military factions who did not want any opening (*abertura*) at all.

General Geisel, a Lutheran, tried to rule the world's largest Catholic country single-handed. Under his rule censorship was softened and political parties restored to legality. But even by the end of the 1970s, before the full effects of the 1979 oil shock had been felt, the "miracle" had gone sour, and in face of increasing unrest repression was again tightened. General Figueiredo, a cavalry officer, tried to appear a man of the people, but the effect of a well-publicized walkabout in a supermarket was rather spoiled by his reported comment afterward that he much preferred the smell of horses to the smell of people. He proved none too impressive at managing the economy either. The debt situation was already out of control, and the discovery of petroleum on the continental shelf some 100 km. off Brazil's northeast coast came too late to help. In fact by the time either it or the military project to replace it altogether by distilling fuel alcohol from sugarcane was able to contribute significantly, the price of oil had again fallen. By 1982, therefore, inflation was again over 100 percent and labor unrest rising. Pressures for *abertura* led to the reintroduction of direct elections for governors of states in November 1982; the opposition won all the major governorships. In the following year, Brazil experienced the most serious riots and demonstrations since 1964, most notably in São Paulo, over the cost of living and rising unemployment, and the final decision was taken to engineer an early transfer of power to an elected civilian president.

The sheer size of the Brazilian economy meant that even with such problems it was still relatively strong. In addition, although the rapid development sought by the military did not occur in the way that they had envisaged, Brazil, among Latin American countries, is still seen as having a tradition of firm economic management. On the political side, the military may have withdrawn from direct participation in government, but it is by no means clear yet that real civilian democracy is in the cards. Despite the expanding electoral participation of 1945–1964, there was still a high degree of military intervention in the political process then, and there is little evidence that intervention will cease in the future. The armed forces cleared the way for the election of Tancredo Neves, the leading opposition candidate, in 1984. On the day of his inauguration, however, Neves, who had disregarded the preliminary warnings of pain for fear that the military would have second thoughts, was rushed to the hospital with a burst appendix and peritonitis and, despite heroic efforts to save him, died a few weeks later. In this way his vice president, José Sarney, became first acting president and then president in his own right. Sarney, however, who owed his position to the fact that at the last moment he had led his faction of the PDS [Partido Democratico Socialista] (a faction of the former pro-military ARENA) into the Neves camp, lacked his running mate's credibility and charm, and was soon deep in trouble with a Congress that he could not control and a Constituent Assembly that tried but failed to cut short his presidency. With direct elections restored for the first time in eighteen years and inflation running at over 1,700 percent, Brazilians in 1989 rejected two strong left-wing candidates in favor of the candidate of the Center-Right, the telegenic Fernando Collor de Mello, who at his inauguration on March 1990 promised drastic economies and a major campaign against corruption.

Controlled Revolution in Peru

Peru followed a distinctive course. The Peruvian Army shared the concerns of its fellows in Argentina and Brazil. However, the ideas taught in its school for senior staff officers, the Centro de Altos Estudios Militares (CAEM), were different. The armed forces, it was said, should not simply seek to resist the pressures building up for change; instead they should carry out a controlled social revolution that would preempt such pressures.

The military government that held office between 1962 and 1963 saw its role as the traditional one: to remove an unsatisfactory president, and "hold the ring" while fresh elections resulted in the choice of a more suitable candidate. But urged on by the junior officers who had helped make the coup, the interim government proclaimed a "Year of Literacy" on the Cuban model. The elections of 1963 gave victory to a very traditional candidate, Fernando Belaúnde Terry, a moderate Catholic, well connected and an architect by profession, and the Army turned to political action programs in the countryside that were to bring many of them face-to-face for the first time with the real problems their country faced.

By 1967 the uneasy compromise was beginning to break down. The government's economic program was in trouble. Demand for copper had been slack and the sol had to be devalued. In military circles there was growing suspicion that the United States was not going to keep its old promises of aid, and when in 1968 Belaúnde proposed compromise in the long-running dispute between the Peruvian government and the International Petroleum Corporation [IPC], who, the government alleged, had been illegally exploiting important oil resources in the La Brea–Pariñas region, the Army acted. In the small hours of October 3, 1968, Belaúnde was carried out of the presidential palace, kicking and shouting, "These are traitors! scoundrels!" It did no good—they removed his shoes and placed him on a plane to Panama.

The military government that took power did so under a secret plan, the existence of which was not publicly known until 1974. It was called, not wholly imaginatively, "Plan Inca." In accordance with it, the new government headed by General Juan Velasco Alvarado immediately expropriated the disputed IPC holdings and proclaimed its independence of all outside influences. To cancel dependency was to be the fundamental objective of Peru's nationalist revolution. As Velasco said, however, the revolution he had in mind was neither capitalist nor Communist, since "capitalism had failed and communism would not work." As for support for its ideas, the new government consulted mainly with its principal constituency, the armed forces, but the changes themselves were widely accepted, and until 1976 the government, though without a popular mandate, had little need of coercion. The effect was to break the economic base of the coastal oligarchy that had dominated Peru, but to set in their place a military corporatist regime directed, like its predecessors, from above.

In 1970 the government inaugurated a major land reform by Decree Law 17,776, enforcing the expropriation of the great coastal estates that were reorganized in workers' cooperatives. Already legislation had begun the systematic development of the manufacturing sector by nationalization of the principal industries, and within four years the government achieved its objective of central control of the primary and most of the secondary manufacturing industries. Workers were given representation on state boards, and an even greater role in determining policy under the provision made for what was termed "social ownership" of many other enterprises. The government's intent to organize workers under its own leadership, and to undercut the popular support Aprismo [political movement] had held since the 1930s, was coordinated by an organization called the National System of Aid to Social Mobilization (SINAMOS), which was to promote community organization and so social mobilization in support of the government's plan throughout the sparsely populated regions of the sierra and in the remote regions of the Amazon basin.

The plan was from the beginning beset by both natural and man-made crises. Over fifty thousand died in an earthquake in 1970, which by especially ill luck caught many people in their homes watching the national [soccer] team playing in the World Cup. The fishing industry was disrupted by the appearance of the warm *niño* current driving the anchovy away from the coast, as well as by overfishing. The price of copper fell on the world market by two thirds between 1974 and 1976 as the Vietnam War tailed to its end. And the government was caught unexpectedly in a storm of controversy when it tried in 1973 to muzzle the press by placing it under workers' control, in a way very similar to that followed in Cuba. The president suffered from circulatory problems leading to an aneurysm of the abdominal artery. He was rushed to the hospital but had to have a leg amputated. As a semi-invalid he welcomed the delegates to the Non-Aligned Summit in Lima in 1975; then while they conferred he was displaced in a bloodless coup by his prime minister, General Francisco Morales Bermúdez, who said good-bye to them at the end of the meeting. Discreetly the delegates made no comment. A year later Morales conceded to U.S. pressures, ending subsidies, denationalized the fisheries, ended agrarian reform before it had reached the sierra, and proclaimed a state of emergency. The Peruvian revolution was over—at least for the time being. Failing to find any other way out, elections for a Constituent Assembly were held, and in 1980, under a new constitution, Belaúnde returned to the presidential palace he had left involuntarily in 1968.

In his second term Belaúnde's one goal seemed to be to finish his term. In this he succeeded, becoming the first Peruvian civilian to do so in forty years. But as the country drifted, weighed down by the debt incurred in the military years, a new threat arose, a Maoist revolutionary movement termed, with reference to the phrase of [José] Mariátegui, Sendero Luminoso (Shining Path). To combat it, civil rights were suspended, martial law proclaimed, and virtually all the departments of Ayacucho and Huancavelica given over to military government, but the movement survived, discrediting the government by a series of simple but effective demonstrations, a favorite being to dynamite the electricity pylons that carried current into the capital and plunge it into darkness while their own slogan was illuminated on the hills above. In 1985 once again Peruvians voted for APRA [Alianza Popular Revolucionaria Americana] and its presidential candidate Alán García [Pérez], who became the first candidate of the country's majority party to be allowed by the armed forces to take office.

Though the *Apristas* hold office, the Army has retained significant power, and García's challenge, that Peru would and could afford to pay no more than 10 percent on its debt, though wildly popular with other Third World spokespersons, has left Peru boycotted by the IMF and so cut off from new private investment that it desperately needs. It will be the greatest of ironies if in this way the guardians of capitalist orthodoxy succeed in establishing in Peru a revolutionary movement that promises to rival the Khmer Rouge of Cambodia in bloodiness if it should ever come to power.

From Democracy to Dictatorship in Chile

In the 1950s, with Jorge Alessandri, son of Arturo, in the Moneda, the presidential palace in the gray downtown heart of Santiago, Chile took on to the outside world that appearance of a stable democracy which was to prove so deceptive. The appearance was not wholly misleading. Both Left and Right in the period after 1946 remained committed to the ideal of electoral democracy. But the Communists could not avoid the temptation of fomenting strikes against the government of which they notionally formed a part, and so played into the hands of their enemies, and with the formal banning of the Communist party in 1948 its support simply passed to the rival Socialist party, also a Marxist party and in some respects more radical. Marxism was widely popular, enjoyed substantial working-class support, union and political organization, and it was natural to believe that its time would come. It very nearly did in 1964, when the candidate of the Socialist party, a country doctor called Salvador Allende, came a very close second to the Christian Democratic candidate, Eduardo Frei, despite the frenetic efforts of the church hierarchy to denounce Allende as a Communist. It came instead in 1970. The more radical elements among the Christian Democrats pressed successfully for the nomination of a more radical candidate than Frei, who was debarred from succeeding himself. They nominated their most able spokesman, Radomiro Tomic, son of Yugoslav immigrants. But their more conservative support, some of which was inherited from the party's unsavory predecessor, the pro-fascist Falange, deserted them, and voted instead for Jorge Alessandri, seeking a second term; the nonsocialist vote was split, and Salvador Allende was elected.

U.S. firms were aghast, and some of them asked their government to intervene to prevent Allende from taking power. No effective action seems to have followed. The military commander, who supported the constitutional order, was assassinated, but no revolt occurred. The Christian Democratic majority in Congress, who had to ratify the election, demanded certain guarantees, but these were given and they ratified it. Allende was sworn in and his coalition government, Popular Unity (UP), immediately embarked on a large-scale program of nationalization and radical reform, which was sufficiently popular to give the UP a narrow majority in the congressional elections of 1972. It was already too late. However sincere in his constitutional beliefs, Allende had failed to realize the dilemma inherent in carrying out such a radical program within the limits of constitutional legality. As a Marxist he might have called for all-out revolution, formed a Red Guard, and fought for dominance in the streets. As a constitutionalist he might have postponed the more radical elements of his program to capture the Christian Democrats. Instead he unwisely lost no opportunity of assuring the Army of his devotion to the constitution, while in the countryside his government either connived at or failed to stop unofficial land occupations and a series of violent acts carried out by the militant Movement of the Revolutionary Left (MIR). The Chilean middle class, and especially the self-employed, began to resist the implementation of government policies. Middle-class housewives stood at the doors of their houses in the evening and beat on the bottoms of empty pots as if to suggest there was never anything in them, while a national truckers' strike disrupted Chile's spinal pattern of production and distribution and brought the economy to crisis point. When the coup that toppled Allende finally came, in September 1973, it was in no way a normal Latin American coup, but with both sides already armed, it was rather a very short-lived but extremely vicious civil war.

The Army, led by its commander, General Augusto Pinochet Ugarte, seems to have been well prepared, apparently with the help of the Central Intelligence Agency, whose agents were active in fomenting resistance to the government. But troops moved into action only when the possibility of a naval revolt forced their hand. Tanks took up position and shelled the Moneda. Allende died as it burned, allegedly by suicide. Troops rounded up large numbers of suspects and incarcerated thousands in the National Stadium. Like many more thousands in the countryside, some were shot out of hand, others tortured with the most revolting cruelty, with beatings, immersion, electric shock, and repeated rape. The nature of these tortures, so consistent with those reported by hundreds of witnesses and victims not only from Chile but also from Argentina, Uruguay, Brazil, and Central America, was evidently not in any sense capable of being regarded as rational; rather it was deliberately intended to humiliate and degrade, especially in its sexual features. Worse still (if that is possible), it was not directed systematically; rather the discretion left to local commanders, and the freedom with which they used it to round up people just because they were young, students, suspects, or even just relatives of suspects shows that the use of torture had the wider purpose of frightening people into conformity with the policies, however evil or absurd, of the dictatorship that was to follow.

From 1973 to 1990, Chile was under the rule of General Pinochet. In the first phase, the country was subdued. To their shame, the Christian Democrats, who had obviously believed that if a coup came they would be allowed to return to power, accepted the coup and made little or no effort to prevent the atrocities. Censorship was established, representative institutions dissolved, and a junta formed of the four service commanders (in Chile the police, or *Carabineros*, are regarded as a military service). In the second phase, the unconstitutional rule continued, while the new regime by decree reversed the nationalization measures of the Allende years and made a determined effort to establish an unrestrained free-market economy on the Chicago model. The sale of public enterprises and the inflow of foreign investment, drawn by the honeypot of a dictatorial regime allowing unlimited profit, brought great prosperity to the middle classes, who closed their ears to the suffering around them. In the third phase, after a pseudoconstitutional regime was established, General Pinochet formally retired from the Army and was appointed president and confirmed as such in a plebiscite, but no Congress existed and the junta remained as the ultimate guarantee of military supremacy. In the early 1980s the boom ended and the bankruptcies began, though as the prosperity ebbed, the middle classes were still able to retain their share as the poor grew poorer. In 1988, to the great surprise of General Pinochet, the Chilean people showed they had not lost the habit of democracy after all. They took the only opportunity they had been given to vote against the unconditional prolongation of his term by plebiscite. Elections were called, and the Christian Democratic leader, Patricio Aylwin, elected, but by the time he took office in March 1990 General Pinochet had already ensured that both enormous power and resources would be retained for himself and the Army he continued to command.

Ecuador's Oil Boom

Ecuador has, for most of the twentieth century, exhibited rather an odd form of political struggle, which has broadly amounted to a tradition of conflict between two élites. Poor communications and the severe limits on the extent and power of national institutions, including the military, have contributed to regionalism. Regional issues have influenced the achievement of power and also policies once power has been achieved.

Regionalism has remained such a powerful force in Ecuadorean politics that it has kept government in the hands of the élites and has limited reforms that might otherwise have been expected.

The economic crisis of the early 1930s in Ecuador hit one of the two rival regional élites, the coastal landowners and traders, particularly hard, and their representatives, the ruling Liberals, found themselves in a political crisis too. The political recovery of the Conservatives, who had dominated the early history of the country and represented the other important regional élite, the sierra landowners, seemed to be in the cards. Nevertheless, the Liberals, who succeeded in using constitutional procedures against the elected Conservatives, moved the political tussle into the military arena, where each party found some factional support. After a four-day civil war in August 1932, the Conservative forces were defeated and the Liberals established a new government. Despite the support of some middle-class elements, this government could only achieve power through electoral fraud and faced a growing opposition supported by the Left.

José María Velasco Ibarra, the lawyer from Quito who was to dominate Ecuadorean politics for a generation, had been born in 1893 and studied at the Central University. A brilliant orator, he needed, as he once said, "only a balcony" to rouse masses and to achieve power. But his self-proclaimed socialism was subordinated to his drive for personal power, and his distrust of organized political parties stemmed from the populist desire to create a vast amorphous "movement" that would raise him to power without the inconvenience of detailed programs or policies. Mobilization of the urban working class by the populist Velasco made further fraud impossible, and he was fairly elected, assuming the presidency for the first time in 1934. But once in power he immediately began to exhibit the pattern of behavior he would display for the rest of his long political career. He set about antagonizing the opposition, beginning with the Right, and, when he was challenged, tried to institute a dictatorship. This led to his deposition in August 1935 and his first period of exile in Colombia.

The political chaos that followed Velasco's departure was met by a period of authoritarian rule by two civilian presidents co-opted by the armed forces. The Central University was closed and political opponents imprisoned or sent into exile on the Galápagos Islands. Direct military rule under General Alberto Enríquez was less repressive and formed a transitional period until the military handed power back to the coastal middle class. Despite growing middle-class and leftist disaffection with the continuing domination of the internationally oriented élite and its policies, Dr. Carlos Arroyo del Río "won" the 1939 elections as the candidate of the oligarchy against Velasco. The scale of the fraud was so massive that nobody could doubt that it had occurred. Velasco's indignation was supported by a brief military uprising, but this was soon quelled and Velasco himself shipped off to exile in Colombia again.

The weakness of Arroyo's fraudulent government was to cost Ecuador dearly. So many troops were needed to support his regime that the country was unable to withstand the 1941 Peruvian invasion of the Marañón River basin and the capture by Peru of half of Ecuador's national territory, which it was then forced to sign away in 1942 under the Protocol of Rio de Janeiro. By 1944, Arroyo was so unpopular that nothing could sustain him in power and he resigned. A coalition of opposition groups was formed and called on Velasco again to assume the presidency, but, in a manner quite characteristic of Ecuadorean politics, this coalition began to fragment as soon as it had achieved its primary purpose. Economic problems, and in particular the rising cost of living, led to public disorder. Hunger marches were, however, forcibly dispersed, and in 1946 Velasco again declared his regime a dictatorship, thus consolidating the opposition, which led in 1947 to his arrest and exile.

Paradoxically, a brief interim presidency was to usher in Ecuador's longest period of stable civilian politics to date. Three full presidential terms punctuated by relatively peaceful elections brought to power in turn a liberal-leaning independent, Galo Plaza Lasso (son of former President Leónidas Plaza, later secretary-general of the OAS [Organization of American States]); the populist Velasco, for the only one of his five presidencies that went its full term and ended peacefully; and a conservative, Camilo Ponce. The economic boom Ecuador enjoyed through production of coffee, cocoa, and bananas certainly contributed to its stability during the 1950s. But at the same time a destabilizing demographic shift to the coast occurred, and the move of workers into urban areas was paralleled by a growth in the middle class. By the end of the decade, commodity prices were already falling and growing labor unrest was met with government repression. The crisis again assured Velasco of a massive majority in the 1960 elections.

Popular belief that Velasco could and would resolve the crisis was, however, misplaced. Demonstrations against the president in 1961 brought out his authoritarian streak and led to the proclamation of a state of emergency. Again the armed forces stepped in to remove him from power. He was succeeded by his vice president, Carlos Julio Arosemena. It was not Arosemena's rather inappropriate personal habits that encouraged the military, the church, and the élites to unite against him—even though they included being drunk at public functions, insulting foreign diplomats, and shooting at waiters in bars to make them move faster. It was his moderately left-wing nationalism that alarmed the armed forces, and the orchestrated campaign against him simply gave them the excuse they needed. In 1963 he was supplanted by a military junta, authoritarian in style, but aware of the need to advocate reformist policies. However, as the fear of "communism" declined, these policies increasingly drew the opposition and resistance of the economic élites. The military abdicated in 1966 in favor of the liberal bourgeoisie who initially had the support of the Left in their opposition to the armed forces, but who faced a growing economic crisis as international demand fell for Ecuador's commodity exports, and for bananas in particular.

With the economy in crisis, Velasco again won in 1968, though with a narrow majority. Within a year, with the crisis deepening, he again resorted to repression in face of popular unrest, and in June 1970 again declared his regime a dictatorship. With age, Velasco appeared to have turned to the right, and the coastal élite, fearing that a military takeover might bring a left-wing, reforming military government like that in neighboring Peru, did not oppose him at this stage. When the coup did come, in February 1972, it was to forestall elections in which the victor was expected to be a new type of left-wing populist leader, Assad Bucaram. Velasco again found himself heading for exile, this time in Buenos Aires. It had been his last experience of power, as he died in 1979.

Bucaram was a populist in the Velasco mold, though the two men were bitter political opponents. His strongest support was among the urban poor of the port city of Guayaquil, but he alienated the middle classes by his Lebanese parentage, his violent and often uncontrolled oratory, and his macho style, which involved occasional public fistfights and, once, waving a pistol on the floor of Congress. It was bad luck for him that his candidacy for the presidency at the head of the Concentration of Popular Forces (CFP) came at a time when the nonmilitary role of the armed forces, in the spheres of agriculture, industry, and trade, as well as politics, had been greatly expanded. The military remained factionalized, with the rival Peruvian and Brazilian examples influencing different cliques within it. But all factions realized the significance of the discovery of oil in Oriente Province in 1967. They wanted the military as an institution to benefit from the wealth that began to flow by pipeline across the Andes in 1972, and they certainly did not want it frittered away by another populist leader with the masses to satisfy.

General [Guillermo] Rodríguez Lara, a highland landowner from Cotopaxi, had been trained in the School of the Americas in Panama and in the United States and was expected when he took power to take a pro-U.S., internationalist position. To the surprise not only of the United States, but also of the domestic élite that had supported the military against Bucaram and the CFP, Rodríguez showed himself to be something of a reformist, and conflicting pressures within the armed forces and the junta of which he was chairman pushed him in the direction of a strident nationalism. Legislation to control the activities of foreign oil companies was introduced, and after Ecuador's admission to OPEC [Organization of Petroleum Exporting Countries] (of which it became a full member in 1973), the government followed OPEC policy with regard to pricing and took steps to assume first a shareholding and then a dominant share in the industry, despite its lack of experience of managing anything like it. The assumption was that the huge revenues that were confidently expected would be ploughed into development, but the Rodríguez government's developmentalism was both capital-intensive and regionally concentrated, leading to unemployment and internal migration. Thus the marginal sectors of urban areas, especially Guayaquil, burgeoned, and shantytowns spread while middle-class wealth went on debt-enhancing luxury imports. Although development of the infrastructure did bring in increased foreign investment at first, increasing controls on both foreign and domestic capital alienated investors along with the élite elements who had helped bring the military to power and now urged them to return to barracks.

By 1975 oil prices had dropped. Oil companies might have boycotted Ecuador in protest at what they saw as the government's nationalist policies, but they had no need to do so; with Alaska and the North Sea coming on stream Ecuador's production was too small and too expensive to attract their interest. A massive decline in government revenue followed and was compensated for by unwise borrowing. The end of 1975 saw an unsuccessful coup; on January 11, 1976, the three service chiefs stepped in and established a new junta under the chairmanship of Rear Admiral Alfredo Poveda, who had previously held the post of minister of the interior under Rodríguez. The new government, then, represented only a modest shift away from nationalism toward the influence of more conservative economic interests. In addition, it came at a time when increasing labor strength and mobilization were expressing themselves in widespread strikes. The new government cracked down hard against labor, but worsening food shortages and other economic problems caused by the government budget deficit and soaring debt charges reduced its capacity to control the political process, and in 1979 Ecuador became the second South American country to revert to civilian rule.

Before this happened, the armed forces were able to secure at least one objective—the amended constitution, by requiring the president's parents to be Ecuadoreans by birth, excluded Bucaram, who in any case died in 1981. But despite fiddling with both electoral procedures and results, they could not prevent Bucaram's son-in-law, Jaime Roldós, from being elected president with 68.5 percent of the popular vote. At thirty-eight, Roldós was Latin America's youngest-ever democratically elected president, but the bright hopes his election raised were soon to prove ill founded. Bucaram soon fell out with his son-in-law and began to oppose his policies. In so doing he removed most of the president's support in Congress, and Roldós had to establish a new, unstable coalition there. He had just done so when, at the end of 1980, he, his wife, and his minister of defense were all killed in an air crash. Vice President Osvaldo Hurtado assumed power and so had the bad luck to be in post to preside over the acute economic crisis of the early 1980s. Initially opposition to government economic policies came primarily from élite groups, but then austerity measures as part of an IMF stabilization package led to increased popular opposition.

The declining popularity of the Hurtado government was, however, only one of several factors that contributed to the electoral success of the political Right in 1984. The greater organization and unity of the Right, which enabled them to field one candidate, helped, as did the regionalism and personalism that have characterized Ecuadorean politics. The right-wing candidate, León Febres Cordero, a businessman, was able to pick up the massive coastal vote in the second round of the election, despite having lost the first ballot. He also used personalist appeals by refusing to debate policies and emphasizing personality differences. He invoked Ecuadorean machismo by arriving at political meetings on horseback. As a U.S.-trained engineer, millionaire, and president of the Guayaquil Chamber of Industry, it came as no surprise that Febres Cordero advocated policies representative of the interests of the coastal oligarchy. He combined an authoritarian style with the economic liberalism of the free marketeer. In fact in his zeal for monetarism he went far beyond anything that had been seen in Latin America in recent years, cutting protective tariffs and encouraging agricultural exports in accordance with the idea of comparative advantage.

Being in power in Ecuador, however, seems to be the sure way of ensuring that one loses the next round of the succession struggle. From the outset the Febres Cordero government faced opposition. But its policies soon brought growing challenges and decreased electoral support. Terrorist attacks, previously almost unknown in Ecuador, began and led to severe repression accompanied by violations of human rights. Not only did congressional opposition flourish in such circumstances, but so, as on previous occasions, did unrest among the armed forces, a group of whom kidnapped the president. Despite his macho image, he immediately capitulated to their demands. By the 1988 elections his popularity had declined so far that his party's candidate came in third with only 13 percent of the vote. The victor in a second-round ballot was Dr. Rodrigo

Borja Cevallos, of the opposition Democratic Left (ID), who secured victory by 1,762,417 votes (46 percent) to 1,572,651 (41 percent) for Sr. Abdalá Bucaram Ortiz, son of the former populist leader. At the inauguration ceremony, the outgoing president characteristically refused to hand the sash of office to his successor, who within hours had announced an emergency economic package devaluing the sucre, placing sharp constraints on nonessential imports, and doubling the price of gasoline to the equivalent of US$0.50 a gallon.

Military Government in Central America

In Central America, military intervention also took place, but in these smaller and less sophisticated societies it took a much cruder form. Only in Guatemala does the characteristic pattern of "military developmentalism" appear, though a decade earlier in El Salvador a series of military-led governments did succeed in bringing about some economic development, but at the cost of creating pressures for further change, which they proved unable to handle even by the most severe repression.

In Guatemala the forces of traditionalism had reasserted themselves in 1963, when the commander of the Army deposed President [Miguel] Ydígoras and assumed power in his own right. Ydígoras, with his sympathy for the United States, had gone too far in accepting U.S. aid to counter the guerrilla movements that had appeared in 1960. The final straw that alienated the Army, however, was his move to allow ex-President [Juan José] Arévalo to return to the country to stand for election. Ydígoras's successor, General Enrique Peralta Azurdia, rejected U.S. assistance in combating the insurgency that earlier U.S. intervention had helped increase. The victory of a civilian in the 1966 elections, and the fact that he was allowed to take office, were the results of tragic circumstances; the candidate of the democratic Left was shot shortly after his nomination, and his brother, nominated in his place, proved too strong to resist. Nevertheless, Julio César Méndez Montenegro (president, 1966–1970) was only allowed to hold office after he had agreed to the Army being given a free hand in the devastating campaign planned and led by his military commander, General [Carlos] Arana [Osorio].

In the next four years terror, countering a wave of kidnappings and assassinations, brought a measure of relative peace, though at the cost of serious losses among the ruling élite. Key figures were killed by guerrillas, rural and urban. In return the death squads killed civilian politicians, trade union leaders, and anyone whose education or social standing made them suspect of left-wing sympathies. General Arana's election to the presidency in 1970 then ushered in sixteen years of military rule under five presidents. During the government of Arana and that of his successor, a descendant of Swedish immigrants with the unpronounceable name of Eugenio Kjell Laugerud, the regime, though authoritarian, was relatively liberal. Guerrilla activity continued, but the groups, split by their adherence to rival versions of Marxism, did not pose a great threat, and measures to carry out some limited cooperative development in Indian districts, though denounced as Communistic by the hard Right, seemed initially successful. In 1976 a serious earthquake struck the central uplands, devastating the capital, making hundreds of thousands homeless, and severing the very inadequate road and rail communications. But reconstruction still lagged when in 1978, at Panzós in the department of Alta Verapaz, soldiers brought in by local landowners fired on a gathering of more than seven hundred Kekchi Indians who were demonstrating peacefully in support of their land rights. Some one hundred forty were killed and over three hundred wounded.

This incident, bad enough in itself, was the catalyst for a horrific onslaught by the armed forces on the Indians who made up the majority of Guatemala's population. The Conquest had driven the Indians up onto the higher and less desirable lands, while the introduction of coffee in the 1880s had reduced their proportion of the available land still further. Then as health and hygiene facilities were improved, the population increased rapidly, intensifying pressure on the usable land to the breaking point and making an ever larger number of Indians dependent on seasonal work on the banana and cotton plantations of the lowlands in order to earn enough to stay alive. The last straw was the decision by the military government to create a development zone across the north of the country, in the area in which, as it soon turned out, oil was to be found. Led by General Romeo Lucas Garcia (president, 1978–1982), who was himself a large landowner in Alta Verapaz, the armed forces, officered by *ladinos* (Guatemalans of predominantly European extraction), fought as if every Indian was a rebel, and the conflict took on an overtly racialist character. Whole villages were massacred and large areas of the country turned into "free-fire" zones. Guatemala was, in effect, in a state of civil war.

Eventually resistance within the Army led to the deposition of Lucas Garcia by General Efraín Ríos Montt. Although the brother of the bishop of Escuintla, Ríos Montt had been converted to one of the charismatic Protestant sects that had spread widely in the country in the previous twenty years, supported by money and missionaries from the United States. Their strongly anti-Communist beliefs made them and their ideas acceptable to the military élite, who in any case saw the Catholic Church as weak and riddled with Marxist ideas. Ríos Montt promised "rifles and beans" (*fusiles y frijoles*) to those who supported him, death to those who did not. But the situation did not change, and a year later he too fell to a military coup by his commander of the Army. With the situation still highly volatile, it was this last who finally made the decision to allow both elections and the choice of a civilian as his successor.

Though the armed forces have traditionally wielded power in both El Salvador and Honduras, in neither case have they taken the lead in promoting development. In Honduras constitutional government has had a fitful existence since the retirement of [Tiburcio] Cariás [Andino] in 1948. Military coups in 1956 and 1957 gave way to civilian government under Ramón Villeda Morales, but he was overthrown in 1963 for fear of a more liberal successor. The military junta that succeeded him then rewrote the constitution to secure the choice in 1966 of a military president, the corrupt and authoritarian General Osvaldo López Arellano. It was he who made the fateful decision in 1969 to launch the "Football War" [that is, soccer war] on El Salvador. The root cause of this savage conflict, which, despite its apparently trivial pretext (a disputed decision in the third qualifying round for the 1970 World Cup), lasted for thirteen days, killed two thousand people, and resulted in serious industrial damage, was the fact that El Salvador, the most overcrowded state on the American mainland, had been receiving a continuous stream of workers from less-developed Honduras in search of jobs. The war itself was brought to an end by the mediation of the OAS. But in consequence of it Honduras withdrew from the Central American Common Market (CACM), thus effectively bringing its development to a halt, while many Hondurans who had been working in El Salvador had to return home.

In 1975 the suicide of Eli Black, head of United Brands (which in a mere six years had grown from a small metal box company until it had taken over the once mighty United Fruit Company), led to the disclosure that López Arellano had been paid half a million dollars to break ranks with the leaders of other banana-producing countries and stop the price increase for which they had been fighting. Within a week he had been deposed by General Juan Alberto Melgar Castro (president, 1975–1980). In 1980, Honduras was still the least-developed country in Central America and one of the poorest on the continent.

In El Salvador the situation was rather different. El Salvador, down to the outbreak of civil war in 1980, was dominated by the same tight oligarchy of leading families, the so-called Forty Families, who had ruled in the early years of the century. But panicked by agrarian unrest in 1932 into support for the bizarre Theosophist dictator, Maximiliano Hernández Martínez (president, 1930–1944), they accepted military rule after his fall for fear that new elements might succeed in breaking into the charmed circle of the élite. In 1948 a coup by junior officers installed a modernizing military regime. Regularized by elections in 1950, the new constitutional order lasted for a decade, until Colonel José María Lemus tried to arrange for his own reelection. He was speedily deposed in 1960 by a fresh revolt of junior officers, while students demonstrated against the government in favor of Cuba. Fearful that even the mildest reform might lead to a Communist takeover, a new civil-military coalition was quickly formed behind a rival junta, who established a new official party, ironically termed the Party of National Conciliation (PCN).

Under Colonel Julio Adalberto Rivera (1962–1967) and his successor, Colonel Fidel Sánchez Hernández (1967–1972), the PCN, with the support of the United States through the Alliance for Progress, became the main beneficiary of the CACM, though at the cost of the social strains that were to lead to the outbreak of the Football War. The leader of the new Christian Democratic Party, José Napoleón Duarte, who had been elected mayor of San Salvador in a landslide in 1964, now emerged as a dynamic rival to the official candidate in 1972. Development had had the effect of mobilizing public opinion in favor of a greater liberalization of politics and more economic equality, and Duarte offered a constitutional alternative. Sadly, however, the armed forces denied him his victory, with disastrous results. On the surface nothing appeared to have changed. The official candidate took office and in 1977 was able to hold fraudulent elections and impose his military successor, General Carlos Humberto Romero. For two more years, until the success of the Nicaraguan Revolution, he was able to maintain order at the cost of a sharp escalation in the use of force. But below the surface it required only a spark to release the explosive potential of frustrated change locked up for nearly four decades.

Lastly in Panama there emerged in the 1970s a military-led revolutionary regime that somewhat resembled that of Peru under Velasco Alvarado. For most of the period since the Second World War, starting with a coup that deposed Arnulfo Arias in 1941, Panama had been firmly in alliance with the United States. Its small élite benefited out of all proportion. After the war, the spread of "flags of convenience" left Panama on paper one of the largest maritime nations in the world. Fortunately, perhaps, it was never called upon to back up its pretensions by providing military escorts for any of its vessels, since this would have been quite beyond the capabilities of its small police force. Yet, as we have seen, the police took over the role in internal politics, which in other Latin American countries was performed by the armed forces, and in 1949, when the presidential succession was disputed, a police coup decided the matter and Arias took office for the second time. In 1952 he was again deposed and power seized by the commander of the police, José Antonio Remón, who in 1953 renamed the police the National Guard, which more accurately reflected what they really were. Remón gave the country three years of reasonably stable government before he was gunned down in his car as he was leaving the racecourse.

Under his civilian successors, in the postwar climate of decolonization, the emotive issue of the U.S. presence in the Canal Zone aroused considerable unrest among students. The Eisenhower administration agreed to a review of the 1936 treaty that increased the annuity paid for the use of the canal and gave Panama a greater share of the revenues raised in the zone. But economic growth left the majority of the population in relative poverty, while unrest continued among students angered at their feeling of inferiority in their own country. Sensitive to the potential dangers, President [John F.] Kennedy made the further important, though symbolic, concession that in future the Panamanian flag would fly alongside that of the United States in the zone. In 1964, however, U.S. Marines fired on students who, to shame their elders into action, marched unarmed into the zone and demanded its liberation. Twenty-one students were killed and more than four hundred wounded, but the Canal Zone was at last recognized as Panamanian territory, since by this time even the U.S. Joint Chiefs of Staff had realized that the important thing was whether they could use the canal, not who owned it.

Meanwhile rival factions had developed within the National Guard, some demanding tough measures and others urging a reforming military regime. In 1968, Dr. Arnulfo Arias was reelected. His first move was to try to rid himself of his commander of the National Guard, General Omar Torrijos Herrera. Instead, only eleven days after he had been sworn in for his fourth term, Arias was again expelled (he died peacefully in exile in Madrid in 1988) and Torrijos headed a military junta, which closed the National Assembly and the university and proscribed all political parties.

It soon became clear, however, that Torrijos himself was one of those who had the determination to carry out far-reaching redistributive reforms and was in addition a leader whose charismatic personality rallied a wide base of support for his policies. He dominated Panamanian politics for the next thirteen years, ruling for his first year through his supporters in the military junta and then, when the hard-liners tried a countercoup during his absence in Mexico, through a series of civilian presidents. In regaining power, his key supporter was Major (now General) Manuel [Antonio] Noriega, who soon became indispensable. Once back in power there followed a series of measures designed to mobilize popular support and distribute wealth more widely among the regime. The funds came from a new source, the emergence of Panama itself as a center for offshore banking under the Banking Act of 1970, for, despite its central position and small population, Panama has never had a surplus on its visible

balance of trade. In 1972 a new constitution was enacted that concentrated power in the hands of Torrijos as head of government with Demetrio
Lakas Bahas as titular president. A Labor Code came into force, and community health schemes and an expansion of social services were also prepared. Plans were also made to carry out a degree of agrarian reform
through a combination of confiscation for debt, expropriation, donation,
and purchase; the amount of land affected was small, about 5 percent of
all available arable land, but in the Panamanian context it was a significant step forward. Abroad, Torrijos pursued a pragmatic, anti-U.S. foreign policy, established diplomatic relations with Cuba and East European
states, and in 1975 joined the Non-Aligned Movement, a decisive break
with his country's traditional posture of subordination to the United States.

In 1978, Torrijos resigned as head of government but as commander
of the National Guard retained ultimate power in the country until
July 13, 1981, when he died in a mysterious air crash in Cocle Province.
A bitter succession struggle raged for the next three years. When the dust
cleared, Colonel Rubén Dario Paredes, who had ousted Colonel Florencio
Flores in March 1982, had in turn fallen and General Noriega had emerged
as commander of the National Guard, renamed the Defense Forces in 1984.
The president and Legislative Assembly, directly elected from 1983, remained under the control of General Noriega, who ousted Paredes's choice
as president, Ricardo de la Espriella (February 1984) and imposed through
rigged elections a trained economist as president. Dr. Nicolás Ardito
Barletta's devotion to President [Ronald] Reagan and to free-market rem-
edies, however, was of no help in dealing with the economy. In due course
he too was dismissed, and in 1988 the economy was devastated by a U.S.
boycott intended to rid Panama of Noriega, but which only succeeded in
bringing widespread hardship on all but the wealthy élite. By then little if
anything was left of the extensive program of reform of the Torrijos years.

The elections of May 1989 were a classic fraud. General Noriega's
supporters, it seems, had calculated that they needed just over one hundred thousand extra votes to ensure victory. So the twenty thousand members of the Defense Forces voted five or six times each, in various areas
and in the name of those recently dead, while known opposition supporters found themselves struck off the ballot or directed to vote hundreds of
miles from their homes. Voting itself was free and exit polls were held,
from which it emerged that even some of the soldiers did not vote for the
official candidate. When, as the count progressed, it became clear how
far the government had miscalculated, and the polls reported the official
candidate losing by a margin of three to one, armed plainclothes police
appeared in the polling stations and seized the official returns, replacing
them with neatly typed lists of their own. Told of this, however, former

President Carter of the United States, who was present as an official observer, called a press conference and within seconds news of the fraud was circling the globe. The government reacted with violence, but failed to suppress the growing anger, and after four days, as armed troops rampaged through the streets striking down opposition demonstrators and smashing their cars, the general declared the election null and void. With breathtaking cheek he blamed the "unpatriotic actions" and irregularities, not of his own supporters but of the opposition, and remained firmly in charge. Subsequently the Bush administration stepped up its economic sanctions against Panama, calling for the replacement of the nominal government of interim head of state Manuel Solís Palma and the resignation of General Noriega, and sent a "brigade-sized force" to the Canal Zone in reassertion of U.S. rights there. Following the failure of an OAS mediation attempt, Francisco Rodríguez was sworn in as president on September 1, when President Barletta's term should have ended, and the U.S. government broke off diplomatic relations. But in the end it was the unwise decision of the new National Assembly to name General Noriega head of government and to proclaim Panama in a "state of war" with the United States (December 15), which was followed by attacks by Panamanian troops on U.S. personnel, that led to the decision of President [George] Bush to order armed intervention in Panama early on December 20. After four days of resistance, General Noriega, who had evaded capture in the initial phase, took refuge in the Papal Nunciature and later surrendered to U.S. troops, while Guillermo Endara, the real winner of the 1989 elections, established a new government. However, despite the fact that democracy had been restored in Panama, the recurrence of U.S. military intervention was deeply resented throughout Latin America.

9

The Latin American Military, Low-Intensity Conflict, and Democracy

Gabriel Marcella

*In recent years most of Latin America has returned to civilian govern-
ment, a phenomenon known as "redemocratization." The region, however, faces many serious political, social, and economic problems, which
may threaten the restored civilian order. If the civil authorities "fail," the
question confounding many observers today is: Will the military once
more feel compelled to "save the nation"?*

*In this selection, Gabriel Marcella examines the challenges posed to
both civilians and the military by the recent economic, political, and social changes in the region. Latin America, which endured a severe economic decline during the 1980s, now must attempt to resolve new and
extremely serious problems resulting from the international drug trade
and the renewed vigor of a virulent insurgency in some countries, while
continuing to address the growing social and economic problems of the
last decade. The new threats to national sovereignty and internal peace,
however, have erupted at a time when the region's armed forces find themselves discredited and politically isolated. Thus, the leaders of Latin
America—civilian as well as military—must forge a new and improved
"civil-military dialogue on national security" to address the region's current crisis. It will be necessary to determine the boundaries of military
responsibility with regard to international and national dangers, including drug trafficking and the insurgencies and other internal unrest, if
civil order and democracy are to flourish.*

From the *Journal of Interamerican Studies and World Affairs* 32, no. 1 (1990):
45–73, 75–82.

> There can be no expression of a desire to return to po-
> litical power when experience tells us that the result is
> totally negative for our country and fundamentally so
> for the armed forces.
> —CHIEF OF STAFF, ARMY OF ARGENTINA (*LAWR*, 1986b)

Introduction

The most remarkable development in Latin America during the economically "lost decade" of the 1980s is the regionwide process of
redemocratization. Close to 90 percent of the people of the region are
ruled by civilian governments. The flowering of democratic, pluralistic,
and participatory systems is still a noble aspiration, but it is radically
different from the bleak political landscape of the 1960s and 1970s, when
military governments prevailed. Nor is the appurtenance of civilian government equal to democracy. There is a large variety of civilian-military
coalitions possible in a democratic setting. Moreover, as a senior Brazilian officer commented, it is not necessarily true that all civilian governments are of a democratic tendency and working for the common good,
or that all military governments are driven by other interests. While the
process of redemocratization is far from complete, a strong foundation
has been established.

The turnaround is explained primarily by the working out of indigenous factors, and only secondarily by the influence of external factors,
such as U.S. policy. The positive trend is part of a worldwide democratic
renaissance and rejection of both authoritarian and totalitarian forms. That
is, it is due to an increasingly universal yearning to hold the governors
accountable to the governed. As redemocratization proceeds, the armed
forces will have a decisive role to play in helping to nurture the institutional bases on which it rests. It is the thesis of this article that democratization is compatible with professionally strong military establishments.
Such compatibility is also consonant with U.S. strategic requirements.
Professionally capable, self-confident, and politically responsible military institutions provide a better security shield for the survival of
democracy than do poorly organized, insecure, and—at the extreme, such
as the Panamanian Defense Forces under Manuel Antonio Noriega—
corrupt institutions distanced from, and at times in conflict with, the larger
civilian society. Such institutions are incapable of carrying out their professional responsibility of defeating external threats and provide little
defense against—and, indeed, may facilitate the victory of—the new
totalitarian revolutionaries.

During the past two decades and in one form or another, the Latin
American militaries faced critical challenges to their institutions and to

their nations, challenges that ranged from how to integrate the national territory effectively to how to fight underdevelopment and/or Communist insurgencies (with or without foreign support). There were also episodes of violence against external enemies: the conflicts between El Salvador and Honduras (1969), Peru and Ecuador (1981), and Argentina and the United Kingdom over the Falklands/Malvinas (1982), and the threatened—though peacefully resolved—confrontation (1978) between Chile and Argentina over the Beagle Channel. There have also been new challenges: the diffuse, unconventional threat posed by Sandinista subversion and the differentiated Soviet-Cuban strategy of alliance with the new revolutionaries of the 1970s and 1980s. Looming over all of these is the new warfare waged by the international drug traffickers against all aspects of the social fabric: moral, ethical, and economic.

Nonetheless, the coercive power of the military, its often superior administrative capability, esprit de corps, and deep patriotism were insufficient attributes for them to win both the internal and external wars and, at the same time, manage complex national economies and political systems. In a number of cases, the exercise of political power exerted a corrosive influence on professionalism, on institutional cohesion, and on civil-military relations. While the military institutions, whether in or out of national power, made important, lasting contributions to national development, they also contributed to antithetical conditions. Illegitimate and ineffective governments were capable neither of retaining popular support nor of making good on promises to meet the demands of the governed: for social change, for improved economic performance, for political participation. The military's penchant for orderly development within a corporatist context may also have stifled the efficacy and/or growth of other mediating institutions able to serve the national interest.

Consequences were twofold. The first was the political isolation of the institution—what Latin Americans call *desgaste* or *desprestigio*—in the context of growing political polarization; the second was the disengagement of U.S. security assistance under the rubric of its human rights policy, later resumed on a more limited, but fitful, basis during the 1980s. In 1987, U.S. security assistance to South America reached an all-time low of only $5 million. In 1988, U.S. security assistance to the area, mirroring global trends, continued the long-term decline, to the point that only three countries—El Salvador, Guatemala, and Honduras—received funding, support that was directly related to defensive efforts against domestic insurgency and Sandinista expansion. In 1989 security assistance was refocused to target Colombian narcotraffickers. Finally, a new wave of revolutionary violence threatens to weaken not only the military institutions but also hopes for the democratic opening of society. It is in this context that the comments of the Argentine army chief of staff, General Hector Ríos Erenu, at the beginning of this paper are understandable.

It is within this same context that Elliott Abrams, then the assistant secretary of state for inter-American affairs, proposed a democratic vision of security to the graduating civilian and military officers from sixteen hemispheric countries of the Inter-American Defense College in Washington, DC:

> Your generation must be a generation of pioneers. You are now the guardians of the new democracies. Your highest calling must be—not to replace failed regimes—but to protect successful democracies. You must succeed in the task of forging a new vision of security in which democracy is the cornerstone, not a luxury; where free and political competition is an ally, not an impediment to peace and development.
>
> In this sense, the rise of democracy in the hemisphere satisfies the imperatives of comprehensive security policy. We will find security in the construction of open, inclusive, and democratic political order. (Abrams, 1986: 1)

Democracy has also been rediscovered by some of the armed forces of Latin America. This stems both from internal institutional developments and from the military's assessment that democracy may offer the best type of political organization to meet the challenges that lie ahead. Some of this thinking emerged at the November 1985 Conference of the American Armies, held in Santiago de Chile, on the theme of "The Role of the Army in a Democratic Society," at which a pluralism of views was revealed along with a grudging consensus that democracy is worth another try.[1] A subsequent Conference of the American Armies, held in the United States (at Fort Benning, GA) in March 1987 pursued the follow-up theme of "How Military Training Enhances Democratic Growth." Exchanging views at this high a level enables communication to take place both across military institutions and throughout the hemisphere. And, of course, they nurture support for the core values of democracy. It remains to be seen whether such support will translate into what John S. Fitch, of the University of Colorado, calls a doctrine of "democratic military professionalism," to better civil-military relations and smoother transitions to democracy.

However, the military faces troubling dilemmas in promoting democracy. This paper will first explore themes common to the region and then focus upon specific national situations. These dilemmas are not unique to the military alone; civilians face challenges of equal dimensions in promoting the institutional bases for democratic military professionalism. Moreover, civilian leaders have yet to develop an effective approach to integrate participation of military professionals into the national decision-making.

The Need for Responsible Civil-Military Dialogue on National Security

In his classic work, *The Soldier and the State*, Samuel Huntington argued that cooperative civil-military relations is the principal institutional component of military security policy. There is increasing evidence that Latin Americans recognize this. Yet it is exceedingly difficult to communicate this concept, given the enormous gap between civilians and the military. One U.S. field commander who is intimately familiar with Latin America refers to the "no-man's-land" that separates the civilian from the military world. Isolation is not uncommon to military institutions. There is always an element of tension between the civilian and military sectors of any society, but it reaches a particular, if not dangerous, intensity in Latin America. The lack of communication is particularly acute with respect to the mission of the military—national security—where few civilians engage in a pragmatic institutionalized dialogue with either military professionals or with the international network of strategic studies. Over the last two decades, national security has taken on a negative connotation within civilian circles because of the excesses associated with military governments in the 1960s, 1970s, and 1980s. The limited amount of dialogue that does take place does so within the environment of war colleges, where the military and civilians have institutionalized the joint study of national security issues. Institutions of this type exist in Brazil, Argentina, Chile, Peru, Ecuador, Colombia, Venezuela, and Bolivia. Absence of such dialogue weakens the claim of the military to a legitimate professional mission within a democracy. It also seriously diminishes civilian understanding of the legitimate concerns of the military profession. Sharing knowledge about national security is a form of democratic empowerment that is sorely needed in Latin America.

National security issues are not openly discussed in a sophisticated manner. Despite the flowering of such institutions as the Superior War College in Brazil and the Center for Advanced Military Studies in Peru, few civilians are serious students of national security. Budgetary constraints will inhibit such efforts in the future even more. National security has become a partisan symbol. As a code word for authoritarian/military government, civilian leaders have felt compelled to turn their backs on it. Because Latin America is a secondary theater in the global military balance, few civilians in Latin America—even fewer in the United States—are familiar with the language and the manner of thinking involved in: 1) defense planning; and 2) the professional concerns of Latin American military institutions. Much of the voluminous writing on the Latin American military makes scarce reference to its primary professional mission of defense. Few are familiar with the seminal writings of Eduardo Mercado Jarrín on strategy (such as *Seguridad, Política, Estratégia,* 1974) or with the planning documents (*Manual Básico*) that have influenced a generation of military officers in Brazil. The military and strategy journals, which are outlets for the expression of military views, have a meager readership. The statements of national objectives and strategies explicit in these writings attempt to develop the art of national and military planning and are compatible, if not convergent, with civilian concepts. They are: democracy, national integration, integrity of the national territory, social peace, progress, and sovereignty. They are to be achieved through a balanced application of the instruments of national power—political, economic, psychosocial, and military. These writings provide keys to understanding the operational code of the military professional: his worldview, his political framework, his concept of civil-military relations, and the definition of his mission.

Some analysts state that such doctrines of national security inevitably involve the military in the very thing they ought to avoid, i.e., running governments. These critics argue that the mission of the military should focus upon external, rather than internal, security. It would be fair to say that few civilians are familiar with the intellectual formation of the Latin American military professional, in particular what he reads, whether in the form of texts on military strategy, military history, economic development, the nation's history, or of international relations. The study of military sociology or of the military as a social institution is practically nonexistent. Such academic sophistication as exists is confined to the political role of the military institution. Analysts who display an intellectual fascination with the military are either unaware of, or unwilling to recognize, its professional mission to defend the nation. There is a small intellectual movement among a few scholars—in Chile, Argentina, and Uruguay—to study the new professional missions of the military.

Philosophical differences are one reflection of the deeply rooted problems of communication between civilians and the military. Even though he had taught engineering at the Salvadoran Military Academy some years before, President José Napoleón Duarte admitted later that he never took the time to study how the military thinks.[2] Sometimes military establishments have seen fit *not* to share military and political intelligence with civilian leaders on national problems. And, upon occasion, military intelligence organizations can be, and have been, exploited for partisan—even personal—political purposes at variance with the national interest, subverting the principle of civilian control. In some countries, the military intelligence organizations provide the only systems for national intelligence. Laws and practices vary from one country to another, yet centralizing national intelligence in the hands of the military, or of individuals autonomous within the institution and within society, is not conducive to accountability nor to effective government. Knowledge is power, and the dissemination of intelligence forms the basis for shared learning and shared decision-making in a healthy democracy. Abuse of this basic principle can compromise both the institutional interests of the military and the national interest.

Cultural distance, institutional resentment, and political excess in the name of safeguarding national security and democracy all play a part in widening the communication gap between the military and civilians, resulting in mutual paranoia and desire for revenge that can seriously diminish the prospects of pragmatic reconciliation necessary for a democratic community.

The New Challenges Facing the Latin American Military

As Latin America approaches the year 2000, it faces enormous social, economic, and political problems: deep economic recession, high levels of unemployment and underemployment, rapidly expanding populations making increasing demands upon the political systems, austerity cutbacks on social expenditures and national defense, the decapitalization produced by the external debt problems (estimated at $440 billion in late 1989), and the explosion of the narcotics traffic. In some countries, such as Peru and Colombia, central authority is being subverted by the twin scourges of insurgency and drugs. These alone are sufficient to place great strains on the national security of any political system, but particularly those of fragile democracies.

The outbreak of social violence in Caracas (Venezuela) on February 26, 1989, with a toll of 246 dead and 1,831 injured, bears witness to the political danger of imposing economic austerity. This event becomes even more compelling when one considers that Venezuela has been a robust democracy for three decades. There is, in addition, the new revolutionary warfare being waged against institutions, governments, and the armed forces. While much of our attention has been focused on insurgency violence in Central America, many Marxist and Marxist-Leninist insurgents are also active elsewhere in Latin America. (See list, Table 1.)

Table 1. Insurgent Groups

Guatemala	Revolutionary Organization of the People in Arms
	Revolutionary Armed Forces
	Guerrilla Army of the Poor
	Guatemalan Workers' Party
El Salvador	Farabundo Martí National Liberation Front (FMLN)
	(5 Groups): Revolutionary Party of the People, Revolutionary Party of Central American Workers, National Forces of Armed Resistance, Popular Liberation Forces, Armed Forces of Liberation
Honduras	Chinchoneros
	Lorenzo Zelaya Popular Revolutionary Forces
Colombia	Armed Forces of the Colombian Revolution
	M-19
	Armed Forces of National Liberation
	Army of Popular Revolution
Ecuador	¡Alfaro Vive Carajo!
Peru	Sendero Luminoso
	Tupac Amaru Revolutionary Movement
Chile	Manuel Rodríguez Patriotic Front
	Movement of the Revolutionary Left

The new revolutionaries have adopted a more sophisticated strategy than their predecessors of the 1960s. They have chosen a strategy of protracted warfare to take advantage of the vulnerabilities of Latin American societies and of the inconsistencies and discontinuities of the principal external support element, i.e., U.S. policy. Encouraged by the example set by the Sandinistas in 1979, of taking power with logistical support from Cuba, the Socialist bloc, and even non-Communist sources, these groups target beleaguered governments. By developing international political support systems, they attempt to isolate governments and the armed forces in order to weaken, and ultimately destroy, intermediate institutions. Their strategic objective is to destroy the sense of legitimacy and consensus which links the people, the government, and the military—or "the triangle," as it has been called by General John R. Galvin, former commander in chief of the U.S. Southern Command in Panama, in a reference to Karl von Clausewitz's counsel from his classic *On War* (Galvin, 1986). The military may inadvertently facilitate this strategy if they respond to violence with indiscriminate counterviolence of their own, an overreaction that may generate the conditions for their own destruction by eroding their legitimacy further, thus risking elimination of U.S. support to the government—and the military institution—so targeted.

The new revolutionaries are quite clear about their objectives with respect to democracy and the role of the armed forces in the new political order, which is: to facilitate civilian control by merging the state, the revolutionary party, and the popular army—as occurs in Sandinista Nicaragua and in Cuba. No doubt, such fusion is anticipated by the FMLN and other Marxist-Leninist groups in the region.

If the government and armed forces meet the insurgent violence with indiscriminate counterviolence of their own, an institutional crisis may ensue in which the government and/or the military lose legitimacy. This will occur unless counterinsurgency measures are carried out with professionalism, restrained use of force, and respect for human rights. The democratic dilemma is that counterinsurgency is war, requiring mobilization of vision, decisiveness, and resources. More often than not this means, at least for the short term, strengthening both the size and political power of the military in order to defeat the insurgents and win the "hearts and minds" of the people. Mobilizing strategic vision, decisive authority, and resources ought to be a joint effort of both civilians and military. Where such cooperation is not effective, the military's political power will increase.

The challenge is intensified by economic crisis, natural disasters—such as earthquakes and floods (Peru 1982, Chile and Colombia 1985, El Salvador 1986, and Ecuador 1987)—and the new threat of drugs. Hopes for a democratic outcome can be thwarted within such a frustrating environment.[3] Under this kind of stress, the very conditions that induced the military to take political power in the first place may return: violence, economic mismanagement, and a renewal of insurgency. In these circumstances, some military officers and civilian supporters may be tempted to plot a coup, particularly those who perceive either the national security or their own institutional interests to be threatened, or those who may be held accountable for conducting a "dirty war" against insurgents. The degree of threat perceived may also be a function of its estimated impact upon the United States, particularly if the latter should opt to disengage from the region, as happened during the 1970s, when the United States eliminated security assistance to many countries, weakening its military-to-military ties in the process. Coups by the military against their civilian governments may resolve a given security problem in the short run, but, at the same time, such actions may only intensify the crisis over the longer term by, among other things, increasing the political polarization, thus eroding the legitimacy of the institution further. Another danger is that prolonged military government and its involvement in the civilian sectors of government tend to deprive civilians of that important political administrative experience that would obviate military intervention in the first place. These dilemmas are understood by pragmatists among the civilian and military sectors of government alike, but mutual suspicion about the governing capacity and intentions of the other can make civil-military cooperation difficult. Some appreciation of how this works out in practice can be gleaned from the following country situations.

The New Civil-Military Relations

The capacity of Latin American military institutions to surmount these challenges will help determine the future of democracy and of relations with the United States. This section addresses, albeit briefly, some contemporary issues in civil-military relations in the following countries: Guatemala, El Salvador, Honduras, Panama, Peru, Chile, Argentina, and Uruguay. Although the challenges are similar in many ways, specific circumstances make each national situation different.

Guatemala

With the election of Vinicio Cerezo in 1985, the Guatemalan military formally exited from the political power it had held for over thirty years (1954–1985). During that time, the military fought two generations of Marxist insurgents, ran the government, and attempted to bring about social and economic development. Finally, the human rights abuses, economic mismanagement, political incompetence, and the international isolation of the government of General Romeo Lucas García (1978–1982) led to the young officers' revolt of 1982 that brought to power General Efraín Ríos Montt. He and his successor, General Hector Mejía Víctores, implemented a successful counterinsurgency strategy of "bullets and beans" to isolate the guerrillas as well as to absorb them.

Before turning the government over to Cerezo, who came to power through a clean election in 1985, the military granted itself an amnesty that reduced its accountability for former human rights violations. Cerezo has steered away from investigating the past involvement of the military in the human rights abuses and from moving too quickly to control the military. Other—potentially divisive—issues remain. These include controlling how the counterinsurgency is conducted and the austerity imposed on the military budget, as well as Guatemala's foreign policy in Central America. Both civilian and military leaders appear to have arrived at a common understanding to cooperate in order to return Guatemala to national dignity and economic development and to set it on a course of democratization. How this cooperation will work out remains to be seen. The military takes great pride in its political and military accomplishments, yet, at the same time, it is eager to see that the democratic alternative succeeds.

On the one hand, there appears to be a coincidence of interests between Cerezo and the military on some issues; on the other, there are tactical disagreements on how those interests should be pursued.[4] The senior leadership of the army is attempting to institutionalize respect for democratic values.

El Salvador

On October 15, 1979, and in the midst of escalating violence, a bloodless coup took place that installed a new government in El Salvador made up of younger military officers and moderate civilians committed to reforming the country's antiquated economic, social, and political structures. The government promised to end repression, create a democratic political system, and implement agrarian reform. Even though the coup resulted in the retirement of approximately 40 percent of the senior officer ranks, the so-called October Junta could not muster sufficient support from the generally conservative military and security forces to carry out its bold program. A new junta, which included José Napoleón Duarte and other Christian Democrats, was formed in January 1980 and soon announced sweeping banking and agrarian reforms. The new government was immediately confronted with a number of formidable challenges. To implement broad socioeconomic reform, a strong government—based on either a widespread consensus or a monopolization of the means of violence or both—was needed. The junta had neither. Its reform programs were attacked by the Left as insufficient and by the Right as threatening. The polarization, and subsequent militarization, of society left the government in a position where it could neither control effectively the terrorism of the Right nor end the guerrilla activities and terrorism of the Left.

In the spring of 1980 it was feared that the fragile coalition could not survive these challenges. Some believed that a Marxist-Leninist takeover of El Salvador was imminent. Others thought the coalition would be toppled by the Right or overwhelmed by the combined efforts of the FMLN. Neither happened. In January 1981, the insurgents launched their "final" offensive, the first of a number of strategic miscalculations on the likelihood of a popular uprising, which was defeated by government forces. This blunted right-wing efforts for a coup. In March 1982, almost 1.5 million Salvadorans went to the polls to elect a new constituent assembly charged with writing a constitution and setting up full presidential elections. Subsequent elections in 1984, 1985, and 1988 have ratified the Salvadoran commitment to democratic evolution and rejected a more violent path.

The Salvadoran armed forces have made remarkable progress in the counterinsurgency. They have improved their battlefield performance immeasurably due, in part, to U.S. support and training. The FMLN has been confined to a minor portion of the national territory and its numbers reduced to an effective core estimated at five to seven thousand. While the military maintains the initiative, the FMLN has by no means been defeated. FMLN strategy now emphasizes prolonged warfare designed to cause maximum destruction to the economy and wear down U.S. support. The guerrillas engage in mine warfare and are attempting to rebuild their urban infrastructure. The military has supported social and economic changes that have altered the character of the political power structure. Slow but steady progress has been made in agrarian reform, to the benefit of over 550,000 people. The armed forces have made some institutional changes in an attempt to eliminate human rights abuses and have adopted more humane tactics in their air and ground operations—in part at the insistence of civilian President Duarte and in part because such tactics make more sense in winning the war. The critical support of the United States hinges on such tactics.

Serious problems remain: progress in judicial reform has been slow, along with that of the National Pacification Program, which has experienced serious setbacks in the form of: 1) the October 1986 earthquake, 2) a shortage of resources, and 3) only weak cooperation between civilian ministries and the military. Potentially troublesome for the long term will be the balance between civil and military power once the fighting is over. Internal war has greatly expanded the military's reach in society. Expansion of the armed forces (from twelve thousand in 1980 to fifty-three thousand in 1988) and their professionalization have given them great resources and enhanced their political stature relative to civilian institutions. The need to reduce the size of the military and to subordinate it fully to civilian authority once the insurgency is defeated will prove a challenge to Salvadoran democracy.

The military's commitment to democracy is expedient politically. Nevertheless, such expediency is not to be denigrated if it can lead to greater cooperation between the military and civilians. Democracy has its uses, not only to retain U.S. support but also to beat the insurgents. When considered in these terms, the military's uneasy alliance with the Christian Democrats and President Duarte is understandable.[5] The parliamentary victory of the right-wing ARENA (Alianza Republicana Nacionalista) party in 1989 is an important test for democracy. At the same time, the military faces internal problems of discipline and poor professional performance, which remain unresolved.[6] The Salvadoran military has a poor record when it comes to removing incompetents and disciplining lawbreakers within its ranks. Moreover, along with other Central American militaries, it shares a distressing history of corruption. For democracy to take root, the Salvadoran military must find a way to make its institutional interest compatible with the national interest.

Honduras

Honduras is a key country for the U.S. policy of democratization in Central America. Because it is a major strategic ally in preventing Sandinista expansion, Honduran civil-military relations are greatly affected by its pivotal role in regional defense[7] and its importance to U.S. policy.

For the most part, relations between civilians and the military have remained relatively free of the kind of excesses found in polarized political societies, such as Guatemala and El Salvador. Honduras has thus far escaped such polarization due to a more egalitarian, less stratified social order and to the recent professionalization of its armed forces. Nevertheless, its civil-military accommodation is not so strong that it does not find the situation of its neighbors—consolidation of communism in Nicaragua and insurgency in El Salvador—threatening.

The Honduran military has exercised its power in a relatively benign fashion and supports civilian control for a variety of reasons: because of strategic imperatives, because it is in its institutional interest to do so, and because it is a critical requirement for obtaining U.S. economic and military support. Honduras is keenly aware of its security vulnerabilities. Until March 1988, when it raided Bocay and provoked the U.S. Army's "Golden Pheasant" retaliation, the Sandinista army had been able to conduct cross-border operations against elements of the Nicaraguan resistance located in Honduras with relative impunity. In October 1986 a small insurgent group, trained by Havana and Managua, appeared in La Ceiba (on the Caribbean coast), where it was quickly disposed of by the armed forces.

However, factional disputes and rumors of corruption within the Honduran military remain a source of concern. Not only do these internal problems compromise the respect of civilians, they also diminish the professional readiness required to deal with threats to security, both internal and external (i.e., Sandinistas). When Army Commander Colonel Guillermo Thuman Cordon was replaced by General Humberto Regalado Hernández, Tegucigalpa Radio commented:

In Radio America, we are deeply concerned about what is taking place
inside the military institution. Because it is an institution that must be
worthy of the respect of all Hondurans, it must be a model of well-
reasoned and strictly professional conduct. We want the so-called absolute unity, which is mentioned by the press bulletin, to be a complete
reality of the Armed Forces. We are not surprised when there are differences of opinion in the Armed Forces because this is to be expected in
an organization comprised of human beings. The only thing that we are
worried about is that as a result of these latest events, the Armed Forces
might again play the lead in stormy situations that would have somber
prospects for the country's peace—situations that we all believed were
things of the past. These situations are only good for those who are on
the side of totalitarian doctrine and who oppose the democratic process
of the country. (FBIS-LAM, 1986d: P5)

On the plus side, any weaknesses within the military are increasingly
finding a counterbalance in the growing professionalism of its younger
officers and the institutionalization of cooperative decision-making by
civilian and military leaders on issues of national security. Relations between these two important components remain sensitive—as in Guatemala and El Salvador—to the evolving security balance in the rest of
Central America. This balance will be seriously affected by the potential
disbanding of the contra forces if no corresponding democratization takes
place in Nicaragua. It remains to be seen whether this balance will
strengthen the insurgent Left, increase the insecurity of the Right, or
weaken the political Center. One key to cooperative civil-military relations, particularly if regional conflict continues, is the extent to which the
military can continue to count on U.S. security assistance in the future.

Panama

The Panamanian Defense Forces (PDF) under the control of Manuel Antonio Noriega represent the ultimate corruption of military professionalism in Latin America. Under the leadership of General Omar Torrijos
[Herrera] (1968–1981) the then National Guard evolved from a small
police force into a nation-building unit that, by virtue of the 1977 Panama
Canal Treaty, was admitted into: 1) a bilateral defense relationship with
the United States; and 2) the promise of a new, and probably unrealistic,
mission: unilateral defense of the canal by the year 2000. Ever since 1968,
Panama has been controlled by Torrijos (until his death in 1981), his successors, and the military. For the last two decades, the symbols of
torrijismo, populism, and anticolonialism have dominated the economic
and political life of the country. Applying one of the most effective civic
action programs in the Third World, the PDF has penetrated into every
niche of society, using its formidable intelligence system to co-opt and

intimidate. As if tradition and practice were not enough, Law 20 of the 1983 Constitution grants "administrative autonomy" to the leadership of the armed forces, thereby codifying the subordination of civilian authority to that of the military. The National Assembly, the judiciary, the police, and all the administrative elements of government are controlled by the military through the instrument of a government party and compliant sycophants. The extraordinary political control is enforced through economic co-optation, intimidation, and military control of the mass media, which subjects the small nation of 2.2 million people to a constant barrage of propaganda and misinformation. Noriega and many of his supporters, both civilian and military, have profited immensely from numerous lucrative legal enterprises, as well as many that go beyond the margin of legality (money laundering, drugs). From the late 1970s to 1987, U.S. military assistance—primarily equipment and training—was a key factor in increasing PDF professionalism and its domestic political base. The PDF exploited this military relationship with the United States to control the people of Panama.

This kind of manipulation plus corruption finally drove thousands of demonstrators into the streets demanding political change in the democratic stirrings of June, July, and August 1987. These efforts proved fruitless against the repressive force employed by Noriega and the military to crush the opposition. Two attempts at a coup (March 1988 and October 1989) failed to dislodge Noriega from power, nor did the elections of May 7, 1989, whose results were brutally annulled by Noriega in a naked display of power that shocked the world.

On December 20, 1989, the United States mounted a military operation designed to liberate the Panamanian people from the repression and viciousness of state terrorism. In the ensuing days, reconstruction, reconciliation, and the building of democracy began.

Creating a democracy will be a novel experience for Panamanians. In the wake of dictatorship, they must learn to live by rules of fair play and consensus making. Military domination, manipulative techniques of control, and official lawlessness have been deeply embedded in the political culture. The military so dominated political life after 1968 that the foundations of democratic community—such as free expression, honest elections, a representative legislature, an impartial judiciary, and a government administrative system at the service of the people—became subverted.

The government of Guillermo Endara (who was elected by an overwhelming majority on May 7, 1989) has taken the first (and, hopefully, decisive) step by dismantling the Panamanian Defense Forces, locus of both power and wealth for the past twenty-one years. Drugs, money laundering, and numerous illicit activities corrupted both people and institutions. The officer corps enriched itself immeasurably. Unconfirmed estimates of Noriega's personal wealth went as high as $800 million while that of his subordinates [was calculated at] $50 million or better. The PDF was contemptuous of democracy and indoctrinated its members to despise civilian authority. Loyalty to the commander in chief, not patriotism, was held to be the highest attribute of a soldier.

Old habits die hard, and it will take time to root out established patterns of corruption and authoritarian domination. The newly organized Panamanian Public Force (PPF) must be purged of such attitudes and practices. Whatever replaces the old military must be smaller and accountable to civilian control. Because the Endara government has no experience in control, it will need support of every kind. The kind of multibattalion organization planned by Noriega (reportedly to reach a size of twenty-two thousand by the year 2000) fits neither strategic reality nor Panama's economic capability. The new military force must be imbued with respect for democracy and the role of civilian control. Latin American militaries who respect such values (in Venezuela, for example) can advise. Costa Rica, which disbanded its military in favor of a police force long ago, may serve as a useful model.

In order to bring what Vice President Ricardo Arias Calderon calls decency to public life, it is essential not only to tame the military but to reform a system that has filled the government's administrative network with political cronies and *botellas* (literally, empty bottles who draw pay for no work) and that has facilitated corruption (such as bank secrecy laws which have enabled drug traffickers to launder money).

Peru

President Alán García Pérez and the Peruvian armed forces face formidable, seemingly intractable problems. High external debt and economic recession have brought crushing austerity to the welfare and defense sectors of the economy. Slow growth in the world economy has caused serious economic and social dislocations. A suffocating bureaucracy stifles economic growth. These add to the frustrations brought about by the inability of civilian ministries and the military to develop and implement an effective strategy to defeat the brutal Maoist Sendero Luminoso insurgency, a movement that rejects Western values, including that of democracy. Insurgents are active in at least 40 percent of the national territory and seriously threaten to eliminate the authority of central government in that area. A smaller group, the urban-focused Tupac Amaru Revolutionary Movement, poses a less serious threat. The narcotraffic adds to the general decline of internal order, since it diminishes the ability of government, police, and armed forces to control the national territory. Indeed, narcotraffickers appear to control the Upper Huallaga Valley. Of great concern is the emergence of a tactical alliance between the traffickers and Sendero Luminoso.

In 1967 the Peruvian military, under General [Juan] Velasco Alvarado, came to power committed to social, economic, and political reform only to exit, in the late 1970s, frustrated by the lack of social and economic progress and eager to relinquish power lest the prestige and internal cohesion of the institution be further compromised. However, Peru's return to civilian government—first under President Fernando Belaúnde Terry and then García Pérez—has proved equally incapable of producing lasting solutions to critical national problems. Although the defense establishment was reorganized and various changes of cabinet ministers made, both the government and the military have come under criticism for their inability to contain, much less eliminate, the guerrillas. Sendero Luminoso pursues a low-tech protracted warfare designed to deprive the government of space and people, isolate cities, and provoke the armed forces into abusive acts that undermine their legitimacy. In June 1986, Sendero Luminoso prisoners were massacred at Lurigancho and Fronton prisons,[8] raising anew the ethical question of how to deal with domestic terrorism.[9] Meantime, the defense budget is being cut in half, forcing the military to stretch its limited resources ever more thinly to combat this threat. Unfortunately, Peru's traditional defense strategy has been devised to meet the possibility of conventional border conflict with Chile and Ecuador, not counterinsurgency, hence its shift in focus has been inadequate at best.

In Peru, the democratic idea is being severely tested. Civilian government is attempting to eliminate terrorism within the context of the nation's laws and, at the same time, promote political and economic development. Meanwhile, the military is trying to find a way to strengthen both national security and its own commitment to democracy. From the perspective of Peru's highly professional military, there is little alternative to civilian government. While desperate economic conditions make it unlikely that Peru can change its dependency on Soviet military equipment (and, consequently, training), this fact has in no way lessened the Peruvian military's respect for democracy and support of the West.

Chile

In 1990, General Augusto Pinochet [Ugarte] and the military will return political power to civilians. During 1988 and 1989, Chileans debated the specifics of this transition. When the military took over political power on September 11, 1973 (by overthrowing the Salvador Allende government), they did so with the support of the majority of the population, and in order to end violence and prevent a Communist takeover. In the mid-1980s violence returned to the streets of Santiago, and the Chilean Communist party, no less strong and with considerable Cuban and Soviet support, espoused the violent road to power to make Chile ungovernable and thus vindicate their strategy. In 1985, Chile experienced the highest incidence of bombings in the world after Lebanon, and violence continued into 1986. Military government and violence incongruent with Chile's political tradition threatened seriously to endanger the prospects for a democratic outcome.

That outcome rested upon the ability of Pinochet and his senior military leaders to work out an agreement with the civilian opposition. On October 5, 1988, a national plebiscite was held to determine whether or not the people wanted Pinochet to continue in power. His bid to do so was rejected. Patricio Aylwin was elected as Chile's civilian president in December 1989, taking office in March 1990. Yet to be worked out is how the balance of power will be distributed between civil government and the military and whether (and, if so, how) the military will be subordinated to civilian authority—through such instruments as the National Security Council, the military educational system, and the process of national defense planning.

Pinochet and the senior military distrust civilian politics. To protect democracy (or their conception of it), they drew up the Constitution of 1980 to protect it from—in their words—the irresponsibility of civil politicians and from those who espouse doctrines of class warfare, i.e., the Communists. The constitution proscribes totalitarian parties from political activity, a ruling that profoundly affects political life among Chile's traditional ebullient political parties. At the same time, the constitution makes the military the guarantor of institutional order through control of the National Security Council and renders the military virtually free of civilian control. Pinochet's opposition wants to subordinate the armed forces to the civilian president, a concept anathema to military leaders desirous of maintaining constitutional provisions that safeguard the tutelary role of the armed forces. Genaro Arriagada, a leading Christian Democratic intellectual, has argued, on the grounds of military professionalism, that these provisions should be reformed:

> The role which the Constitution of 1980 assigns to the Armed Forces is damaging for the military institution, in particular, and unacceptable from the point of view of what a democratic political system is. It institutionalizes constant involvement and political activity by the three Commanders-in-Chief and the Director-General of the *Carabineros*

through the National Security Council and the decisive role of this organization in the Constitutional Tribune and the Senate. The National Security Council consecrates in an unmistakable manner a military tutelage over the autocratic political government. This destroys the principle of political domination of civil power over the military, which is the essence not only of democracy but also of a mature and stable political system, whether democratic or not. Moreover, permanent political activity by the military will likely have destructive effects on the military profession. Armies involved in politics degrade their military professionalism, diminish their military capacity, suffer the destruction of military values, and soon become divided.

The military is a tremendously complex profession, which must develop apart from undesirable political interference, and which has an ethical code and responsibility to its society. The military has the monopoly of arms and, therefore, there should not be any other armed group in society. Despite its monopoly, the military should never use its arms against the state and civilians. (Arriagada, 1988: 34)

Most Chileans are fully committed to a democratic transition, and signs are good that the more offensive authoritarian elements of the Constitution of 1980 will be amended. Chile's economic miracle of the 1980s provides a strong foundation for sustaining democratization into the future. A process of civil-military rapprochement is under way, assisted by an increasingly sophisticated dialogue on defense policy and the respective roles of civilians and military.

Argentina

Civil-military relations in Argentina, Chile, and Uruguay have had a similar evolution over the last fifteen years. In all three countries, the military intervened to preserve public order and prevent a perceived Marxist takeover. After entering politics to protect a democracy that "went wrong," so to speak, the military then found it exceedingly difficult to extricate itself with institutional unity intact and democracy secure. Clausewitz once warned that this was a characteristic of war: easy to get into, but difficult to get out of.

Argentina's military was unsuccessful on two fronts: it found itself increasingly unable to govern at home and it failed to win a war (the 1982 Malvinas/Falklands War). As a result, the military regime lost the confidence of the people and was faced with a rising demand for the return of civilian government—which culminated in the free elections of 1984 that brought Raúl Alfonsín to the presidency. In May 1989 he was succeeded in office by Carlos Menem, another freely elected civilian, apparently consolidating Argentina's return to democracy. Subsequently, some of the military leaders—those responsible for the human rights abuses incurred during the internal "dirty war" of the 1970s as well as for incompetent leadership in the 1982 war—were tried in court and punished. Argentina's crushing defeat in the war exposed the weakness of the military in the exercise of their prime professional responsibility and raison d'être and, in so doing, of the institution itself. To remedy this situation, the Alfonsín government determined to reform and modernize the military establishment, both intellectually and operationally. Defeat in war also underscored the necessity for civil control of the institutional means of applying force. Since coming to power, President Menem carried this program forward by pardoning (in October 1989) over 280 military officers, along with leftist subversives. The *New York Times* quoted Menem as declaring this step to be necessary to heal the wounds left by the "dirty war" of the 1970s.

As the armed forces undergo reorganization, the military budget has been cut severely. Argentina is attempting to establish a modern military organization capable of joint operations, a major deficiency in the 1982 war. These changes have caused bitterness within the ranks of the military. A 1986 army report cited the following budgetary impact on defense:

> noncommissioned officers outnumber conscripts by twenty-eight thousand to twenty-five thousand;
>
> the army's strength was at a ratio of 1 to 5 compared with Brazil and 1 to 3 [compared with] Chile;
>
> low pay has reduced the number of officers and noncommissioned officers by 35 percent since 1983;
>
> equipment could not be maintained; and
>
> students entering the noncommissioned officers' school dropped from two hundred fifty in 1985 to only forty in 1986.

Passage of the April 1988 Defense Law redefined the military's role in national security as responsibility for defense against external aggression, taking away its mission of internal security and intelligence-gathering for internal political matters.

The political dilemma in Argentina is how to balance military requirements for institutional survival and modernization/professionalization of the armed forces against political requirements of: 1) economic austerity; and 2) primacy of civilian control over the military within an effective democratic order. For Alfonsín and Menem, some sort of national reconciliation is basic to the establishment of a functioning democracy. In 1986, Alfonsín began promoting his *punto final* (full stop) strategy, i.e., setting a three-year time limit, after the beginning of legal proceedings in 1983, for bringing charges against military officers for human rights violations (FBIS-LAM, 1986b). The chief of the Joint Staff of the Armed Forces, Brigadier General Tedoro Waldner,[10] reflected on the problems of the military in politics as follows:

> regardless of whether the handling of public affairs, something for which we are not trained, was correct or not, this led to the discredit of the Armed Forces, to its separation from the people, and to the inexorable loss of morale and discipline within the Armed Forces themselves. (FBIS-LAM, 1986a: B2)

Uruguay

In 1973 the Uruguayan military came to power, taking pride in having successfully liquidated the Tupamaros (urban guerrillas) between 1967 and 1972. Like the Chilean military, the Uruguayan military attempted to institutionalize a political role of "protecting" democracy from what it perceived to be civilian irresponsibility and the threat of totalitarian government. This effort, rejected by the profoundly democratic Uruguayan people, caused dispute even within the military. Finally, in 1984, the Naval Club agreement was worked out with the political parties, providing for a democratic transition. In November of that year, elections were held that brought Julio María Sanguinetti, a civilian, to the presidency. The military, having accomplished its mission of restoring order and democracy, was anxious to be relieved of the burden of government. But all was not smooth. Many members of the military were unwilling to relinquish economic perquisites and political influence acquired during the years of military rule, while avoiding recriminations (or retaliation) for human rights violations committed during the same period. This gave rise to long-standing debate between the military and civilians over how to deal with mistakes of the past and prevent their future recurrence, and centered around a civilian-sponsored bill to resolve the emotional issue of amnesty. The debate took place within the context of economic recession, military concern over recurrence of political instability, and general lack of confidence in civilian politicians, and cuts in the defense budget. The amnesty law under discussion:

limited trials to the thirty-eight most serious cases;

allowed prosecution of military officers in civilian courts in cases of homicide, grievous injury, "disappearances," or rape;

excluded from human rights trials those violations committed during the campaign against the Tupamaros;

granted the Supreme Court exclusive jurisdiction over human rights cases;

established sanctions on any future attempts at a coup;

exempted civilians from being tried in military courts;

established torture as a crime. (*LAWR*, 1986a: 7)

Though initially rejected by the Uruguayan Congress (October 1986), President Sanguinetti believed that the bill provided a basis for national reconciliation between a military establishment that had ended (in 1973) Uruguay's democratic tradition with reluctance and a public seeking to understand not only why democracy had failed in the past but also how to make it succeed in the future.[11] Finally, and only after heated debate, the Congress approved (on December 22, 1986) a military amnesty bill that barred further prosecution of military and police officials accused of human rights violations occurring prior to March 1984 (*New York Times*, 1986: A3).[12] On April 16, 1989, a referendum reconfirmed the amnesty law by a vote of 57 percent to 43 percent.

Conclusion: Implications for U.S. Policy and Democratic Military Professionalism

A democratic vision of security makes sense in Latin America. It makes political sense because it offers an effective alternative to totalitarian doctrines and/or practices. It also makes sense in terms of U.S.-Latin American relations. Because democracy is a value prized by the U.S. Congress and public, appealing to this value expands the policy options available to the United States in dealing with Latin America. U.S. ideals and institutions are more likely to respond sympathetically to requests for economic and military cooperation when the value to be defended is democracy, making possible greater bilateral and multilateral cooperation and encouraging Latin Americans to realize a community of interests with the United States. U.S. public opinion and the Congress are reluctant to support causes perceived to be unjust and at variance with democratic values.

The security of Latin America and that of the United States are inextricably linked. Latin American military establishments, in particular, form an important part of that linkage, and they will bear a critical responsibility to ensure that democratization prospers. It may be, as numerous civilian and military leaders fear, the final opportunity that democrats have in these troubled times. Another round of coups and military government would only assist opponents of the very democratic values that the inter-

American security system was created to defend. A single coup not only assists the enemies of democratic values but is a success, in and of itself, for antidemocrats of both the Left and Right simultaneously, but for different reasons.

The United States can best support redemocratization by holding fast to its own values and by being alert to opportunities for assistance. Democratic professionalism can be communicated through sophisticated military diplomacy, requiring sustained, skillful interaction via security assistance and military-to-military relations. As security assistance funding declines, the United States must seek out new forms of influence or lose effectiveness. Increased interaction between the military forces of the United States and countries in Latin America is one such form. While the United States can try to foster professionalism in its military-to-military dealings with Latin America, civilian and military leaders of the region must learn to work together to formulate a doctrine encompassing a role for the military in which it serves as guardian of the renascent democracy.[13]

Of what would such a doctrine consist? Following are some tentative working proposals:

1. Definition of the security requirements of emerging democracy. Such a healthy reexamination is under way in Argentina, Uruguay, and Guatemala—and is required in El Salvador, Panama, Peru, and Chile. The task should be undertaken jointly by civilians and military. It entails a clearer, more precise delineation of the boundaries of military responsibility in national defense and intelligence-gathering. This task will be the most difficult, for it involves both democratization of power and subordination to civilian authority. With the potential withering away of the East-West divide, national security strategies will have to adapt to more realistic assessments of threat.

2. Modernization of military and civilian views of one another. While the old adage "se puede militarizar a un civil pero no se puede civilizar a un militar" (you can militarize a civilian but you can't civilize a military man) is useful at cocktail parties, it seriously misreads the need for more cooperative attitudes. Cooperation is in order, founded on the following concepts.

3. Legitimizing national security and military studies in civilian universities and research centers. This would improve the climate for mutual dialogue on the most important issue of national security. National security and military affairs are too important to be left to the military alone.

4. Expanding linkages and feedback mechanisms between the military and civilian society to reduce their isolation from one another.

A military institution isolated from the larger society can be a serious threat to democracy and to itself. Civilian control of the military implies establishing links to communicate professional expertise from one sector of society to the other.

5. Recognition that the military, despite the troubles of recent history, will remain an actor in national affairs. Power sharing is not incompatible with democracy. The legitimate role of the military in contemporary society is expanding into areas such as technological research and development, communications, search and rescue, fighting the narcotics traffic, countering terrorism, arms control, and peacekeeping. Properly understood, such an expansion of their role is to be welcomed rather than feared.

6. Expanding opportunities for civilians and the military to share learning experiences through educational programs. Among other possibilities, this would mean requiring university education for advancement in the officer corps. It may require greater integration with the civilian educational system following graduation from the military academy. Increased university education is an imperative, given the expanding role of the military to deal with the complex challenges that their societies face. While the U.S. Army is quite a different institution from its Latin American counterparts, it long ago understood the value of university education. The United States Military Academy authorized the bachelor degree in 1932. Out of 189 Army students in the U.S. Army War College Class of 1987, 6 held doctorates, 177 had master's degrees, 3 had law degrees, 2 had medical degrees, and 1 some study at the university level. Today the contemporary military officer must be capable of greater technical proficiency than was formerly the case, as well as be able to interact successfully with civilian professionals.

7. Capacity to learn from past successes/failures and incorporate such lessons through constructive, professional self-criticism. In the United States, both military and civilian leaders experienced the debacle of Vietnam. To understand what happened and why, military officers—such as General Bruce Palmer (1984) and Colonel Harry Summers (1982)—have written some of the most penetrating analyses of the mistakes that civilian and military leaders made. Such self-criticism is not to be confined to the classified environments of war colleges, but should be open to the national security and foreign policy dialogue of the entire society in order to inform responsible decision-making in a democracy.

8. Civilians and military must cooperate to develop a counterinsurgency doctrine appropriate for a democracy. The new warfare facing Latin America requires mobilization of both civilian and military assets to develop a composite strategic vision and the decisive authority to implement that vision. Constraint in the use of force combined with and respect for human rights are critical for success. Absent such civil-military coordination, measures to counter insurgencies are apt to fail.

Implementing these proposals will be far from easy, but the key is to expand interaction between the civilian and military establishments. Such efforts will reduce the mutual paranoia and distrust that now divide and weaken the society. Improving civil-military relations will lead to wider recognition of the legitimate role of the military in national security, development, and democracy. No doubt, there will always be some tension between military and civilians, even where relations are well established, as in the United States where the military subordinates itself willingly to civilian rule. The challenge in Latin America today is to perceive some level of tension as natural, manageable, even desirable—given the alternatives.

Notes

1. At this meeting, the various delegations (including the U.S. Army chief of staff) presented formal papers on the subject, which were discussed extensively in working groups and then distributed throughout the armies of the hemisphere. The documents presented by Brazil, Uruguay, Peru, and Colombia, among others, offer especially eloquent statements of military views on civil-military relations in the context of democratic transition. They also constitute excellent primers on how the military defines national security and how they formulate strategy in the context of the contemporary threats.

2. With respect to the "philosophy" of the military, Duarte states:

> I came to the conclusion that if I were forced to choose between converting the Marxist guerrillas to my democratic philosophy and trying to convince the officers, I stood a better chance with the armed forces. If I had understood the armed forces better years ago, my work would have been easier. My prejudice against the military was deeply rooted in the history of El Salvador, and I regret not having learned how to analyze the philosophy of the military much earlier. It is hard to categorize officers. They move along the spectrum of political thought, responding to a particular issue or to whom they spoke to last. But it is this flexibility that has led to the changes that now are evident in the Salvadoran armed forces. (Duarte, 1986: 106)

3. An example of this frustration is to be found in the reflections of a retired Peruvian army major, J. Salvatteci (Salvatteci, 1986).

4. Cerezo's principled pragmatism can be seen in the following interview:

> JULIO MILLER. Mr. President, it seems that there is a sudden turn toward democracy in Latin America. However, military sectors remain as guardians, and, in many countries, the civilian governments do not have the right aggressive attitude. In your opinion, what is the direction, the path, that democracy is taking in Latin America?

VINICIO CEREZO. It is true. There are certain places where doubts and distrust exist between the civilian government and the armies that continue—just as in all countries of the world—to play a predominant role in the country's political life. This is of special importance. Having weapons means having political power.

However, I think that the direction being taken is one of consolidating civilian governments to the extent that the president of the republic, as coordinator of the national effort, does not isolate the Army from the political and social processes.

I think that, historically, the error made by civilian governments was trying to isolate the military sector from the political and social process. The military officers must not belong to parties, but they must never be apolitical. They must share the responsibility of the country's economic and social development with the civilian governments.

The Army is not an institution that is detached from national problems. The military's had been (*sic*) traditional separation from the problems, and detachment from its shared responsibility kept converting the military officers into judges who wanted to correct situations. Conservative groups kept pushing them, and this resulted in the traditional coups d'état in Latin America.

However, if they share responsibility and join the social and political process in each country, they will also consolidate democracy instead of being on alert to interfere and interrupt democratic processes when they are provoked by certain groups.

JULIO MILLER. Cerezo is a clear example of the transition from a military to a civilian government. How has Cerezo achieved this while it has not been accomplished in certain countries?

VINICIO CEREZO. By discussing very clearly with the military officers their responsibility within the democratic process. We have not meant to cut them off or corrupt them, and we have not refused to discuss the country's problems with them. We have established clear discussions with them, demanding that they fulfill their historical responsibility that links them together with the civilian government: Strengthen democracy and accept the only formula that establishes the legitimacy of a regime, which is answering to the people, who are sovereign, and exercise this right through the government that they have freely elected. The open discussion of the problems with the military officers, their constant contact with the country's problems, the honest and frank discussion of all their problems and the problems of the civilian government have allowed us in Guatemala to have a president who is truly the General Commander of the Army. (U.S. Department of State, 1986a)

5. For further information on developments in El Salvador, see U.S. Department of State (1986b); for the political-military lessons learned, see Manwaring and Prisk (1988).

6. [Due to its length, the account of barriers to reform in El Salvador's small military officer corps by a U.S. military attaché to that country is not reproduced here. It may be consulted in the original article.]

7. For the views of a senior Honduran Army officer on civil-military relations and the nation's defense policy, see Nuñez-Bennett (1986), who was an International Fellow at the War College for the 1985–86 academic year.

8. On June 18, 1986, Sendero Luminoso prisoners held by the government in these prisons mutinied and took seven hostages. The following day government forces retook the prisons. In so doing, 244 prisoners were killed; government losses included one policeman and three marine infantry (for a detailed report, see Ames, 1988).

9. For the views of a senior Peruvian Army officer on the Sendero Luminoso and the strategy to deal with it, see Zubiaga (1985) and Jarama Davila (1987).

10. The sentiments of Waldner and Ríos Ereñu remarkably echo the views expressed by General Luis Rodolfo González, in September 1956, in the aftermath of the overthrow of Juan Perón (González, 1968: 193–227).

11. For a perceptive analysis of Uruguayan civil-military relations, and the views of the military on the crisis of the 1970s and the current democratic transition, see Rial (1986); on how the military perceives itself and democratization, see Perelli (1986).

12. For some provocative speculation on the future of civil-military relations, see Perelli (1987). To understand the intensity of the military's sentiments on the defeat of the amnesty bill, see the communiqué of six military social institutions (FBIS-LAM, 1986c).

13. The term "democratic military professionalism" is proposed by Professor John S. Fitch of the University of Colorado in numerous writings on the subject of civil-military relations in Latin America (see, for example, Fitch: 1987 and 1988).

References

Abrams, E. (1986) "A Democratic View of Security." (Current Policy No. 844) Washington, DC: U.S. Dept. of State, Bureau of Public Affairs.

Ames, R. (1988) *Informe al Congreso sobre los Sucesos de los Penales.* Lima, Peru: Talleres y Gráfica.

Arriagada, G. (1988) "Los Políticos y las Fuerzas Armadas." *Que Pasa* 891 (5 May): 34.

——— (1986) *Pinochet: The Politics of Power* (Nancy Morris translation of *La Política Militar de Pinochet*). Boston, MA: Unwin Hyman.

Duarte, J. (1986) *Duarte: My Own Story.* New York, NY: G. H. Putnam Sons.

Duryea, Col. L. (1986) "U.S. Foreign Policy and Local Corruption." Paper presented at conference sponsored by VECINOS and the Lyndon B. Johnson School of Public Affairs, University of Texas-Austin, 4 March.

Fitch, J. (1988) "The Armed Forces and Democracy in Latin America: Towards a New Relationship." Transition team document prepared for the Inter-American Dialogue, Washington, DC, December.

——— (1987) "The Armed Forces and Democracy in Latin America." Discussion Paper presented at the Plenary Session of the Inter-American Dialogue, Washington, DC, 16–18 October.

Foreign Broadcast Information Service—Latin America (FBIS-LAM) (1986a) "General Waldner Comments on 'Full Stop' Proposal." *Noticias Argentinas*, 6 December, FBIS-LAM-86-236, 9 December: B1–B3.

———— (1986b) "Alfonsín Speech Explains 'Full Stop' Proposal." Buenos Aires Televisora Color Network, 6 December, in FBIS-LAM-86-235, 8 December: B1–B5.

———— (1986c) "Military Social Institutions View Amnesty." Montevideo Radio Carve, 3 October, in FBIS-LAM-86-193, 6 October: K1.

———— (1986d) "Armed Forces Changes Reviewed." Tegucigalpa Cadena Audio Video, 29 September, in FBIS-LAM-86-189, 30 September: P5.

Frente Farabundo Martí de Liberación Nacional (FMLN) (1986) *Concerning Our Plans: The Military Strategy of the FMLN* (Document captured and transcribed by the Atlacatl Battalion, near Perquin, El Salvador; translated and edited by Gabriel Marcella, U.S. Army War College, May).

Galvin, Gen. J. R. (1986) "Uncomfortable Wars: Toward a New Paradigm." *Parameters* XVI, 4 (Winter): 2–8.

González, Gen. L. (1968) "Ideas Contrary to the Spirit of May and Their Repercussion in Argentine Political Life: A Military Operation at the Service of Definitive Pacification." Speech given September 1956 and reprinted in pp. 193–227 of Kalman H. Silvert's *The Conflict Society: Reaction and Revolution in Latin America*. New York, NY: Harper and Row.

Huntington, S. (1981) *The Soldier and the State: The Theory and Politics of Civil-Military Relations*. Cambridge, MA: Harvard University Press.

Jarama Davila, Lt. G. S. (1987) "Bases para el Diseño y Planeamiento de una Estratégia Contrasubversiva." Paper prepared by chief of Peruvian delegation for the Interamerican Defense Board, Washington, DC (mimeo).

Latin American Weekly Report (LAWR) (1986a) "Uruguay: Congress Agrees on an Amnesty." WR-86-39 (9 October): 7.

———— (1986b) "Argentina: Army Sympathy." WR-86-38 (2 October): 9.

Manwaring, M., and C. Prisk (1988) *El Salvador at War: An Oral History*. Washington, DC: National Defense University Press.

Mercado Jarrín, E. (1974) *Seguridad, Política, Estratégia*. Lima, Peru: Ministerio de Guerra.

New York Times (1986) "Uruguay Approves a Military Amnesty." 23 December: A3.

Nuñez-Bennett, Lt. Col. J. (1986) "Honduras Defense Policy" (paper prepared for International Fellows Program, 1985–86). Carlisle, PA: U.S. Army War College, Carlisle Barracks.

Palmer, Gen. Bruce (1984) *The 25-Year War: American Military Policy in Vietnam*. Lexington, KY: University Press of Kentucky.

Perelli, C. (1987) "Amnistía Si, Amnistía No, Amnistía Puede Ser . . . La Constitución Histórica de un Tema Político en el Uruguay de la Posttransición" (paper prepared for Kellogg Institute, 7 January). South Bend, IN: University of Notre Dame.

———— (1986) "Someter o Convencer: El Discurso Militar en el Uruguay de la Transición y la Redemocratización" (paper prepared for Kellogg Institute). South Bend, IN: University of Notre Dame.

Rial, J. (1986) *Las Fuerzas Armadas: ¿Soldados Políticos o Garantes de la Democracia?* South Bend, IN: University of Notre Dame Press.

Salvatteci, J. (1986) *Terrorismo y Guerra Sucia en el Peru*. Lima, Peru: Punto Rojo.

Summers, H. (1982) *On Strategy: A Critical Analysis of the Vietnam War*. Novato, CA: Presidio Press.

U.S. Department of State. (1986a) Retransmission of interview 2 November on Panama City Circuito RPC Television, reported in Telegram R190245. 18 November.

—— (1986b) *The Situation in El Salvador* (Special Report No. 144). Washington, DC: U.S. Dept. of State, April.

Zubiaga, Col. V. (1985) *Shining Path: Peruvian Peasants' Rebellion* (Military Studies Program paper). Carlisle, PA: U.S. Army War College, Carlisle Barracks.

10

Military Professionalism and Nonintervention in Mexico

William S. Ackroyd

The violent Revolution of 1910 threatened to reignite the rampant militarism that had plagued Mexico during much of the nineteenth century. Within two decades, however, the country's armed forces were brought under civilian control. Mexico's contemporary experience stands in sharp contrast to that of most other Latin American countries where military involvement in politics is the norm. Since the successful depoliticization of the military during the postrevolutionary period, symbolized by the removal of the military as a sector of the official party in 1940, the armed forces have remained under civilian control while becoming increasingly professionalized. Mexico's experience contrasts with the Latin American pattern wherein professionalization is frequently associated with increasing rather than decreasing political activity by the military.

William Ackroyd explores Mexico's enviable record in the area of civil-military relations by comparing the nature of the country's military education and professionalization with those in Brazil and Peru. The author's analysis indicates not only that Mexican officers acquire a different type of professionalization than their South American counterparts—one that emphasizes the primacy of civilian institutions—but also that they recognize the greater efficacy of civilian structures in their country.

Compared to other Latin American countries, Mexico has been a model of civil-military tranquility. No successful coup has occurred in

From *Armed Forces and Society* 18, no. 1 (Fall 1991): 81–96. ©1991 by Transaction Publishers. Reprinted by permission of the author and Transaction Publishers.

Mexico since 1920, and no serious threat has manifested itself since the late 1930s. Civilians dominate the political life of the nation. This article examines this atypical situation—namely, the reasons for civilian political control and the absence of coup behavior.

The problem of relations between civilians and the military, however, is complex.[1] Hypotheses have presented a broad spectrum of causal factors ranging from international structural features down through external national structure to internal military institutional characteristics.[2] Because of this broad scope, an analysis of all such possible factors is felt to be beyond the capabilities of a single article. This study therefore concentrates on internal characteristics of the military.

The rationale behind the choice is that ultimately the military makes the final decision on whether or not to carry out a coup. Outside forces may influence the coup decision, but the interpretation of environmental stimuli and the selection of socially appropriate responses by individual officers are foremost in the causal sequence. How the military perceives its environment and what reactions the military deems socially appropriate therefore intimately affect its behavior.[3] Since perception and response result from a social learning process, analysis should focus on the individual officer, his professionalization, and the military educational system.

Most of the information used in this study comes from direct observations of Mexican officers. This includes multiple formal and informal conversations with forty-nine different officers in Mexico over a period of fifteen years and the observed interaction of officers among themselves and with civilians.[4] Additional information for analysis is supplied by their writings and institutional rules. Interviews with civilians and other military personnel familiar with both the military in Mexico and the other Latin American republics provide data from still another perspective.

The methodology and data are not, however, without their problems and limitations. The secrecy and suspicions of Mexican army officers frequently made structured interviews impossible. This may reduce the validity of the responses to some degree. The fact that the officers interviewed were not randomly chosen may also cast some doubts on the reliability of the data.

Nevertheless, the length of the study period and the reliance on informal, open-ended questions and interviews also produced a greater number of frank and honest responses, less influenced by individual career considerations. In addition, the data were verified as frequently as possible through the use of multiple sources. Obviously, however, further work remains to be done on the subject.

The Current Paradigm of Professionalism[5]

Currently, the most widely accepted explanation for professionalism's effect is the "new professionalism" model developed by Alfred Stepan. Stepan integrates the past, classical model with the reality of the Brazilian and Peruvian coups of 1964 and 1968, suggesting that there are actually two types of military professionalization. One type focuses on an external threat and the other on an internal threat.[6] Professionalization for an external mission depoliticizes the military by forcing officers to devote their time to studying subjects associated with international war. The result is a military with no time for politics and consequently no interest in the subject. This is similar to the classical model.[7] An internal mission, however, teaches officers that threats to the nation result from inadequate national development. Any government failing to promote national development encourages such threats and must be removed. The military's perspective of civilian political performance therefore determines coups, and this perspective is the product of the values inculcated by the professionalization process. In the cases of Brazil and Peru, these values are well articulated in their national security doctrines, but as Samuel Fitch points out in his study of Ecuador, values and perspectives may vary from country to country.[8] This is the new professionalism model.

Mexican Reality

While the coups of the highly professionalized Brazilian and Peruvian militaries in 1964 and 1968 gave considerable credence to the new professionalism model, Mexican civil-military relations do not appear to support all the model's hypotheses. Over the last seventy years, coups and coup attempts have continually declined in Mexico. The Mexican situation therefore suggests three possible explanations. First, Mexico has not professionalized its military. Second, Mexico's military has not professionalized for an internal threat. Third, the new professionalism model needs modification.

Examining professionalism first, since education is the primary method of professionalization, the degree of complexity (number of levels, total time in school, etc.) of the military educational system is a good indicator of institutional professionalism. Under this criterion Brazil, Peru, and Mexico have similar rankings. All three countries have a four-tier military educational system: a military academy, junior officers' school (branch specialization), general staff and command school, and a superior war college. In all three systems, entrance to the schools is based on competitive universalistic criteria, and completion of progressively higher school levels is necessary for career advancement.

At the highest tier, the Brazilian Superior War College (Escola Superior de Guerra [ESG]), founded in 1949, and the Peruvian Center for Higher Military Studies (Centro de Altos Estudios Militares [CAEM]), established in 1951, are older than the Mexican Defense College (Colegio de Defensa [CD]), begun in 1981. This indicates that in some respects the Mexican system may lag in development compared to Brazil and Peru. The capacity to transfer experiences and technology rapidly, however, somewhat mitigates this apparent inequity. The Mexicans have had the advantage of drawing upon the Brazilian and Peruvian examples and, therefore, did not have to develop their defense college from scratch.

All three countries also use universalistic procedures for recruitment and promotion, and their activities are coordinated by highly developed general staffs. Mexico's military, however, appears a more national force than Brazil's, which suffers from regionalism, and Peru's, which exhibits racial factionalization.[9] Considering these criteria, Brazil and Peru may be somewhat more professional by virtue of their earlier educational development. The difference, however, does not appear great.

With regard to the relationship between Mexican professionalization and military mission, it is clear that Mexico has professionalized for an internal threat.[10] For example, the former secretary of defense, Lt. Gen. Felix Galvan López, has asserted that it is the responsibility of the armed forces to maintain national security. This involves "the maintenance of social, economic and political equilibrium" (i.e., internal security).[11] Similarly, as a governmental document states, "the Mexican army has the great responsibility of maintaining tranquility and internal order under the rule of the Constitution . . . . It guarantees, moreover, that the nation will continue harmonious development."[12]

Furthermore, the military has refined the concept of national strategy into a doctrine integrating all aspects of social behavior and development. According to one senior officer, the increasing complexity of war has forced the military to integrate into its strategy such traditionally nonmilitary concerns as economics, psychology, morale, politics, and technology.[13] The concept of national strategy also appears in the doctrine of the ESG. According to an ESG publication, "strategy is to set up in peace and conduct in war all the resources of a people to satisfy their political objectives."[14] General strategy, according to the school, "is an integration of military and political strategies with national politics and the doctrine of the military."[15]

Therefore, while the new professionalism model is intuitively appealing and explains the Brazilian and Peruvian cases, it does not seem to fit the Mexican case. The problem appears to be that the new model focuses too extensively upon the mission of the military and too little on the actual process of officer learning and socialization (i.e., professionalization). The linkage between macrolevel behavior and individual decision making is therefore never fully or adequately examined, and cross-national patterns of institutional behavior may appear contradictory. In the case of Mexico, then, identification of causality requires knowledge of the interaction between the primary agent of military socialization (i.e., the military educational system) and individual officers.

The Mexican Military Educational System

The Mexican military educational system has basically two functions: to inculcate the values and norms necessary to function within the military institution and to teach necessary skills while restricting political knowledge, interest, and efficacy.[16] Of the two, the teaching of values and norms, especially discipline, is the most visible.

Discipline's centrality to the military value system is suggested by the first page of the admissions manual of the Heroic Military College (Heroico Colegio Militar [HCM]): "Discipline is the norm to which the military must subject its conduct: it has as its foundation obedience and a high concept of honor, justice and morality, faith and the exact completion of those duties prescribed by military laws and regulations."[17]

The Mexican concept of discipline, however, has been widely misinterpreted by North American and North European officers and scholars, who at times claim that the Mexican officer corps lacks discipline.[18] In the Mexican context discipline means unquestioning, unyielding deference and personal obedience to superiors. This means that no order is questioned and no action is taken independently of a superior.[19] Discipline, however, does not mean "self-discipline." The individual officer might break some written rules, but this is winked at and sometimes even encouraged by peer esteem (i.e., admiration for someone who can get around the rules).[20]

Order and authority closely relate to discipline. Order means conformity and obedience to law. This interpretation encourages nonchallenging political behavior similar to the behavior between an individual officer and his superior. Order, though, can only be achieved through authority. According to one senior officer, "authority is first, since order cannot exist if there is no authority which sustains and imposes it."[21] The importance and meaning of these values encourage Mexican officers to follow the orders of their superiors, the president, and his civilian agents. To do otherwise would produce a discordant, nonorderly situation, the anti-thesis of military values.[22]

Closely related to the concept of order/disorder is the need for reso-lute action. From the military's perspective, government's purpose is to govern, and in Mexico, the military is taught that civilian politicians gov-ern.[23] Brazil and Peru inculcate the value of resolute action, but do not teach the corresponding perception of strong civilian behavior.[24] This inhibits intervention in Mexico and encourages it in Brazil and Peru.

The military educational system also inculcates the values of loyalty and patriotism. Through these two values the system mandates a progres-sion of loyalties, placing the nation, the state and its institutions, and finally the military in descending order of importance. Furthermore, the superior position of the state, vis-à-vis the military, is reinforced by the ideological fusion of nation and state created by the Revolution.[25]

The effect of these values is twofold. First, officers are taught to place the nation before the individual. This, combined with discipline, has dis-couraged the predatory militarism prevalent in the nineteenth century and the immediate postrevolutionary period.[26] Second, the progression of loy-alties firmly places civilian institutions ahead of the military in impor-tance. To attack the state would be to attack the nation and the Revolution, an almost sacred event and ideal in Mexico. The order of progression, together with authority, therefore inhibits military intervention and rein-forces civilian control of the polity.

Brazil and Peru reverse the order of importance between national political institutions and the military. The officer corps in these countries is taught that the military is the institution that has the greatest capability of determining the interests of the people.[27] In addition, the concepts of nation and state are separated, with the nation being a permanent entity and the state a temporary one.[28] Military values in Brazil and Peru, there-fore, tend to encourage intervention, while the opposite order in Mexico inhibits it.[29]

The second function of the school system, the teaching of skills, focuses upon course subjects and content. A course analysis of the HCM reveals that 10 to 13 percent of the courses are devoted to social sciences; only 4 to 5 percent, though, have any political content. Another 4 to 5 percent of the courses are devoted to civic and moral values—the proper behavior of officers in relation to their institution and society.[30]

The ESG follows a pattern similar to that of the military academy. During the first two of the three years at the school, 77 and 71 percent, respectively, of the curriculum are devoted to general tactics, such as those used in World War II and the Korean War. Only 6 percent of the first-year and 5 percent of the second-year courses teach general strategy and other subjects having sociopolitical content. Discipline and group behavior, however, are heavily stressed.[31]

The course content analysis, therefore, indicates little political information or stimulus in the curriculum. Instead, the educational program forces students to devote the vast majority of their time to nonpolitical matters. This inhibits the development of political interest and efficacy and, in turn, discourages political participation. The use of military officers, rather than civilians, as teachers further exacerbates the trend towards low political interest and efficacy by preventing any "tainting" of cadets through civilians and their ideals and interests.[32]

The Mexican ESG's third-year curriculum, however, begins to resemble the curriculum of the Brazilian Army Command and General Staff School (Escola de Comando e Estado Maior do Exercito [ECEME]).[33] The time devoted to general tactics, for example, drops to 53 percent, while general strategy and related courses rise to 30 percent of the curriculum. Civilian lecturers are also more prominent, and the year culminates in a class study of some sociopolitical problem facing Mexico.[34]

The curriculum pattern continues at the Mexican Defense College, where about twenty-five brigadier generals, or their equivalents, from all branches of the armed forces spend one year. The students study exclusively political-military subjects such as the situation in Central America, Mexican foreign policy, and development of Mexican natural resources. Civilians provide most of the instruction in a seminar-type format. The year ends with the submission of individual position papers by each officer.[35]

The Mexican military educational system therefore appears to screen officers and restrict political knowledge to only a few at the highest ranks.[36] This screening process begins with application to the HCM but becomes most apparent with selection for the ESG and the school's third year. At each step, tests are administered, but the entire process is shrouded in secrecy, with only ESG graduates seeing and grading tests. As a result, entrance and advancement seem to place considerable emphasis upon personal recommendations from senior officers, while continuation to the ESG's third year and graduation seem to be predicated upon having the "right attitude" in the eyes of the ESG instructors. Those who fail or drop out inevitably lack this high degree of conformity and adaptation to the system. About half of the original entering class makes it to the third year and graduates to become the future generals and leaders of the military.[37] The officers who receive political training at the CD have survived the selection process at the ESG and have the institution's values most deeply ingrained. They also have prospered the most from the entire military system and, therefore, have the most to lose from any challenge to the system.

Only 7 percent of the officer corps have graduated from the ESG and received moderate political instruction. Only 2 percent of the officer corps have graduated from the CD and received more extensive political training. The remaining 91 percent have little exposure to political subjects, consequently developing little interest in politics and exhibiting little political efficacy.[38]

An analysis of the subject matter of the *Revista del Ejército y Fuerza Aérea Mexicanos* indicates the military's success in inhibiting political interest. Only 1.7 percent of its articles have some political content. About 16 percent have the theme of loyalty to the nation and its institutions. Civic action, however, represents the largest category, with the remainder being devoted to technical, nonpolitical, and frequently nonmilitary scientific subjects.[39] The subjects overwhelmingly stress either loyalty to the present system or nonpolitical activities.

In the Brazilian and Peruvian military journals the opposite situation exists. Stepan, for example, found that over 50 percent of the articles in the Peruvian *Revista de la Escuela Superior de Guerra* were in the New Professionalism category—that is, sociopolitical.[40] In Brazil, a similar situation is indicated by the titles of the major military publications.[41] Content analysis would therefore seem to indicate relatively little exposure and interest in politics in Mexico and substantially higher levels in Brazil and Peru.

Military Political Efficacy

The amount and method of the educational experience also affect political efficacy and participation. Studies indicate that as education increases, the level of political efficacy and participation also increases.[42] In Mexico, graduation from the military academy is the highest education most officers receive. No college degree is granted for completion of the four-year military academy program. It is considered to be the equivalent of the *preparatoria*, a preuniversity, high-school level in the United States.[43] The vast majority of Mexican military officers therefore probably do not reach educational levels generally associated with increased political efficacy.

This condition, however, is relative to the educational level of competing groups. The university education of the civilian political leadership tends to give the civilians greater confidence in their dealings with the military and exacerbates the lower level of political confidence and efficacy of the officer corps. This further inhibits military participation in the polity.[44] In Brazil, where military officers are educated as well as or better than their civilian counterparts, the opposite condition is true.[45]

The condition is reinforced by the roles officers and civilians play in the system. Nowhere in the three levels of this educational system do officers interact with civilians as equals. What contact does occur is limited to a student-teacher—in other words, an inferior-superior—relationship. This is the opposite of the Brazilian system, which encourages interaction between civilians and military, and uses military personnel to teach civilians, as well as civilians to teach officers.[46] This encourages interaction and integration of civilians and military as equals. In 1966, for example, about 51 percent of the graduates of the Brazilian ESG were civilians.[47] According to Gen. Emilio Garrastasú Médici, former president of Brazil, the ESG is "one of the most effective instruments in the integration of the Armed Forces and of the identification between civilians and military."[48]

The educational experience in Mexico, therefore, psychologically places the military below civilians in rank and inhibits military assumption of civilian roles. In Brazil the experience ranks the two groups as equals and imposes no military inhibitions. The psychological result limits Mexican military efficacy, and therefore political participation, while generating the opposite condition in Brazil.

The Mexican military's educational methods also discourage efficacy and political participation. The extreme importance placed upon discipline and obedience to authority in the school system restrains student participation in the classroom. This is indicated by an individual student's fear of any response that might be regarded as a challenge to the instructor or the system.[49] The common instructional method of rote memorization also inhibits participation. Such a lack of classroom participation decreases the probability of participation in other modes of behavior, such as politics.[50] The Brazilian system, on the other hand, encourages participation in areas of substantial importance, such as national security doctrine.[51]

Control of the student's environment and of the elements affecting his self-esteem also enhances the Mexican military educational system's ability to influence the behavior of the student. In any educational system the power to modify values comes from the student's need to be accepted by his peers. Public exposure opens the student to either praise and acceptance or criticism and rejection by peers.[52]

In the civilian school system, though, the power of peer pressure may be diminished. The school has control over the student for only about 25 percent of the time, five days per week, and provides no food, clothing, or shelter. The student also has the option of seeking solace in the family. The system, therefore, has potentially strong competition from parents and siblings.

In contrast, military educational systems do not have the counter-vailing influences of the civilian system. No optional refuge in the family exists for the military student, especially the cadet. The HCM, for example, controls the student from the moderately young age of fifteen to about nineteen years of age. During these four years, the academy pro-vides the cadet with food, clothing, and shelter and controls approximately 80 percent of the cadet's time, seven days a week. Students are allowed to have visitors only on Thursday evenings from 6 to 9 P.M. On Sundays, the cadets may leave the school to visit family or friends or to sightsee.[53]

In practice, though, the academy's control is even more pervasive than the visiting schedule indicates. Students may not be allowed to leave the school if they are involved in parades or other duties. Further-more, the school is located a considerable distance from the center of Mexico City on its southern outskirts, which makes it difficult and time-consuming for cadets to go into the city. Also, for cadets from other parts of the nation, the distance makes family visits prohibitive, especially since most families have relatively little wealth. Cadets therefore are isolated and totally dependent on the military educational system for food, shel-ter, and social contacts.

The environmental conditions that influence cadets' behavior extend beyond isolation and physical dependence. Behavioral norms are strictly regulated within a physically demanding environment. Such a combina-tion works to break the individualism of the cadet and to produce institu-tional conformity through physical exhaustion and commonality of peer experiences. A typical cadet's day, for example, begins promptly at 5:30 A.M. and continues until 9 P.M., when cadets return to their dormito-ries for the night. Fridays and Saturdays, cadets go on a thirty-six-kilometer march and bivouac. Hazing by upperclassmen and physical and mental punishment by peers for nonconformity are common. The system, in effect, resembles the Chinese method of mass behavior modification in such ways as the isolation of students from the outside world, exacting and rigorous physical routines, physical punishment, and social pressure.

In such an educational environment, the conditions normally operat-ing in a civilian school system are intensified, exaggerating their normal effect and influence. This encourages stronger bonds of loyalty, friend-ship, and monolithic uniformity in political views among classmates. The role of the parents as opinionmakers therefore diminishes and upperclass-men, peers, and instructors supplant the parents, especially on questions of national policy.[54]

Conclusions

The findings of this study suggest two possible relationships between professionalization and military coups. First, political efficacy appears to affect the political behavior of the military. Studies in the United States and Mexico indicate that as education increases so does political efficacy. Since political efficacy and participation are heavily correlated, increases in military professionalization through education lead to increasing probabilities of military political intervention. This explains the Brazilian and Peruvian cases, in which the political confidence of the military as an institution increased and led to the 1964 and 1968 coups. The new professionalism model correctly predicts this relationship but stresses national security doctrine and mission, thereby masking the impact of political efficacy and values.

The problem manifests itself in Mexico, which has an almost identical national mission and level of professionalism but exhibits different behavior. The Mexican case indicates that professionalization (i.e., education) may not always lead to increased levels of efficacy. Education's impact, while generally positively related to efficacy, is also dependent on method and content of instruction. In Mexico's case, educational processes actually tend to inhibit the growth of political efficacy and military intervention. Furthermore, professionalization's impact is relative to civilian professionalism, which, if higher than the military's, as in Mexico, tends to diminish military efficacy and decrease demands for participation.

Equally important to method and content is the relational context in which the educational experience occurs. In Brazil, civilians interact with officers as both instructors and students. This encourages an officer perspective of civilians as equals and does not decrease the relative efficacy of others. Mexico, on the other hand, has established a strong superior-inferior relationship by restricting civilian participation in the military education system to the role of instructor. Mexico's interaction, therefore, builds an image of superior civilian politicians and diminishes the relative political efficacy of Mexican officers.

Another consideration is the values taught by the system. In Brazil and Peru, officers are taught that loyalty to the military institution comes before loyalty to the government. In Mexico, the order is reversed. In addition, the mythology of the Revolution encourages officers to think of nation and government as one. An attack on the government would therefore be an attack on the Revolution and the nation. In contrast, the national security doctrines of Brazil and Peru separate the concepts of nation and state and encourage intervention, while Mexico's inhibit it.

Professionalization, then, determines military values and efficacy. As the military's political efficacy, relative to civilian politicians, increases, the probability of military intervention also increases. The amount of political efficacy is dependent upon the method of education and political content, as well as the amount of education; the amount of political efficacy and probability of coup behavior may therefore vary among military institutions with equal amounts of professionalism. Values that affect order of loyalties, the relationship of nation and state, and the presence or lack of revolutionary legitimacy will, in part, determine the amount of efficacy disparity the polity will tolerate between civilian and military institutions before military coup behavior occurs.

Finally, while this study indicates that professionalization influences military coup behavior, it also suggests that the relationship is very complex and subject to change. The study indicates, for example, that the military is taught the values of discipline, order, and authority, thereby implying that if the government and civilians do not act in accordance with these values, any military, including Mexico's, may intervene to restore them. The idea of efficacy also implies group comparisons. Such a comparison requires an examination of civilian institutional strength vis-à-vis the officer corps. A decline in civilian institutional strength, change in the method and content of the military educational system, or the military's reassessment of civilian values and norms could transform Mexican civil-military relations into the South American model.

Such a transformation currently may be occurring as a result of the apparent policy reversals of many of the Revolution's ideals. The decline in the strength and splintering of the PRI and the use of the military in the Chiapas area also appear to be potentially contributing factors. Whether such modification in Mexican civil-military relations is under way, however, remains unclear and requires further examination.

Notes

1. See, for example, Habibul Haque Khondker, "Bangladesh: Anatomy of an Unsuccessful Military Coup," *Armed Forces & Society* 13 (Fall 1986): 125–43; and Claude E. Welch, Jr., "Civil-Military Relations: Perspectives from the Third World," *Armed Forces & Society* 11, 2 (Winter 1985): 183–98.

2. See, for example, Robert D. Putnam, "Toward Explaining Military Intervention in Latin America," and Abraham F. Lowenthal, "Armies and Politics in Latin America," in *Armies and Politics in Latin America*, ed. Abraham F. Lowenthal (New York: Holmes & Meier, 1976), 87–113; Edward N. Muller, "Dependent Economic Development, Aid Dependence on the United States, and Democratic Breakdown in the Third World," *International Studies Quarterly* 29 (December 1985): 445–69; Alfred Stepan, *The Military in Politics: Changing*

Patterns in Brazil (Princeton, N.J.: Princeton University Press, 1971); and John Samuel Fitch, *The Military Coup d'Etat as a Political Process: Ecuador, 1948–1966* (Baltimore: Johns Hopkins University Press, 1977).

3. See Fitch, *Military Coup d'Etat.*

4. This includes conversations at parties, breakfasts, lunches, and dinners as well as at military installations. Trips to military installations include three visits to the HCM, six to the ESG, six to La Defensa Nacional, and one to Campo Militar Numero Uno and the military zone command in Queretaro.

5. Professionalism, as used in this paper, means the level of technical knowledge, articulation of and adherence to institutional norms and values. As the process of professionalization (learning/socialization) increases, so does the level of professionalism.

6. Alfred Stepan, "The New Professionalism of Internal Warfare and Military Role Expansion," in *Authoritarian Brazil* (New Haven, Conn.: Yale University Press, 1973), 47–53.

7. Samuel P. Huntington, *The Soldier and the State* (Cambridge: Harvard University Press, 1957).

8. Fitch, *Military Coup d'Etat.* See also John Samuel Fitch, "Military Professionalism, National Security and Democracy: Lessons from the Latin American Experience," *Pacific Focus* IV, 2 (Fall 1989): 107–12.

9. The author has observed individuals with strong Indian features at interviews, at La Defensa Nacional, and in the pictures of the alumni of the ESG; see *Escuela Superior de Guerra* (Mexico City: Secretaría de la Defensa Nacional, 1982). Additionally, both army units and individuals are transferred around the nation. For a discussion of the regional character of the Brazilian army, see Stepan, *Military in Politics*, 13–14. The conclusion about racial factionalization in Peru comes from an interview with an officer intimately familiar with the Peruvian military.

10. Officer interviews with author, Mexico City, summer 1974 and 1980. Also, Stephen J. Wager, "Basic Characteristics of the Modern Mexican Military," in *The Modern Mexican Military: A Reassessment*, ed. David Ronfeldt (San Diego: Center for U.S.-Mexican Studies, University of California at San Diego, 1984), 89.

11. Roberto Vizcaino, "La Seguridad del Pais, Fin Primorial el Estado," *Proceso* (September 22, 1980), 6.

12. "Cuarto Informe de Gobierno, Anexo Programatico II-A," *Proceso* (September 22, 1980), 8.

13. (Col.) Luis Garfias Magana, DEM, "¿Que es la estrategia?" *Revista del Ejército y Fuerza Aérea Mexicanos* (May 1977): 9; see also (Lt.) Augusto Garcia Ochoa, "Historias de las operaciónes psicologias," *Revista del Ejército* (September 1975): 29.

14. Garfias, "¿Que es la estrategia?" 10–11. The elite nature of the ESG and its close relation with the Mexican General Staff also magnify the significance of such statements. The definition is also similar to Brazil's. For a comparison see Golbery do Couto e Silva, *Geopoliticas do Brasil* (Rio de Janeiro: Jose Olympio, 1955), 251, and Umberto Peregrino, *Historia e projecao das instituicoes do exercito* (Rio de Janeiro: Jose Olympio, 1967), 115.

15. *Escuela Superior de Guerra: Programa de Estudios, 1977–1978, Curso de Mando y Estado Mayor*, vol. 3 (Mexico City: Secretaria de la Defensa Nacional, 1977), 9.

16. Based on estimates from officers' biographies and interviews, it takes Mexican officers approximately thirty years to reach brigadier general, by which time they will have spent between 7.5 and 8.5 years in the educational system. This represents 25 to 30 percent of total time in the military.

17. Heroico Colegio Militar, *Instructivo de Admisión, 1980–1981* (Mexico City: Secretaría de la Defensa Nacional, 1980), 5.

18. This view is discussed in Michael J. Dziedzic, "Explaining Civil-Military Relations in Mexico: The Politics of Co-optation," 1984–1985.

19. In interviews with foreign officers during 1980 and 1982, the opinion was expressed that discipline, in this sense, was the highest in Latin America.

20. See Dziedzic. "Explaining Civil-Military Relations."

21. (Maj. Gen.) Gilberto Barriquete Soto, DEM, "Principio de Autoridad," *Revista del Ejército* (March 1975): 47–48.

22. There is an additional implication to these values: if the civilian politicians do not accept and follow these values, they may not be fit to govern. The implication, however, requires an additional study of civil-military interaction.

23. Author's personal interviews with officers, Mexico City, summers 1974 and 1980–1984.

24. The Brazilian military's perception of civilian weakness appears in the national security doctrine. The doctrine distinguishes between permanent and current national objectives, corresponding to the nation and the government. Accordingly, the nation has a permanent existence, while the state exists only as long as it promotes the welfare of the nation. It is therefore not an aberration to replace the state, and, indeed, it is the military's duty to remove any government that threatens the well-being of the nation. For further discussion see do Couto e Silva, *Geopoliticas*, 251–56; Peregrino, *Historia e projecao*, 115; and Roland Schneider, *The Political System of Brazil: The Emergence of a "Modernizing" Authoritarian Regime, 1964–1970* (New York: Columbia University Press, 1971), 247–48.

25. Author's interviews with officers, Mexico City, summers 1980 and 1982; also, see *Instructivo de Admisión*, 5–7; Heroico Colegio Militar, *Sintesis Histórica, Objectivo y Activides* (Mexico City: Secretaría de la Defensa Nacional, Dirección General de Educación Militar y de la Universidad del Ejército y Fuerza Aérea, January 1980), 5–6; and Escuela Superior de Guerra, *Visita del Colegio Nacional de Guerra de los Estados Unidos de Norte América* (Mexico City: Secretaría de la Defensa Nacional, April 2, 1982), 2–3.

26. This is also similar to the pattern anticipated by Abraham F. Lowenthal in his introductory chapter of *Armies and Politics*, 19–20.

27. Pedro Aleixo, "Conceito de seguranca nacional no regime democratico representativo" (paper presented to the fourth series of conferences on national security, Belo Horizonte, 1968), 5; see also (Maj.) Joao Bina Machado, "The Making of Brazilian Staff Officers," *Military Review* 50 (April 1970): 80.

28. Do Couto e Silva, *Geopoliticas*, 251–56; Peregrino, *Historia e projecao*, 115; Schneider, *Political System of Brazil*, 247–48.

29. This is also similar to Fitch's findings in Ecuador, where, he notes, the values and norms taught by the military educational system influence the military's perception of crisis and the proper response. See Fitch, *Military Coup d'Etat*.

30. HCM, *Sintesis Histórica*, 26–31, and author's interviews with officers, Mexico City, 1982–1984.

31. *Escuela Superior de Guerra: Programa de Estudios*, 91–97; also author's interviews with officers, Mexico City, 1980–1984.

32. Author's interviews with officers, Mexico City, 1982–83.

33. Stepan indicates that the New Professionalism content of ECEME courses is 94 percent. Stepan, *Military in Politics*, 181.

34. *Escuela Superior de Guerra: Programa de Estudios*, 91–97; also, author's interviews with officers, Mexico City, 1980–1984.

35. Author's conversations with officers and civilians who have taught at the school, Mexico City, 1982–1984. And Wager, "Social Contributions and Political Influence," 19.

36. Author's interviews with officers, Mexico City, 1980–1987; see also Dziedzic, "Explaining Civil-Military Relations," 16.

37. Ibid.; see also *Escuela Superior de Guerra, 1932–1982* (Mexico City: Secretaría de la Defensa Nacional, 1982), and Wager, "Social Contributions and Political Influence," 17–19.

38. These figures on rank structure are taken from the Estado Mayor (General Staff) and from the author's interviews of officers, Mexico City, 1980–1984.

39. The analysis was compiled from a study of *Revista del Ejército* between March 1973 and December 1976. No formal analysis was conducted on the López Portillo period, but an examination of the table of contents of several issues reveals no apparent deviations from the earlier findings. Also, see Wager, "Social Contributions and Political Influence," 10–11.

40. Alfred Stepan, *The State and Society: Peru in Comparative Perspective* (Princeton, N.J.: Princeton University Press, 1978), 131–32 and 140–41.

41. For example, see *Seguranca e Desenvolvimento: Revista da Associacao dos Diplomatos da Escola Superior de Guerra*. This is the alumni publication of the graduates of the ESG. The title (Security and development: review of the association of graduates of the ESG) indicates the concern of this publication, which contains the best papers of current ESG students as well as those by military and civilian alumni. See also the *Boletim de Informacoes* published by the Brazilian General Staff; and Stepan, *Military in Politics*, 177–78, 181.

42. M. Kent Jennings and Richard G. Niemi, *The Political Character of Adolescence: The Influence of Families and Schools* (Princeton, N.J.: Princeton University Press, 1974), 40 and 98; Sidney Verba and Norman H. Nie, *Participation in America: Political Democracy and Social Equity* (New York: Harper & Row, 1972), 97–99 and 287; Rafael Segovia, *La Politicización del Niño Mexicano* (Mexico City: El Colegio de Mexico, 1975), 79–83; and Roderic A. Camp, *Mexico's Leaders: Their Education and Recruitment* (Tucson: University of Arizona Press, 1980), 5, 90–91.

43. The exceptions are air force officers who after two years at the military academy and two years at the air force academy are granted a college degree. Author's interviews with military officers, Mexico City and Guadalajara, 1980–1984 and 1988.

44. Verba and Nie, *Participation in America*, 97–99; those officers who are graduates of the ESG are exceptions to this statement. The concept of relative efficacy is suggested in Abraham F. Lowenthal's Relative Institutionalization hypothesis. Lowenthal argues that the relative institutional strength—as measured by professionalism, cohesion (a product of professionalization), and resources—of civilians and military is the determinant of intervention; see

Abraham F. Lowenthal, "Armies and Politics in Latin America: Introduction to the First Edition," *Armies and Politics in Latin America*, rev. ed., ed. Abraham F. Lowenthal and J. Samuel Fitch (New York: Holmes & Meier, 1986), 19–20; Fitch also suggests the impact of relative institutional professionalism when he argues that it is the high degree of civilian professionalism vis-à-vis the military that has prevented a coup in Mexico; J. Samuel Fitch, "Armies and Politics in Latin America: 1975–1985," *Armies and Politics in Latin America*, rev. ed., 37.

45. Stepan, *Military in Politics*, 32, 35, and 40.

46. For a more complete discussion of the Brazilian military and civilian integration into the military educational system, see (Gen.) Emilio Garrastasú Médici, "Objectivos, politicas, y estrategias del gobierno de la revolución," *Estrategias* (January–February 1970): 60; Stepan, *Military in Politics*, 177; Schneider, *Political System of Brazil*, 250–51; and Marcio Moreira Alves, *A Grain of Mustard Seed: The Awakening of the Brazilian Revolution* (Garden City, N.Y.: Doubleday Anchor, 1973), 62.

47. Stepan, *Military in Politics*, 177; see also Schneider, *Political System of Brazil*, 250.

48. Garrastasú Médici, "Objectivos, politicas, y estrategias," 60. It should also be noted that civilians are integrated into the Brazilian armed forces by bestowing the rank of colonel on each civilian graduate of the ESG and through the alumni association of the ESG which teaches courses and disseminates information favorable to the armed forces.

49. Author's interviews with cadets and officers, Mexico City, 1980–1984.

50. Verba and Nie, *Participation in America*, 275, 287–90, and 295. This behavior has been witnessed by the author and confirmed in conversations with officers, Mexico City, 1980–1984.

51. Schneider, *Political System of Brazil*, 251.

52. Robert Dreeben, "The Contribution of Schooling to the Learning of Norms," in *Socialization and Schooling*, ed. Bunnie Othanel Smith and Donald E. Orlasky (Bloomington, Ind.: Phi Delta Kappa, 1975), 31.

53. Author's interviews with officers and cadets, summers 1980 and 1982; see also *Sintesis Histórica*.

54. M. Kent Jennings, Richard G. Niemi, and Suzanne Koprince Sebert, "The Political Texture of Peer Groups," in *Political Character of Adolescence*, 238, 242–45.

Suggested Readings

Although the Spanish conquered highly developed Indian societies, such as the Aztecs, the Mayas, and the Incas, which possessed large and well-organized armies, the colonial order established by the Europeans was not based on military force. Local militias, frontier garrisons, and coastal fortresses sufficed to maintain internal order and to defend the empire from both nomadic Indians and foreign assaults. The situation changed in 1763, after the Seven Years' War, when both England and Spain created standing armies in their colonies.

The most extensive and sophisticated treatments of the eighteenth-century military reform in Spanish America have focused on the Viceroyalty of New Spain, the largest and wealthiest part of the Spanish empire. Lyle N. McAlister, *The "Fuero Militar" in New Spain, 1764–1800* (Gainesville: University of Florida Press, 1957), is a pioneering study that examines the contradictory role of corporate privilege in the new colonial army. Christon I. Archer, *The Army in Bourbon Mexico, 1760–1810* (Albuquerque: University of New Mexico Press, 1977), not only expands and refines our understanding of the institutional reform, but he also situates the military within the broader political, economic, and social context of the colony. Studies of other parts of the empire, such as Allan J. Kuethe, *Cuba, 1753–1815: Crown, Military, and Society* (Knoxville: University of Tennessee Press, 1986), and *Military Reform and Society in New Granada, 1773–1808* (Gainesville: University Presses of Florida, 1978); and Leon G. Campbell, *The Military and Society in Colonial Peru, 1750–1810* (Philadelphia: American Philosophical Society, 1978), demonstrate that the level and impact of military modernization varied between and within the viceroyalties.

After the conquest in the early sixteenth century, independence (1810–1826) constituted the most extensive and most violent military conflict in Latin America. The best general analyses of the military in Spanish America during the struggle for independence are Jorge I. Domínguez, *Insurrection or Loyalty: The Breakdown of the Spanish American Empire* (Cambridge: Harvard University Press, 1980), and John Lynch, *The Spanish American Revolution, 1808–1826* (New York: W. W. Norton, 1973). There is a vast literature focusing on the "heroes" of independence but not treating the martial institution itself. Among the best examples of this genre are: Hugh M. Hamill, Jr., *The Hidalgo Revolt: Prelude to Mexican Independence* (Gainesville: University of Florida Press, 1966); Gerhard Masur, *Simón Bolívar* (Albuquerque: University of New Mexico Press, 1969); and Jay Kinsbruner, *Bernardo O'Higgins* (New York: Twayne, 1968). Although his protagonist was a royalist officer, Stephen K. Sloan, *Pablo Morillo and Venezuela, 1815–1820* (Columbus: Ohio State University Press, 1974), fits that mold. Surprisingly, few scholars have written analytical studies of the military in this crucial period. Among the exceptions are Christon I. Archer and Brian Hamnett, who have published numerous articles on the process of insurgency and counterinsurgency in New Spain. See, for example, Christon I. Archer, "The Royalist Army of New Spain, 1810–1821: Militarism, Praetorianism, or Protection of Interests?" *Armed Forces and Society* 17, no. 1 (Fall 1990): 99–116; and Brian R. Hamnett, "Royalist Counterinsurgency and the Continuity of Rebellion: Guanajuato and Michoacán, 1813–20," *Hispanic American Historical Review* 62, no. 1 (February 1982): 19–48. Comparable works are lacking for other Latin American regions.

Although nineteenth-century Latin America was characterized by considerable internal upheaval as well as international warfare, few studies of the military have appeared in English. Among the best are: William F. Sater, *Chile and the War of the Pacific* (Lincoln: University of Nebraska Press, 1986); Frederick Nunn, *The Military in Chilean History: Essays on Civil-Military Relations, 1810–1973* (Albuquerque: University of New Mexico Press, 1976); Robert L. Gilmore, *Caudillism and Militarism in Venezuela, 1810–1910* (Athens: Ohio University Press, 1964); and Charles Kolinski, *Independence or Death: The Story of the Paraguayan War* (Gainesville: University of Florida Press, 1965). Other useful works on foreign intervention in the region include: John Eisenhower, *So Far from God: The U.S. War with Mexico, 1846–1848* (New York: Anchor Books, 1990); J. A. Dabbs, *The French Army in Mexico, 1861–1867: A Study in Military Government* (The Hague: Mouton, 1963); William C. Davis, *The Last Conquistadores* (Athens: University of Georgia Press, 1950); and John F. Cady, *Foreign Intervention in the Río de la Plata, 1838–50* (Philadelphia: University of Pennsylvania Press, 1929).

There is a vast literature on the armed forces in Latin America during the twentieth century. Early interpretations include: Edwin Lieuwen, *Arms and Politics and Latin America* (New York: Praeger, 1961), who argued that the military played a negative role in national development, and John J. Johnson, *The Military and Society in Latin America* (Stanford: Stanford University Press, 1964), who portrayed the armed forces in a more positive light, arguing that the officers had the potential to contribute to national development. For recent general introductions to the subject, see Peter Calvert and Susan Calvert, *Latin America in the Twentieth Century* (London: MacMillan Press, 1990); George Philip, *The Military in South American Politics* (London: Croom Helm, 1985); and Alain Rouquié, *The Military and the State in Latin America* (Berkeley: University of California Press, 1987).

Studies of twentieth-century wars and foreign interventions include: Hans Schmidt, *The United States Occupation of Haiti, 1915–1934* (New Brunswick: Rutgers University Press, 1971); Neill Macaulay, *The Sandino Affair* (Chicago: Quadrangle Books, 1967); David Zook, *The Conduct of the Chaco War* (New York: Bookman Associates, 1960); Don L. Etchison, *The United States and Militarism in Central America* (New York: Praeger, 1975); David Zook, *Zarumilla-Marañón: The Ecuador-Peru Dispute* (New York: Bookman Associates, 1964); Piero Gleijeses, *The Dominican Crisis: The 1965 Constitutionalist Revolt and American Intervention* (Baltimore: Johns Hopkins University Press, 1978); William H. Durham, *Scarcity and Survival in Central America: Ecological Origins of the Soccer War* (Stanford: Stanford University Press, 1979); Ivan Musicant, *The Banana Wars: A History of United States Military Intervention in Latin America from the Spanish-American War to the Invasion of Panama* (New York: Macmillan, 1990); Robert Leiken, ed., *Central America: Anatomy of a Conflict* (New York: Pergamon Press, 1984); and Fritz L. Hoffmann and Olga Mingo Hoffmann, *Sovereignty in Dispute: The Falklands/ Malvinas, 1493–1982* (Boulder: Westview Press, 1984).

English-speaking scholars generally have been interested in the political role of the military. Among the most valuable country studies are: Robert A. Potash, *The Army and Politics in Argentina, 1928–1943: Yrigoyen to Perón* (Stanford: Stanford University Press, 1969); Alfred Stepan, *The Military in Politics: Changing Patterns in Brazil* (Princeton: Princeton University Press, 1971); William F. Sater, *The Heroic Image in Chile: Arturo Prat, Secular Saint* (Berkeley: University of California Press, 1973); Liisa North, *The Military in Chilean Politics* (Toronto: York University Press, 1974); Frederick M. Nunn, *Chilean Politics, 1921–1930: The Honorable Mission of the Armed Forces* (Albuquerque: University of New Mexico Press, 1970); Richard Maullin, *Soldiers, Guerrillas, and Politics in Colombia* (Lexington: Lexington Books, 1973); Winfield J. Burggraaff, *The Venezuelan Armed Forces in Politics, 1935–1959* (Columbia: University of Missouri Press, 1972); Louis A. Pérez, *Army and Politics in Cuba, 1898–1958* (Pittsburgh: University of Pittsburgh Press, 1976); John Samuel Fitch, *The Military Coup d'Etat as a Political Process: Ecuador, 1948–1966* (Baltimore: Johns Hopkins University Press,

1977); G. Philip, *The Rise and Fall of the Peruvian Military Radicals, 1968–1976* (London: University of London, Institute of Latin American Studies, 1978); Robert A. Potash, *The Army and Politics in Argentina, 1945–1962: Péron to Frondizi* (Stanford: Stanford University Press, 1980); G. Pope Atkins, *Arms and Politics in the Dominican Republic* (Boulder: Westview Press, 1981); Carmelo Mesa-Lago and June Belkins, *Cuba in Africa* (Pittsburgh: University of Pittsburgh Press, 1982); Maria Helena Moreira Alves, *State and Opposition in Military Brazil* (Austin: University of Texas Press, 1985); and Roderic Ai Camp, *Generals in the Palacio: The Military in Modern Mexico* (Oxford: Oxford University Press, 1992).

The question of professionalization has been the subject of considerable debate in recent years. See, for example, Alfred Stepan, *Rethinking Military Politics: Brazil and the Southern Cone* (Princeton: Princeton University Press, 1988); and Frederick M. Nunn, *Yesterday's Soldiers: European Military Professionalism in South America, 1890–1940* (Lincoln: University of Nebraska Press, 1983), and *The Time of the Generals: Latin American Professional Militarism in World Perspective* (Lincoln: University of Nebraska Press, 1992).

The problem of the transition from military to civilian rule has generated considerable discussion. Some of the best analyses are found in: Howard Handelman and Thomas Sanders, *Military Government and the Movement Towards Democracy in South America* (Bloomington: Indiana University Press, 1981); Guillermo O'Donnell, Philippe Schmitter, and Laurence Whitehead, eds., *Transitions from Authoritarian Rule: Latin America* (Baltimore: Johns Hopkins University Press, 1986); J. Malloy and M. Siligson, eds., *Authoritarians and Democrats: Regime Transition in Latin America* (Pittsburgh: University of Pittsburgh Press, 1987). The process of change has been made more difficult by the human rights record of the various military regimes. See, for example, Margaret Crahan, "The Evolution of the Military in Brazil, Chile, Peru, Venezuela, and Mexico," in *Human Rights and Basic Needs in the Americas*, ed. Margaret Crahan (Washington, DC: Georgetown University Press, 1982).

The changing nature of Latin American arms procurement and production has also attracted scholarly interest. See Joseph E. Loftus, *Latin American Defense Expenditures, 1938–1965* (Santa Monica: Rand Corporation, 1980); Augusto Varas, *Militarization and the International Arms Race in Latin America* (Boulder: Westview Press, 1985); Bishara Bahbah, with Linda Butler, *Israel and Latin America: The Military Connection* (London: MacMillan; Beirut: Institute for Palestine Studies, 1986); and Edward S. Milenki, "Arms Production and National Security in Argentina," *Journal of Interamerican Studies* (August 1980).

Several important issues regarding the Latin American military in the twentieth century are treated in edited volumes. See, for example, Georges Fauriol, ed., *Latin American Insurgencies* (Washington, DC: Georgetown Center for Strategic and International Studies and National Defense University, 1985); Abraham R. Lowenthal and J. Samuel Fitch, eds., *Armies and Politics in Latin America* (New York: Holmes & Meier, 1986); and Brian Loveman and Thomas M. Davies, Jr., eds., *The Politics of Antipolitics: The Military in Latin America* (Lincoln: University of Nebraska Press, 1989).